Colchester United
From Conference to Championship

DESERT ISLAND FOOTBALL HISTORIES

	ISBN
### CLUB HISTORIES	
Aberdeen: A Centenary History 1903-2003	978-1-874287-57-5
Aberdeen: Champions of Scotland 1954-55	978-1-874287-65-0
Aberdeen: The European Era	978-1-905328-32-1
Bristol City: The Modern Era – A Complete Record	978-1-905328-27-7
Bristol City: The Early Years 1894-1915	978-1-874287-74-2
Bristol Rovers: The Bert Tann Era	978-1-905328-37-6
Cambridge United: The League Era – A Complete Record	978-1-905328-06-2
Cambridge United: 101 Golden Greats	978-1-874287-58-2
Carlisle United: A Season in the Sun 1974-75	978-1-905328-21-5
The Story of the Celtic 1888-1938	978-1-874287-15-5
Chelsea: Champions of England 1954-55	978-1-874287-94-0
Colchester United: Graham to Whitton – A Complete Record	978-1-905328-35-2
Colchester United: From Conference to Championship	978-1-905328-28-4
Coventry City at Highfield Road 1899-2005	978-1-905328-11-6
Coventry City: The Elite Era – A Complete Record	978-1-874287-83-4
Coventry City: An Illustrated History	978-1-874287-59-9
Derby County: Champions of England 1971-72, 1974-75	978-1-874287-98-8
Dundee: Champions of Scotland 1961-62	978-1-874287-86-5
Dundee United: Champions of Scotland 1982-83	978-1-874287-99-5
History of the Everton Football Club 1878-1928	978-1-874287-14-8
Halifax Town: From Ball to Lillis – A Complete Record	978-1-874287-26-1
Hereford United: The League Era – A Complete Record	978-1-874287-91-9
Hereford United: The Wilderness Years 1997-2006	978-1-905328-22-2
Huddersfield Town: Champions of England 1923-1926	978-1-874287-88-9
Ipswich Town: The Modern Era – A Complete Record	978-1-905328-24-6
Ipswich Town: Champions of England 1961-62	978-1-874287-63-6
The Old Farm: Ipswich Town v Norwich City	978-1-905328-12-3
Kilmarnock: Champions of Scotland 1964-65	978-1-874287-87-2
Leyton Orient: A Season in the Sun 1962-63	978-1-905328-05-5
Luton Town at Kenilworth Road: A Century of Memories	978-1-905328-10-9
Luton Town: The Modern Era – A Complete Record	978-1-874287-90-2
Luton Town: An Illustrated History	978-1-874287-79-7
Manchester United's Golden Age 1903-1914: Dick Duckworth	978-1-874287-92-6
The Matt Busby Chronicles: Manchester United 1946-69	978-1-874287-96-4
Motherwell: Champions of Scotland 1931-32	978-1-874287-73-5
Northampton Town: A Season in the Sun 1965-66	978-1-905328-01-7
Norwich City: The Modern Era – A Complete Record	978-1-874287-67-4
Peterborough United: The Modern Era – A Complete Record	978-1-874287-33-9
Peterborough United: Who's Who?	978-1-874287-48-3
Plymouth Argyle: The Modern Era – A Complete Record	978-1-874287-54-4
Plymouth Argyle: 101 Golden Greats	978-1-874287-64-3
Plymouth Argyle: Snakes & Ladders – Promotions and Relegations	978-1-905328-34-5
Portsmouth: The Modern Era	978-1-905328-08-7
Portsmouth: From Tindall to Ball – A Complete Record	978-1-874287-25-4
Portsmouth: Champions of England – 1948-49 & 1949-50	978-1-874287-50-6
The Story of the Rangers 1873-1923	978-1-874287-95-7
The Romance of the Wednesday 1867-1926	978-1-874287-17-9
Seventeen Miles from Paradise: Saints v Pompey	978-1-874287-89-6
The Southend United Chronicles 1906-2006	978-1-905328-18-5
Stoke City: The Modern Era – A Complete Record	978-1-874287-76-6
Stoke City: 101 Golden Greats	978-1-874287-55-1
Potters at War: Stoke City 1939-47	978-1-874287-78-0
Swansea City: Seasons in the Sun	978-1-905328-02-4
Third Lanark: Champions of Scotland 1903-04	978-1-905328-03-1
Tottenham Hotspur: Champions of England 1950-51, 1960-61	978-1-874287-93-3
West Bromwich Albion: Champions of England 1919-1920	978-1-905328-04-8
West Ham: From Greenwood to Redknapp	978-1-874287-19-3
West Ham: The Elite Era – A Complete Record	978-1-905328-33-8
Hammers Through the Looking Glass	978-1-905328-23-9
Wimbledon: From Southern League to Premiership	978-1-874287-09-4
Wimbledon: From Wembley to Selhurst	978-1-874287-20-9
Wimbledon: The Premiership Years	978-1-874287-40-7
Wrexham: The European Era – A Complete Record	978-1-874287-52-0
### WORLD CUP HISTORIES	
England's Quest for the World Cup – A Complete Record	978-1-905328-16-1
Scotland: The Quest for the World Cup – A Complete Record	978-1-897850-50-3
Ireland: The Quest for the World Cup – A Complete Record	978-1-897850-80-0
### MISCELLANEOUS	
Blinded by the Lights: A History of Night Football in England	978-1-905328-13-0
Red Dragons in Europe – A Complete Record	978-1-874287-01-8
The Book of Football: A History to 1905-06	978-1-905328-00-4
Football's Twelve Apostles: The Making of the League 1886-1889	978-1-905328-09-3
Football's War & Peace: The Tumultuous Season of 1946-47	978-1-874287-70-4
Freestaters: Republic of Ireland 1921-39	978-1-905328-36-9

Colchester United

From Conference
to Championship

Series Editor: Clive Leatherdale

Rob Hadgraft

DESERT ISLAND BOOKS

First published in 2007
by
DESERT ISLAND BOOKS LIMITED
7 Clarence Road, Southend-on-Sea, Essex SS1 1AN
United Kingdom
www.desertislandbooks.com

© 2007 Rob Hadgraft

The right of Rob Hadgraft to be identified as author of this work has been
asserted under The Copyright Designs and Patents Act 1988

British Library Cataloguing-in-Publication Data
A catalogue record for this book is available from the British Library

IBSN 978-1-905328-28-4

Printed in Great Britain
by
Biddles Ltd, King's Lynn

Contents

Author's Note

It was a mighty long time ago, but I still recall my first day back at school after the 1966 Easter Holidays. In the sunlit classroom at St Luke's Primary School in Tiptree, headmaster Gordon Ambridge was in charge of our motley group of ten-year-olds that day. His instruction for our English Composition lesson was to write an essay entitled 'What I Did On My Holidays'.

Tales of chocolate eggs and Easter bunnies were probably what he expected, but my effort was an account of a football match which I head-lined: 'Colchester 0 Aldershot 0'. A goalless draw at Layer Road may not have been everyone's idea of a holiday highlight, but it was good enough for me. Mr Ambridge, a keen football fan, seemed to approve of the essay and even suggested I might make a football reporter later in life. Now there was a thought. A seed was planted that morning and twenty years later I did indeed find myself reporting Colchester United matches for a living. Now, another twenty years further on, my views on the U's make up the pages of this book.

Some habits are hard to shake, and my interest in Colchester United is now in its 42nd year. That Aldershot game in 1966 was my fourth visit to Layer Road, but I still hadn't seen the U's win. Those early games ended up 3-3, 2-2, 1-1 and 0-0. Bizarre or what? Despite the lack of vic-tories I was hooked, and schoolboy and early adult years involved many trips to Layer Road, with plenty of wins and losses to add to those draws.

One learns to expect the unexpected with Colchester United, but I never thought I would get the chance to write a book which tracks the club's progress from non-league football to the upper echelons of the Championship, with a new stadium thrown in for good measure.

In completing this task I would like to gratefully acknowledge the assistance of everybody at the football club, particularly Matt Hudson and Peter Heard, and not forgetting devoted and knowledgable support-ers Jim French and Paul Ost. I also thank publisher Clive Leatherdale and my wife Katie for support and advice. Although I was able to call on many personal memories and records, my research also required refer-ence to the published work of authors and journalists young and old: Bernard Webber, Hal Mason, Jeff Whitehead, Carl Marston, Jonathan Waldron and Francis Ponder, to name but six. Many of the photographs were taken by Rob Sambrook and are used with the permission of Colchester United FC, with some by myself and others taken from pri-vate collections.

I hope U's fans will see this book as a companion to the excellent 1999 work by Jeff Whitehead (see list below), which features full statistical data about all U's games from 1968. Where my match statistics and Jeff's overlap, I have produced abbreviated versions in this book.

BIBLIOGRAPHY: *Colchester United: From Graham to Whitton – A Complete Record* by Jeff Whitehead (Desert Island Books, 1999), *The Official History of the U's* by Hal Mason (Yore, 1993), *The Way U's Were* by Bernard Webber (Tempus, 2004), *Playing Extra Time* by Alan Ball (Pan, 2005), *We All Live In A Perry Groves World* by Perry Groves (John Blake, 2007), *Rothman's* and *Sky Sports Football Yearbooks* (various), *The PFA Premier and Football League Players' Records 1946-1998* by Barry Hugman (Queen Anne Press, 1998), *Nine Minutes of Magic* (CUFC, 2006).

ROB HADGRAFT
Chelmsford, September 2007

Foreword by Peter Heard

In November 1991 one of my partners in my surveying firm in London did some work for James Bowdidge, chairman of Colchester United FC, a man who worked for Robert Frasier, a merchant bank in London, and who had a property company. Mr Bowdidge invited me to lunch, knowing of my interest in football through refereeing, and having been told by my partner that Colchester was my birthplace. Mr Bowdidge took me to a posh lunch in Mayfair, which was probably the most expensive lunch I ever had! He asked if I would put £25,000 into the club and join the board of directors.

On my first tour of the Layer Road offices I asked the club secretary what the pile of paper was adjacent to her desk. She told me they were outstanding bills, and I asked when they would be paid. She said they were normally not paid until receipt of a writ! Without a cash injection I believe the club at that point was close to bankruptcy.

One year on, with the commercial property slump beginning to bite, the chairman could not devote further time to the club and stood down. In that year the club was in the Conference and went to Wembley for the FA Trophy final, where we beat Witton Albion and went on in our final league game against Barrow to clinch the Conference title. Interestingly, Graham Poll refereed that game, as he also did our first home game back in the League against Lincoln in 1992. Our manager, Roy McDonough, always deserves credit for leading us back into the Football League. Two years later I presented him with a silver salver on the pitch at Carlisle for playing 500 League games – not many reach that milestone. A few days later Roy lost his job and we then opted for a bright young manager in George Burley. He got off to a very poor start, losing the pre-season friendlies and his first four League games. Just before an away game at Scarborough he asked if a former colleague who had been coaching in America could be his number two. Some of the board were not keen, but I was much in favour and the late Dale Roberts arrived. We duly won at Scarborough and had a fantastic autumn run, losing only one game, to Chesterfield, with George Burley playing his last competitive match as a player at Doncaster.

Little did I know that this ideal period was about to be shattered by the intervention of our old rivals Ipswich Town and after a huge tug-of-war George Burley resigned over Christmas 1994. A bitter legal fight then ensued, eventually resulting in substantial compensation being paid to this club. Into the managerial breach stepped our former captain Steve

Wignall, who calmed things down and served us for over three years. There was an unsettling period when Brentford tried to acquire his services. Mr Wignall's achievements included promotion via the Wembley play-offs against Torquay United in 1998 and a visit to Wembley in the Auto Windscreens Shield final against Carlisle a year earlier.

Our first ever away match at Manchester City coincided with the day of the FA Cup first round draw for 1998-99 which for the first time was not regionalised. We drew Bedlington Terriers, based in Northumberland, away. Half the board thought we were going to Bridlington! Perhaps we should have done, for we lost heavily to a team seven levels beneath us in the football pyramid. Although we won our next game at Notts County, we were to win no more games under Steve Wignall's stewardship. He resigned in the following January.

Then came a tumultuous six months at the club. The board was split between appointing Steve Cotterill and Mick Wadsworth. The latter got the vote and, with his onfield general Warren Aspinall, steered us to safety from relegation. We ran into difficulties with an agent, receiving a blizzard of legal documents, and after six months – which included the appearance of a Brazilian known as Fumaca (Portuguese for 'flaming torch'), who played part of one televised home game against Manchester City, was knocked out, carried off and never seen again – Mr Wadsworth resigned and we moved on to the era of Steve Whitton, previously assistant manager. He steadied the ship and had plenty of honest endeavour, but eventually ran out of steam.

In 1998, having been vice-chairman for a number of years, I took over the chair and sought a meeting with the chief executive of Colchester Borough Council, Mr John Cobley. At that time nothing really moved in Colchester unless John Cobley was behind it. Although he had no interest in football he was receptive to my plea that he tell the club where a new ground should be located, rather than the Council keep turning down specific sites suggested by the club (which seemed to have been going on since the Second World War). He agreed to this and shortly afterwards a Memorandum of Understanding was signed by all three political parties on the Council. Nine years later, in July 2007, documents were signed for the new 10,000-seater Community Stadium to be built on the northern approaches of the town. It is scheduled for opening for the 2008-09 season.

Following the departure of Steve Whitton we took a chance on appointing the completely untried Phil Parkinson. His explosive energy and his 'pied piper' personality meant we got off to a wonderful start and this charismatic, but impatient young man in over three years took the club significantly forward. However, in June 2006 this all abruptly ended when he left for Hull City for what turned out to be only a very brief stay. Perhaps it is too soon to comment further on his fiercely resisted departure, following our first promotion to Championship-level football. Few will forget the tension of the game at Yeovil when promotion was clinched.

Geraint Williams, our assistant manager, took over as manager in difficult circumstances and we finished our first season at this level in a credible tenth position. In September 2006 I disposed my controlling shareholding to local successful businessmen Robbie Cowling, and I write this Foreword shortly after announcing my decision to retire. The club has moved in my time from the Conference to the Championship – from the foot of the mountain to one rung from its peak! Can Robbie Cowling take it to the summit? Who knows? All I can say is that he has the youth, drive, and financial resources to give it a jolly good try. Only time will tell.

PETER HEARD
Chairman, Colchester United FC 1998-2007

'Roy Keane, Your Boys Took a Hell of a Beating …'

It is five to three on Saturday, 21 April 2007. An area to the south-west of Colchester, bordering the town's huge British Army base, is alive with noise and colour. A helicopter buzzes overhead, security is tight. Road blocks are in place, police are everywhere.

Zoom in closer and there, in dark suit and tie, and looking every inch the business executive, is Niall Quinn, taking his place in the Visiting Directors and Guests section of Colchester United FC's tiny, rather rickety main stand. If he feels uncomfortable in such ramshackle surroundings Quinn isn't showing it. Enjoying his first full season as Sunderland FC's chairman and saviour, the 40-year-old Dubliner is the epitome of hospitality, greeting fellow grandees with a massive smile, and signalling to more than one passerby that he would like to buy them a drink at half-time. These expansive gestures might be a trifle ambitious, for he has clearly never experienced the queues that can build up at Colchester's embarrassingly inadequate refreshment facility.

But, for now, Quinn is the picture of a contented chairman, unbeaten in four months and on his way to the Coca-Cola Championship title. Sitting just three seats away from Quinn, and in rather more restrained mood, is Sunderland celebrity fan Steve Cram, looking tanned and healthy as would be expected of a former Olympic athlete. Many eyes glance in his direction as a tribute to his recently deceased uncle Bobby, a former Colchester skipper, crackles out of the public address system. As the ground falls quiet, Cram's expression gives little away.

Less inhibited are the travelling Sunderland fans situated to Cram's right, packed into the quaint Layer Road end of the ground, singing lustily in praise of their famous manager Roy Keane, and apparently undaunted by their confinement to barely a dozen steps of terracing behind the goal. Maintaining their carnival mood of the past six months or so, this colourful mob is actually squeezing extra enjoyment out of today's visit to the sort of ground they had previously only heard about. To them, this feels more like a cup-tie at the home of 'minnows' than a crucial Championship fixture. They are here to have a good time, no matter what, buoyed by the knowledge that their side is virtually certain to be returning to the Premiership whatever the result today.

Earlier the Sunderland hordes packed into the nearby Drury Arms, a short walk from the ground, to sink the obligatory pre-match lagers and sing

the songs of a proud invading tribe. Some went to the trouble of seeking out
the Queen's Hotel on Berechurch Road, a little further afield, but which is
run by a fellow 'Mackem'. The police helicopter circled over the whole area,
adding to the sense of occasion, but there were no outbreaks of trouble
inside or outside the ground. A thunderous roar greets the arrival of the two
teams, briefly drowning out the ancient strains of the *Post Horn Gallop* coming from the public address system. This old signature has been revived as
part of the tribute to the late Bobby Cram, stalwart of 35 years ago. For
older fans in particular, this whiff of nostalgia adds to the general excitement
and provides a spine-tingling moment.

As expected, the game proved to be a passionate affair, played at a furious pace. Colchester knew that to win this home match, as they had fourteen
of the previous 21 so far this season, would put them within a single point
of the top-six play-off zone, with just two games to play. The impossible
dream of reaching football's promised land – the Premiership – was no
longer a far-fetched fantasy, it was tantalisingly within reach. The general wis-
dom was that Colchester were punching above their weight by merely surviving in League One, let alone reaching for a top place in the Championship.
After years of struggle, for little Colchester United the big time was finally
beckoning.

There was less pressure on mighty Sunderland, who looked assured of
the promotion whatever today's outcome, but manager Keane was determined to extend an unbeaten run that went back sixteen weeks. For United,
only a win would do.

After the first frantic 45 minutes, some spectators started to slip out early
to beat the rush for hot dogs and fizzy drinks. This proved a big mistake, for
they missed defender Wayne Brown meeting Kevin Watson's free-kick with
a thundering finish to put the U's ahead. The half-time whistle came just second later, meaning Keane suddenly had to compose a revised set of instructions for his troops.

Whatever he said in the cramped and gloomy away dressing room was
effective, for soon after the restart they drew blood – Dwight Yorke heading
in a Daryl Murphy cross to equalise. The contest then became deadlocked
for the best part of 30 minutes, but swung Colchester's way after substitutions by manager Geraint Williams. He threw on bustling Jamie Guy in place
of Chris Iwelumo and the tricky Hogan Ephraim in place of Johnnie
Jackson. Ephraim found the space to regularly turn left-back Dean
Whitehead inside out and, as the pressure mounted, Sunderland's usual swag-
ger became noticeably absent.

Suddenly the title-favourites began to crack. When the Colchester goals
came they were worthy of the occasion. Richard Garcia's slick turn and finish was from the top drawer, and Jamie Cureton's penalty clincher bore the
mark of a man who knew what he was going to do and how he was going

to do it. Another crack Championship side had succumbed to the might of little Colchester United.

The roar which greeted the final whistle was enough to shake the foundations of the old ground and must have nearly set off the security alarms in the nearby garrison. Who was the most dignified person in the place? Roy Keane, who took defeat manfully and proceeded to provide the waiting TV crews with a calm and measured assessment of the game. All was not so composed in the Colchester ranks, as players, officials and supporters came to terms with the fact that the team had left itself with a realistic, if outside chance of making the play-offs for a place in the Premiership with just a fortnight of the season to go. After 54 seasons of perennial struggle in League football, this position represented an all-time high. The situation took some believing: after all, this club was enjoying its very first taste of this level of English football, having been tipped for relegation in every one of the past nine campaigns.

Just fifteen years earlier Colchester had been a non-league outfit and in the intervening years the gap between the rich and the poor in English football had grown ever wider. Clubs like the U's had long accepted that in the modern game the odds are stacked heavily against the little guys and, as ever more money pours into the coffers of the elite clubs, those odds lengthen yet further. Wimbledon did manage to climb from non-league football into the top flight, but that was back in the 1980s and miracles like that simply didn't happen any more. And certainly it couldn't happen to a club like Colchester, which had never spent more than £50,000 on a single player, whose gates had averaged below 5,000 for the last 30 years, and whose tiny ground was frankly a source of amusement to visiting fans.

Colchester 3 Sunderland 1: how the mighty had fallen. It was a monumental victory and proved that giant-killing is not a footballing phenomenon confined merely to cup competitions. Perhaps the spirit of the recently deceased Bobby Cram was gazing approvingly over Layer Road that afternoon. Cram had played a major role in the single most famous day in Colchester United's history – captaining the 1971 FA Cup victory over Leeds United. In those days the U's were down in the old Fourth Division, struggling to make a promotion challenge with a team of veterans and journeymen, but able to rise to the challenge of a big cup-tie. Those of us who witnessed the 3-2 defeat of the mighty and much-disliked Leeds find it hard to believe that more than 35 years have passed since that great day. Particularly when you consider that 35 years before the Leeds game, Colchester United didn't even exist.

Since the club's formation as a professional outfit in 1937 there had been many notable ups and downs but, in terms of the U's national standing and prestige, April 2007 represented a new peak. In terms of the English football 'pyramid' they were now one of England's top 30 clubs. Yet as recently as the early 1990s their 'ranking' was in the low 90s. The expected relegation battle in this first Championship season of 2006-07 had not materialised, despite a distinctly shaky start. They had proved over the course of the campaign that they were no flash in the pan at this level, beating just about everyone in the top half of the table at least once, with brilliant home form turning Layer Road into a real fortress that filled visiting opponents with fear and trepidation.

As Sunderland fans made their way out of the tiny away end with tails firmly between legs, this was a time to reflect on how times had changed at this footballing outpost. Even the most optimistic Colchester follower cannot have expected a promotion challenge in 2007 – the bookies had predicted a finish of 22nd place, and they rarely get things this badly wrong. Those grey Layer Road days of goalless draws against the likes of Rochdale in front of 1,500 people were still clear in many memories, but they suddenly seemed like an awful long time ago.

Football supporters are liable to get over-excited at victories such as this over Sunderland, but most managers like to remain calm and not get carried away when asked for their views. And so it was for United's stoical and likable manager Geraint Williams, who did his post-match interviews looking as composed and unfazed as ever. Skipper Wayne Brown was a tad more excited, however, as he spoke for the players: 'Layer Road has rocked this season, and that was the case against Sunderland. It was a fantastic atmosphere. Before the match we said this was a must-win game to stand any chance of getting into the play-offs. Well, we've won it, so we have a hell of a chance now.'

The results of the various remaining games in the closing days of the campaign went largely to form, and the lack of any further miracles meant that Colchester did ultimately fall just short of a play-off place, but, curiously, this didn't seem to matter too much. The U's had exceeded expectations to such an extent, and provided the fans with so much to enjoy and mull over, that there were no gloomy faces to be found when the final League placings were ultimately settled.

It had been a campaign dotted with stunning victories and the win over big-spenders Sunderland will surely live longest in the memory and be regarded as the zenith of an incredible season. In years gone by, Colchester had often made national headlines with outstanding one-off cup giant-killings, but finishing in the top ten of the Coca-Cola Championship was an achievement that surely outstripped all of those.

Perhaps the club 'peaked' that week in April 2007, over-achieving in a way we will never see the likes of again? An optimist might beg to differ, for there is now a new owner on board in the shape of successful young businessman Robbie Cowling, and building work is finally underway on a brand new stadium, meaning the potential is there for many more days like the Sunderland visit. Ever since Queen Boudicca and her rebels came to Colchester in Roman times, away victories became common occurrences in this part of the world. Not any longer!

## CHAPTER 1

50 Years of Ups and Downs

1937-1987

A few U's fans basking in the success of 2007 were old enough to have been around when it all started 70 years earlier. For Colchester United FC is a relatively young club, born in 1937, a year in which Manchester City won the League, Sunderland the FA Cup, George VI was crowned and Neville Chamberlain became Prime Minister. Across the Channel a certain Adolf Hitler was reportedly developing plans to acquire 'more living space' for the German people. Football in Colchester was also expanding its horizons, albeit with less frightening consequences.

The plan in Britain's oldest recorded town was for Colchester United to operate as a professional outfit, sharing the homely Layer Road ground with established amateur club Colchester Town, who'd been in residence since 1909. Before long, however, the older club (nickname The Oysters), folded due to financial problems.

The new professional team had the stage to itself. Neighbours Ipswich Town had turned professional just a year earlier and had lofty ambitions of breaking into the Football League as soon as possible. The U's didn't want to get left behind and plans were made at Layer Road to shape the new organisation into one fit for League status. Ipswich were able to gain admission remarkably quickly, so in 1939 Colchester boldly tried their luck too, but were rebuffed, receiving not a single vote in the poll of other clubs.

So Colchester United were forced to serve an apprenticeship in the Southern League, their first competitive match coming at Yeovil, a town to which they would return 69 years later for arguably the most important League game in their history. By the time the 1939-45 War was over, Colchester were an established force in the Southern League and during 1947-48 went on an historic FA Cup run which saw them become the first non-league outfit ever to reach the competition's quarter-finals. Led by Ted Fenton, a deep-thinking manager who devised the much-publicised 'F-plan', they beat Wrexham and Bradford from the Second Division and then, astonishingly, the Division One giants Huddersfield. The Cup adventure ended when Stanley Matthews and company put five past them at Blackpool.

The footballing world had by now sat up and taken notice of this brash new club from Essex, and the U's good attendances, solid League form and Cup heroics inevitably combined to enable election into the Football League, the successful application coming in 1950, even though they finished behind Merthyr in that year's Southern League. They were accepted into Division Three (South), alongside Gillingham, with Scunthorpe and Shrewsbury elected to Division Three (North) – the four clubs benefiting from the League's expansion to 92 clubs. The U's polled 28 votes, some way behind Gillingham's 44, but well ahead of local rivals Chelmsford City, whose pre-election confidence was deflated when they polled just eight votes.

After adapting to the brave new world, Colchester made a steady if unspectacular start to life in the Football League. They were managed by Jimmy Allen, who in 1948 had been given the unenviable task of replacing the revered Fenton, who had been recruited by West Ham. Allen, it emerged later, had got the job chiefly through being pals with the departing Fenton and his appointment was not universally welcomed at Layer Road.

Star player Bob Curry had been promised the role of player-manager and was not pleased to be overlooked. Allen was a man with a fiery temper, outspoken and never afraid to give even the club's directors a piece of his mind. His time in charge saw mixed results on the field. He introduced the high-scoring local boy Vic Keeble to the side but his finishing positions in Division Three (South) were decidedly unspectacular – 16th, 10th and 22nd.

After three years in the League the club had failed to make the expected impact and things came to a head at the end of 1952-53 with Allen having rows with the board and others. At one point even the supporters club publicly criticised Allen for allowing his players to 'stroll around the town at all hours'. Eventually, under fire from all sides, Allen fell on his sword and resigned in May 1953. Having struggled on the field and desperately short of cash, the club was not in great shape over the summer of 1953, and things reached crisis point when the attempt to recruit a new manager resulted in one of the most embarrassing fiascos in the club's history.

The directors fancied taking on a player-manager to save money, but Johnny Carey of Manchester United said no and George Hepplewhite of Preston suddenly withdrew his interest. Looking at the list of remaining applicants, the directors were dismayed to see a distinct lack of experience and well-known names. They came up with a desperate shortlist of three, each interviewed in early June – former Chelsea goalkeeper Harry Medhurst, ex-Arsenal player Les Henley, and a mystery man from Wales called Ron Meades.

After the interviews were over, club secretary Claude Orrin announced that 32-year-old Meades was the chosen one. The local press were flabbergasted. The *East Anglian Daily Times* called it a 'bombshell', and their reporter asked Orrin: 'Do you seriously think a 32-year-old non-league player, out of League football since the war, can lead and inspire United in the Third Division?' A flustered Orrin is said to have made no reply. He also refused to comment when asked what the U's players would think of such an appointment. Meades was described as 6ft tall, under 12st and looking fit and young for his age. He had described himself as a family man who had coaching and masseur qualifications. He had apparently turned out for Cardiff City a few years earlier and had player-manager experience at non-league level. After getting little change out of Orrin, the man from the *EADT* decided to make his own investigations into the shock appointment of this unknown.

Enquires were made in South Wales and the West Country and it was discovered that Meades had in fact mostly been a reserve player at Cardiff City in the war years – hardly a glittering career – but did have a handful of first-team games to his name. He'd also been player-manager of Welsh minnows Treharris and later held the same role at Wadebridge Town FC in Cornwall. In the year before his appointment at Layer Road he had been mostly 'based at home, while coaching locally'.

So, it seemed that not only was Meades clearly under-qualified for the job of United manager, what little experience he did claim had been vastly exaggerated. The situation caused an almighty fuss in the press, with the U's directors accused of incompetence. Not surprisingly, within a few days the club did a complete U-turn and cancelled Meades' contract. A statement was issued saying the appointment was now void owing to the unsatisfactory outcome of enquiries made. Red-faced club director Major Gerald Benham told the *EADT*: 'We shall have to start all over again.' Hence, just four days after starting his new job at Layer Road, Meades was chased out of town. To this day, he remains the only Colchester manager never to lose a match (or to win one)!

The embarrassed directors now acted quickly, but more carefully, and recruited Jack Butler, a 56-year-old former Arsenal player who had managerial experience at Torquay, Crystal Palace, Royal Daring of Belgium and briefly with the Belgian national side. Butler arrived with a personal recommendation from Arsenal's secretary-manager Tom Whittaker and – compared to Meades – his qualifications and CV looked impeccable. On arrival in Colchester, Butler was quick to dismiss the controversy surrounding the Meades fiasco. He said: 'I don't want any ballyhoo about this job. All I can offer is 100 per cent effort.'

Despite the U's, as ever, being severely cash-strapped, they splashed out a relatively lavish salary of £12, plus £5 expenses, per week on Butler and rented him a club house at £1 a week. However, despite his impressive CV, Butler did not prove an instant success and by the end of his first season (1953-54) the U's had slumped to 23rd place and amassed just 30 points.

Fortunately the other League clubs were sympathetic when it came to re-election and Colchester retained their status, polling 45 of a possible 48 votes. Many players departed that summer and the club built new offices and a boardroom – modest facilities that were still operating in 2007. On the field, however, things went from bad to worse, and after eight successive defeats in the autumn of 1954, the stress became too much and Butler suffered a nervous breakdown. He took sick leave and then resigned in January 1955.

It was crisis time again at Layer Road, but this time the choice of manager would ultimately prove a huge success. The job went to 36-year-old Benny Fenton, younger brother of former manager Ted, who accepted the role of player-manager. As a teenager Benny had turned out for Colchester Town and later starred as a wing-half for Millwall and Charlton. Inheriting a dispirited bunch of players and with more than half the 1954-55 season gone, Fenton couldn't prevent the U's finishing bottom, but was relieved when re-election was again secured. The following campaign was one of consolidation, with a twelfth-place finish in Division Three (South).

The 1956-57 season, however, would prove to be the most successful in the club's history thus far, and would remain so for a further 49 years. United missed out on promotion to the old Second Division by a whisker, pipped by Ipswich and Torquay, who amassed 59 points to United's 58. It was a monumental improvement on previous seasons, yet Fenton himself was blamed for the failure to clinch promotion, because he'd missed a penalty in a 0-0 draw with Alf Ramsey's Ipswich. Had it been scored, the U's would have finished above the Suffolk club, who have remained in the top two divisions ever since. Shell-shocked Colchester, meanwhile, went on to spend another half-century outside the top divisions.

The following campaign saw a mid-table finish before Fenton hung up his boots in 1958 to concentrate on managing. United held mighty Arsenal 2-2 in the FA Cup and finished fifth in 1958-59, but a slump followed and in 1961 led to relegation to Division Four. In those days, relegation didn't necessarily put the manager in severe danger of the sack, and Fenton's position remained secure. He repaid the faith shown in him by leading his team to instant promotion, finishing 1961-62 as runners-up with a remarkable 104 goals racked up, a club record 38 of them from local boy Bobby Hunt. After a mid-table finish in 1962-63, Fenton was tempted away to manage Leyton Orient.

Neil Franklin, the former Stoke City and England centre-half whose playing career had been blighted by his brief defection to South America, took Fenton's place. Like his predecessors, there was no honeymoon period for Franklin and, after a 17th-place finish in 1963-64, the following season ended in relegation back to Division Four. However, Franklin was able to emulate Fenton and engineer an instant return with promotion in 1966, on goal-average. Despite impressive performances by Derek Trevis, Duncan Forbes and Reg Stratton, a mid-table finish in 1966-67 was followed by yet another relegation the following year. Colchester were establishing a reputation as a real yo-yo side, and a dreadful run-in to the end of 1967-68 saw Franklin sacked. Disillusioned, he returned to his native Midlands to take charge of a pub.

The next four years saw the U's under the charge of former Crystal Palace and Orient boss Dick Graham, a period that produced mixed results but in which life was never dull. Disciplinarian Graham built a new side from the wreckage of the Franklin era, largely using cut-price bargains from his former clubs. During his tenure (1968-1972) Graham's teams remained in the upper half of Division Four (6th, 10th, 6th and 11th), without ever looking convincing promotion material.

League disappointments during this period were overshadowed by dramatic events in cup competitions. The club re-established its reputation as giant-killers in a big way, notably when Don Revie's mighty Leeds United were beaten 3-2 in the fifth round of the FA Cup on an unforgettable day in February 1971. The result meant manager Graham had to honour a rash pre-match pledge to climb the walls of Colchester Castle if Leeds were beaten.

The ageing U's team (dubbed Graham's Grandads) ultimately went out in the quarter-finals at Everton, but no Fourth Division club has ever gone further in the competition. The U's became the talk of the nation and just a few months later won the Watney Cup, overcoming West Brom in a thrilling final at The Hawthorns. BBC TV's *Match of the Day* viewers marvelled at a contest that ended 4-4 after extra-time, and was won by inexperienced teenager Phil Bloss in one of the very first penalty shoot-outs to be seen in this country.

Despite all the cup excitement, League success continued to elude the club. A memorable Layer Road era ended when Dick Graham quit in the autumn of 1972, storming out of a shareholders meeting after hearing what he considered ill-informed criticism of his team from a local police officer, who had reportedly won his shares in a raffle. Graham, recently suffering from health problems, walked out for good.

Most fans were horrified by this turn of events and were doubtful about the choice of his successor. Before long, however, it became clear the new man had actually been an inspired choice. Jim Smith, a no-nonsense, balding Yorkshireman, player-manager of non-leaguers Boston United, took charge at Layer Road. The way Smith confronted the challenge of reviving a Colchester side languishing at the bottom of Division Four marked him out as a man to be reckoned with. After turning his no-hopers into promotion-winners in eighteen months, he was tempted away in 1975 to Blackburn Rovers, an early step in a long and celebrated managerial career that continues to this day.

A major factor in Smith's success at Colchester was his partnership with coach Bobby Roberts, a Scot who had served Leicester City as a useful defender. Long-serving goalkeeper Mike Walker reckoned Smith and Roberts formed a phenomenal combination: 'Bob was the quiet, thoughtful side of the partnership and players could take their problems to him,' he says. 'But if you tried to cry on Jim's shoulder he would probably clump you round the head.' Roberts took over the reins after Smith set off for grander horizons, and oversaw a period (1975-82) in which the U's yo-yo reputation was reinforced. Roberts experienced two relegations and a promotion before a fall-out with the board of directors saw him leave the club after seven years in charge.

For once, relegation to the Fourth Division in 1980 did not spark an immediate return, and throughout that decade the club toiled in vain to get out of the football basement. Former Ipswich and Northern Ireland skipper Allan Hunter had a brief spell at the helm after Roberts' departure, but quit after just nine months in charge, stating that the enjoyable aspects of his job were far outweighed by the unpleasant ones.

Unlucky Hunter even had to deal with the tragic death of striker John Lyons, who took his own life after experiencing personal problems and having suffered from crowd barracking. The post-1980 slump at Layer Road would only temporarily be halted by the efforts of subsequent managers Cyril Lea and Mike Walker, who both briefly hoisted the club into the upper reaches of Division Four, but couldn't achieve the target of promotion.

The urbane Walker, with 522 appearances in the U's goal to his credit, appeared to be getting things right in 1987 but suddenly left his post in bizarre circumstances – more about this in the next chapter. With hindsight, Walker's exit signalled the start of a real decay in Colchester's fortunes. The U's embarked on an inexorable downward slide and less than three years later the hardy Layer Road fans suffered the ultimate horror – watching their club demoted out of the Football League.

## CHAPTER 2

Another Fine Mess

1987-1991

After 40 years and 1,838 games as a Football League club, Colchester United suffered banishment to the wilderness of non-league football on a depressing weekend in April 1990. Fellow strugglers Hartlepool and Doncaster both chalked up victories, while the U's stumbled haplessly to a 0-4 thrashing at Cambridge.

The season still had a week to go, but these results meant survival was now impossible and Colchester were demoted to the Vauxhall Conference. No longer could the club finishing 92nd be saved by the old boys re-election network – automatic demotion had recently been introduced and Colchester found itself an early victim.

For the devoted football fan, relegation to a lower division is a cataclysmic event; demotion out of the League is even worse. U's supporters were shell-shocked, even though this calamity had been feared for some weeks. Surely this sort of thing only happened to eternal strugglers like Newport or Hartlepool? How on earth had it happened to Colchester, a club with a rich giant-killing transition for whom 'normality' meant bouncing between Divisions Three and Four?

Storm clouds had been deepening over Layer Road for some years but at what point did a drama become a crisis? Looking beyond the emotion and the recent calamities, it seems the source of the decline can be traced to the day five years earlier when a brash young businessman walked into the club brandishing his cheque book.

Back in 1985 locally based marketing man Jonathan Crisp – the son of a former Test cricketer – had failed to buy his way into Ipswich Town and decided to turn his attention to their hard-up neighbours Colchester, over the Suffolk-Essex border, eighteen miles to the south. Millionaires were an unfamiliar sight at humble Layer Road and Crisp nearly had his hand bitten off.

He was welcomed with open arms and quickly seen as a messiah who could lead this cash-strapped club out of the doldrums. Sadly, it would prove a false dawn. Crisp and Colchester would not make a happy marriage and history shows that his six-year period in control of the club was little short of disastrous.

I clearly recall attending the meeting at which his bid for control was approved, and being infected by his wholehearted enthusiasm as he promised that within five years he would get the club into football's second tier and have them operating from a new stadium. It seemed an exciting and plausible pledge, and spirits were lifted both within the club and out on the crumbling terraces.

Little did we know then, but the things Crisp was promising would actually take more than twenty years to materialise and it would be bad times, not good, that were just around the corner. Not only would Crisp be unable to deliver the success he promised, but fortunes would go dramatically in the opposite direction.

South African-born Crisp was a charismatic and well-connected figure, and head of a highly successful marketing empire. A lover of art and fine wine, he couldn't have presented a more contrasting figure to his predecessor as Colchester chairman, Maurice Cadman, a salt-of-the-earth builder, born and bred in north Essex. Crisp was, in fact, unlike anyone who preceded him in the cramped Layer Road boardroom. He was driven to be a high-achiever, a trait surely inherited from his father Bob Crisp, DSO, MC, an extraordinary figure whose heroics as a Test cricketer were just a part of his own life story.

Bob Crisp resembled a figure from the pages of *Boy's Own*. A hostile pace bowler, he remains the only international cricketer to have taken four wickets in four balls, twice. In 1935 he bagged five wickets for South Africa against England at Old Trafford, just days after climbing Mount Kilimanjaro.

According to *Wisden's Almanac*, Bob Crisp was 'essentially an adventurer with something of an attention span problem'. During the Second World War he was an outstanding but turbulent tank commander, fighting his own personal war against better-armoured Germans in Greece and North Africa. He had six tanks blasted from under him in a month but carried on fighting and was awarded the DSO for outstanding gallantry. Crisp hated authority so much that General Montgomery intervened personally to prevent him being given a Bar a year later – this, his second honour, being downgraded to an MC. Crisp was mentioned in despatches four times before being invalided out of Normandy. The King asked if his bowling would be affected by his war injuries. 'No, sire,' he is reported to have replied. 'I was only hit in the head.'

After the War he returned to South Africa where son Jonathan was born, and took up journalism. He founded the now well-established black newspaper *Drum*, before settling in England where he tried mink farming before becoming a leader writer for the *East Anglian Daily Times*. He published books on his war exploits – *Brazen Chariots* (1957) and *The Gods Were Neutral* (1960) – before going off to live in a Greek hut for a year.

Informed that he was now suffering from incurable cancer, he spent a year walking round Crete, selling accounts of his adventures to the *Sunday Express*. Crisp died at his home near Colchester at the age of 82, reportedly with a copy of the *Sporting Life* on his lap, having just lost a bet. A risk-taker to the last.

Son Jonathan inherited his father's bullishness but directed his energies into marketing before alighting on the idea of building a brighter future for Colchester United. After securing ownership of the club for an initial outlay of just £150,000, his first high-profile action at Layer Road was to sack team manager Cyril Lea and coach Stewart Houston. Crisp wielded the axe as the 1985-86 season began to peter out with the club again treading water.

Mediocrity was not good enough, said Crisp, and he would only tolerate success. Reserve coach and former goalkeeper Mike Walker was put in caretaker charge and instantly transformed results, with five wins and three draws from the final eight games. Crisp and others were surprised at Walker's aptitude for the task, which was rewarded by him being given the job full time.

Thirty-nine-year-old Crisp had friends and contacts within sport and show-business, and he made full use of these to aid his new football project. Former Arsenal manager Bertie Mee was recruited as Colchester's football consultant and comedian Frank Carson joined the board. Carson visited the ground and gave the players what was described as a 'pep talk', but as time went on he was rarely seen at matches. Nevertheless his arrival initially stirred up interest and publicity, which was presumably Crisp's main aim.

Other famous faces – including singer David Essex – were spotted in the stands at Layer Road from time to time, but perhaps the sight of a half-empty, poorly appointed stadium deterred potential investors from dabbling in Crisp's little enterprise.

Mike Walker's first full season as manager saw a measure of improvement on the field. The team squeezed into the Fourth Division play-offs, only to lose to Wolves in the semi-finals. On paper, at least, things seemed to be moving in the right direction. However, Crisp was not satisfied with this snail-like progress and had a few more bombshells up his sleeve. Ostensibly to improve life for loyal U's fans, Crisp announced that the club's 50th anniversary would see the introduction of a 100 per cent ground membership scheme, effectively meaning away fans and neutrals were banned.

Naturally the idea provoked incredulity and hostility, both locally and from other clubs, but Crisp insisted he was creating a better environment for the people who mattered – home fans – who would eventually turn up in greater numbers attracted by the safe and pleasant surroundings. Luton Town had introduced something similar in the top division a season earlier in a bid to combat hooliganism, reducing the number of arrests at games to zero, and Crisp was keen to follow suit.

Crisp seemed baffled and frustrated by the negative response to his scheme: 'Needless to say, most of the comment that has been published has been negative, some even going so far as to equate club membership to South Africa's pass laws. I have personally been described as everything from a rabid Tory to an ego-tripping maniac.'

Applications to become a member (costing £5) were screened to ensure only home fans were accepted, but the response from the Essex public was so poor that just 1,600 signed up before the first game of the 1986-87 season. One of the lowest gates in the club's history (1,372) attended an occasion that normally would have attracted around three times that number.

Even with such a small turnout, large queues built up outside the ground. Confusion reigned, with a few foreign tourists standing around looking baffled at not being allowed in. The whole thing was evidently a fiasco. In subsequent weeks record-low crowds of fewer than 1,200 turned up for matches with Peterborough and Swansea. Inevitably, the idea was subsequently scrapped, and Jonathan Crisp's standing in the eyes of many fans had taken a fatal knock.

Crisp's next trick outdid the away fans ban. During the autumn of 1987 Mike Walker led the team to joint-top of Division Four, only for his chairman to respond by giving him the sack. To be fair to the chairman, he had presumably decided much earlier that a change of manager was required to bring success, and it was while searching for Walker's successor that the team (rather embarrassingly for Crisp), began to win football matches on a regular basis.

With classic timing, Crisp summoned Walker and his deputy Allan Hunter to his home on the weekend that Colchester had gone joint-top after beating Darlington. Conflicting stories abounded over what was said but, whatever the truth, Walker and Hunter went in with a job and came out without one – the official line being that a conflict over a 'matter of principle' had arisen.

The popular version that became established later was that the pair refused to concur with Crisp's vision that the only way out of Division Four was to kick your way out. The media had a field day, marvelling at how Walker had won the manager of the month award and got sacked within hours.

As a member of the local press corps at that time, I had the dubious pleasure of 'door-stepping' a shell-shocked Walker the next day. Grim-faced, he emerged from his home in Bures to say he was unable to comment on what had happened because the matter was in the hands of his legal people. The sacking shocked the world of football but the urbane Walker was soon offered work elsewhere, accepting a coaching job at Norwich. His assistant Hunter, meanwhile, gave a metaphorical two-fingered salute to his former employer and went off to work on Felixstowe Docks. Within a few years Walker had risen to become manager of the Canaries, leading them to a spell at the top of the Premier League and a memorable run in Europe.

Many U's fans thought chairman Crisp had gone completely bonkers. Even more so when he announced the name of Walker's replacement, a certain Roger Brown, manager of the none-too-successful non-league side Poole Town. 'Roger who?' screamed the headline in the *Evening Gazette*.

Thirty-five-year-old Brown was a big, blond-haired former centre-half who'd played for Bournemouth, Norwich and Fulham. His managerial qualifications looked rather flimsy, but apparently he had been recommended to the chairman by his new 'consultant' Bertie Mee.

Without wishing to insult Brown, most people found his appointment strange, although it gave credence to rumours that Crisp intended to create a team with a more physical presence. In his playing days Brown had been a no-nonsense defender who struck fear in opposing defences when he stormed forward for set-pieces. He'd never been a quick, skilful player but had certainly been effective after entering the professional game late in life. Until he was 25, Brown had played for AP Leamington as a part-timer, combining his football with a job in industry.

Reflecting his own playing style, Brown tackled his new job with determination and gusto. He appeared at a press conference to announce that he would take little Colchester from Division Four to Division One in three years. He looked deadly serious as he uttered these words, and local hacks like myself were astonished to be confronted by a man who apparently made even more rash promises than Crisp. In a less positive moment later on, however, Brown showed his melancholy side: 'If we get promotion this season, the credit will go to the previous manager, and if we fail it'll be down to me.'

Brown's press conferences could certainly be lively events. I recall one occasion when he launched into me for the crime of 'smirking' at something he had said (in reality, it was probably astonishment and not disdain showing on my face). On another occasion he announced his intention

to single-handedly invade the terraces to sort out one particularly vocif-
erous critic.

Apparently these were not empty words, for he came close to carrying out this threat, I was told, but fortunately got no further than verbal
ripostes from twenty yards or so. Later on, a friend of mine, concerned
about recent U's results, wrote to the club offering his views and was startled the next day to receive a personal phone call from Brown who vocif-
erously defended himself. For all his faults, Brown was not a man afraid
to confront issues head on.

By a twist of fate, Brown's first game in charge of Colchester would
be an FA Cup-tie against his home-town team, non-league Tamworth, for
whom his brother played. Brown got off to a 3-0 winning start and
results continued to go well over his first few weeks. United even hit top
spot after beating Cardiff, leading to Brown winning the manager of the
month whisky which, given what happened to Mike Walker, might have
been a rather ominous development. Before long, however, results took
a serious downturn and a run of nine games without a win dropped the
U's from first place to halfway in a matter of weeks.

Attendances remained embarrassingly low and an air of unrest per-
vaded Layer Road. Serious questions were being asked. How could a winning side suddenly slump so badly? Were the players not fully behind their
new manager?

The U's eventually finished ninth and the subsequent summer of 1988
proved unhappy. Major cash losses were announced at the club and season ticket sales were poor. Only 1,664 watched the opening game of
1988-89 and only three of the opening ten games produced victories.
Brown worked long and hard – he sometimes looked stressed and unwell
– but couldn't turn things around no matter how he tried.

One of the most miserable eras in the club's history finally came to an
inglorious end in mid-October 1988 when a U's team bereft of spirit and
inspiration were hammered 0-8 by a very moderate Leyton Orient. This
disaster could only have one outcome. Roger Brown resigned, subsequently leaving the professional game altogether, and youth team coach
Steve Foley found himself in temporary charge. Critics of Jonathan Crisp
were in full cry. Things were going from bad to worse for the beleaguered
chairman. Just to rub more salt into gaping wounds, a local farmer came
forward to lay claim to a plot of land within the proposed Turner Rise
development in the town, thus scuppering plans which included a much-
needed new stadium.

Roger Brown's exit failed to halt the bad times on the field. The next
sixteen League games failed to produce a win and the U's found them-

selves marooned at the bottom of Division Four for weeks. There was a measure of light relief thanks to unexpected progress in the FA Cup, but when one of the team's few saleable assets, Rudi Hedman, departed to Crystal Palace for £100,000, fans questioned the ambition of the board. As a sign of the times, fewer than 1,000 turned out for a local derby with Southend in the Sherpa Van Trophy, even though former favourite Ian Allinson was making his return to the club.

An end to League football in the town looked very likely after the turn of the new year, prompting the *Evening Gazette* to launch a 'Save Our Soccer' campaign to try and galvanise players, officials and fans into preventing such a calamity.

Meanwhile, chairman Crisp searched high and low for a new manager to stop the rot. His previous choices had been untried at League level, so now he decided it was time to go for experience. Through his footballing social circle he tapped up a high number of well-known names, most of whom were frightened off by United's predicament as the 92nd club in the Football League ladder.

Then somebody told Crisp that Jock Wallace, the legendary former boss of Glasgow Rangers, was no longer working and was spending his days at a villa in Spain, playing golf and enjoying an early retirement in the sun. Wallace was a respected figure who frightened the life out of those he confronted, credentials which greatly appealed to Crisp. Before long the chairman was off to Spain, to work his charm on the battle-hardened 53-year-old Scot.

It was suggested that Wallace had suffered health problems and was now enjoying life away from the pressures of football with his wife. Nevertheless, Crisp's persuasive tongue somehow talked him into giving up the sun and sangria in favour of the grey January skies of north Essex and the stiff challenge of hauling the U's out of trouble. For once, Crisp had taken a radical step that met with approval. He'd apparently been pumping money into the ailing club with little appreciation from the supporters, but appointing Wallace was something that would surely halt the slide and win back the missing thousands.

And so it proved. Wallace quickly transformed the club, recruiting new players and creating a sense of purpose that saw results improve and attendances soar. Among his minor miracles was an instant profit on Irish winger Paul McGhee: he purchased him for £35,000 from Bohemians and after just four appearances sold him to Wimbledon for £150,000. But perhaps the most remarkable stroke he pulled was to persuade World Cup winner Alan Ball, until recently manager of Portsmouth, to come to Layer Road as first-team coach. Long-suffering U's fans struggled to believe the news that one of the most famous names in football was on his way to join the rescue act.

Ball later recalled the day he was approached to come to Colchester: 'When Jock Wallace rang he said he needed some help at Colchester United and asked if I fancied going there as his assistant. I told him I had to visit Qatar and that when I came back I would get back to him, but that his offer was very appealing. I didn't know where Colchester were in the league – when I looked in the paper, trailing my finger down the two lower division tables, I stopped at the last place. There they were, Colchester United, bottom of the Fourth Division. It was April 10 and I rang him to say I would be over to see him. It was the beginning of long weeks of absolute fun. I have never laughed so much in all my life, because Jock Wallace had an enthusiasm for life and football that was incredibly rich. He was everything you wanted in a football man. He was Bill Shankly, he was Harry Catterick, he was my dad, and he was Sir Alf Ramsey, all rolled into one.

'The players loved him like a father, but there was always a fearful respect for him. Winning, not that Colchester had much experience of it, was a deadly serious matter. I was not impressed with the team in our first away match [1-1 at Hereford] and I remember going home and wondering aloud just what I had got myself into. For the next match [1-1 at Lincoln], on a Tuesday night, the situation was still dire but I had not yet seen Jock in full flow in the dressing room before a match. As the lads filed in, Jock, with his rich rasping Scottish accent, announced the team and told them to get ready. "We are going to war" he said, like a Rob Roy commander in some Highland battle. "This is war".'

Driven on by the passion of Wallace and Ball, United started picking up points. From being adrift at the bottom, they caught 23rd-placed Darlington by April. However, Brian Little's Quakers were also enjoying a mini-revival and for a while the two clubs were neck and neck, caught up in a desperate two-cornered fight for survival.

With barely a fortnight to go, the two sides met at Feethams in late April 1989 for what would be a death or glory encounter. A huge following from Essex headed up the A1 for the showdown and witnessed a thrilling 2-1 victory, which provided the springboard for a dramatic finish to the season.

A week later, the biggest Layer Road crowd of the season, four times the paltry number attending earlier games, turned out to see United take on Exeter. Points were still essential to avoid the drop, but by now confidence abounded and the earlier gloom was truly banished. As the Layer Road terraces rocked to the sound of fans chanting Wallace's name, Alan

Ball recounted the astonishing scenes inside the home dressing room before this game:

'When they were stripped, I did my spiel. It was obvious stuff and Jock just sat on the side silently as I launched into my tactical plan in coach-speak. We were going to play tight and push up as a unit. I was doing my rousing best and Jock was saying nothing. Good, I thought, he is letting me get on with it. Just as I finished he stood up and the no-frills, no-nonsense Scottish voice announced: "You, Tony English, my skipper, stand in the middle of the dressing room and sing. By the way, I dinnae like the name, son." Tony stepped forward looking slightly embarrassed and heard another strident order to sing. "Sing what?" he said, desperately puzzled. "Nae surrender," commanded Jock. The lad started quietly murmuring "No surrender" and Jock exploded. "It's nae surrender," he shouted to Tony. "Louder," roars Jock, and gets the rest of the team in a huddle all singing. I could not contain myself and escaped to the physio's room to peep through a little cubbyhole. Jock was in the middle of them with his "Nae surrender" and then suddenly he hit his captain a full blow in the stomach, elbowed somebody else, gave another a crack and the buzzer went for them to get out on the pitch. They ran out and walloped Exeter 4-0 and I cried laughing.'

Wallace and Ball had achieved their aim to keep United in the League, but the exciting six months under their command proved to be another false dawn. Before 1989-90 started Ball left to become Mick Mills' deputy at Second Division Stoke and, without his trusty lieutenant, Big Jock found himself unable to maintain the momentum. Just one win, against hapless Maidstone, was chalked up over the opening months and, after horrendous defeats by Aldershot and, later, Torquay at home, Wallace called it a day, relinquishing his job but agreeing to remain as a director. It emerged later that he was suffering from Parkinson's Disease, a condition first spotted after he described his symptoms one day to the U's physio Charlie Simpson. Wallace returned to Spain and died of his illness in 1996.

Although Wallace had signed promising youngsters like Mark Kinsella and Martin Grainger, the team he left behind ended December 1989 rock bottom, with just two wins to its name. Once again United's League status hung by a thread. In the first days of 1990 Crisp appointed former Ipswich and England stalwart Mick Mills as his new manager. Curiously, Mills had recently parted company with Stoke, with his job at the Victoria Ground going to Alan Ball. The managerial merry-go-round was certainly in full swing. Mills was a dapper and articulate character who had excellent credentials as a player but who would never quite get to grips with the crisis at Layer Road. His appointment meant the U's had been managed over the past eight years by footballing legends from each of the four British nations – Mills (ex-England skipper), Wallace (ex-Rangers manager), Hunter (ex-Northern Ireland captain), and Lea (ex-Wales international).

Although home results improved in the second half of 1989-90, the side remained marooned in the bottom three throughout Mills' reign, hitting the floor again in mid-March, this time never to recover. Dismal defeats in April against Southend and Torquay killed hopes of a late revival. By the time the U's surrendered 0-4 at Cambridge it was all done and dusted – Colchester were Conference-bound.

There was a late ray of hope when Aldershot's financial plight threatened their existence, but when the Shots survived a High Court winding-up order and retained their Division Four status, demotion for the U's was confirmed. It meant Jonathan Crisp's great five-year plan had not only failed to materialise, it had backfired spectacularly. It was a black period, especially for the long-standing supporters who'd enjoyed the good times. Many wondered whether United were on their way to obscurity, never to return. Losing League football felt like a big part of their lives was being taken away. The club announced it would remain fully professional and would fight to get back, but this did little to console the doomsayers.

Despite his good intentions, and all the money he apparently poured into the running of his pet project, the charming and eminently clubbable Mr Crisp had overseen a footballing disaster. He took much personal abuse, but must surely have accepted this as inevitable after the inglorious way his ambitious pledges had failed. It was hoped to sell the Layer Road ground back to Colchester Borough Council for £1.2 million to ease club debts, but this proved yet another controversial move which only stirred up further discontent.

Mick Mills didn't hang around, so Crisp appointed another of his Ipswich cronies, former Town midfielder Ian Atkins, to be player-manager in the first season of the non-league era. United remained a professional outfit and achieved a degree of consistency in their new surroundings, battling near the top of the table with Barry Fry's Barnet throughout the season.

Many loyal fans even admitted the drop had not proved the disaster they had anticipated, for the upturn in results was welcome and they were having plenty of fun visiting new places on away trips. There were surprisingly high turnouts of U's fans at footballing outposts such as Runcorn, Slough and Sutton.

As new kids on the block in the Conference, the U's found themselves involved in the FA Trophy for the first time. This led to the previously unimaginable sight of the club entertaining local side Wivenhoe in front of a near-5,000 crowd. Wivenhoe had been the subject of considerable investment and were full of well-paid, fading Football League stars, yet a few years earlier it had been little more than a north Essex village team. To see them competing on a level playing field with Colchester was a real sign of the times.

Not long ago the likes of Newcastle, Manchester United and Leeds visited Colchester for cup-ties – now teams like Wivenhoe squeezed into the cramped away dressing room at Layer Road. Local pride was retained when Wivenhoe were well beaten, and indeed 1990-91 saw nineteen of the 26 visiting teams leave with tails between their legs. But, despite all Ian Atkins' efforts, it was Barnet who won the race for the GM Vauxhall Conference title, pipping the U's by two points. Results had improved, attendances were roughly the same, but the bottom line was no immediate return to the Football League.

Crisp said a second-placed finish was not good enough: winning had been the only aim and runners-up was a failure. Not returning to the League meant cash was urgently needed to save the club from going bust. He put the entire squad up for sale, and watched as manager Atkins was lured away to become coach at his home-town club Birmingham City. Rumours began to circulate that Crisp would soon be on his way too. Sure enough, shortly after axing some long-serving office staff in a cost-cutting exercise, Crisp decided enough was enough and stood down as chairman, giving way to another young locally based businessman. James Bowdidge, a 30-year-old farmer, merchant banker and property developer was a very different character to Crisp. The grandson of a former club chairman and a genuine long-standing U's fan, Bowdidge said some complimentary things about his predecessor, praising his good intentions, but now he had to pick up the pieces.

There was no denying the vast wreckage of the Crisp years. Bowdidge inherited a club that had recently been aiming for Second Division football but was now marooned in non-league waters. He had to contend with the aftermath of a disastrous members-only scheme, the dismissal of a manager who took the club to the top of Division Four, not to mention the lost ownership of the ground and debts said to have peaked at £1.5 million. As the calendar year of 1991 drew to a close, Crisp revealed his plans to the local press:

'I am leaving the country, but it is to take up an interesting business opportunity in Africa. It has always been my intention to go to Africa and then Australia.' He added that he had written off £1 million of his own fortune when pulling out of Colchester United.

Perhaps appropriately, Crisp exited the club for the very last time with a dramatic screech of tyres and a puff of smoke. According to Francis Ponder's irreverent diary column in the *Evening Gazette*: 'It is customary for the last person to leave the ground to make sure everything is secure, but it seems the former U's chairman – at his last match before setting out for South Africa – simply drove out of the ground leaving his former empire open to the world and his cousin.'

## CHAPTER 3

'Red-Card Roy' and the Tabloid Years
1991-1994

The U's youthful new chairman James Bowdidge, younger than a number of the players under his employment, made a bold promise when he took office in 1991: Colchester United FC would be 'handed back to the people'. One of his first initiatives certainly underscored this intention, for he placed the club's wayward striker Roy McDonough in charge of team affairs. Perhaps 'allowed' the extrovert McDonough to take charge would be a more appropriate description.

Few inside or outside the game had viewed McDonough as potential management material – here was a man who liked a pint or six, relished the physical side of football and had enjoyed run-ins galore with authority. He was dubbed 'Red-Card Roy' and was elevated perhaps as the cheap option for a club with no money. After all, his job title would remain nothing more grand than 'first team coach' even though, to all intents and purposes, he had become the club's player-manager. McDonough's promotion to head honcho was something of a turnaround, for barely six months earlier his fearsome reputation worried a section of the Layer Road hierarchy so much they had tried to block his return to the club from Southend United when manager Ian Atkins recruited him as a player-coach.

Atkins recalled: 'I grew up in Birmingham with Roy McDonough and I put my neck on the line when bringing him back to Colchester to try and help us win the Conference. Jonathan Crisp, the chairman at the time, told me then that under no circumstances would McDonough come to this club. I stood my ground because I knew Roy wouldn't let me down – he didn't. He is the type of character who will bounce back again and again.'

After Atkins had got his way, McDonough, typically, scored and was then sent off in his first full game back in Colchester colours. Nobody imagined that here was the next manager of the club. However, his ever-positive attitude and gung-ho style rubbed off on his colleagues and, given the club's circumstances, he would prove a highly successful choice as leader of the pack.

With McDonough in charge, there was certainly never a dull moment at Layer Road. Perhaps it was his presence that helped persuade *The Sun* to sign a shirt sponsorship deal with the club. Perhaps the paper guessed they were linking up with a man who would be a source of future copy. Big Roy would certainly make more headlines in the tabloids than in the broadsheets, and most of them would be nothing to do with his goalscoring ability. One of his special skills was said to be consuming a pint of lager, without spillage, while standing on his head. His ever-increasing collection of red cards from referees, and a much-publicised relationship with a colleague's wife, were among other topics that would bring him publicity, not to say notoriety.

But all this aside, what an inspiring leader he proved to be on the field. United spent the crucial 1991-92 season locked in a battle with Wycombe Wanderers at the top of the Vauxhall Conference, the outcome in doubt until the very last game. Only the champions would be promoted to the Football League and the two clubs went at it hammer and tongs throughout the season. The consistency of both sides was remarkable, for they ended up with 94 points apiece, leaving third-placed Kettering 21 points adrift. Colchester lifted the title through superior goal difference, returning to the League in magnificent style when more than 7,000 squeezed into Layer Road to roar them to a 5-0 triumph over Barrow on the final day. As if these scenes of jubilation weren't enough, McDonough led the team to a notable double when winning the FA Trophy against Witton Albion at Wembley. Few long-standing U's supporters ever thought they'd see the blue-and-white stripes performing beneath the twin towers, and there was many a moist eye that afternoon in May 1992.

The most important aspect of 1991-92 was, of course, the return to the League arena, but one unexpected legacy of that glorious season was the long-lasting rivalry that has developed between Colchester United and Wycombe – who were promoted a year later. It all began in 1991 as a consequence of that thrilling Conference title race, and now, more than sixteen years later, is still accepted by both clubs as the sort of established rivalry normally only associated with local derbies. Things got really serious through the antics of the mischievous McDonough, who decided his more restrained opposite number, Wycombe boss Martin O'Neill, was ripe for a spot of winding-up. McDonough publicly questioned O'Neill's 'bottle', which led to the Northern Irishman quietly branding him arrogant. McDonough also repeatedly taunted Wycombe players on the pitch. In one game he instructed the U's to 'showboat' as much as possible after they had built a good lead, and then in a minor cup confrontation against Wycombe he played an entire team out of position, apparently treating the game as a training exercise.

McDonough recalls the period fondly: 'The rivalry between us was strong. I made a couple of remarks in the local paper saying Wycombe would bottle it [the title race] and they got back to Martin. He called me and wanted to know why I was winding people up. In the December we beat them 3-0 at home and when we were three-up the ball went out and a ball-boy threw it back to me. I looked at Martin on the bench and shouted to my players "No more goals, let's play keep-ball". We must have strung together 27, 28 or 29 passes and Martin knew then we were just taking the p***. The following week we played Wycombe again in the Bob Lord Trophy, which was a Mickey Mouse competition. So I played myself as sweeper and put the defenders up front. Wycombe won 6-2 and the Conference wanted to fine me £500, but they couldn't because I had fielded my first team. We made it to the FA Trophy final that year as well and Martin was the commentator for Sky. He called me an arrogant so-and-so on live TV!'

In recent years McDonough had become 'Essex Man' personified (despite his Birmingham roots), and although he didn't impress everyone with his laddish behaviour, most Colchester fans loved him for it. The Wycombe episode was typical of Colchester United's 'tabloid years'. The dapper O'Neill, an erudite and articulate young manager, found himself suffering a season of torment from this big, loud herbert wearing *The Sun* emblazoned across his shirt. It couldn't have been a pleasant experience, but time has shown what an outstanding manager O'Neill would turn out to be.

Both sets of fans exploited this rivalry and it slowly intensified. Years later, in a magazine survey, each set of fans would name the other club as their biggest rivals, despite the 100 miles by road between the two towns. In a subsequent encounter at Wycombe, United won 5-2 on an afternoon the visiting fans would never forget. McDonough recalled: 'I put a left-footer in the top corner. Afterwards I waved goodbye to the Wycombe fans, who were going mental, and Alan Parry, the TV commentator who is a director there, tried to get me arrested for starting a riot.'

Wycombe fans have bitter-sweet memories of that non-league rivalry with Colchester. An editorial in their fanzine 'When Skies Are Blue' explained: 'Under O'Neill, we had become a real force in non-league terms. We had won the FA Trophy the season before and had set our sights on promotion to the Football League. In our opinion we were the unstoppable force. With the best ground, largest support, best manager and a board with vision and will and means to realise that vision. Then came Colchester. They were the bad guys in the story. Just relegated from the League, they remained full-time aiming to bounce straight back as Lincoln had done previously. They had an arrogant player-manager with a motor mouth, Roy McDonough, or "McDonut" as he was rightly known. They had a reputation as trouble-makers – and not just because of McDonut – and generally considered themselves too good for non-league football.'

Fans from both sides recall clearly the eventful first meeting in 1991-92, during which some Colchester supporters deliberately infiltrated the Wycombe end to cause trouble. The home fans' discontent was compounded when United won the game with virtually the last kick – a 90-yard punt downfield from goalkeeper Scott Barrett which sailed straight into the Wycombe net. There were allegations that after the game a jubilant McDonough had made remarks to the press which seemed to condone the terrace disturbances. With both teams level on points at the season's end, Barrett's freak winner was seen as the moment that decided the title. In the final game, with Colchester just needing to beat lowly Barrow to confirm first place, McDonough sent a cheeky message to Wycombe saying that victory would be so easy that his team might as well turn out in fancy dress like the fans.

McDonough's demeanour may have struck others as loutish, but to Colchester he was a passionate figurehead who led his troops into battle with enthusiasm and vigour. His combative style as a bustling old-style centre-forward upset non-league defences immensely and inevitably landed him in trouble with referees. Eventually he would amass a grand total of 21 sending offs during his career, a total which remains the joint highest in the UK professional ranks, alongside the former West Brom and Scotland winger Willie Johnston. Thirteen of McDonough's red cards came in Football League games, putting him well ahead of more famous 'bad boys' such as Vinnie Jones, Dennis Wise and Mark Dennis. Later, when the U's were finalising new ground plans, it would be suggested by one supporter that McDonough be commemorated by the home dressing room bath being named in his honour – 'The Roy McDonough Early Bath'.

He may have been an unlikely manager, but winning the non-league 'double' in 1992 was a fine achievement. He had to banish the hangover from years of recent disappointments, and had little or no cash to work with. His key talent was his power of motivation, and this helped persuade experienced players such as Ian Stewart and Paul Roberts to join the club. Colchester banged in 98 goals in the 42 Conference games of the 1991-92 season, 26 of which came from McDonough himself, and he also helped set up many of the combined 44 scored by Steve McGavin and Gary Bennett. A personal highlight for McDonough was the foursome he scored inside 37 minutes at Slough. When attempting to claim the match-ball as souvenir afterwards, he was told by the home club that they were too hard-up to give it away, so his wife Jackie had to be summoned with her purse to cough up the necessary payment.

Veteran journalist Bernard Webber, who reported Colchester games in six different decades, reckoned that despite McDonough's wretched disciplinary record and all the other fuss that surrounded him, he deserved much credit for hauling United out of the non-league mire: 'It was no mean feat and I doubt that managers with better credentials would have fared better. Roy, a real Brummie with an accent to match, proved just the right man for a difficult job. Without him, the U's might have been stuck in the non-league wilderness for years.'

When Colchester had been demoted in 1990, it was rightly seen as the end of an era, and many feared the slow decay evident at the club would worsen, and that League status would not be regained for many years – if ever. McDonough and his troops quickly banished such fears and nobody was more proud of their achievement in bouncing back than local boy Tony English, the team's skipper. Versatile English, a reliable and popular performer for many years, recalled: 'I captained the team out of the League and I captained them back in again and during our time in the Conference every game was like a cup final. The fans were fantastic then and rallied behind us magnificently. Our ground was a fortress.'

United's return to the League was not without its worrying moments in terms of off-the-field matters. When Jonathan Crisp sold the stadium to Colchester Borough Council, the club agreed to three years security of tenure at Layer Road. But with a new stadium looking highly unlikely in the near future, this situation did not impress the Football League. They insisted upon ten years of security of tenure as a minimum requirement for League membership, and for a while it looked that the U's might be barred from returning to the League because of this technicality. After talks with the Council, the lease was extended to ten years and everyone breathed a sigh of relief. It was still necessary, however, for chairman Bowdidge to organise a 'Back to the League' appeal to raise funds to help bring the ground up to the required safety standards. This money was spent on new safety barriers and conversion of wooden terracing to concrete. The open end of the ground looked a mess, but it was passed fit for action in the League.

Shortly after McDonough was named 1992 Conference manager of the year and McGavin its player of the year – a double success Bowdidge called 'the perfect end to a perfect season' – the chairman stood down after just a year at the helm. Money was still desperately scarce, but there was certainly more optimism about the place when he left than when he had arrived. His twelve months of 'transparent government' had proved remarkably successful, considering the parlous financial state of the club. He confessed that without the FA Trophy trip to Wembley, the club's position would have been worse than desperate.

On the return to the League, Bowdidge gave way to Gordon Parker, who became the club's eleventh chairman since they first attained League status in 1950, but the first to have actually played for the club. Parker, 58, had been a regular presence at Layer Road since the War, as schoolboy fan, ball-boy, reserve team player and then director. 'If you snapped me in half you would find Colchester United running right through the centre of me,' he said. 'The U's are in my blood you see. I can remember coming here as a snotty-nosed kid one winter, praying that it would snow so hard that I could stand on it and be able to see over the fence behind the top goal.'

In many people's eyes, the oddest aspect of Parker's arrival as chairman was the fact that he happened to be the manager's father-in-law. His twin daughters had both married U's players – becoming Mrs Roy McDonough and Mrs Tony Adcock. Fans speculated over what would happen when McDonough became ripe for the football manager's inevitable day of reckoning – for he would have to be sacked by his own father-in-law.

The start of the Parker era didn't bring any fresh money for team strengthening, but the ever-cheerful McDonough didn't appear to complain. He vowed his team would continue to play attacking football and keep the big smile on the faces of the fans: 'I'll never forget those 24,000 fans cheering us on at Wembley and I want to keep that spirit going. But most of all I want to reward those wonderful people who have sweated blood throughout the summer, working so hard to get this ground up to Football League standard. I've said it before and I'll say it many times again – keep the fans happy and together we can go places.'

Once the first season back was underway, the dismantling of the side which won the non-league 'double' accelerated. Results were mixed, with much of 1992-93 spent in mid-table. Such consolidation represented a solid achievement in difficult circumstances, but many U's fans seemed to harbour ideas of instant promotion. There was a distinct air of anticlimax on the terraces when play-off hopes disappeared after heavy defeats at Rochdale (2-5) and then, embarrassingly, at Crewe (1-7). McDonough, still playing fairly regularly despite being in his 35th year, became the target of terrace abuse – less than a year after he'd been everybody's hero. After being sent off in the thrashing at Rochdale, the old warhorse announced he was retiring from playing. It was his second red card of the season for 'use of the elbow' and his continuing ill-discipline on the field was not viewed as appropriate for a manager. At this point the team had the worst disciplinary record in the division – 70 yellow and three red cards after around 35 games – and the manager was clearly not setting a good example. McDonough defended himself, claiming he was suffering at the hands of referees purely because of his reputation. Opponents were 'taking liberties' with him, he claimed, and he was not being protected by the men in black.

Perhaps the biggest setback the team faced in 1992-93 was not the manager's disciplinary problems, but the fact that American Mike Masters had not been adequately replaced in attack, nor had the club found a permanent goalkeeper. The U's created a Football League record by using no fewer than seven keepers in all matches (Munson, Parks, Newell, Monk, Green, Emberson and Barber), all of them on loan or triallists.

The fans might have been critical of certain on-pitch failings, but things remained up-beat behind the scenes. For example, Sue Smith was recruited as the club's new football secretary, the thirteenth female to take such a role in the Football League. She recalled her startling first week at the club, during which she was greeted by the sight of three apprentices running around the pitch stark naked, apparently paying the penalty for a misdemeanour against a senior player.

Despite the looming danger of a substantial fine for the team's ill-discipline, manager McDonough decided to recruit yet more 'steel' to his forward line in the shape of notorious ex-Birmingham hard-man Robert Hopkins. By common consent, Hopkins had been part of a 1980s City side that was the scariest outfit ever to lace up boots. Under grim-faced manager Ron Saunders, City fielded the so-called 'Birmingham Six' – Mick Harford, Mark Dennis, Noel Blake, Howard Gayle, and Tony Coton, along with Hopkins.

This rowdy bunch were regularly in the papers for misdemeanours on the streets of Birmingham, not to mention contravening the laws of football during their working hours. At Colchester, Hopkins proved to be a speedy forward with a fiery temper, trying to fan the embers of a fading playing career that had taken him into the top flight with Birmingham and Aston Villa. He helped the U's win half their final fourteen games of 1992-93, scoring on his debut at Shrewsbury, but the team finished four points adrift of the play-offs and Hopkins' time at Layer Road proved short-lived.

'I've been in a bit of bother in my time,' admitted Hopkins. 'While it lasted, playing in that [Birmingham] team and hanging around with those blokes was the most fun I've ever had. I don't care how much it cost me or how much trouble I got into, it was a brilliant time and I wouldn't change a thing. The other day Mick Harford said that we made the [1990s] Wimbledon side look like pussycats.'

There had been some concern that McDonough was trying to recreate that notorious Birmingham side at Layer Road, and there were certainly one or two relieved faces when the manager decided to hang up his boots after his thirteenth red card, at Rochdale. Sadly, much of the damage had already been done and shortly afterwards the club was asked to appear before the FA to explain their appalling disciplinary record. They were hit by a suspended fine of £7,500.

These were tricky times for club chairman Parker, even more so when cracks appeared in the marriage of McDonough to his daughter Jackie, who worked as the U's lottery manager. Eventually the pair would separate amid an unwanted glare of publicity, and the player-manager began living with the wife of another Layer Road employee, causing even more tension at the ground. It sparked a new wave of salacious gossip and added yet another colourful episode to the club's 'tabloid years'. Even the top-selling women's chat magazine *Take-a-Break* was attracted by the curious goings-on at Layer Road, featuring a two-page colour spread about Roy, Jackie and the new woman in his life. By that time, the CUFC love triangle had become big news and had already been covered in detail by *The Sun* and other tabloids.

For all his faults, McDonough certainly achieved more publicity for little Colchester United than probably any other single player in its history. Not since the days of Ray Crawford in 1971 had the national media been so obsessed by the U's. Even award-winning author Tony Parsons was despatched to profile Red-Card Roy for the *Telegraph Magazine* and find out what made him tick.

Parsons described McDonough as football's version of Vlad the Impaler, and seemed surprised at how likeable and placid he was off the field. Parsons asked him to reflect on his career at Colchester and the big man went all misty-eyed: 'People can never take the memories away from you. I've got videos of the double winning year – we scored 129 goals that season and set a record for the least number of defeats. The best day of my football career was when I led my team out at Wembley, going on for 34 years of age. I've enjoyed life, Tony. I would do my work – and then I would drink as much lager as I possibly could.'

McDonough made hopeful noises in the press about the team's prospects at the start of 1993-94 season and some of his optimism seemed justified when he recruited goalkeeper John Keeley from Premier League Oldham. United made a moderately good start to the campaign. The early wins, including the above-mentioned 5-2 party at Wycombe, saw the heady heights of the top four attained by October, but sadly the momentum was not sustained. Having decided to don his boots again, McDonough was constantly under fire whenever standards slipped. The classic fickleness of football fans was exposed when an awful 2-5 home defeat by Rochdale saw the team jeered off amid calls for McDonough's head. Just seven days later United trounced Wycombe by the same score and he was feted like a favourite son again.

The ups and downs continued all season, with some rare comedy in a 0-5 collapse at Hereford. The U's created a new record by having two goalkeepers sent off in the same game. McDonough himself went in goal for a spell and Hereford's Chris Pike netted a hat-trick, with each goal going past a different goalkeeper – another League record. Other remarkable events this season included a 19-0 victory for the reserves against St Albans, and a fans demonstration against the board for not investing in new players.

After Martin Grainger and Steve McGavin were sold for relatively large fees, McDonough was given limited funds for new faces, but mostly failed to get the men he wanted – one notable exception being Steve Whitton from Ipswich. Whitton signed just before the transfer deadline in March 1994, joining as player-coach, and helped steer the team clear of any lingering danger of finishing bottom and disappearing back out of the League again. The final resting place of seventeenth was, overall, disappointing and just a few days after celebrating his 500th League game in the season's final match at Carlisle, McDonough got the news he must have been dreading but possibly half-expecting.

'This is not the most pleasant of days nor the most pleasant of tasks,' said chairman Gordon Parker, as he announced that he had sacked his son-in-law following board deliberations at their end-of-season meeting. 'The board felt it would probably be best if a more experienced man was the manager.' After the decision was made and it became clear no other directors were available to break the news to his son-in-law, Parker realised he would have to do the dirty deed himself and admitted his 'worst nightmare' had finally arrived.

McDonough reflected that he had probably clashed with the board too many times, but admitted he was bemused at how they agreed a budget with him for the next season, only to sack him a few hours later: 'The way things had been going I was fearing the sack at any time, but I was only trying to express my honest opinion all the time,' he said. 'I have just experienced the three hardest years of my life as player-manager trying to make this club successful. I brought in something like £270,000 in transfers while only spending around £18,000. I told the board the budget they were offering me would only fund a team of youngsters and that would be a recipe for disaster.'

His Football League days over, McDonough went on to drift around senior non-league clubs in the region, as player, manager or coach, or a combination of the three. He enjoyed a series of highs and lows in the colours of Bishop's Stortford, Dagenham & Redbridge, Heybridge Swifts, Braintree, Chelmsford City and Canvey Island.

In his three colourful years steering the Colchester ship, McDonough had provided untold entertainment and interest, and had propelled a damaged vessel out of non-league waters in swashbuckling style. The board was probably right to let him go by May 1994, but 'Red-Card Roy' and the tabloid years would certainly be missed.

## CHAPTER 4

Out of the Mire

June 1994 – January 1999

A fortnight of wild speculation followed the May 1994 sacking of Roy McDonough, with a vast number of well-known football names touted as being in the frame for the managerial vacancy. Former Manchester City supremo Mel Machin was offered the job and apparently agreed terms, but then had a change of mind for geographical reasons.

Ultimately the winner of the race to become the U's nineteenth manager since their formation in 1937 would be an unfancied outsider who came up unexpectedly on the rails.

Step forward George Burley, the former long-serving Ipswich Town and Scotland full-back who had recently spent five years as player-coach and player-manager with Motherwell and Ayr United. Burley, who turned 38 in the week of his appointment, barely had more managerial experience than McDonough, but was obviously seen as a man with greater potential. Having lived in Essex during his fourteen-year Ipswich stint, Burley still owned a home in the county and settled back into the region with ease.

His first steps seemed positive enough. He reintroduced a playing kit of blue-and-white stripes, recruited former Ipswich manager Bobby Ferguson as a part-time coach, and reappointed local favourite Tony English as captain – rescuing him, literally, from the scrapheap, for the player had spent part of the summer working as a council dustman. Any illusions Burley had about the task ahead were quickly shattered, however, when a pre-season friendly with part-time neighbours Sudbury Town ended in a 0-5 humiliation. Burley admitted, friendly or not, this had been a shock to the system and gave him a sleepless night, but urged against talk of a crisis.

The 'c' word would be bandied about a few weeks later, though, for the team lost all the first six competitive games under Burley, four League games and two in the Coca-Cola Cup, conceding thirteen and scoring just one in the process.

It was a grim start that dumped the U's to the bottom of the League. Burley responded by bringing in former Ipswich colleagues Trevor Putney and Dale Roberts, the latter as his assistant, and even made a couple of playing appearances himself, something he'd never intended to do. To his credit he managed to turn things round in spectacular fashion.

After nicking a 1-0 win at Scarborough, confidence soared and United promptly embarked on a run of fifteen League games with just one defeat, which saw them rise to fifth place by Christmas. Highlight of that run was the five-day spell when home fans enjoyed eleven Colchester goals flying in, seven in the FA Cup replay with non-league Yeading and then four more against Scunthorpe at Layer Road.

As Christmas 1994 approached, everything in the garden looked rosy – plans were even announced to build a stand at the windswept open end of the ground. But bad news was again lurking just around the corner. In early December the club's struggling Premier League neighbours Ipswich parted company with manager John Lyall, and inevitably the U's new miracle worker Burley was mentioned as a possible replacement. The old enemy from eighteen miles up the road would be the last club United fans wanted to lose their promising young manager to.

In Christmas week, Burley was reportedly busy strengthening the U's defence by signing Paul Stoneman from Blackpool, and on Boxing Day, more than 5,000 filled Layer Road, expecting to see an unbeaten run stretched to nine games against lowly Northampton. Most fans had no inkling of what had been going on behind the scenes and were in for a big shock. Right up to the morning kick-off, many supporters – out of touch and perhaps hung-over from Christmas – were blissfully unaware that Burley was no longer manager of Colchester United. He had walked out on the club around 48 hours earlier.

Slowly the facts of this sorry episode would filter out. Ipswich had sought permission from Colchester in mid-December to speak to Burley about their vacancy. Permission was granted by U's chairman Gordon Parker, but subject only to a compensation package being agreed between the two clubs first. Ipswich made an offer, thought to have been £100,000, but Colchester turned it down flat. Ipswich did not come back with an improved offer and the situation was deadlocked. Then, a few days before Christmas, Burley reportedly handed a letter of resignation to Parker. It would emerge later that Burley had been interviewed by Ipswich at the Talbooth Hotel and Restaurant at Dedham earlier in the week. Around seven candidates were considered by the Town board, a list that included Mick Mills, Mike Walker, Graham Turner and Paul Goddard.

Gordon Parker refused to accept Burley's resignation and told him to go away and think about things. Burley still had eighteen months of his two-year contract to run, but telephoned Parker on December 23rd to confirm the resignation. The U's board were furious – they'd lost their manager and the compensation issue hadn't been resolved. The players were informed on Christmas morning, and the sensational news made some newspapers on Boxing Day just hours before the Northampton match. Colchester accused Ipswich of poaching, a dishonourable if commonplace football crime that would have been unimaginable a few years earlier in the days when the Cobbold brothers ran things at Portman Road.

The U's chairman said he had no intention of emulating Ipswich by approaching clubs with managers under contract. Meanwhile, Ipswich, struggling at the bottom of the Premier League, handed out a statement in the Upton Park press box during their Boxing Day match with West Ham. It pointed out that their manager's vacancy had been well known in football and they had received an enquiry from Burley. In accordance with accepted practice they contacted Colchester to establish their view and to seek permission to speak to him. This was granted, said the statement, but subsequent negotiations did not lead to an agreement. They had since been informed that Mr Burley had resigned his position at Layer Road and as he had renewed his enquiry for the Ipswich vacancy this was now being considered.

There was widespread sympathy for the U's and for Gordon Parker in particular. 'I warned George not to jump ship until he had somewhere safe to land,' said Parker. One paper suggested Colchester should have simply turned down Ipswich's approach and then this ugly situation wouldn't have occurred. A week or two earlier Ipswich had apparently asked Luton permission to approach David Pleat, but Hatters' chairman David Kohler said no and the matter ended there.

Ipswich Town didn't formally announce George Burley's appointment until three days after Christmas, although the man himself broke his silence from his Great Dunmow home, confirming he was bound for Portman Road. He added: 'Colchester United must realise that football can change so quickly, but I am disappointed to leave them in the way I did.'

While Burley was being unveiled on the morning of 28 December, Parker confirmed he had not been contacted by Ipswich. No compensation had been agreed and Colchester would not let the matter drop. The more Colchester fans heard about what had gone on, the more they felt aggrieved by the actions of neighbours Ipswich.

In a distinctly subdued atmosphere, the U's winning run came to an end against Northampton on that Boxing Day morning, a penalty sending them to a 0-1 defeat. There was talk of disenchanted U's fans attending the next Ipswich home game to stage a protest, but this appears not to have materialised. One fan wrote later: 'There was a strange mood at

Layer Road for that Boxing Day game against Northampton. We may not be one of the biggest clubs about, and probably never will be, but we are passionate about our club and feelings run high when someone stitches us up. Ask anyone at Layer Road who the name Judas applies to, and you'll only get one answer.'

The only consolation for the bitterly disappointed Colchester fans was that Ipswich continued to lurch from defeat to defeat, even with their new manager on board, and looked certainties to drop out of the Premier League. They shipped nine goals at Manchester United, which produced a massive cheer when announced over the public address system during a Layer Road match.

So once again the hunt for a new U's manager began, and for the second time in six months the directors ultimately sprang a surprise, choosing someone who proved popular with supporters, yet had barely been mentioned as a contender beforehand. This time the successful interviewee was Steve Wignall, the 40-year-old Liverpudlian who had made 281 League appearances at the heart of the Colchester defence between 1977 and 1983. Recently Wignall had been doing an impressive job leading little Aldershot Town on its journey up football's non-league 'pyramid'. The club had been formed from the ashes of Aldershot FC, the Football League outfit that was wound up in the High Court in 1992.

In Aldershot Town's first season (1992-93), Wignall led them to the Diadora League Division Three title by a massive eighteen-point margin. A further promotion and long run in the FA Vase followed in 1993-94 and Shots fans knew it was probably only a matter of time before Wignall would be snapped up by a higher club. In early 1995 Colchester United became that club. Wignall's qualifications to manage at Football League level were modest, but he was a popular figure at Layer Road and his appointment was greeted with cautious optimism.

With no one at the helm, the team had begun to falter, and by the time of Wignall's arrival they were slipping away from the play-off zone. The potential to mount a promotion challenge still existed, however, as was amply illustrated by an excellent display at Selhurst Park in the FA Cup, where the U's gave Premier League Wimbledon a real run for their money, only going down to a Mick Harford goal. The large contingent of travelling U's fans outsang their counterparts and enjoyed a memorable day out.

Regular goalkeeper John Cheesewright was laid low with a mystery virus, which meant Wignall was forced to call on Carl Emberson, who had cost £20,000 from Millwall – a large fee by Colchester standards – but had languished in the reserves under Burley. Wignall felt his attack needed spicing up and recruited Canadian international Niall Thompson and loaned beefy Carl Asaba from Brentford.

However, in Wignall's early weeks things only really clicked once, a stunning 4-3 win at Scunthorpe in which the team recovered from the horror of going 0-3 behind in under twenty minutes. Thompson snatched two goals in the final eight minutes to complete this remarkable feat.

Wignall made significant changes to the squad he inherited, with modest results. The fans had to be satisfied with his plea for patience while he built the side he wanted. Promotion within the League hadn't been achieved by Colchester in eighteen years and Wignall warned that he needed a little more time.

Colchester tried a unique experiment towards the end of 1994-95 when they joined forces with local businesses to allow spectators into a home game free of charge. The 1-0 win over Darlington attracted a bumper 6,000-plus. To get in, spectators had to produce a coupon from the local paper, in return for which they received 90 minutes of football, a ride from the town centre on a shuttle bus, a cup of tea and a subsidised match programme. The turnout pleased the U's commercial department, whose main aims had been to remind former fans what they were missing and to attract new ones into the bargain.

United finished this traumatic season in tenth place with a symmetrical record. Home and away they won eight and lost eight. Wignall's player-coach Steve Whitton, who had bags of experience in the top divisions, settled well in his new surroundings and ended up leading scorer and player of the year. Unexpectedly, Wignall was able to retain promising Irish midfielder Mark Kinsella, who had seemed certain to move to a bigger club in the summer of 1995.

The U's made a decent start to the 1995-96 campaign and were in the top four by the end of October. However, a dreadful tackle by Darlington's Sean Gregan wrecked Whitton's knee and the big man's crucial presence was lost for more than six months. Despite this blow, United remained between fourth and ninth in the table throughout the season. The only serious blip was the horrendous FA Cup surrender at non-League Gravesend & Northfleet, where Colchester caved in and lost 0-2, prompting the normally unruffled Wignall to brand his players as 'cowards'.

Inspired from the back by giant centre-back Peter Cawley, a former member of Wimbledon's Crazy Gang, the Cup embarrassment was soon forgotten and by the final week of the season a play-off place remained within reach. For the final game, at home to Doncaster, United needed to win and hope that either Hereford or Wigan slipped up elsewhere. That would ensure sixth place. In a lively atmosphere the U's achieved the first task, courtesy of a freak goal from full-back Paul Gibbs, whose intended cross from the flank sailed into Rovers' net to clinch a 1-0 victory. When Wigan's defeat at Northampton was announced over the loudspeakers the ground erupted in jubilation.

The play-off semi-final pitted the U's against Plymouth, whose outspoken manager Neil Warnock raised the stakes with antagonistic statements in the media, which only made U's fans and players all the more determined to see the Devon side put away.

Plymouth had splashed out more than £1 million to get where they were, while Wignall's side cost £2,000, a contrast which helped create a cup-tie atmosphere in which the U's were clear underdogs. A thundering strike by Kinsella, one of the best goals of his career, gave the U's a 1-0 win in the first leg at Layer Road. In the return things went pear-shaped in the first half and Argyle steamed into a 2-0 lead. Kinsella pulled one back, which could have proved a decisive away goal, but Colchester hearts were broken in the dying minutes when a cross was forced past Carl Emberson by Paul Williams.

That elusive promotion would escape Wignall again the following season when United ended 1996-97 one point adrift of the play-off zone. The consolation prize this time was an appearance beneath Wembley's twin towers in the final of the Auto Windscreens Shield. More than 45,000 – a crowd not bettered anywhere else in England that weekend – saw the contest against Carlisle end goalless, the U's cursing a glaring miss by a weary Joe Dunne. In the subsequent penalty shoot-out, misses by Cawley and the rookie Karl Duguid meant the U's came away empty-handed.

The season had other consolations, however, including a 7-1 thrashing of John Beck's Lincoln and a 3-1 Coca-Cola Cup triumph at First Division West Brom, the latter featuring an entertaining cameo between the sticks by emergency keeper Steve Whitton.

The single most joyful moment of an intriguing season was probably during the second, home leg of the Auto Windscreens Shield semi-final, when a 0-2 deficit against Peterborough United was clawed back, with locally born winger Paul Abrahams then firing Colchester to Wembley with a glorious 'golden goal' from 25 yards out. Earlier, Abrahams had promised his team-mates that if he scored the winning goal he would run straight down the tunnel and out to the pub without stopping. Fortunately he got caught up in a mass pitch invasion, which prevented such a transgression.

If that win over Posh produced the biggest excitement, then the home win over League leaders Fulham a few weeks earlier provided the biggest laugh. To U's fans' amusement it emerged that the empty spaces at the visitors' end were down to a blunder by a coach driver. Instead of driving Fulham fans to Colchester, the driver had got mixed up and taken them to Cambridge United instead.

Perhaps, with hindsight, the victims would be glad of his error, for the match saw Fulham's promotion hopes take a dent. After the U's went down to ten men when David Greene was sent off for an elbowing offence (the U's might have seen two red cards but the referee was lenient when Emberson handled outside his area), Fulham levelled through Simon Morgan's deflected shot on the slippery pitch. The battling ten men hit back, however, and won the points with a well-taken breakaway goal by nippy Chris Fry.

Fulham skipper Morgan had painful memories of that game, in more ways than one: 'Near the end Colchester played keep-ball near our corner flag. Paul Parker lost his head and, having already been booked, committed three reckless tackles within a minute. The referee couldn't send him off because he had already been lenient in allowing Emberson to stay on. The whole evening had been a disaster and to top it all off I was on the receiving end of a flying elbow in the last minute. More scar tissue to look forward to. The major surgery was performed in the Colchester physio's room, which at least removed me from the bitter inquest going ahead in our dressing room. The truth was, however, that despite our feelings of injustice, Colchester had out-fought us on a tricky surface and fully deserved to inflict only our fifth defeat of the season.'

The fighting spirit evident in that hard-earned win, plus the ruthless 7-1 destruction of Lincoln, showed the U's were capable of turning over the best teams in the division in 1996-97. Indeed, over a three-year period they had proved themselves to be one of the better-equipped Third Division sides, but taking that extra step to mount a serious promotion challenge was proving difficult.

Wignall needed to strengthen his hand for 1997-98, especially after losing the services of performers like Kinsella and Tony McCarthy, but, as usual, he had little to spend in the transfer market. Extra funds did come in when Ipswich were ordered to pay £135,000 compensation for taking George Burley – some of which was invested on midfielder Aaron Skelton from Luton, defender Guy Branston from Leicester, and striker Neil Gregory from Ipswich (for a club record £50,000).

The Burley saga was vividly recalled when Brentford came along seeking permission to speak to Wignall about becoming their new manager.

Having had his fingers badly burnt over Burley, chairman Gordon Parker adopted a hard line and insisted on the Bees first agreeing to a £300,000 compensation package. This figure was way out of Brentford's price range and Wignall, albeit a tad disenchanted by the whole episode, stayed in Essex.

Wignall's new signings played their part in an excellent late run – ten wins from the final fifteen League games – which saw United soar into the play-offs. They finished fourth, just a single point adrift of automatic promotion. After surviving two frantic and closely contested play-off semi-finals with Barnet, the U's reached Wembley for the third time in six years, and this time the reward for beating Torquay would be promotion to Division Two. Excited fans of both clubs made plans for the big day, but were dismayed when the FA decided to stage a friendly between England and Saudi Arabia at Wembley on Saturday, 23 May, meaning the play-off final would have to shift to the Friday evening. This made it far more difficult to get to the game, particularly for those from Torquay, most of whom lived up to 200 miles away.

As a result, the attendance was less than 20,000 and a little of the gloss was missing thanks to the vast areas of empty seats. The game itself was tense and scrappy, decided by a first-half penalty from David Gregory, a prolific scorer from midfield who'd been born in Colchester, but spent much of his career at Ipswich. The referee denied the U's a second, more blatant penalty later on, but the team clung defiantly to their lead and skipper Richard Wilkins was able to head for the Royal Box to collect the trophy. The lap of honour was long and noisy and nobody wore a broader smile than manager Wignall. With two Wembley appearances and a promotion under his belt, he had, on paper at least, become Colchester's most successful manager ever.

The subsequent 1998-99 season was Colchester's first as a 'Division Two' club, although of course they were actually playing in English football's third tier under its new name. The U's had in fact last played at this level in 1980-81, meaning their younger fans had never witnessed such heady heights before. Lining up in the same division as Colchester would be big-spending clubs such as Manchester City, managed by Joe Royle, and Kevin Keegan's Fulham. Working with the inevitably tight budget, Wignall would have his work cut out to compete with such opposition. And so it proved.

Five goals and six points in the first week of the new season promised much, as did the arrival of quality players like Geraint Williams and Jason Dozzell, but life proved tough and points hard to come by over the autumn of 1998. By early November Colchester were languishing down in twentieth place. At this point, after a 1-2 defeat by Manchester City at Maine Road (the first competitive meeting of the clubs), United's next away trip would be to a somewhat less celebrated stadium – Doctor Pit Welfare Park in the Northumberland village of Bedlington.

The FA Cup draw had placed Colchester, the famed giant-killers of yore, in the unfamiliar position of having to tackle opponents some 100 places and five divisions below them in the football pyramid. Even U's fans used to their own humble little ground were amazed by what they found awaiting them 300 miles north in Bedlington.

They were greeted by a peeling Main Entrance sign, a disintegrating papier maché model of the indigenous terrier hanging from the club-house roof – sculpted by the 78-year-old groundsman, Jack Carter – and dressing-rooms that looked worthy of a National Trust preservation order. As banana skins go, this was big and very slippery. As if the bleak little ground wasn't frightening enough, the snarling Terriers' side looked worryingly unfamiliar too.

Once upon a time this team would have been full of local coalminers, but these days it was a motley collection of factory workers, builders, computer boffins, electricians and fitters. Leading scorer John Milner was a TV repair man. Five of his colleagues, including coach Tony Lowery, had recently received redundancy notices from the local Wilkinson's razor factory. Sponsored by the local Asda supermarket, the Terriers were man-aged by Keith Perry, a builder with good motivational skills, but who had never kicked a ball himself. A few months earlier they became Northern League champions but had to decline promotion because they had no money. The proceeds from the Colchester United cup-tie would go towards buying floodlights and building a new stand behind one of the goals.

Every dog has its day, and the eager Terriers duly overwhelmed the uncomfortable Colchester professionals on that chilly November after-noon. It ended up as a 1-4 rout, which is by some distance the most embarrassing defeat in the U's history, outranking earlier losses at Dover, Leatherhead and Gravesend. It was a display that Wignall said 'will scar me for a very long time'. Eric Young, Bedlington's secretary, was in dreamland: 'We were 2-0 up at half-time and one of their lot said they'd turn us over in the second half, and it would end 4-2 at least. But I told him he hadn't seen the Terriers when they're going downhill with a lead. When our third goal went in, the bloke from Sky TV nearly fell off his wagon.'

It was a major humiliation, the impact made worse by the opponents' quaint name and remote location. Wignall was incandescent and deeply troubled at how his men had caved in, and even an away win at Notts County the following week didn't erase the bad memories. United went on a dismal run of eight games without win, four draws and four defeats, and all was clearly not well inside Layer Road. Unable to sign the new forwards he wanted, Wignall gave multi-talented teenager Lomana Tresor Lua-Lua a debut at Chesterfield and the little genius scored within four minutes of coming on.

But not even the emergence of Lua-Lua cheered Wignall up. He complained bitterly about how players' agents were making his life a misery and was also said to be unhappy about the lack of money available for purchases. Even a cash windfall from the FA – compensation for the Wembley dates fiasco – didn't seem to help. Given Wignall's unhappy frame of mind, perhaps it was not so surprising when, shortly after a Friday night home defeat by Wrexham in mid-January, he tendered his resignation. Dignified as ever, he simply stated: 'I don't think I can take the team any further.'

Perhaps a clue to his intentions might have been gleaned from his programme notes for that Wrexham game: 'Neil Campbell's agent has decided that [Campbell] is staying at Scarborough, which I say in a sarcastic manner and make no apologies for it. I genuinely fear for the game with the Bosman ruling and agents involved at all levels. Things are beginning to get out of hand and many clubs will suffer the same fate as my previous club Aldershot did in 1992, when they went out of business.'

Some observers felt that disillusionment wasn't the only reason for Wignall's 1999 departure: it was rumoured that a job had been promised him at neighbouring Southend United. Whether or not this was true, his coach Steve Whitton was quickly put in caretaker-charge of a Colchester side that was looking set to drop back into Division Three after just one season. They sat nineteenth in the table and looked jaded and demoralised to say the least.

Wignall had been one of only five managers to guide United to promotion as a League club, following in the footsteps of Benny Fenton, Neil Franklin, Jim Smith and Bobby Roberts. Apart from his final two months in the job, he enjoyed a good four years in the hot seat and, overall, his achievements were very highly rated by other former Colchester managers.

Dick Graham reckoned that what Wignall achieved on a limited budget in the lower divisions was on a par with what Alex Ferguson and other Premiership managers had achieved with millions at their fingertips to spend: 'Two Wembley finals, two promotion play-offs and just missing out on the play-offs again by a point, is a fantastic feat,' said Graham. Jim

Smith concurred: 'Without a shadow of doubt, working in the lower divisions is getting harder and harder by the season. The expectations of the fans are for ever mounting, but Steve has clearly done a great job with little room to manoeuvre and little cash to throw around. When I was at Colchester I was able to go into the non-leagues and pull out players of the calibre of Bobby Svarc and John Froggatt. You can't do that sort of thing these days – little clubs want massive fees for their players.'

## CHAPTER 5

Enter the Foreign Legion

January-September 1999

For a spell in January 1999, Colchester United's hard-won third tier status appeared to hang in the balance. Having slumped to a season's low of nineteenth place, the team looked demoralised, there was little cash for new players, and the fans were grumpy. To cap it all, Steve Wignall gave up the struggle and resigned, frustrated at every turn in his attempts to strengthen the squad.

Coach Steve Whitton was put in temporary charge, assisted by backroom staff Micky Cook and Paul Dyer. Many believed Whitton would soon be confirmed in the job. However, the directors felt someone with more managerial experience was needed to steer the club away from the relegation trapdoor, and they whittled their shortlist down to two – Steve Cotterill of Cheltenham and Mick Wadsworth of Scarborough. They plumped for the older man, Wadsworth, a dogmatic Northerner and former schoolteacher who had never hit the heights as a player, but who possessed impressive coaching qualifications.

Wadsworth's appointment provoked a mixed reaction, as summed up by supporter and fanzine writer Jason Skinner: 'The trouble was, as [he] received the vestments of power, half of the U's fans hadn't heard of him, and the other half had noticed with some concern that his previous job had seen him skilfully pilot Scarborough to the lofty position of only being the second-worst club in the entire Football League. He did have his good points though, having taken the very same Boro to the play-offs the previous season on a budget that even our own chairman Gordon Parker would consider mean.'

After caretaker Whitton had guided the team to battling away draws at Stoke and Bristol Rovers, Wadsworth assumed command and proceeded to turn Layer Road upside down. This was some feat, considering he often worked from his home, 190 miles away in Pontefract. Whereas his predecessor Wignall had struggled to find the men he wanted on the transfer market, Wadsworth was ready to launch into a frenzy of buying and selling, many of his negotiations involving foreign players. The shake-up left the club in a spin. It felt as if Colchester United was suddenly being dragged kicking and screaming into the modern world. Until now, most locals only associated foreign players with the glamorous world of the Premiership, but all that was changing.

Over the next six months or so, no fewer than fifteen new players turned out for the U's, nine of them having been born outside England. To balance things up, Wadsworth's clear-out saw fifteen players who featured in the first team during 1998-99 depart by the start of the following campaign. It represented, by a huge margin, the biggest turnover of playing staff ever seen at the club in such a short period.

Wadsworth was working his contacts to the full, and never before had Colchester had so much involvement with that scourge of the modern game – the footballer's agent. To many onlookers, all these comings and goings added up to exciting times, but more circumspect supporters wondered where it would all end. Surely there would be long-term implications for all this extravagance? Perhaps we should have expected something unusual from a man who said his heroes were poet Khalil Gilbran and miners' leader Arthur Scargill.

Veteran reporter Bernard Webber was one of those with reservations: 'Wadsworth was a dogmatic personality with whom it was often difficult to communicate, and he was not especially popular. He made dubious signings and had a shock clear-out of established favourites. Neither did the fact that he conducted some of the club affairs from his home in the North help endear him to the fans.'

The net result of the Wadsworth Revolution was that relegation was avoided by two points in 1998-99, the team chalking up six wins and five draws from their final eighteen matches. They captured 23 points from a possible 54 under Wadsworth, having managed 29 from 84 under Wignall and Whitton – a success rate of 42 per cent compared to 34 per cent. The best results in Wadsworth's early weeks were successive 1-0 home wins over Preston and Walsall, who were both lying second when they visited Layer Road. United finished the campaign with two losses, but had amassed enough points to stay clear of the dreaded drop. It had not been pretty to watch, but Colchester scratched and clawed their way to safety, their six wins under Wadsworth all by single-goal margins, and the immediate objective of everybody at the club was achieved.

So, who exactly was this no-nonsense and controversial character who had steered bewildered Colchester to safety? Wadsworth, 48, hailed from Barnsley and had been a winger in his playing days. His only Football League playing experience had come with Scunthorpe United, where he made around 30 appearances in the late 1970s. He later had a spell as player-manager at Frickley Athletic and taught as a schoolteacher. Moving into coaching, he worked with Barnsley's youth team before joining the Football Association in 1985 as a regional coach for the North-West of England, a position he retained for six years before becoming a Technical

Co-ordinator on the FA's Excellence Programme, working on the futures of promising youngsters. He filled FA coaching roles in Europe, Africa and the Caribbean and between 1988 and 1992 worked behind the scenes for the national team under Bobby Robson and then Graham Taylor. During this period he coached at Barnsley and also travelled as one of Robson's aides to the 1990 World Cup in Italy. Wadsworth spent two years as manager of the England non-league team, five years as manager of the England youth team, and also coached the Under-21s. In 1993 Bobby Robson recommended him for a coaching role at PSV Eindhoven, but this opportunity disappeared due to a lack of Dutch coaching credentials. He joined Carlisle under controversial owner Michael Knighton, where he took charge of the team in the role of Director of Coaching. In 1995 he led them to the Division Three title, but couldn't sustain the success the following season and quit. In January 1996 Wadsworth became assistant to Gary Megson at Norwich and six months later left to become Scarborough manager. It is easy to see how his FA credentials and history of working with cash-strapped clubs must have impressed the Colchester directors when they were seeking to replace Steve Wignall. Nevertheless, they can't have expected the whirlwind that would follow their decision to appoint him.

Wadsworth installed a metaphorical revolving door at the entrance to the Colchester dressing room, and new recruits started coming in thick and fast, including four Frenchmen and a Brazilian. However, with hindsight, it is fair to say that only three of the fifteen new faces made any significant impact in those early months – and even they lasted less than a year at the club. The French pair of Stephane Pounewatchy and Fabrice Richard claimed regular places in the U's defence for a spell, while the stout and somewhat intimidating figure of 31-year-old Warren Aspinall played a key role in the midfield engine room. Aspinall was an experienced campaigner who possessed the competitive mean streak that Wadsworth felt Colchester needed. He'd played at the top level with Everton and Aston Villa and was immediately made captain on arrival at Layer Road.

Apart from Aspinall, Pounewatchy and Richard, the rest of Wadsworth's imports only had bit parts to play, although young midfielder Thomas Pinault did come good much later on. Pounewatchy, it seems, was very much a short-term investment, recruited purely to shore up the defence and help the club avoid relegation, before moving on again. Born in Paris, this 32-year-old giant central defender tipped the scales at a hefty 15 stones. Having served French clubs Martigues and Geugnon, he'd had short spells at Dundee and Port Vale and, most notably, at Carlisle under

Wadsworth, where he made nearly 100 appearances. After leaving the U's he would become a players' agent. Fellow Frenchman Fabrice Richard, 25, would last longer than Pounewatchy, enjoying an extended spell in the first team at full-back. The third French import, the teenage youth international striker Steve Germain, arrived from AS Cannes but failed to impress during his stay. The other member of the Gallic quartet was Thomas Pinault, another youngster, who had to be patient before getting his first start much later on, encouraged, no doubt, by Steve Whitton's remark that 'Pinault could be the future of this club'.

The club packed Richard, Germaine and Pinault off to the Grey Friars Adult Community College in Colchester town centre for a course of English language lessons in a bid to improve dressing room harmony and on-field communication. The trio had been struggling with the instructions from Wadsworth, who had a broad Yorkshire accent. With a little help from tutor Anita Tuddenham, Pinault confessed: 'I only understand the coach when he speaks slowly.'

Richard may have tried hard to learn the language, but he struggled to learn how to keep out of trouble. He was banned from driving for exceeding the blood-alcohol limit after his Renault Clio was stopped by police. On another occasion he was fined by the club after he was seen to spit at visiting Walsall supporters.

Players came and players went, the verdict of the home fans being a mixture of thumbs-up and thumbs-down as they were paraded in the blue-and-white stripes. The jury remained firmly out on ex-Irish youth international and Derby starlet Brian Launders, who only played one game, at the end of 1998-99, and even that was away from home. But a thumbs-up was given to nippy striker Bradley Allen, who arrived on loan to pep up the attack, but only stayed one month. Pint-sized Allen went back to Charlton after a March defeat at Macclesfield, leaving Wadsworth with a hole in his forward line. The man chosen to fill it came from thousands of miles way in the Bahian region of north-eastern Brazil – and his subsequent stay at Colchester would be so short it would make Bradley Allen's four-game stint seem like a lifetime. The much-heralded Brazilian came, saw, but failed to conquer. For Colchester fans it was almost a case of 'blink and you miss it'. Fumaca's U's debut – his first senior game in English football – would last a full fourteen minutes. He then disappeared to hospital and was never seen in Essex again.

That was a strange episode, occurring during a strange period in the U's history. The player's full name was Jose Rodriguez Alves Antunes, but, in true South American fashion, he preferred to be known by a single-word name. Fumaca was a nickname that translated as 'smoky' and was originally given to him by his mother who, shortly after his birth, described his hair as resembling strands of smoke spiralling up from a fire. Fumaca had come to England desperately trying to find a club, but discovered that potential employers were deterred by the seven-figure price tag put on his head by his agent. Fumaca's agent was a certain Barry Silkman, a man whose name would become well-known at Layer Road. A number of Wadsworth's signings were on the books of Silkman, and as events unfolded during 1999, this agent – an ex-Manchester City midfielder – would subsequently become *persona non grata* at Layer Road.

In the meantime, Silkman was vigorously trying to find a British club for 22-year-old Fumaca and apparently told anyone who would listen that his player was the best uncapped Brazilian footballer in the world. The very fact that he was Brazilian made people sit up and take notice but, on looking deeper into the facts, it soon became clear Fumaca was not an established superstar back home in the land of the samba. Born in Belem, he was on the books of Catuense, a club from the Bahian city of Catu. 'Catuense are fourth in the top league in Bahia,' announced Silkman. 'What you have got to understand is that Bahia is bigger than England. There are four full-time leagues and he is in the top one. He's not with a dummy club.'

Among the first to take notice had been West Ham earlier in 1998-99. They took Fumaca on trial but when manager Harry Redknapp heard about the £100,000 apparently required by Silkman to enable a three-month loan arrangement, he showed him the door.

Next stop was Birmingham City, whose manager Trevor Francis offered a trial and was impressed enough by the tall Fumaca to agree to a loan deal. Fumaca soon discovered that Birmingham's chilly Wast Hills training ground, beside the busy A441 Redditch Road, did not compare favourably with the palm-fringed beaches of Bahia – particularly in December. He admitted he was finding it tough going to adjust: 'The ground has been hard and the weather different to what I'm used to, but these are not obstacles I can't overcome,' he said. 'I have a great desire to do well in England.' He had not played for five weeks when he arrived and things did not go well in the Midlands. By the end of January 1999 Birmingham had seen enough and allowed Fumaca and Silkman to look elsewhere by ending the loan period prematurely. Fumaca had made just two unimpressive appearances for their reserves in the Pontins Premier Division. The Brazilian was under pressure to live up to all the hype, which came mainly from Silkman, who said his man was 'potentially a £2 million player'. Birmingham's co-owner David Sullivan admitted that coughing up the £100,000 to pay for the loan had been a gamble which failed, and gave his blessing for Fumaca to leave early to try and get fixed up elsewhere.

To the rescue came Colchester, who jumped in and secured Fumaca's temporary services while he was having another trial at Grimsby Town. The U's agreed a short-term deal whereby Fumaca could leave immediately if a bigger club came in for him. His arrival startled many observers, not least the acerbic football writer Des Kelly of *The Mirror*, who wrote: 'Daftest story of the week: Colchester have signed Brazilian midfielder Jose Antunes Fumaca. Manager Mick Wadsorth spotted him playing for Grimsby reserves. Must be good then.'

Fumaca arrived at Layer Road on Wednesday, 17 January in a blaze of publicity and he was plunged into a hastily arranged game that evening against Crystal Palace reserves. He did well in a 2-1 win, was taken off after 55 minutes, and promptly named in the first-team squad for the club's first-ever home match against Manchester City on the following Saturday. It was an occasion notable enough to attract live transmission by Sky TV and their new pay-per-view scheme. Wadsworth needed a strike partner for Neil Gregory after losing the services of Bradley Allen, did not fancy the lanky Mark Sale, and felt Lomana Tresor Lua-Lua, a promising reserve with remarkable dribbling skills, was not ready. And so he took a chance on Fumaca in the No 11 shirt.

In front of 6,544, the biggest home crowd of the season, the U's poured forward, with Fumaca revelling in the big-match atmosphere and showing some nice touches. Disaster struck with less than fifteen minutes on the clock, however. A mid-air collision with the robust defender Andy Morrison left the Brazilian unconscious in the penalty area. After lengthy treatment he was stretchered off to Colchester General Hospital with severe concussion. Without their new star, the U's were beaten by a second-half Shaun Goater goal. Wadsworth had hoped to keep Fumaca, but shortly after the game agent Silkman fixed up a transfer to First Division Barnsley, exploiting the get-out clause in Fumaca's contract with United. Depending on which way you look at it, he'd been a Colchester player for five days or for fourteen minutes.

Said Wadsworth: 'Fumaca is a great lad, a lovely fellow. He liked it at Colchester and he's one hell of a talented footballer – one of the best players I have ever worked with. It was very worrying [when he was knocked unconscious], the boy was out sparko, but he did enough in those fourteen minutes to prove to me just how good he is. I am very relieved he's okay now.'

Things didn't work out at Barnsley and, without playing a first-team game there, Fumaca had trials elsewhere before joining Crystal Palace and then Newcastle, making three and five League appearances respectively. Eventually he and Silkman gave up on England and headed for continental Europe. Football fans can be cruel to players, and poor Fumaca later featured in a poll to find the Top 50 'worst players ever' to appear in the top flight of English football. Newcastle fans who nominated him described Fumaca as the only Brazilian player in history unable to trap a bag of cement.

After Fumaca's departure, Mick Wadsworth's honeymoon period in charge of Colchester looked to be over. He'd started his stint with six unbeaten games, but three successive losses sucked the U's perilously close to the relegation trapdoor once again. As the season drew to an end, the team looked unconvincing but somehow scraped together four wins (all by the odd goal) from their final nine matches. It proved enough to maintain Division Two status by two points, and everyone breathed a huge sigh of relief.

There would be no respite from the hectic comings and goings, however, and, if anything, the activity behind the scenes gathered momentum over the summer. Among the new faces introduced was the splendidly named defender Osagyefo Lenin Ernesto Burton-Godwin, usually known as Sagi Burton. Others signed on the dotted line, too, but it would be departures that made the biggest headlines during the early days of the 1999-2000 season. First, Wadsworth chose to release popular Irish fullback Joe Dunne and hard-working striker Tony Lock, a decision that went down badly with the fans. Then, with the rumblings of discontent at Layer Road getting louder, the club's managing director Stephen Gage quit less than 24 hours before the first game of the new season. The official reason given was a disagreement over the speed of implementation of plans for the club's future. This sounded a little ambiguous and only served to increase the fans' worries that the scheme to get United into a new stadium was as far from completion as ever.

All these problems were put in the shade when, on the morning of Wednesday, 25 August, less than three weeks into the season, manager Wadsworth followed Gage out of the club. It came as a huge shock and once again the supporters were left guessing the true reasons behind the departure. A statement was issued explaining that Wadsworth could no longer tolerate commuting from Pontefract. This appeared risible, particularly when Wadsworth immediately took up a coaching role at Crystal Palace, a club even further away from Pontefract, with the extra hassle of crossing London added on.

The U's had got off to a poor start and suffered three straight defeats when Wadsworth quit. In his seven months at Colchester he had presided over 23 competitive games – seven wins, six draws and ten defeats. The fans were distinctly disenchanted with the majority of his new signings. Added to this was the feeling that he spent too much of his time in the North of England, meaning few were sad to see him go. The icing on the cake was his decision to join Crystal Palace so soon after the U's visited Selhurst Park in the Worthington Cup. Some asked whether he'd used the occasion to find himself a new job. After hearing his sorry tale of travel weariness, this was a bitter pill for the fans to stomach.

A veil of secrecy hung over Layer Road the day after the Palace game, but it emerged that Wadsworth and assistant manager Steve Whitton had been summoned to a meeting with U's chairman Peter Heard in London only hours before the 1-3 defeat. The team coach's departure for home was delayed after the match because Whitton was called into another meeting. It was beginning to look as if the 0-4 thrashing at Bournemouth a few days earlier had in fact been the last straw, and the board had decided time was up for the high-spending Wadsworth.

Wadsworth certainly got himself fixed up quickly, and his new Palace job did not appear to be a stop-gap, for he told the *Evening Standard* he wanted the role permanently. With disarming honesty, he said: 'Problems with travelling were supposed to be why I left Colchester, but that was just the official reason. I don't make the trip every day, and I have no problem getting to training at Palace.'

After all the trauma, it was clear Colchester needed calm and stability to get the club back on an even keel, and in the best possible shape to retain Division Two status. They needed someone to steady the ship and so turned to assistant Steve Whitton, who many felt had been unlucky not to get the job six months earlier. It was a popular choice.

As for Wadsworth, he seemed destined to be the eternal football itinerant. His time at Crystal Palace only lasted two weeks before Bobby Robson invited him to become assistant manager at Newcastle United. After less than two years with the Geordies, Wadsworth headed south to work with Stuart Gray at Southampton. This proved another short-lived task. Next stop was seven months as manager of Oldham, before another parting of the ways. Next came six months in charge of Huddersfield, after which Wadsworth was reportedly dismissed, only to be reinstated for a few more months when the club found it could not afford his severance package.

Before long, Wadsworth was off to coach the Democratic Republic of Congo national side for several months, and then had a brief spell at Portuguese club Beira Mar. Then, back to England he came, to assist Gary Peters at Shrewsbury Town, before a move north of the border to

Gretna. As Gretna commenced their inaugural Scottish Premier League season in August 2007, Wadsworth was again the focus of intrigue, taking joint-charge of the team after manager Rowan Alexander was suspended due to what was described as a stress-related condition.

Wadsworth remains a controversial figure among supporters of the many clubs who experienced his short-term leadership skills. Not least among these is Colchester, as witnessed by reporter Francis Ponder, who wrote in one U's matchday magazine: 'After almost breaking the bank with his controversial signings, our dear old friend Mick Wadsworth has enjoyed lucrative coaching roles at Newcastle and Southampton since walking out on the U's. His brief flirtation with the Saints ended with the sack [and] he walked away from St Mary's Stadium with a handsome £300,000 golden handshake only three months into a four-year contract. With decisions such as these, does football and its club chairmen deserve all the aggro they get?'

The fall-out at Layer Road from the crazy Wadsworth era was long-lasting. One of the most significant issues surrounded Brian Launders, an Irish midfielder captured by Wadsworth on transfer deadline day in 1999. Launders remained with the club after the manager had departed, but before long hit the headlines when the club sacked him for 'gross misconduct'. This led to months of legal wrangling, appearances before football authority tribunals, and then the High Court, and left a thoroughly nasty taste in the mouth.

Born in Dublin, Launders had joined Crystal Palace as a seventeen-year-old from Irish club Cherry Orchard and made the London side's first team in September 1994, appearing against Chelsea. After just four games for the Selhurst Park club he had a fruitless loan spell at Oldham before moving on to Crewe, where he played nine League games. A spell in Holland with First Division Veendham led to a move back to English football with Derby County in September 1998. He only made the Rams first team once, as a second-half substitute against Leeds, before embarking on his ill-fated move to Colchester.

Launders was reportedly plagued by a mystery blood problem, which apparently sidelined him on a number of occasions. Loaned to the U's in March 1999, he was injured on his debut at Bournemouth and unavailable for the remainder of the season. By now, Launders had turned 23 and had been in the game since his teens, yet had only made fifteen League appearances in six years as a professional. Despite all this, a lucrative two-year full-time contract at Colchester was negotiated and he became the highest paid player in the club's history. His weekly wage was reportedly £1,200 and he received a signing-on fee of £40,000, paid in eight instalments. He also stood to gain appearance and incentive bonuses and have his accommodation paid for. The entire two-year package could have cost the club in excess of £150,000.

After Mick Wadsworth hailed him as a highly talented individual who could well become the U's' leading scorer for 1999-2000, he appeared in midfield in each of the first six League games. Sadly, Wadsworth was way off the mark with his prediction, and in October, with Wadsworth long gone, Launders was summoned from the training ground one day and sacked for what the club called 'gross misconduct'. It was reported that Launders was being punished for failing to answer questions put to him by U's officials relating to his association with his agent Barry Silkman.

Launders and Silkman lodged a claim for unfair dismissal. In January 2000 a Football League tribunal threw this out, along with the player's claim for damages. Silkman appealed, which if successful would have seen the U's lose a fortune. It was reported that Silkman himself also had an action pending against the club for 'introducing players' to Layer Road for which he alleged he was owed in excess of £100,000. U's director Peter Powell said: 'We were surprised the [Launders] action was brought in the first place. We acted in good faith and took the appropriate legal advice at all times and of course we would be very confident if we had to fight the case all over again.'

In March 2000, Silkman and Launders' appeal was turned down. A tribunal ruled that the club did have justifiable and ample grounds to terminate the player's contract. Undaunted, Silkman said he would now take the matter to the civil courts. He explained: 'It has cost us and Colchester United a lot of money taking the case through the Football Association and the Football League, but the FA insisted we had to go through that procedure first. We have done that and have been over-ruled both times, but they can no longer keep it within the confines of the FA and the League.'

And so the saga dragged on. Eventually, in June 2001, two years after Launders first signed his ill-fated contract, Colchester were ordered to pay an estimated £200,000 after a High Court judge found in favour of Silkman's claim that Layer Road chiefs had refused to pay £40,000 plus interest for Launders' transfer from Dutch club Veendam in May 1999. Mr Justice Morland awarded Silkman's agency damages, including interest, and ordered CUFC to pay most of his legal costs – a total bill of about £150,000. So, ultimately both sides enjoyed partial success in this sorry saga, although the biggest winners were the lawyers.

Launders' career in England fizzled out after he left Colchester, but the real legacy of the Wadsworth era at Layer Road was the club's renewed determination to be wary of involvement with players' agents. Wadsworth's successor in the manager's chair, Steve Whitton, was particularly vocal on this subject:

'I never had an agent throughout my playing career. I did all the dealings myself and was always happy with the way things turned out. Ninety-nine per cent of agents don't care about the game. Their involvement may ruin the relationship between a club and a player, especially a small club like Colchester where there's not a lot [of money] to go around in the first place. But now they are involved I'm not sure if they can ever be kicked out. We have probably got to put up with them. In my view their only place in the game should be for players' outside interests, such as boot, kit and clothing endorsements. They should not have any involvement in the game of football itself.'

## CHAPTER 6

The Whitton Wisdom

August 1999 – January 2003

Coach Steve Whitton was elevated to the manager's chair in late August 1999, signalling the end of a turbulent era in Colchester United's history. His brief was to steady the nerves and, ultimately, ensure the club stayed in Division Two. Players and fans generally welcomed the appointment of the 38-year-old east Londoner. His first match in charge saw a determined performance, the team twice coming from behind to notch up a thrilling 3-2 win over Reading. Sadly this enjoyable afternoon was not a sign of things to come. The U's failed to win any of their next eleven League games and spent most of the autumn at the foot of the table.

These were difficult times and team spirit seemed lacking, but things slowly improved once Whitton was able to rebuild with his own men. A number of Mick Wadsworth's signings headed out of Layer Road, and among these was defender Sagi Burton, whose lucrative two-year contract was torn up by mutual consent after just five months. The player said: 'I just wasn't happy at the club any more. On reflection the club were not as ambitious as I first thought. The only reason I signed in the first place was for Mick Wadsworth. He sold Colchester United to me as a club that was ready to go places. No reflection on the current manager, but when Mick left the ambition didn't appear to be there any longer. The club were happy to let me go, so it's best for all concerned that we parted company.'

Along with the sacked Brian Launders, Burton's exit meant another of Wadsworth's high earners was off the wage bill, and Whitton was happy to plug gaps by welcoming back some familiar faces. Tony Lock and Joe Dunne, rejected by Wadsworth, returned to the club, as did striker Steve McGavin, following his five-year sojourn with Birmingham, Wycombe, Southend and Northampton. Wadsworth's choice of skipper, Warren Aspinall, was swapped for Brighton's Andy Arnott, and Richard Wilkins came off the transfer list now that the new era had begun.

Whitton preached attacking football and deserved the breaks that started to go his way as the 1999-2000 season passed its halfway point. By early January the U's had gathered enough points to claw their way out of the bottom four and the smiles were coming back to the faces on the terraces. Highlight of the winter months was undoubtedly an epic 5-4 win over promotion-chasing Bristol Rovers, a game which will go down

as a Layer Road classic. The encounter passed the hour mark with United
1-3 down, but a marvellous comeback was climaxed by Lua-Lua's last-
minute winner. During Colchester's 48 seasons as a Football League club
– that's some 1,100 home League matches – there had never been a 5-4
scoreline at Layer Road before.

Lua-Lua was fast making a name for himself as a highly skilled performer, possessing a lethal shot and a spectacular line in acrobatic goal
celebrations. Hordes of scouts from bigger clubs monitored his progress
and marvelled at how he could suddenly and unexpectedly bring a match
to life with a mazy run or an explosive shot out of the blue. Whitton was
occasionally criticised for starting matches with Lua-Lua on the bench,
but the evidence suggested that the player was most effective when coming on a substitute to add instant impact to a game that might not be
going Colchester's way. Lua-Lua was by no means the finished article, to
coin a well-worn cliché, but he certainly had the weaponry to frighten
Division Two defenders to death when he chose to use it.

Watching his repertoire of tricks, United officials must have blessed
the day when this unique talent was given a second chance at Layer Road.
Youth team supremo Micky Cook had earlier let him leave the club after
the player displayed attitude problems and poor time-keeping. But when
Lua-Lua and his family pleaded that he would change his ways, he was
cautiously allowed back, a decision that would ultimately prove wise and
lucrative. The player later recalled the depressing period when his career
had hung in the balance: 'As was often case back then, my attitude was
wrong and although they thought I was a good footballer, they turned me
down. They wanted me to sign YTS forms, and although I was supposed
to be there at 10am, I eventually turned up at 11.30 and that made their
minds up for them. I went back to college and my work experience was
spent at McDonald's cleaning the toilets. It was at that moment that I
realised I had to sort myself out so I went back to Colchester United begging for another chance.'

Lua-Lua's astonishing athleticism came from his childhood obsession
with gymnastics. Growing up in the Democratic Republic of Congo, he
did gymnastic training with other youngsters at an army camp on the out-
skirts of Kinshasa. Facilities were limited and, with no proper spring-
boards or high beams, the kids would take off from vehicle tyres buried
in the sand or from the top of brick walls. They had to be fearless and
Lua-Lua recalled breaking his arm three times. Back then his ambitions
lay with becoming a stuntman rather than a footballer, he admitted:

'I initially came to England as a nine-year-old to visit my aunt in Forest
Gate [east London]. As my parents had separated, it was decided that I

would have a better chance in life in England and I never returned. I went to Leyton College to study media studies and performing arts and it was at this point that my football career started to take off. My school PE teacher phoned up and told the College they had to push me into playing for the College team and I also joined a Sunday side. We had a lot of scouts watching our Sunday games, but as a Christian it is deemed a day of rest and my aunt didn't let me play that often, so I thought my chance had passed me by. Thankfully I was able to make an impression for the College team and, having played against a Colchester college, I was given a chance at Layer Road. The referee that day was Geoff Harrop, who was also a scout for Colchester United and he invited me along for a trial.'

Colchester had unearthed a real diamond with extraordinary skills, although in the early days it was clear Lua-Lua needed to work on aspects such as tactical awareness and team play. Promotion to the first team didn't come quickly, and Lua-Lua admitted it took a visit to a local factory to convince him to be patient at Layer Road and work harder at making his football career take off. Youth team boss Micky Cook took him and other youth players to sample life on a production line so they could see how 'the other half' lived. Lua-Lua said that day helped change his attitude and he quickly knuckled down. Shortly afterwards he scored with his first kick in senior football when coming on as sub at Chesterfield in January 1999, just a few weeks after his eighteenth birthday. A year later he was being pursued by a host of Premiership clubs and seven-figure transfer fees were being suggested.

Lua-Lua's exciting form coincided with the goals beginning to flow again for Steve McGavin, and the memorable 5-4 win over Bristol Rovers sparked a run of four straight victories, which banished relegation worries for the time being and hoisted United into mid-table. Dramatic victories over a trio of promotion-chasers – Wigan, Stoke and Preston – followed shortly afterwards and safety was assured. The season petered out somewhat, with just one win from the final seven games landing the club eighteenth. However, Whitton had achieved his main target and the U's could anticipate another campaign in the Second Division. The scheme to move to a new stadium was said to be inching forward again, so a degree of optimism returned to Layer Road.

Whitton shored up his defence for 2000-01 by signing experienced centre-backs Simon Clark (Leyton Orient) and Alan White (Luton), and he also secured the services of long-serving Ipswich midfielder Mick Stockwell. He proved an inspired capture, for despite his advancing years Stockwell rarely missed a game over the next three seasons, winning player of the year and leading scorer accolades to boot.

Early in the season Lua-Lua grabbed a wonderful hat-trick at QPR in a Worthington Cup-tie. Having lost the home leg 0-1, United were indebted to Lua-Lua, who ran Gerry Francis's defence ragged and handed Rangers their most embarrassing home defeat in years. Lua-Lua's display only intensified the interest in him. Newcastle, managed by Bobby Robson and spending money as if there were no tomorrow, were particularly keen. U's chairman Peter Heard drove a hard bargain and was able to insist on a club record fee of £2.25 million, which by mid-September Newcastle agreed to pay.

Although he appeared in the U's' next two League games – forgettable encounters at Wigan and Bury – Lua-Lua's one-man show at Loftus Road is widely remembered as his real farewell performance, capping a year of high entertainment. His pace and trickery would be sadly missed by the fans, but the huge transfer fee was some compensation.

Perhaps it was playing in London on a bigger stage, and knowing that scouts were out in force, that inspired the youngster that night at Loftus Road. For once, he didn't frustrate his manager by only playing in fits and starts. He was in the thick of it from the kick-off and fully justified his starting place. A long ball towards the Rangers' goal saw Matthew Rose leave it to goalkeeper Lee Harper and Lua-Lua was on to it in a flash, curling the ball under Harper for the first goal of the night. The aggregate scores were level and Rangers were hardly over the shock when Lua-Lua struck again, skipping past Mark Perry, Tim Breacker and Steve Morrow and firing into the far corner. The small band of away fans were ecstatic, while their depressed opposite numbers greeted the strike with a mixture of abuse for their own defence and applause for the skills of Lua-Lua.

Chris Kiwomya nudged Rangers level on aggregate but ten minutes after half-time Lua-Lua set up Steve McGavin to restore U's' advantage. Lua-Lua was in his element, and might have had half a dozen himself. A QPR fan wrote later that by this stage the match was turning into a farce with QPR's ineptitude helping to make Colchester look like Brazil and Lua-Lua like Pele. There were some experienced and talented men on the field, future England star Peter Crouch for example, but none could hold a candle to Lua-Lua that night. His final flourish came with four minutes left on the clock. With Rangers' players desperate for the final whistle to end their torment, Lua-Lua cheekily skipped around Harper and tucked the ball into an empty net to complete a wonderful hat-trick. Before the start Lua-Lua had often been hailed as a £1 million player, but this display had pushed his price tag past the £2 million mark, thanks to just 90 minutes' work.

After Lua-Lua departed for St James' Park to play alongside his hero Alan Shearer, another rising star stepped forward at Layer Road – this one not quite as young and nimble, but just as important. The club announced that its new chief executive was to be Marie Partner, a local woman who had served the U's in many capacities over the previous twelve years or so. In her early days, Marie had carried out the humblest of tasks around the offices, brushing off chauvinistic jibes that women didn't belong in football, and her ascent to the chief executive's office represented a remarkable feat. The list of jobs she carried out over the years behind the scenes at Layer Road is endless, and if ever there was a classic example of someone working their way from the bottom to the top of a single organisation, then this is it.

Asked about her time at the club, she almost found it easier to list jobs she hadn't done rather than those she had: 'I haven't mowed the pitch, or picked the team yet,' she said. Among the things she can tick off are stints working as a steward, turnstile operator, a ticket seller, club shop-girl, the players' beans-on-toast chef, door-to-door lottery saleswoman, programme compiler, mail-opener and receptionist, club secretary and commercial manager. Marie started work at Layer Road in the late 1980s after a spell at a building society. At that point working at the football club was just another job, but later it became a compulsion: 'It becomes a habit. It's like wearing a nicotine patch. I need the fix. Even on holiday I never switch off.'

She recalled making a rather inauspicious start to a career in the world of football. On her first day, working in the ticket office, she encountered gruff manager Jock Wallace, definitely one of the old school: 'He didn't agree with females in football and he gave me six months,' said Marie. 'Eighteen years later here I sit and he has probably twisted and turned in his grave many a time.' Marie grew up in a house near to Layer Road and clearly recalls the fuss and excitement of the day Leeds United were beaten in the famous 1971 FA Cup-tie. She was a mere slip of a girl in those days, hadn't a clue about football and thought all the celebrations were because the Queen had come to town. Her first visit inside the ground is said to have been as part of a teenage dance group called Chirpy and the Cheep Cheeps, who performed a display at a charity event. After that she began to take an interest in football, but admitted it was only 'to see how pretty the players were'.

Since her unique career at Layer Road began, it is thought Marie has seen off around fifteen managers, four chairmen and eleven managing directors. She has a clear perception of being a woman in what can be a man's world: 'For me it works, it opens doors. I believe women are better organised – I don't say they do a better job – but I'm regarded as the agony aunt, the financial adviser, the marriage guidance counsellor. There's something about a woman that makes her more approachable. There's a lot of players who have come and gone who say I'm firm but fair, but can be more sympathetic to problems. I admire Karren Brady, for example. She's done a fantastic job at Birmingham City, has a good business head and turned that club around. Seventy-five per cent of their success is down to her.

'We all muck in here at Colchester because we are very strict with our housekeeping,' she said. 'If the cleaner doesn't turn up I will be the first to empty people's bins. We take it in turns making tea, and I have been known to sweep up after a game because we are a small staff – there's just twenty of us, apart from the playing squads.'

Marie's story as the unsung heroine of Colchester's rise out of non-league football has from time to time attracted the curiosity of the national press. One paper summed her up as 'the lorry driver's daughter who liked dancing, had no interest in her local team but ended up running the whole show with such enterprise that she became Essex Businesswoman of the Year'. It was also pointed out that by becoming chief executive she became the first Essex girl – complete with cheeky sense of humour – to join the select band of female football grandees, which includes Delia Smith (Norwich), Karren Brady (Birmingham), Lorraine Rogers (Tranmere) and Brenda Spencer (Wigan). 'You can't have prissy females in this role, you must have a sense of humour and a spine of steel,' she insisted. 'There's more to Essex girls than white Ford Escorts, stockings and white stilettoes.'

And so it came to pass that the year 2000 ended with Colchester United being steered by a team manager and a chief executive recently promoted from within. Results on the field were seen as satisfactory if not spectacular – the U's went into 2001 halfway in the table – while behind the scenes the club was gearing up to push forward its proposal to build a new ground at Cuckoo Farm, just off the A12 trunk road to the north west of the town.

A body-blow in 2000-01 had been the early and humiliating exit from the FA Cup at the hands of non-League Yeovil. The 1-5 hammering was an embarrassment that evoked memories of the Bedlington Terriers fiasco, but the team responded by embarking on a run of three League wins and a draw which pushed them up the table. This mini-revival was halted by a 1-6 thrashing at leaders Millwall, but once again Whitton and his troops bounced back and were soon on an even keel. There was never any danger of getting too closely involved with the relegation dog-fight, and a fine display in beating Alan Pardew's promotion-chasers Reading in the final home game banished any lingering fears. The final resting place of seventeenth was an improvement of one place on the previous campaign. One source of delight among the Colchester faithful had been the relegation from the Premiership of local enemy Ipswich, this being the second time George Burley had taken Town down from the top flight since his defection from Layer Road in 1994.

Steve Whitton celebrated his second anniversary as U's manager by getting the side off to a tremendous start in 2001-02. Three wins and eleven goals from the first four matches meant that by the end of August the U's were sitting proudly at the top of Division Two. On top of this, they beat First Division Portsmouth at Fratton Park in the Worthington Cup, which confirmed the finest start to a season since the club joined the Football League. Key to the confidence surging through the team was the opening-day 6-3 win at Chesterfield.

United fans thought Whitton would be a dead cert for the manager of the month award, but saw it awarded to Bristol City's Danny Wilson. This was hard to fathom, for although the Ashton Gate club had, like the U's, also won three and drawn one of their opening four League games, they had scored fewer goals and had a much easier passage in the Worthington Cup. Some fans concluded it was just another case of the smaller, more unfashionable club being overlooked. It was hard to disagree.

The great start, which featured lively front-running by the newly formed strike partnership of Scott McGleish (signed from Barnet) and Kevin Rapley (Notts County), was not maintained through the autumn of 2001. By Christmas, United were back in mid-table and by January skipper and centre-half Simon Clark unexpectedly walked out on the club, asking for his contract to be cancelled for personal reasons. In addition, injury robbed the side of full-back Joe Dunne's services, although the lively Graham Barrett came in from Arsenal and proved the club's best loan capture for many years. Not quite as effective was the introduction of lanky centre-forward Adrian Coote, a club record-equalling £50,000 signing from Norwich, who was mainly only used as a substitute.

United wound up fifteenth at the end of the campaign, another slight improvement on the previous year, and comfortably clear of the danger zone. Gates increased slightly over the season as a whole, but averaged below 4,000 per home match, which meant the club remained one of the poorest supported in the division. The money from the Lua-Lua transfer a year earlier helped balance the lack of income from the turnstiles. That windfall had assured the club's short-term future and banished talk of a financial crisis – at least for the time being.

There was no room for complacency on the money front, however, for in March 2002, just before the season ended, the beleaguered ITV Digital company went into administration. This situation created what the Professional Footballers Association called a 'doomsday scenario' for hard-up clubs like Colchester. ITV Digital, launched in 1998, had been hit hard by a slowdown in advertising revenues, and struggled to compete with Rupert Murdoch's satellite broadcaster BSkyB for viewers. This led its two parent companies to pull the plug on their loss-making business. PFA chief executive Gordon Taylor said the consequent loss of TV revenue would cripple some of the 72 clubs outside the Premiership and players' livelihoods would be under threat because many wage deals were being funded by clubs' income from TV: 'If a club hasn't got the money and can't pay wages and can't function then the club will have to go into administration and then it will have a real knock-on, domino effect.'

The stunned Football League sued ITV Digital's parent companies, Carlton and Granada, claiming they had breached their contract in failing to deliver the guaranteed income to the clubs. The League lost the case, with the judge ruling it had 'failed to extract sufficient written guarantees'. The Reuters news agency asked Marie Partner how the crisis might affect a club like Colchester and she said: 'It will have a great impact at this stage of the season. It's a huge chunk of our income – about 25 to 35 per cent – which at a small club such as ours would have a great impact when you're budgeting to talk to players about contracts. It does mean seriously having to revisit how you're going to fill that gap – commercially here at Colchester we don't have the facility to fill it.'

Under Steve Whitton, United had finished eighteenth, seventeenth and fifteenth, not bad considering their recent history and general lack of resources. However, the fans demanded that income from the Lua-Lua transfer be spent on the team to provide a better finish for 2003-04. Frenchman Thomas Pinault got the U's off to winning start, cracking home the only goal of the opening day at home to Stockport. Sadly this would prove to be just one of six victories in the first 30 games, a dismal run that included first round exits in all three cups. Once again a non-league outfit, this time Chester, ousted the U's from the FA Cup. The ever-growing list of such cup embarrassments was evidence that the gap between League and non-league was closing.

Whitton began picking skilful young forward Dean Morgan on a regular basis but the U's suffered through a lack of fire-power, with the strikers McGleish, Coote and Rapley only producing six goals between them in the first 30 games. Three successive defeats in January 2003 meant United were looking like serious relegation candidates and Whitton must have felt the writing was on the wall when the board demanded improvements, particularly as gates were slipping ever lower.

Sure enough, a depressing home defeat by Blackpool – the U's sunk by two second-half goals and Karl Duguid sent off into the bargain – spelt the end for Whitton. After more than three years in the manager's chair, the axe finally fell. As is often the case in football, this parting of the ways was described publicly as being 'by mutual consent', but it was clear that Whitton hadn't resigned.

After the departure the 42-year-old angrily told the *Evening Gazette*: 'I think everyone knows by now that I would never have walked away from it. I knew exactly what was going to happen when the phone went asking me to attend the meeting. But there were eighteen games left for us to turn things around and I was prepared to fight it out and take the stick for the players. Sadly that option has now been taken away from me. I've just experienced my first sacking and I'm out of a job for the first time in my life. I'd gone through the ranks at Colchester as a player, player-coach and manager, but the moment you become the manager you know there is nowhere to go if things don't work out.'

Whitton, who played at top level with Coventry, Birmingham, West Ham, Ipswich and Sheffield Wednesday, was generally a popular figure at Layer Road, and the players expressed surprise and disappointment at news of his departure. Full-back Joe Keith, one of a crop of players to establish themselves under Whitton, said: 'Myself and the rest of the lads never had any doubts we'd get out of this trouble under Steve. That's why the timing has come as quite a surprise.' Karl Duguid admitted he had not seen this coming: 'I can't believe it. Spirit and confidence was not a problem in the camp – the only thing missing was the results. Even so, we were all in it together and the feeling was definitely that we could turn things round.' Supporters' club official Jon Burns spoke for most fans when he pointed out: 'Steve Whitton deserves a lot of credit for everything he's achieved at the club, both as a player and manager, but there's no denying the club is in a rut. Something needed to change in order to reignite that spark again. I wouldn't say I'm glad to see him go but I understand it was probably a necessary step.'

As is par for the course, a host of well-known names in football were soon being linked with the vacant job. Coach Geraint Williams was put in temporary charge and helped inspire a string of good performances as the board spent a month searching for a new manager. Under Williams, the U's beat Bristol City away, Mansfield at home, and drew with Cheltenham and Stockport. In many peoples' eyes, this sudden improvement ought to have been sufficient for him to get the job permanently.

Meanwhile, in the media gossip columns, the hot tips were two non-league managers, Nigel Clough of Burton Albion, son of the legendary Brian, and Garry Hill of Dagenham & Redbridge. Former U's managers Steve Wignall and Roy McDonough were also mentioned as candidates, but few expected the club to look to the past. A month after Whitton's departure the identity of the new man was finally revealed and – not for the first time at Colchester – it was an unfamiliar name that raised more than a few eyebrows.

CHAPTER 7

Young Man in a Hurry

February 2003 – February 2006

There's an old corporate maxim which says if you want a job done well, give it to a busy person. Perhaps this was in the minds of the Colchester directors when they handed the job of manager to the untried Reading midfielder Phil Parkinson in February 2003.

Hyperactive 'Parky', one of the most popular figures ever to play for the Berkshire club, had just about reached the end of his playing days, but his burning ambition to become a coach and manager meant he had not been idle recently. Although he turned up for his Colchester interview bereft of managerial experience, he had recently dipped his toe into the world of coaching by assisting Alan Pardew at Reading's training ground. Furthermore, he had an array of coaching certificates earned during his spare time, not to mention a hunger to succeed that meant he came highly recommended as a man with a big future in the game.

Parkinson had never been one for the snooker halls and daytime TV once morning training was over. While at Reading he'd gained a host of top qualifications, including UEFA 'A', 'B' and 'C' coaching badges and a Bachelor of Science degree in Social Science from the Open University. He was only 35 but his penchant for coaching and leadership, and a deep determination to get on, had already caught the eye of leading figures within the game. He came to Colchester having already been identified as one to watch.

Unveiled four weeks after Steve Whitton was shown the door, the face of Colchester United's future spoke enthusiastically about his passion for the task ahead: 'I feel honoured to be given the job. It is an opportunity that I couldn't turn down. I feel that I am coming into the club with my feet already running, but I am ambitious and I am very keen to make my way in the game. Last year I played in a team that won promotion out of this division and although I haven't played much football this season, playing is an option that I want to leave open. As a player I like to perform with passion and that's what I will be looking for the lads to do here. I am sure we can all achieve what we are looking for with the fans' backing. I learned a lot under Reading managers Mark McGhee and Alan Pardew and I will be taking little things from both of them. I know some of the Colchester supporters may have mixed feelings about my appointment, but this is a fantastic opportunity for me.'

Parkinson had been a regular in the No 6 shirt at the Madejski Stadium the previous season when Reading were promoted to Division One, but so far in 2002-03 had been limited to six appearances as a substitute. At 35, playing had now taken a back seat in his career, and shortly before the Colchester job came up he had agreed a three-year deal to become a coach at Reading.

Married with three children, Parkinson was born in Lancashire, and started his senior football career as a trainee at Southampton. He failed to make the Saints' first team and was the subject of a £12,000 transfer back to his native area to play for Bury in March 1988. He spent more than four years at Gigg Lane, making 169 appearances in all competitions, before Reading paid £37,500 for his services in the summer of 1992. Roaming the centre of midfield, he was a fearsome tackler who always led by example and was named player of the year two seasons in a row (1997-98 and 1998-99). He captained the Royals to promotion from the Second Division in 2002 and soon afterwards celebrated his testimonial year with a memorable night at the Madejski, when 20,000 fans paid tribute in a match featuring the likes of Paul Gascoigne, John Barnes and Chris Waddle. Parkinson notched up a massive 452 appearances in all competitions in a Reading shirt – placing him ninth on their all-time appearances list. Always a busy fellow, he'd been the club's PFA representative as well as skipper and part-time coach.

The chance to manage Colchester had come out of the blue, and to secure the role he had to beat off the challenge of 65 other 'serious' applicants, many of them better known. He was eventually named on a shortlist that included current U's caretaker-manager Geraint Williams, Dagenham & Redbridge boss Garry Hill, former Barnsley and Rochdale manager Steve Parkin, and Southend coach Stewart Robson. Despite speculation to the contrary, a non-starter was former West Ham and Liverpool defender Julian Dicks, whose recent move to the Shepherd & Dog pub in Langham, on the edge of Colchester, had sparked rumours that he was in the running.

Reading, who at the time were ploughing an inexorable furrow up towards the Premiership, seemed genuinely sad to lose Parkinson. One fan said: 'There are few troopers of Parky's calibre left in the game and it is unlikely in the modern era that Royals' fans will ever again see a player so totally committed to their club for such long dedicated service. Phil Parkinson is from a rare mould and will always be remembered fondly in the hearts of Reading supporters everywhere. There is no doubt that whenever he returns to the club, in whatever capacity, he will receive a rousing reception of appreciation.'

U's chairman Peter Heard described his new man as having 'explosive energy and a pied piper personality' and this was evident from the start. After spending his first day at Layer Road taking training and then working behind his desk, Parkinson took off to the Midlands to watch Port Vale, the club's next opponents. One of his first decisions was to keep 'caretaker' Williams at the club as his second-in-command. Many fans felt Williams unlucky not to get the top job himself, having just ended a poor run by overseeing four unbeaten games. Chief executive Marie Partner said: 'Geraint Williams was impeccable in his four weeks as caretaker-manager and we were keen to keep him at the club. Phil had done his homework on the club and decided that himself and Geraint would make a good team.'

Fired up by the presence of their new young boss, the U's ripped into Port Vale and chalked up their biggest win of the season, on-loan striker Gareth Williams bagging a hat-trick in a 4-1 success. This superb start was maintained three days later with a 2-0 home win over Northampton and the U's were positively soaring clear of the relegation danger that had seemed so imminent. Over his first eleven games in charge, Parkinson only tasted defeat once, at the home of Ian Dowie's promotion-chasing Oldham. His first month in the job saw him win the divisional manager of the month award. A new-found sense of purpose had been instilled at Layer Road which pleased the fans and saw attendances begin to creep upwards.

The U's were brought briefly down to earth in April when, now safe from the drop, Parky made some experimental team changes for the visit of Luton and watched in horror as the Hatters won 5-0, the worst home defeat in Colchester's League history. With lanky youngster Greg Halford making his debut, young goalkeeper Richard McKinney had a game to forget as big centre-forward Steve Howard trampled all over United's tentative young defence, thumping a hat-trick. Normal service was resumed the following week, however, United licking their wounds and bouncing back to hold old rivals Wycombe to a draw at Adams Park. The 2002-03 season finished a week later, Wigan winning the title with 100 points. Parkinson had steered United to a finishing position of twelfth, their highest on the Football League ladder for 23 years.

Parkinson was in no mood to rest on his laurels. Before long he was off seeking further certificates by participating on the UEFA Pro-Licence Course, the game's highest coaching qualification, mandatory for Premier League bosses. It gave him the chance to 'network' with football's biggest names: 'It's a good learning curve for me, not just the content of the course, but working with other people on the course and making contacts which will hopefully stay with me for years to come. We interact with other people on the course regularly and learn a lot from each other. I'm in regular contact with quite a few of the other coaches on the course and that can only be good. The profile of the English coach and manager is rising all the time and I think there are some highly talented individuals coming through and this Pro-Licence has helped them all.'

Parkinson acquired his Pro-Licence in company with well-established names such as George Burley, Bryan Robson, Sam Allardyce, and Steve McClaren.

Preparing his squad for his first full season (2003-04), Parkinson paid special attention to strengthening his front line. In came Wayne Andrews from Oldham and loanees Craig Fagan from Birmingham and Rowan Vine from Portsmouth. The revamped line-up lost narrowly at Barnsley on the opening day when Joe Keith skied a penalty. At home a week later came another defeat, this time to a late Swindon goal, and for Colchester fans the worry beads were out. A third successive defeat, in a seven-goal thriller at Port Vale, left the U's in the bottom four, but the tide began to turn in the fourth game when Scott McGleish netted a brilliant overhead kick against Bristol City at Layer Road. United won 2-1 and embarked on an unbeaten run of eight games that lifted all the gloom. All was well with the world by the time a win at Wrexham saw the U's enter November in third place.

By the turn of the year, League form began to stutter, perhaps due to various distractions cropping up in cup competitions. In the LDV Vans Trophy, Cheltenham, Yeovil, Wycombe and Northampton were all beaten away before United came up against Southend in the southern final. The prospect of an appearance at Cardiff's Millennium Stadium receded when Southend netted three at Layer Road after falling behind early on. Managed by former U's favourite Steve Wignall, the Roots Hall club hung on in the second leg and the U's were left to rue a bad week in which they'd been beaten in three different competitions.

Two days before that LDV exit, the U's had travelled to First Division promotion-chasers Sheffield United to contest a place in the last eight of the FA Cup. They reached Bramall Lane courtesy of earlier victories over Oxford and Aldershot, plus a blood-and-thunder affair with Accrington Stanley, and a demolition of First Division Coventry through a Rowan Vine hat-tick in a Layer Road replay. A large following accompanied the U's to Sheffield. They witnessed a spirited display against Neil Warnock's men, but Paul Peschisolido's second-half header proved decisive.

At the height of the cup runs United tumbled from fifth to fourteenth in the Division Two table. When free from cup distractions, however, the

League position soon improved. The play-offs were never realistic after Christmas, but four wins in the season's final month yielded a finishing position of eleventh, one better than a year earlier. Parkinson's first season had seen a one-off home disaster when Luton won 5-0, and his second featured another, Port Vale romping to a 4-1 win. This game apart, mid-table was respectable, given Colchester's attendances and resources. Plymouth won the divisional title and were promoted with QPR and Brighton.

Perhaps inevitably, the pundits again had Colchester down as relegation candidates for 2004-05. This was no surprise, for it had happened before every season since the club reached the League's third tier in 1998. The U's management were happy with this situation for it meant they were perennial underdogs perceived as punching above their weight. The ultra-positive Parkinson, of course, was not happy merely to survive and his sights remained set on the unlikely-looking feat of winning a place in the newly named Championship.

Managers everywhere always stress the need to get off to a good start, and Colchester did just that, winning their first three games to go top of the division – now known as Coca-Cola League One. In terms of status, it was still the good old Third Division, of course, but Colchester's lofty position in first place represented the highest point they'd ever attained in the League, matching brief spells back in 1957 and 1975. It was heady stuff for the fans, although being top in August doesn't actually count for much. The cynics who said it wouldn't last were proved right in the fourth League match, at Chesterfield. Two goals by Senegalese Tcham N'Toya-Xoa sent United to defeat, and Stephen Hunt, given his debut, was sent off for a challenge that sparked an ugly brawl.

United kept within touching distance of the play-offs, enjoying victory over West Brom in the Carling Cup into the bargain, and the good form of the defence was a noticeable feature. Wayne Brown and Liam Chilvers looked as good as anyone in the division, with Pat Baldwin doing a good job when called upon. Parkinson had also introduced two reliable and experienced men in veteran keeper Aidan Davison and midfielder Kevin Watson. Davison, now 35, was at his thirteenth League club, having started out with poetically named non-leaguers Billingham Synthonia. Watson, 29, was a former Reading colleague of Parkinson, but had also worn the colours of Spurs, Swindon and Rotherham. Essex-born teenager Greg Halford had by now settled into a regular first-team spot, his tall and rather awkward frame disguising fine skills and shooting power. The team looked well-balanced and defensively stronger than for many years. Not a single League One opponent scored more than twice against the

U's throughout 2004-05, the heaviest losses being a couple of 0-2 reverses in the second half of the season.

For the second season in a row, a cup run would hamper progress in the League. This time, the team reached the fourth round of the FA Cup and a meeting with Premiership side Blackburn, which coincided with a major mid-season dip in League form. Between early October and early March, League wins were hard to come by, just four in 25 games. The Cup-tie at Ewood Park saw United sunk 0-3, demoralised early on when Aidan Davison's blunder gifted Mark Hughes' men the lead.

Once the Cup fever was extinguished, it needed an unbeaten sequence at the end of the campaign – four wins and six draws – to ensure the U's steered clear of relegation. Victory over Torquay on the season's final day sent the visitors down and landed Colchester in fifteenth position, a little disappointing after the progress of previous years. Away form had been satisfactory – just six defeats and the joint-meanest defence in the division – but nine home defeats was worrying.

Starting his third full season in charge, Phil Parkinson knew he needed more fire-power and made two significant acquisitions in big striker Chris Iwelumo and pacy Mark Yeates. Scotsman Iwelumo was signed after a spell on the Continent, having earlier turned out for St Mirren, Stoke and Brighton. Yeates came on loan from Tottenham and both went straight into the team for the start of 2005-06. Parkinson opted for what was essentially a 4-5-1 formation at relegated Gillingham and at home to promoted Swansea, and saw his men lose both 1-2.

It was a depressing start and fans were critical of what they perceived as negative tactics. Parkinson switched to 4-4-2 for the visit of Barnsley, pushing the versatile Halford into attack, and saw Iwelumo's first goal for the club – a downward header – prove to be the winner. To run the clock down U's players took the ball into the corners, more negativity to rile the Layer Road fans. Those in the main stand let their feelings be known and from the dugout Parkinson was seen to remonstrate with them. He later apologised for his reaction: 'I know we are here to entertain but we are also here to win. I apologise for shouting at the crowd but I want to win. We're in the winning business. If you're one up with two minutes to go you have to be professional about it.'

Parkinson had been desperate for this first win, but it proved to be the only victory in the opening eight games and for a while another season in the doldrums looked on the cards. Most pundits had predicted that relegated Nottingham Forest would challenge for promotion this time round, accompanied by Tranmere, Bristol City and Gillingham. Very few fancied Colchester to avoid relegation, and Southend were also expected to find life tough in League One, following the previous season's play-off pro-motion under Steve Tilson.

Parkinson had by now become used to battling against the odds and he worked hard to create the right blend. Things didn't really begin to click until well into September, perhaps kick-started by the four minutes in which Doncaster helped the U's with two spectacular own-goals to set up a 3-2 win at Layer Road. Things were starting to go Colchester's way. Swansea, Southend and Huddersfield made most of the early running at the top, but as the evenings started to shorten Colchester began to slow-ly creep up the table.

Occasionally, Parkinson reverted back to the unpopular 4-5-1, which proved effective in snatching a point at Bradford City, for example. But United got a taste of their own medicine when Bournemouth employed the same tactics to steal a 1-0 win at Layer Road. Broadly, though, results were positive and the win at Blackpool was particularly pleasing, against a 'bogey' side who had not been beaten for years. Parkinson swooped to borrow tiny goal-poacher Jamie Cureton from Swindon in October. The first time Cureton was paired with big Iwelumo, the duo managed three goals between them to send Yeovil to a 3-2 defeat.

Halford celebrated his 100th game with a brace in the 5-0 mauling of Gillingham. This represented the first time six straight wins had been chalked up for seventeen years, and the U's were now soaring into the top half – very much the division's in-form side. A grand total of 73 hardy U's fans made the long trip to Hartlepool and were rewarded by a single-goal victory thanks to Cureton's strike, a result that lifted the U's into the top six for the first time. Four days later the team embarked on another lengthy trip, this time to leaders Swansea. Victory would establish a club record-equalling eight successive wins. In the event it ended deadlocked at 1-1, the in-form Neil Danns having his late penalty saved by Willy Gueret.

With Christmas 2005 fast approaching, winning ways were regained against lowly MK Dons. Remarkably, considering the shaky start, the U's found themselves in the top four. Plenty of imagination went into goal celebrations – ranging from Iwelumo's 'front-crawl' to bizarre affairs involving Yeates and corner flags. Even more bizarre was the sight of topless (male) U's fans shovelling snow from the pitch in what would ulti-mately be a vain bid to get the Scunthorpe match played after heavy snowfall. Despite the jovial efforts of the scantily-clad hordes, the refer-ee reluctantly ruled the pitch unplayable.

Swindon put a spanner in the works on Boxing Day, their 1-0 win end-ing a twelve-match unbeaten run, but United signalled the strength of their intent on New Year's Eve with an eye-catching 2-0 win at fellow chasers Brentford. It featured a starring performance from two-goal Yeates, who was proving a slippery customer for League One defenders. Nottingham Forest were the first opponents at Layer Road in 2006 and a packed ground reverberated in the dying moments. Danns' opening goal was cancelled out on 90 minutes when Nathan Tyson streaked clear, but the U's hit back directly from the restart, Yeates netting Iwelumo's flick and then Australian Richard Garcia firing an excellent third deep into added time.

Colchester were looking better and better, brimming with confidence and now playing attractive, passing football. Managerless Walsall were seen off 2-0 and Bristol City beaten by the odd goal in five at Layer Road. It meant United's prodigious run had now brought fifteen wins from seventeen games. Top spot was reached on the evening of 21 January, when late goals by Garcia condemned Port Vale to a 2-1 defeat. Over the next weeks Essex football fans could glory in the unlikely sight of Colchester and Southend sitting proudly at the top of League One – at one time six points clear of the rest.

A new U's club record was created on 4 February, when mid-table Bradford City were beaten 3-1, the ninth successive win in all competitions. A 1-0 success over Scunthorpe three days later stretched the record to ten (and equalled the club League record of seven), and jubilant fans were now thinking seriously about making the Championship the following year.

Life has rarely been predictable at Layer Road and perhaps those fans should have known better than to get too carried away. The glorious run (all in all it was 24 wins and four draws from the previous 30 games in all competitions) was set to end with a bang. And this wouldn't be just a temporary blip either – the next thirteen games yielded just a single win.

There was no obvious cause for the crash; it couldn't be blamed on a spate of injuries, suspensions or departures. The only possible explanation was that old bugbear, fixture congestion caused by simultaneous cup runs. While Colchester had soared up the table between September and February, they were also enjoying long runs in both FA Cup and LDV Vans Trophy. Cup success had affected League form in the past two seasons, and now it appeared to be happening again.

The U's were not knocked out of the LDV Vans Trophy until March – in the southern final against Swansea over two legs. Added to the five games played in this competition were another five in the FA Cup. Fellow promotion chasers Southend, meanwhile, had no such distractions, making early exits in all three cups. Not that U's fans were complaining about involvement in the FA Cup, of course, for it ultimately brought about one of the biggest occasions in the club's history – a fifth round meeting with Premiership table-toppers and reigning champions Chelsea. The Chelsea tie was scheduled for Sunday, 19 February, and as the big day edged closer, so United's League season appeared to go pear-shaped. Defeat at Huddersfield was followed by a tepid goalless draw at home to Walsall. A team with a winning habit was suddenly wobbling.

The FA Cup run had begun in early December when non-leaguers Leamington came to Layer Road. The tie was so one-sided it resembled 90 minutes of shooting practice. Goals flew in from all angles and the 44-year-old club record victory of 9-1 (against Bradford City in Division Four) was equalled. Seven different United players got on the scoresheet that afternoon, and as Leamington caved in near the end the U's were disappointed that the referee played only a minimum of added time, thus probably preventing double figures. Well-earned 2-1 away wins at Second Division Shrewsbury and Championship leaders Sheffield United saw the U's progress to a fourth round tussle with another Championship outfit, Derby. The Rams were outplayed 3-1 and a dream pairing came out of the velvet bag when the televised draw for the fifth round was made – the U's would be away to either Everton or Chelsea. Jose Mourinho's glamour boys won their replay as hoped and expected, and so little Colchester began preparing for a day out at Stamford Bridge and their first-ever competitive game against Chelsea.

The media interest and general hullabaloo surrounding the tie even overshadowed the famous 1971 Leeds game. The press descended on Layer Road in droves, demanding soundbites and off-beat pictures. Marie Partner even found herself fobbing off requests to pose in her 'lucky' underwear. She wisely decided this might not be appropriate behaviour for the Essex Businesswoman of the Year. Fully attired, she told the cameras that the entire nation, minus Chelsea fans, would be baying romantically for Colchester in a match that would be televised live to the nation by the BBC.

She was probably right, for the humble Colchester team had cost around £150,000 compared to the £225 million reportedly paid to put Mourinho's outfit together. Statistics like these fed the media's hunger and helped build the hype. The newspapers marvelled at how a club that played in 'the ground that time forgot' would be earning more from their Cup run than their current annual operating loss of £300,000. 'We are a Championship team with Conference facilities,' Marie admitted. 'When people say our ground is the worst in the League, I prefer to say it's the oldest, most old-fashioned.'

When Chelsea dished out the allocation of away tickets, there were bitter complaints from Colchester – ground capacity 6,143 – that the handout of just over 6,000 tickets was nowhere near enough to cater for the demand. Some fans queued all night at Layer Road, complete with their sleeping bags and cans of lager, but inevitably some locals were disappointed. One fan, based in North Carolina, USA, somehow got hold of a ticket and made plans to fly in just before kick-off and then fly back straight afterwards. With BBC screening the game live on the Sunday afternoon, and satellite channels ESPN and Fox Sports involved, there would be a global TV audience, and Colcestrians exiled in all corners of the world would have the chance to see the game from afar.

Statistics were bandied about to emphasise the gulf in status of the opponents – Chelsea's wage bill was £115 million, while Colchester's was £750,000; Chelsea had the bigger professional squad by 35 to 21; a Stamford Bridge season ticket could cost as much as £1,150, while Colchester's most expensive was £390; average crowds were 42,630 compared to 4,200. It was also reported that, to keep Jose Mourinho sweet, Parkinson had sent him a gift pack of twelve jars of jam, kindly supplied by United's sponsors, Tiptree Preserves.

After all the build-up, some U's fans feared that the game itself might prove an anticlimax. They needn't have worried. When the big day finally arrived, there were huge crowds outside Stamford Bridge as the U's team bus inched its way through. Blaring from the vehicle's music system was Johnny Cash's *Ring of Fire*, the choice of goalkeeper Aidan Davison, which even the younger and trendier squad members agreed was a stirring and appropriate pre-match tune to fire the adrenaline.

United took the field in their yellow away kit to be greeted by a mass release of yellow balloons. They were not overawed by the occasion and the first half became a glorious roller-coaster ride that would live long in the memory. Underdogs Colchester were fearless and made the champions look tentative and anxious. The U's looked the more cohesive side before the interval, and showed just why they had won twenty of their previous 24 games. Some of the tension was lifted when the ball went for a goal-kick, only to disappear entirely under the sea of balloons released earlier. The hapless ball-boy simply couldn't locate the ball and stood around bemused and helpless.

United settled remarkably quickly, given their lack of familiarity with such surroundings. Mark Yeates came within a whisker of putting them ahead when he latched onto Karl Duguid's precision pass. He drove the ball across goal, beating Carlo Cudicini, only for the effort to slam against the far post. Then, with 27 minutes gone, came the moment Colchester fans had dreamed about. Halford lifted a first-time ball over Chelsea's makeshift left-back Glen Johnson for Garcia to burst onto and slip a cross along the six-yard box. Centre-back Ricardo Carvalho stumbled as he raced back to cover, and could only deflect the ball at speed past Cudicini. 'Chelsea 0 Colchester 1' read the scoreboard and TV captions across the globe.

The air of disbelief didn't last long. Stunned Chelsea responded with an equaliser as the interval approached, in what was their first decent attack since the opening minutes. A corner from the left found its way to Paulo Ferreira and he bundled the ball over the line. United's lead had lasted only nine minutes – a fact that prompted the club to later issue a lavishly illustrated 52-page commemorative booklet called *Nine Minutes of Magic*.

After the break, Jose Mourinho turned to his big guns and brought on substitutes Joe Cole, Frank Lampard and Hernan Crespo. Stuttering Chelsea clearly needed a boost and Mourinho abandoned his initial plan to leave these three idle on the bench to rest them for Champions League action. Undaunted, Colchester continued to defend stoutly, occasionally launching a dangerous looking foray themselves. As the final ten minutes approached they looked well worth a replay, but on 79 minutes the home side's class finally told. Argentine Crespo's shot was well parried by Aidan Davison, only for Cole to swoop and net the rebound. It was a demoralising time to concede and the exhausted defence succumbed again a few minutes later when Cole netted a curler. The 1-3 scoreline didn't begin to tell the full story, and praise for Colchester was fulsome.

Mourinho was generous: 'I have a lot of respect for the Colchester club, for the team and the manager, who I believe is a good manager. They are top of the League almost and maybe in a few years they can come back to Stamford Bridge to play us in the Premiership. They had some nice pieces of football in the game and the big boy in attack caused problems in the air. They have some players that also caused problems in the box and some quick players as well. The Colchester crowd was unbelievable, this is the only country where the away team bring 6,000 supporters who believe it is possible to win.'

Colchester's celebrity supporter, Radio One disc jockey Steve Lamacq, had an unforgettable day: 'The thing I'll remember most is the singing. Wherever you went you could hear the Colchester fans in full voice. Right from the moment you emerged into the light at Fulham Broadway. It was incredibly uplifting and good humoured and defiant.'

After the dust settled, the task for manager Parkinson was to make sure his troops didn't suffer a cup hangover. The wonderful League form of earlier weeks had dipped, and the team couldn't afford to fall too far off the pace if Championship football was to become a reality. On the day Colchester were losing to Chelsea, Southend recovered to win 4-3 at Chesterfield, opening a four-point gap above them at the top, although the U's did now have two games in hand. With the clubs due to meet at Layer Road in early March, the scene was set for a fascinating climax.

CHAPTER 8

Farewell to the Lower Divisions

February-May 2006

Once the strength-sapping excitement of the Chelsea cup adventure had died down, manager Phil Parkinson could focus on the bid for promotion to the Championship. The League table that mid-February weekend showed United with a fine chance of going up, even though Parkinson believed his team were 'punching above their weight' by even surviving in League One.

The U's remained second in the table, four points behind Southend but with two games in hand. However the four teams immediately behind them (Huddersfield, Swansea, Brentford and Barnsley) in the play-off slots were snapping at their heels. In fact, this top six would never change and would slug it out to the death.

Colchester's fourteen remaining matches would include eight away trips, five of them to opponents in the the top half. This was a prospect that didn't unduly worry Parkinson, however, for United had been looking surprisingly solid and resolute on their travels. In fifteen away games thus far, they'd only lost four and had conceded just thirteen goals – less than a goal a game, and the best record in the division.

As the first shoots of spring appeared, automatic promotion was still attainable. The only cloud on the immediate horizon was the dip in form that dated back to the visit of Scunthorpe in the first week of February. On that Tuesday night, the U's struggled to win 1-0 in unconvincing fashion, and in the games that followed the points began to slip away. A ten-week period would produce just one Colchester win in thirteen matches, cup-ties included, which was hardly promotion form. This was not just a 'blip', it was a crisis.

Perhaps the pre-Christmas dazzle had all been a flash in the proverbial pan. Were Colchester heading back to the mid-table comfort zone that was more 'appropriate' to a club of this size and potential? Or could Parky arrest the slide in time? Many fans, if honest, would have said the former. United slipped back as far as sixth during this worrying period, but never quite lost touch with the play-off zone altogether. Parkinson even took the squad on a mini-break to Portugal to re-charge batteries, but sadly to little effect. The trip to sunnier climes preceded the worst setback of all – a disastrous first half in the long-awaited home derby with Southend. After just 32 minutes the U's found themselves three goals down, a desperate situation that meant the promotion feelgood factor had disappeared out of the window. Even the jovial bunch who frequent the Barside terracing were subdued. Freddy Eastwood's header had eluded a packed six-yard box to drift over the line after just eleven minutes, and Steve Tilson's men followed this up with well-worked goals from Kevin Maher and Che Wilson that left Layer Road stunned.

The goals had really dried up for the U's and Parkinson decided it was time to pep up the attack before the promotion dream fizzled out altogether. As usual he had to find free-transfer bargains or loan men, and over the next week or two signed up experienced poacher Tony Thorpe from Grimsby, borrowed nippy Jamal Campbell-Ryce from Southend (though officially still a Rotherham player), young Irish starlet Billy Clarke from Ipswich, and rangy Scott Vernon from Blackpool. The sixth successive League game without a Colchester goal came at chilly Oldham. United even hit the bar, but had Kemi Izzet sent off and were pole-axed by a last-minute winner from Richard Butcher.

Newcomer Thorpe fell expertly to win a penalty during the visit of Swindon and once again Iwelumo converted sweetly. The U's somehow hung on to record their first win in five weeks and followed up with hard-earned goalless draws at Doncaster and Scunthorpe. Brentford then came to Layer Road for a real six-pointer, the Bees having snatched the second spot in the table previously occupied by Colchester. The U's deserved to win on chances created, but a 1-1 draw at least kept the promotion pot boiling.

The form team was Nottingham Forest, who had stormed up the table to challenge for a play-off place, and they welcomed United for a vital clash in early April. Lady Luck went missing once again and a tense encounter was decided when Wayne Brown lashed at a clearance, only for the ball to fly into the U's net after ricocheting off both Karl Duguid and Forest's Chris Perch.

Neil Danns, who missed a sitter at Forest, was nevertheless doing well in his attacking midfield role, and became the hero in United's 41st match of the League season – a 2-0 win over Hartlepool. It was a huge relief all round, for that win used up the U's' last game in hand. Plucky Hartlepool were battling to avoid relegation and struck the woodwork three times, yet Danns scored twice in the final seven minutes to push the U's back up to third. This left them one point behind Brentford, but eight behind Southend, with everyone having played 41 games. With seventh-placed Oldham five points adrift of Colchester, a top-six finish and a play-off place was there for the taking, but maybe automatic promotion could still be salvaged. The title seemed certain to be heading to Roots Hall.

The determination not to let things slip again was evident at Saltergate when Colchester battled back from two goals down to pick up another precious point. On the same afternoon Brentford drew 2-2 at Rotherham and Huddersfield 1-1 at Bournemouth, so nothing changed within the top four. On Easter Monday, United overcame rugged Tranmere 1-0 thanks to a superb goal by Brown from a nifty free-kick, by which time Rovers were down to ten men after Stephen O'Leary was red-carded for a lunging studs-and-all tackle. Blackpool's last-gasp equaliser at Brentford meant United leapfrogged them back into second place. The excitement was mounting and the U's seemed to be back in top gear. Southend only picked up a single point over Easter but still seemed destined to lift the title, while the U's and Brentford looked to be battling it out for the runners-up spot.

There was no margin for error with three games left. The U's travelled with a big following to the south coast to take on middling Bournemouth. Brentford faced a similar task when visiting Swindon, while Southend were at home to Doncaster. The trip to Dorset proved memorable for the U's contingent, with many a cold lager consumed near the sea front after the team chalked up a 2-1 win. Liam Chilvers' header and a fine finish by Scott Vernon kept the U's in the top two. Despite Brentford's 3-1 win, Southend's slip-up by 0-1 to Doncaster meant they were now catchable. Just four points separated the top three.

Top of the table (22 April 2006). All teams had played 44 games:
1 Southend 78pts, 2 Colchester 75, 3 Brentford 74, 4 Huddersfield 72, 5 Barnsley 68, 6 Swansea 67, 7 Nott'm F 67, 8 Bristol C 64, 9 Oldham 64, 10 Doncaster 63.

So, with two games left Colchester were as close as they had ever been to climbing out of the lower divisions. Southend had two tricky-looking games, so the U's could even dream of winning the title. During the midweek lead-up to the penultimate game – at home to Rotherham – U's fans mused on the various permutations. There were two outcomes that would produce a 'definite': if Southend won at Swansea (barring a mathematical miracle), they would be champions. If Brentford lost and Colchester won, the U's were definitely up. Anything else and it would all go down to the last day. Being a point clear in second place, Colchester knew that it was in their own hands – win both games and they were up. The visit of relegation-haunted Rotherham attracted a full house to Layer Road and the air was thick with anticipation. The last time Colchester had been this close to promotion to football's second tier, they had messed things up completely, losing 1-4 to relegation candidates Swindon in April 1957. Surely lightning wouldn't strike twice?

United laid siege to the Millers' goal with Danns and Yeates in typically lively mood. Visiting centre-back Shaun Barker then looped a header high and handsomely over his own goalkeeper. Remarkably it was the second time this season Barker had own-goaled against Colchester. The points were made virtually safe after the interval when Yeates fired into the corner of the net. Yeates, always a highly enthusiastic and athletic celebrator of goals, set off at speed towards the corner at the right hand end of the main stand and launched himself into an airborne headlong dive towards the corner flag. Those watching closely will have noticed that his landing on the bone-hard surface was far from smooth, the grin on his face replaced by a grimace. For a second or two he seemed to have aborted the celebration, but then as the adrenaline kicked in and his teammates arrived on the scene he leaped back to his feet, whirling his arms around. He had actually dislocated his shoulder, which he somehow disguised for a while, but ultimately forced him from the pitch. He would miss the crucial final game of the season. Surely the most bizarre and unnecessary injury suffered in football this season?

Once the news filtered in from elsewhere, the jubilant Colchester fans and players were able to calculate where they stood. Brentford had again thrown away a 1-0 home lead in the dying seconds, while Southend twice came from behind to draw 2-2 at Swansea. Those results confirmed promotion for Southend, but not yet the championship. Colchester simply needed one point at Yeovil on the final day to be promoted. If Brentford drew, Colchester would go up even if beaten at Huish Park. However, if Colchester won and Southend didn't, the U's would be champions.

Top of the table (29 April 2006). All teams had played 45 games:
1 Southend 79, 2 Colchester 78, 3 Brentford 75, 4 Huddersfield 72, 5 Barnsley 69, 6 Swansea 68, 7 Nott'm F 68, 8 Doncaster 66.

And so it all went down to the wire. Yeovil had rarely been on the Colchester fixture list but had hosted the U's first match as a professional club, almost 70 years earlier. On that occasion Yeovil won 3-0 on the famous old sloping pitch at The Huish. U's fans who had travelled to that historic game shelled out 13s 6d (67.5p) for a special cheap day return rail fare. Those who chose to go by rail for the 2007 game wouldn't even get a sandwich from the buffet car for that sort of money. The ground in use back in 1937 nowadays houses a Tesco, the football club having moved to a brand new Huish Park in 1990.

While the fans and media discussed all the possible permutations, Phil Parkinson insisted he would not listen out for results from elsewhere and would urge his team to concentrate solely on getting a result at Yeovil: 'Training has been light this week and we can't wait. We've blocked out any additional media coverage and we're ready. We looked hungry and committed, but also relaxed, against Rotherham and that's the key against Yeovil. I think it would be dangerous to sit back and play for the draw, so we will go down there on the front foot in positive fashion and go to win the game. All we've done at present is just put ourselves in a good position, there's no pats on the back or congratulations at the moment.

'Last weekend [against Rotherham] we blocked it all out and we didn't know anything from elsewhere until we got back into the dressing room after the game. There's nothing that can happen around the country that would change our approach during this game, so there will be no thinking about that. Pressure? There's three places you can be: down at the bottom with status and livelihoods at stake; in mid-table with nothing to play for; or where we are now. I know where I'd rather be. We prepared the same way for the cup game with Leamington as we did for the one with Chelsea – we watched them both three times in advance. It's the same for this game. 1,600 fans are going down there with us and it will be like a home game for us – we'll approach it in that way. We got terrific backing at the Bournemouth game and it will be the same here.'

A long trek down the A12, around the M25 and then along the M3 confronted the majority of the 1,600-plus travelling U's fans. Yeovil, the vibrant market-town home of The Glovers, was still regarded as something of footballing outpost, for they were about to complete only their third season as a Football League club. There were sunny intervals and a few light showers, but weather conditions were of little consequence as the boisterous band wound its way on their 200-mile journey, stopping in large merry groups at various Little Chefs and other service areas. In particular, the Fleet Services beside the M3 resonated to Colchester songs throughout the morning. The mood was upbeat, flags and scarves waving optimistically from car windows throughout a journey that took most people in excess of four hours.

Many were clad in the U's yellow away kit, others preferring replica shirts in blue-and-white stripes. Bright yellow curly wigs proved particularly popular, and there were flags and banners galore. Many arrived at the small, modern stadium in Lufton Way hours before kick-off. For the vast majority it was their first visit. They found the ground positioned a mile to the west of the town centre, in a suburb known as Houndstone, full of business and commercial premises, with plenty of parking and open spaces. It looked a far cry from the traditional British football ground, surrounded by terraced houses and narrow streets. U's fans converged from all directions and milled around noisily, but it was only on entry to the ground that there was any real football atmosphere. Ushered into the open end, the visitors found the prevailing breeze often carried the noise away, so there was not the same volume as there would have been with a roof. It would not be until the end filled and the singing really took hold that the appropriate atmosphere was created.

Some early-arriving fans headed straight for the players and officials' entrance, where stewards manoeuvred barriers to prevent a crush as the U's coach drew up and the players emerged. Huge cheers greeted them as they stepped off the bus. One or two grabbed a bottle of mineral water from the front of the bus as they alighted, others stopped to sign autographs. Anything to keep occupied and keep the nerves at bay. Some looked serious and thoughtful, others acknowledged the fans with smiles. Chris Iwelumo received a rousing cheer, striding into the building clutching his precious white boots.

Big queues built up at the away end turnstiles. There at the centre of the throng was Bob Russell, Liberal Democrat MP for Colchester and a U's follower for 49 years. It would have needed House of Commons business of the gravest nature to have prevented Russell making this trip. He was sporting a yellow replica shirt underneath a splendid blue-and-white striped waistcoat for the occasion. No Westminster formality here then.

U's fans packed the open away end, roofless and exposed to the elements. The other three sides of the ground were also full as a bumper crowd of 8,785 assembled. It was one of Yeovil's highest gates of the season, despite the fact that for them the result was meaningless. The weather was good and the atmosphere electric. Colchester fans released shredded paper and coloured balloons at various points, and waved flags and banners as they bounced along happily to endless renditions of 'Who Needs Mourinho? We've got Phil Parkinson', a song composed earlier in the season for the Chelsea trip.

As the teams emerged, the United players heading for the away end to warm up, Parkinson leaning on the dug-out, trying to look relaxed as he sipped water and occasionally acknowledged the chanting of his name. He must have been slightly concerned that his team was without regulars Wayne Brown and Mark Yeates due to injury, meaning Pat Baldwin was called into defence and loanee Jamal Campbell-Ryce was enjoying his first full game in U's colours. Referee Andre Marriner signalled proceedings to begin and it was soon clear Yeovil were up for it. The visitors' plan to keep a clean sheet came under immediate threat.

Phil Jevons' quick turn created space and he lashed a shot goalwards, only to see young Dean Gerken deflect the ball against a post. The away end breathed a collective sigh of relief.

The sighs soon turned to screams of protest when Skiverton won a header inside the Yeovil area, flooring Scott Vernon in the process, but Mr Marriner waved aside the penalty appeals. Kindly Yeovil fans in the Westland Stand did the gentlemanly thing upon hearing that Brentford had gone a goal up at Bournemouth and launched into a rousing chorus of '1-0 to the Brentford', which was greeted with grim-faced abuse from the away end. As long as Colchester didn't lose, Brentford could win by a hatful and it wouldn't matter. Nevertheless, beneath the bravado it was an ominous development.

Iwelumo beat Skiverton to a Halford cross, but landed his attempt among the advertising hoardings. At the other end, David Poole whipped the ball across the Colchester goal to Jevons, who flashed his shot a yard wide. The half-time whistle arrived with news that Bournemouth had equalised against Brentford.

Upon the turnaround, the unmarked Paul Terry – brother of England captain John – headed over United's crossbar. The home side looked more likely to break the deadlock, but Colchester worked furiously to keep them out. The clearest chance of the second half saw Poole lob the advancing Gerken, but the ball dropped agonisingly wide.

Yeovil boss Steve Thompson sent on his youth-team skipper Dale Williams for his debut, while United took off loanees Campbell-Ryce and Vernon, replacing them with Izzet and Thorpe. The Westland Stand generously spread the news that Brentford were by now 2-1 ahead. The nail-biting apprehension on the terraces seemed to transmit to the pitch, with signs of desperation appearing in the Colchester back line. Clearances were ballooned into the air or whacked into the stands unnecessarily. For a spell the U's failed to keep possession and seemed unable to keep the ball out of their own half. Some of those behind the goal could hardly bear to look as the clock ticked towards 4.50 and the final whistle loomed. Lindegaard caused an almighty scare when his wicked cross spun across the face of the Colchester goal, leaving keeper Gerken back-pedalling in panic, but the ball veered beyond the post.

There were muffled screams from the away end every time the whistle went near Mr Marriner's mouth. Then, as the ball was pumped over the halfway line, his high-pitch blast signalled scenes of mayhem. Against all odds Colchester United were promoted out of the lower divisions for the first time. It was hard to take in, and it seemed impossible that 1,600 people in an open space could make such a noise. For a second or two players ran in circles, not sure what to do. Karl Duguid, thirteen years with the club, simply clutched his head and wept. The players ran towards each other like headless chickens, hugging whoever came close.

Parkinson embraced Geraint Williams on the touchline before they raced on to join the fun. The players galloped towards their fans, the first to arrive being Neil Danns, who skipped along like an excited child before hurling himself to the ground and laying there prostrate, face down and apparently sobbing with joy. The huge figure of Greg Halford then belly-flopped on top of him.

Within seconds all the U's players and officials had found their way to the away end. Police and stewards lined up anxiously in front of the wall, but there were no signs of trouble or pitch invasions. The chaotic scene was recorded for posterity at close quarters by the club's media men, Matt Hudson and David Gregory, who wandered around pointing video cameras. At one point, defender Baldwin mugged Gregory for his camera and filmed his own segment, but in the excitement seemed unable to hold the instrument still. Everybody hugged everybody, and Duguid and fans' favourite Danns looked particularly emotional.

Duguid, who had known long-term injury and years of mid-table drudgery, was seen wandering off alone, head down, unable to join in for a few moments while his tears flowed. Parkinson earned a huge ovation as he marched up and down acknowledging the supporters. Iwelumo accepted a huge yellow wig and plonked it on his head. Halford's boots and shirt went flying into the crowd and the player himself very nearly followed. Dean Gerken went one better and flung himself into the fans like a rock star performing a stage-dive. Little Kemi Izzet was seized by colleagues and nearly went the same way.

Suddenly an official-looking Coca-Cola 'congratulations' banner appeared. By the time of the players' obligatory mass 'belly-flop' into the goalmouth, some shirts had gone missing, yet the press photographers somehow marshalled the players for the joyful team picture which adorns the dust jacket of this book.

It took some time, but back in the dressing rooms the party resumed, with the champagne and silly songs in full flow. Messrs Hudson and Gregory made creditable efforts at interviewing during this chaos. Asked what it all meant to him, Duguid croaked: 'I can't explain. I've been crying and everything. It wasn't the best of games, in fact it was terrible.' The injured Wayne Brown concurred: 'I can't really grasp it – little Colchester in the Championship. That was probably the worst game of football I've ever seen in my life. I was sitting there kicking every ball with them.'

The point earned left Colchester second, automatically promoted with Southend, whose 1-0 victory over Bristol City confirmed them as champions. Brentford's game with Bournemouth ended 2-2, meaning Martin Allen's men would tackle (and fail in) the play-offs.

Local-boy-made-good Paul
Abrahams, a speedy forward
who had two spells at his
home-town club, either side
of a stint with Brentford

Midfielder Brian Launders is challenged by Bournemouth's Peter Grant, later to become
manager of Norwich. Launders' stay at Colchester ended in acrimony

Chelsea's Didier Drogba shields the ball from U's defender Wayne Brown during the 2006 FA Cup-tie at Stamford Bridge

Jamie Cureton in action against Stoke City at Layer Road in December 2006. He scored twice in a 3-0 victory

Richard Garcia shows his delight in netting Colchester's second goal in the thrilling 3-1 win over Sunderland in April 2007

David Gregory is swamped after netting the winning goal from the penalty spot in the May 1998 play-off final against Torquay at Wembley

Jamie Moralee joined the U's in 1999, but the former Millwall, Watford, Crewe and Brighton forward found goals hard to come by

Karl Duguid (centre) in action against Bournemouth in September 2000, watched by Gavin Johnson (left) and Lomana Tresor Lua-Lua (right)

The Layer Road ground from the air: a humble little stadium hemmed in by suburbia

Popular Steve McGavin celebrates a goal for the U's. He had two spells at Layer Road, either side of stints with Birmingham Wycombe and Southend

Player-coach Roy McDonough finds himself closely marked during a GM Vauxhall Conference game

Layer Road celebrates after David Gregory scores in the May 1998 Division Three play-off semi-final against Barnet

Steve McGavin turns on the style against Wrexham during his second spell as a Colchester player

Skipper Tony English, a loyal servant for more than 11 years, shows his skills in pre-season training at Layer Road

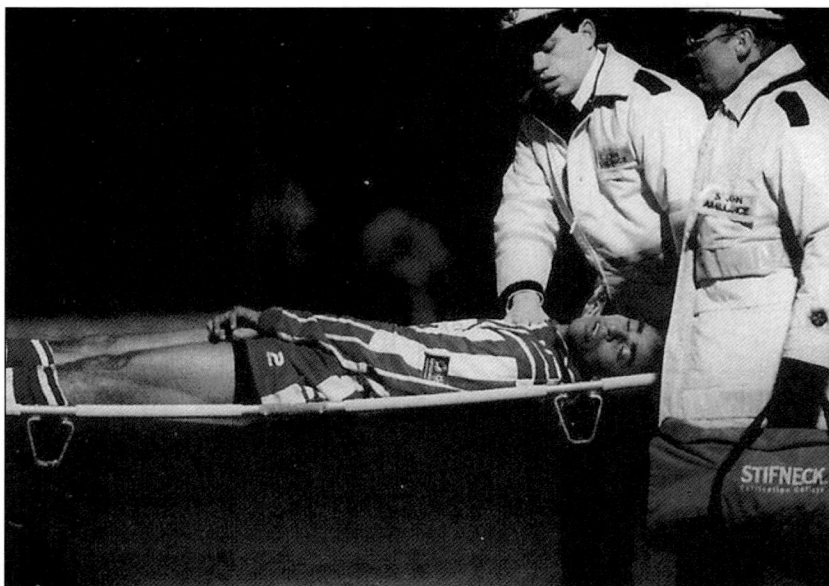

Brazilian Fumaca is carried off unconscious in the early stages of his Colchester debut against Manchester City in 1999. He never played for the U's again

Experienced Steve Whitton, who served the U's for nine years as player, coach, caretaker-manager, and then manager

Centre-half Gus Caesar arrives in the Torquay penalty area for a corner-kick, during his U's debut in August 1994

Chris Keeble, the son of former Colchester, West Ham and Newcastle forward Vic, signed for Colchester from Ipswich in 1999

Ex-Arsenal and England favourite Ian Wright in action at Colchester in Burnley's colours, watched by Jason Dozzell (left) and Richard Wilkins

Gavin Johnson, a polished former for the U's past his 30th birthday, who previously served Ipswich, Luton, Wigan and Dunfermline

Big Chris Iwelumo posed plenty of problems for Ipswich Town during the local derby at Portman Road in January 2007

Gus Caesar (centre) and Mark Kinsella in action against Plymouth, during the May 1996 Division Three play-off semi-finals

Joe Dunne, who played more than 200 first-team games at full-back, before joining Colchester's coaching staff

Tony Lock (No 19) congratulates Steve McGavin on another goal at Layer Road

Record signing Neil Gregory (No 10) in action at Wembley in the
May 1998 play-off final with Torquay

Defender Sagi Burton, one of
the many new faces to arrive
at Colchester during Mick
Wadsworth's short stint as
manager in 1999

Manager Phil Parkinson and Karl Duguid celebrate promotion to the Championship in 2006 from a balcony at Colchester Town Hall

Steve Wignall, a stalwart U's centre-half, whose four-year stint as manager (1995-99) included promotion and two Wembley appearances

Full-back Chris Barker fends off an Ipswich challenge during the local derby at Portman Road in January 2007

Jubilation among U's players as the final whistle at Yeovil in May 2006 heralds promotion to English football's second flight for the first time

Former West Ham midfielder Alan Dickens in action for the U's against Wycombe Wanderers in March 1994

Roy McDonough heads goalwards during an evening game at Layer Road in the Conference era

Jamie Cureton celebrates one of his two goals in a 3-0 victory over Stoke in December 2006. Cureton ended the season with 24 League and FA Cup goals

David Gregory scored many vital goals during seven years at Layer Road. He arrived at his home-town club via Ipswich, Hereford and Peterborough

Colchester's successful 2006-07 managerial partnership of Geraint 'George' Williams and Mick Harford

The U's Greg Halford in action against Ipswich in January 2007, the first League meeting between the sides at Portman Road for 50 years

Full-back and midfielder Joe Keith joined
Colchester from West Ham in 1999 and
played more than 200 times in six seasons

Striker Steve McGavin in Second Division action at Layer Road against Northampton

Mark Kinsella, a Layer Road legend between 1989 and 1996, who went on to play for Charlton, Aston Villa, West Brom and the Irish Republic

Essex boy Mick Stockwell served Colchester superbly for three years (2000-03) after a long career at Ipswich

New floodlight pylons are swung into place at Layer Road during a summer recess

Steve Germain, a French striker signed by Mick Wadsworth, failed to establish a regular place in the U's line-up

Striker Tony Adcock, who quit Colchester aged 36 in 1999, falling narrowly short of Martyn King's club record goal tally of 130

The Colchester squad get a taste of the Wembley atmosphere, shortly before the FA Trophy final with Witton Albion in 1992

Skilful midfielder Adam Locke, who spent three years with the U's in the mid-1990s, and also served Crystal Palace, Southend, Luton and Bristol City

Popular Brian Owen, who first arrived at Colchester as a player in 1970 and has since served the club as a coach, physio and scout

Full-back John White beats England's Shaun Wright-Phillips to the ball in the 2006 FA Cup-tie at Chelsea

Skipper Karl Duguid in action in February 2007 against West Brom. The 2007-08 season is his 13th in the U's first team squad

Goalscorer Aaron Skelton is buried under joyous teammates after netting against
Bournemouth in September 2000

Jason Dozzell added a touch of class to
the U's midfield when he signed in
October 1998, having previously
starred for Ipswich and Tottenham

Karl Duguid at the heart of the action in the 3-1 win over Bournemouth in September 2000

Mick Stockwell fires a shot at Billy Dearden in the Wrexham goal during the 1-1 draw in September 2000

Manager Steve Wignall displays the play-off winners' trophy to the crowds in Colchester High Street in May 1998

Thomas Pinault, a French-born midfielder who served United between 1999 and 2004, before departing for Grimsby

Striker Chris Iwelumo in action at Loftus Road against QPR on New Year's Day 2007

Skipper Richard Wilkins raises the 1998 Division Three play-off trophy at Wembley, watched by chairman Peter Heard (left)

Well-travelled Irishman Barry Conlon terrorises the Oxford defence during his 2001 stint in Colchester colours

Wembley here we come! Celebrations in the U's dressing room in May 1998 after the play-off semi-final victory over Barnet

David Greene is sandwiched by the opposition. The centre-half made more than 200 first-team appearances for Colchester, scoring 18 goals

The Colchester fans enjoying their promotion party at Yeovil in May 2006

Phil Parkinson barks out orders from the touchline during
his eventful three-year stint as U's manager

Layer Road mascot Eddie The Eagle
doing his thing before kick-off

French full-back Fabrice Richard, one of the few Mick Wadsworth signings who lasted more than a few months at Colchester

Chris Iwelumo battles with Wolves' Gary Breen during Colchester's 2-1 win at Layer Road in December 2006

Parkinson encapsulated what it all meant: 'It is a marvellous achievement for a small club like ours. Everyone throughout the club has worked hard to get us where we are and I can't describe what it feels like to think we will be playing teams like Sunderland, West Brom and Birmingham next season. I'm absolutely ecstatic to get a club of our size into the second tier of English football. People within the game know what an achievement this is. We were punching well above our weight to even stay in this division, let alone get promoted – it's an absolute dream. It was a long 90 minutes today, Brentford were winning at two stages, but when the pressure was on we produced. It's easy to play mid-table and mid-season, but these players produced when it mattered. Others have got to the top and floundered, and we had a little dip after the cup run but came back when it counted. Dean Gerken gave an immaculate performance today, and all those who missed out today but played a massive part, I don't want to forget their contributions. Any team that is successful has a good goalkeeper and back four and that is down to hard work on the training pitch. This will take some beating as an achievement for me. We're going to drink Yeovil out of champagne now.'

Parkinson, architect of the success, deserved all the praise he was now getting, according to central midfielder Kevin Watson, himself a star of the show at Yeovil. Watson had played alongside the manager when they were at Reading and spotted his managerial potential early on: 'Phil had all the ideas and the determination to succeed. I knew that he would go on to make a good manager and now I just hope that he stays at the club for next season. He's a fantastic fellow and this promotion success couldn't have happened to a nicer man. Winning promotion tops it all off for me. The bookmakers had us in the bottom four at the start of the season, we weren't given a chance by anyone. We have the smallest budget in the division and the smallest ground. In fact we're one of the smallest League clubs in the land. I think we have thoroughly deserved it as well. It's not as if we have come with a late run to steal promotion; we have kept up our challenge all year. I have been lucky enough to be involved in four promotions but this one is ever so special.'

Congratulations from around the globe poured in over the next days and supporters who hadn't been able to get to Yeovil reacted on websites, radio phone-ins and messageboards. Some just screamed and whooped, while others were inspired to voice their thoughts in more articulate fashion, an example being 23-year-old Witham student Ed Jenkinson: 'The fabric separating reality from utterly ludicrous fantasy was terminally ruptured. Yes. The impossible happened. Colchester United, instead of faithfully following the tragic narrative of the past 68 years (i.e. spectacularly self-imploding and snatching a series of humiliating thrashings from the jaws of desperate draws), were promoted into the second tier of the professional football structure. Hilariously, the ridiculous comedy of this extraordinary event is even further exacerbated by the fact that teams such as Birmingham and Sunderland who regularly play host to crowds of 25,000 or more will be forced to play at Layer Road, a ground which can only be described as a small landfill site surrounded by three cow sheds and a large ditch. The [Yeovil] match itself was a terrifyingly nerve-racking affair, featuring almost incessantly suicidal defending and some miraculous good fortune.'

The celebratory scenes on the pitch at Yeovil were resumed back in Colchester later that night, with many of the players and fans converging on the town centre with midnight approaching, after completing the long journey from Somerset. This was a mere rehearsal for what was to come – an official civic parade to the Town Hall on an open-topped bus. Thousands turned out, crushed into shop doorways and hanging out of upper floor windows as the bus slowly made its way by. The throng particularly enjoyed the medal presentations as they emerged, one by one, on to the balcony of the Town Hall to receive their accolades. Some, like Sam Stockley and Mark Yeates, his arm in a sling, gave the moment the full Oscar nomination performance, while others looked a little more dignified and restrained.

For now, long-suffering Colchester fans couldn't possibly have been happier. What they didn't know was that bad news was lurking just around the corner. The principal hero of the hour was about to walk out.

Into a Brave New World

June-September 2006

It was mid-June 2006, less than six weeks after Colchester's magic day in Somerset, when the harsh reality kicked in. The club's huge achievement had inevitably meant 38-year-old manager Phil Parkinson was now being touted as a top man, and being sized up by a number of covetous bigger clubs with existing or looming managerial vacancies. The news that U's fans didn't want to hear began to emerge on Tuesday, 13 June. Parkinson had apparently handed in his resignation.

U's fans who had lived through similar scenarios knew what this meant. Somebody, somewhere had tapped the manager and this was the first stage in his departure. Speculation was rife that Hull City wanted Parkinson to replace Peter Taylor, who had curiously said no to Charlton but yes to neighbours Crystal Palace. The Colchester board refused to accept the resignation and issued this statement: 'We have asked him to reflect upon the position and to discuss matters with us further on his return from holiday in a week's time. Should we be unable to stop him from resigning the board will do whatever is necessary to protect the club.'

It was a case of once bitten, twice shy for the U's board. Following the protracted battle for compensation from Ipswich after George Burley's acrimonious exit in 1994, chairman Peter Heard did not intend to allow his man to leave until compensation was agreed. Charlton, Ipswich and Derby were all said to have been denied permission to talk to Parkinson, who still had another year of his Layer Road contract. It seemed only a matter of time before the energetic young manager would be on his way to a bigger club, but for U's fans the timing could have been better, with the club's first season in the Championship just weeks away. The League Managers' Association vice-chairman Frank Clark publicly urged Parkinson to resolve the situation amicably.

As expected, Hull City were the target, but if their wealthy chairman Adam Pearson thought he would get his man without a struggle, he was wrong. After Parkinson and Heard returned from their respective holidays, instead of being quickly settled, the row intensified. United won a temporary High Court injunction which prevented Parkinson from leaving. The club said it hoped it would allow both parties time to resolve the matter. This angered Hull, who confirmed they had been attempting to negotiate compensation in order to hold talks with Parkinson, describing the U's chairman's actions as 'shockingly vindictive'.

Colchester United were applauded in some quarters for insisting that even the football world, with all its quirks and other-worldly ethics, should take employment contracts seriously. After winning the injunction, the club issued this statement:

'This verdict vindicates our decision to take this stand to protect the interests of the club. There are legal procedures in place in football concerning managerial positions, including how and when managers can leave their employers. Should any club wish to pursue Mr Parkinson as their manager, we hope that correct protocol will be observed. Phil will continue to be the manager of Colchester United until such a time that his contract expires, Colchester give him permission for another club to speak to him, or the temporary injunction is lifted.'

Hull – soon to be facing United on the pitch – attacked Colchester for not accepting their offer of compensation (reportedly under £100,000) and said they would try to overturn the injunction: 'Despite the fact that Mr Parkinson has formally resigned and does not wish to continue his employment with Colchester, their board are reluctant to negotiate compensation with us for his services. They have put the matter in the hands of their solicitors, even though the compensation on offer is extremely generous. This club categorically denies any wrongdoing, but we believe we have been more than reasonable in our attempts to resolve the matter with Colchester.'

Hull accused Peter Heard of 'preventing Mr Parkinson from making a living when he has done so much for Colchester United'. It was a sad state of affairs which left a dark cloud hanging over Layer Road, at a time when all energies should have been directed towards the exciting challenges ahead. There was further grim news when popular Neil Danns was sold to Championship rivals Birmingham City for a reported £850,000, and centre-half Liam Chilvers left for Preston.

It was eventually announced that compensation of around £400,000 had been agreed and Parkinson was formally released. Colchester stipulated that Parkinson could not raid the U's for any of their players. He left for the KC Stadium having won 79 of his 187 matches in charge of the U's, with 54 draws and 54 defeats during a 39-month tenure. Parkinson's trusty deputy Geraint Williams was put in temporary charge, his second spell as caretaker, and was also a leading candidate to get the job on a full-time basis. Williams spent part of the summer qualifying for his UEFA Pro Licence, alongside the likes of Micky Adams, Lennie Lawrence and Ian Rush.

At the end of July, United confirmed that the popular Williams – known throughout football as 'George' – would indeed be the new manager. Some fans were disappointed that a bigger, more glamorous name hadn't been found, but many felt Williams deserved his chance. He knew the club inside out and would provide continuity and stability. Bookies William Hill reacted by making Williams second favourite to be the first Championship manager to get the sack. Hot favourite was Niall Quinn, chairman and manager at Sunderland.

With Danns and Chilvers gone, and loanee Mark Yeates returned to White Hart Lane, Williams recruited striker Jamie Cureton from Swindon and midfielder Johnnie Jackson from Spurs. Both men were familiar with Layer Road, having had earlier spells as loan players – Jackson's four years earlier. Williams did not have the time to do much more, but was raring to go, with only a week left before the historic first match in the Champion-ship. He appointed as assistant manager former Derby County team-mate Mick Harford, 47, who had been out of football since being sacked as Rotherham boss eight months previously.

Colchester's Championship baptism could hardly have been tougher – a trip to Birmingham, freshly relegated from the Premiership. And as Williams had barely a week to prepare, it must have been a hectic time: 'With a week to go, I felt the players at the club needed clarity and there needed to be a decision on the manager,' he said, adding that while the fans would enjoy seeing their favourites in unfamiliar surroundings at massive clubs like Sunderland and Wolves, everyone had to recognise the season ahead should not become a sightseeing tour: 'For the fans, it will be fantastic but for myself, the staff and players, we want to make sure we have a second visit next year.'

Born near Treorchy in the Rhondda Valley, the career of 44-year-old David Geraint Williams had passed through all levels of the professional game. As a combative midfielder he had won thirteen full Welsh caps between 1988 and 1996, and played at the top level with Derby County (277 League games) and Ipswich (217), but started out as an apprentice at Bristol Rovers, where cleaning the toilets and washing kit was par for the course. When a knee injury ended his playing career at Colchester, his future had looked to be in computer programming, a subject he had studied in his spare time. But the then manager Mick Wadsworth suggested he try his hand at coaching the U's reserves and new horizons suddenly opened up. Williams soon developed a burning ambition to become a club manager, and now that he was being given that chance he cited his own former bosses Arthur Cox and John Lyall as his biggest influences – Cox for his passion and Lyall for his calmness and knowledge.

There was to be no honeymoon for Williams. The first five matches of 2006-07 all ended in defeat and William Hill's odds now looked ominously realistic. The opener at Birmingham ended in a 1-2 loss, although the second half performance gave everyone heart for the battles ahead. Three days later, in the first home game at this level, Plymouth were given a pounding by the U's, who did everything but score. Argyle debutant Luke Summerfield showed them how it was done, netting the winner. The third game was a visit from Barnsley, promoted with the U's (via the play-offs).

This proved to be an occasion enjoyed by U's fans only for the chance to jeer at referee Graham Poll. The official was taking his first game since his blunder with yellow cards in the 2006 World Cup, and the wags on the Layer Road terraces didn't let him forget it. Greg Halford headed the U's in front, but two second-half goals sent them spinning to another defeat. Williams then shuffled his pack for the trip to West Brom, giving Chris Iwelumo his first start. Bryan Robson's men were run close, but two first-half goals proved decisive and the U's slipped to their fourth defeat out of four, and the third by a 1-2 scoreline. Three days later a visit to Second Division MK Dons seemed to be the ideal chance to get into winning ways, but an extra-time goal by Izale McLeod fired Colchester out of the Carling Cup.

All five defeats had been by one goal and in none were the U's outclassed, but with no points on the board there was no disputing it had been a nightmare start for Williams. Soon afterwards he reflected on the horror of it all. He recalled how the more experienced people on his UEFA coaching course had warned him that moving from coaching to the manager's position was a big step. They told him that the stresses and strains of being a manager were very hard to appreciate until they had actually been experienced. Williams admitted that when he first heard all this, he and his fellow coaches just laughed and convinced themselves the managers were just saying that to make it all sound 'mystical':

'But after those first five matches I knew exactly what they meant. When you are coach you care for the man in charge, you work closely with him, but you go home and say "Phew, we weren't good today". You don't realise he's gone home, he's got the video out, he's analysing it. He's thinking "Did I pick the right team? Have I got the right tactics? Did I have the right subs? What do I do for the next game? What do I do for training?" All those things. Then he goes in on the Monday morning ready to start work and someone rings up and says the bulbs have gone somewhere, or it is too wet to train, so he is ringing round looking for somewhere.

'[The losing run] was a hard time and I needed the support of people around me. My wife was fantastic. You wake up at 4.30 in the morning to make a cup of tea and she wonders what is going on, you can't eat your breakfast in the mornings. She's never seen me like that but her support was fantastic and so were my children. They were saying "Go on dad, you can do it". You need those people around when you are away from the job. Then you come to the club and you need people who will tell you the truth.' He admitted that after the Carling Cup defeat by MK Dons the squad and management had a heart-to-heart, although it wasn't a bad-tempered crisis meeting: 'There were no tantrums, no looking for some-one to blame.'

This miserable start to 2006-07 saw United slump to 23rd, with only Sunderland below them (which suggested William Hill knew a thing or two). Having lost their manager, two key players – Danns and Chilvers (to Preston on a 'Bosman') – not to mention their first five games, Colchester seemed solid certainties for immediate relegation. However, the string of losses was about to end in dramatic style. For the visit of his former club Derby, Williams decided to pair Cureton and Iwelumo in attack for the first time at home this season. It worked a treat, the duo notching four goals between them to give the U's a 4-1 lead well into the second half. After the earlier gloom, this was dreamland. Cureton had signalled his intentions with an overhead kick which crashed against the bar. He went on to bag a hat-trick, with Iwelumo's penalty opening an unassailable-looking lead. But Derby pulled two goals back to make it 4-3 and create a nail-biting ending. The three points were manna from heaven for Colchester and proved the turning point.

Off the field it was announced that wealthy local businessman Robbie Cowling had bought the club, having acquired the majority shareholding of chairman Peter Heard, owner for the previous nine years. The sums involved were not disclosed but Cowling said: 'The structure of the deal reflects Peter Heard's devotion to the club and my long-term commit-ment to help support the club financially.' A 45-year-old lifelong sup-porter of West Ham, Cowling said he had tremendous respect for the current board and staff at Colchester for their achievements. For this rea-son, he said, he had asked Heard to stay on as chairman and to continue to run the club with the existing board.

Self-made Cowling grew up with eight siblings in Jaywick Sands, a fad-ing seaside resort ten miles from Colchester. He was a born entrepreneur who worked in his grandmother's fish-and-chip shop as a five-year-old and by the age of twelve was carrying holiday-makers' luggage to guest-houses on an old set of pram wheels and earning himself £20 a day in tips. He left Colbayns High School in Clacton at sixteen with no qualifications and worked as an apprentice at a Vauxhall garage. After four years he stumbled across Sir Clive Sinclair's newly introduced home computer, the Sinclair Spectrum. It was a crude machine that the user had to programme himself, but it caught Cowling's imagination: 'Somebody I knew had one and I found that I could do it. And I enjoyed doing it.'

Cowling told the *Sunday Times* that his brother had worked as a settler in a betting shop, calculating how much the punters had won. Cowling wrote a programme for the Spectrum that could do this work for him: 'I remember telling him that one day it would all be done this way. He didn't believe me.' After four months at college studying IT, Cowling found work with building societies, first in Clacton and then Milton Keynes, and then, in 1993, started work as an IT contractor for the Ministry of Defence in Bracknell. He rode to work each day by motorbike, a passion he shared with another contractor working on the site, John Witney. The two became friends and would meet in the canteen regularly, throwing ideas back and forth. One of these ideas would become the hugely successful Essex company Jobserve.

'One of the things that got me as I was riding the 70 miles to Bracknell in the pouring rain on my motorbike was that I was convinced there would be some bugger going the other way,' said Cowling. 'When you were contracting at that time it was very hard to find out where the jobs were.' The two men started by finding out what contract work was available locally. They then set up an e-mail service, sending the list out to people who subscribed to the service for free. A year later they had about 3,000 subscribers. Jobserve was on its way. In another year, this number had doubled and so had their profits. Before long the business was growing so fast that it was spilling out of the bedroom he used as an office and Cowling decided to dedicate himself to it full time. He moved to a bigger house in the village of Tiptree, south of Colchester, but the business soon needed an office of its own. Cowling bought out his partner in 2001 as the business thrived on the back of the 'dotcom boom' and fears over the millennium bug. Annual turnover and profits were soon in the millions. Jobserve won awards and became a remarkable success story, and now employs scores of workers at its base on a business park just outside Tiptree.

Cowling, who keeps fit though running and triathlons, has been named in various newspaper 'rich lists'. He has regularly used his money to fund sporting ventures, and had lengthy spells as the main shirt sponsors for Colchester and West Ham, his favourite clubs. As he watched the U's rise from the Conference to the Championship and observed the new stadium plans take shape, he decided to go one step further and buy into the Essex club.

In the meantime, matters on the field were taking a dramatic upturn. From early September onwards the 2006-07 season took off in grand style. Colchester and their new manager may have been novices at this level, but it was soon clear the club was not in the Championship just for the ride. The Derby victory sparked a run of six games without defeat, including 2-1 victories at Burnley and at home to QPR. Precious points were also collected at Luton and Leicester, where the U's bravely hung on for a draw in the face of sustained pressure. The first three home games had pulled in crowds of fewer than 5,000, but the sudden improvement saw gates slowly rise, and the stadium was packed to the seams for the long-awaited visit of Ipswich in late September – the first time the East Anglian clubs had met in a League match for 49 years.

With just eighteen miles separating the rivals, this was Colchester's true local derby, but meetings had been so rare in recent years that most supporters harboured a keener dislike for Southend and Wycombe. Now, however, the intense Colchester-Ipswich rivalry that had blossomed in the mid-20th century was alive and kicking. Sky TV chose the match for live coverage and there was an electric atmosphere for the Friday evening meeting under the Layer Road lights.

Appropriately, skipper Karl Duguid, the club's longest serving player, netted the goal that sunk Ipswich, his first in a League game in over three years. Nobody wanted to beat Ipswich more badly than Duguid, and he was jubilant when he told the *East Anglian Daily Times*: 'My cousin had me down as first goalscorer in a 1-0 win at 75-1 and when he told me I just laughed at him. It has come off, so the drinks are on him this weekend. This win has been a long time coming and the fans will love it. Forget Southend – this is the one they wanted to win and I'm just glad to be a part of it. We may have a small ground but we have players here that are good enough to be in this division.'

Duguid's winner came in the first ten minutes. The U's had started brightly, but Ipswich – managed by Geraint Williams' golfing pal Jim Magilton – created the first chance when Sylvain Legwinski drilled wide. Colchester quickly made them pay, Jamie Cureton firing in a skimming drive which was only parried by keeper Lewis Price, and Duguid, under pressure, side-footed the loose ball home. Jason De Vos got close to an equaliser from a Darren Currie corner but at the other end Cureton was unlucky with a curling effort and also flashed a half-volley past the right-hand upright. A long punt upfield found Ipswich's Alan Lee, who bustled his way through and fired in a shot which was well blocked by Aidan

Davison. Jon Macken slid in with the goalkeeper and forced the loose ball home, only for the referee to whistle for a foul. It was a debatable decision but Colchester rode their luck and hung on grimly for the final whistle. Even if relegation was just around the corner, this single result was enough to keep most Colchester diehards happy for years to come.

## CHAPTER 10

A Fortress in Camulodunum

October 2006 – Summer 2007

Colchester's largely unexpected rise up the Championship table during the autumn of 2006 was in direct contrast with the fortunes of Hull City, where U's defector Phil Parkinson was experiencing tough times. The stadium and budget might have been bigger at Hull, but the grass was definitely not proving greener. Just two wins from their opening fourteen games saw the Tigers slide to bottom of the table by late October. It was a remarkable predicament for the man who had quit Colchester for supposedly grander horizons, and U's fans couldn't wait to greet their former boss when Hull came to Layer Road in November.

As expected, Parkinson received what the media like to call 'a mixed reception'. Any lingering affection was quickly forgotten as his side was trounced 5-1 by a rampant and unforgiving U's team. This went one better than the 4-0 drubbing handed out to Sheffield Wednesday a few weeks earlier, and big Iwelumo – brought to Layer Road by Parkinson – taunted his old boss by smashing in four goals. It was United's eighth consecutive home League win and underlined Layer Road's growing reputation as the ground nobody wanted to visit. The old stadium had become a fortress worthy of the town's historic traditions. This was Camulodunum all over again.

Parkinson's return to Colchester had actually got off to a promising start, for Nicky Forster gave Hull a sixteenth-minute lead. Parkinson celebrated exuberantly in front of the dugouts, which he probably regretted as events unfolded. His delight was stifled within three minutes as Kevin McLeod delivered a swirling free-kick which Iwelumo headed powerfully past Boaz Myhill. The U's surged ahead after half-time when Damien Delaney brought down rampaging Iwelumo and the Scot made no mistake from the spot. When Michael Turner failed to clear his lines he was robbed by Iwelumo who headed on for Jamie Cureton to smash home. The roof of the Barside was shaking by now, and Iwelumo's hat-trick was completed in the 66th minute after more poor defending. Duguid strolled past Delaney before picking out Iwelumo to side-foot home from close range. Iwelumo completed the rout in the 79th minute, heading home a Johnnie Jackson cross.

It was a Tuesday night to remember for Colchester, but for Phil Parkinson and Hull it was the beginning of the end. After the unsavoury tug-of-war during the summer, it had not proved a marriage made in heaven. Within a week of the hammering at Colchester, the man who had led the U's into the Championship was out of work. His Humberside dream job had become a nightmare and his employment at the KC Stadium was terminated 'by mutual consent' on Monday, 4 December, less than six months after his arrival. Hull chairman Adam Pearson said the result at Colchester had been 'totally unacceptable' and when City shipped another four goals at home to Southampton just four days later, action had to be taken. Four wins from 21 games was a mystifyingly bad record, especially as Parkinson had spent £2 million on new players. Perhaps he deserved longer to get things right, but Pearson was not a chairman known for his patience.

After a month out of football, Parkinson would be recruited as assistant manager to his former team-mate Alan Pardew at Charlton in the Premiership. His reputation had apparently suffered only minor damage by his experiences at Hull, for early in 2007 he was offered the manager's job at Huddersfield. It was reported that he accepted, only to have a late change of mind an hour before his appointment was announced. Within a few days he had signed an extended contract with Charlton.

Back at Layer Road, everyone was in buoyant mood at the turn of the year. Further emphatic victories over Crystal Palace and Luton, and a tighter win over Mick McCarthy's Wolves, pushed Colchester into the top six play-off zone. These were heights that were hard to fathom, for here was a club universally expected to struggle. With the season past halfway, the anticipated relegation fight had descended on Southend but not on Colchester, and the 'impossible dream' of chasing the Premiership was now a reality. Inevitably, the hypothetical question arose of where the club would play its home games if the impossible happened and the U's stormed into the Premiership. Layer Road would clearly not meet minimum requirements (by a country mile), which left the unappealing option of temporarily sharing Ipswich's Portman Road.

Whether or not a serious play-off bid could be sustained, there was no doubting that Colchester were in a great position to finish as the best placed club in East Anglia for the first time. By mid-January, the U's were sixth, well ahead of regional rivals Ipswich (fifteenth), Norwich (seventeenth) and Southend (bottom). The region's other clubs – Peterborough, Northampton and Cambridge – were all in lower divisions. Champions of East Anglia had a nice ring to it and it would prove a satisfying consolation prize if the club didn't reach the play-offs.

United's progress and an upcoming clash at Ipswich attracted plenty of press interest. Glenn Moore of *The Independent* visited Layer Road to assess humble Colchester's prospects among the bigger boys of football. He described the scene as the club prepared for the visit to Ipswich: 'It was a worrying day to be manager of Colchester United yesterday. Geraint Williams was not concerned about a Premiership club luring away one of his increasingly admired players, nor did the physio have bad news. Williams was nervous about the high winds. His office is a hut perched atop a similar temporary structure at the club's decrepit Layer Road ground. When someone walks up the iron stairs outside it vibrates; when a lorry drives past it wobbles; when the wind blows, said Williams, "It's scary." His office is much as you would expect at a club whose ground holds 6,000 with terracing on three sides and has barely been embellished since being built in 1937, and who were in the Conference 15 years ago.

'What you would not expect is that this team are sixth in the Championship, a position which, in May, would mean a place in the play-offs and a shot at being the smallest team in the top flight since Wimbledon. All this despite Williams, 45, only being given the job a week before the season started, having been caretaker-manager for pre-season while the club interviewed more experienced candidates. He then opened with four League defeats and another in the Carling Cup, to League Two Milton Keynes. To outsiders it is the most remarkable story of the season. The home form – 34 points from the last 36 – may owe something to the facilities. Colchester are due to move to a new 10,000-seat stadium on the edge of town, but that is unlikely to happen until August next year. So the possibility of Thierry Henry squeezing into the dark corners of the pokey away dressing room, and Roman Abramovich balancing his dinner on his lap in the boardroom, has been investigated. Early indications are that the club would have to ground-share, probably with Ipswich. Even providing 50 press seats with power and phone lines is a problem. At present, said one senior employee, "if you turn two fan heaters on in the hospitality area you blow the lights. As for the dressing room, Fergie would probably think it about the right size for a boot room".'

United lost 2-3 at Portman Road, a result that seemed to restore some sort of logic to a surreal season, but it would be only a temporary set-back. Apart from a six-match winless run in February and March, they collected enough points to stay firmly in the division's top ten. Even the loss of versatile Greg Halford to Premiership Reading for a £2.5 million fee (a record for both clubs) had minimal impact. The strike partnership of Iwelumo and Cureton had gelled superbly and the goals flew in, particularly at home. In mid-March a 2-1 win at Southampton kick-started a run of five wins and a draw from six games which rekindled play-off hopes. Southend and Norwich were both humbled by 3-0 during this spell and even the once-mighty Leeds succumbed to the irrepressible U's.

A well-balanced, confident side refused to wilt in the closing weeks and after the delicious 3-1 humbling of champions-elect Sunderland on 21 April, Colchester were just one point outside the play-off zone, with just two games to play – and one of these was a six-pointer against their nearest rivals.

Top of the table (21 April 2007).
1 Sunderland played 44 82 points, 2 Derby 44 81, 3 Birmingham 43 80, 4 Preston 44 71, 5 West Brom 43 70, 6 Wolves 43 70, 7 South'ton 44 69, 8 Stoke 44 69, 9 Colchester 44 69, 10 Sheff Wednesday 44 68.

Although they had risen as high as sixth earlier on, this was really the high point of the season, for the finish line was so close and Colchester so close to a play-off place. As it transpired, a top-six finish would prove just beyond them, the final two games both ending in defeat, 1-3 at Stoke and 0-2 at home to Crystal Palace. Remarkably though, things would only be settled on the final day, and Colchester, albeit by now outsiders, were still in the mix. A finishing position of tenth looked like an anticlimax but there was still no disputing the fact that finishing 30th on the English football 'ladder' and being the leading Eastern region club was a remark-able and unexpected feat. There were many accolades for rookie manag-er Williams, with some pundits and fellow managers suggesting he should be named the Championship's Manager of the Year. He had certainly worked with fewer resources and in less opulent surroundings than the likes of Roy Keane and Steve Bruce.

The first season in the Championship saw United lure average League crowds of 5,466, which meant they were the poorest supported club in the division by a considerable margin. Relegated Luton – who pulled in 8,580 per game – were the only other club at this level to average below 10,000. However, the bare facts don't tell the full story: Colchester could take heart that their average still represented a jump of more than 37 per cent on the previous season, the third-biggest increase in the entire 92-club League. The figures certainly confirmed that Colchester were the division's 'smallest' club. The only other club of comparable size to estab-lish itself at this level in recent times has been Crewe, who were relegat-ed in 2006 after a decade or so. They operated on gates that generally hovered around 7,000.

A burning question over the summer of 2007 surrounded the U's' capability to maintain the momentum. Many supporters began to doubt this when the club's star players seemed to be forming a queue to leave the club. Twenty-four-goal leading scorer Jamie Cureton – whose fading career had been reborn at Colchester – departed for his former club Norwich, while his eighteen-goal strike partner Chris Iwelumo joined relegated Charlton. As if losing the main strike force wasn't bad enough, the third-leading scorer, Richard Garcia upped sticks for Hull and defensive kingpin Wayne Brown followed Garcia to the KC Stadium. To all intents and purposes the heart had been ripped out of the 2006-07 side.

Geraint Williams, already used to battling against the odds, had to find replacements, for if the club hoped to repeat their heroics they would have to do it the hard way. Club record £300,000 payouts were made to MK Dons for big striker Clive Platt and to Tottenham for former U's loanee Mark Yeates and – to cap it all – in came the former Manchester United, Tottenham and England star Teddy Sheringham. The 41-year-old was a friend of owner Robbie Cowling and signed a one-year deal as a player, and not as a coach as the football world initially expected. For little Colchester to capture such a household name was a real coup, despite Sheringham's age, and was exactly the boost needed with Cureton, Iwelumo, Garcia and Brown now departed. Mega-star Sheringham joined pre-season training late due to other commitments, and began arriving each day in his huge Bentley.

The big question was whether these and other new signings would prove adequate replacements. Only time would tell, and maybe the defectors would find, like Phil Parkinson, that the grass is not necessarily greener on the other side – even though the wages are probably higher. Of those who quit, Iwelumo and Garcia had become free agents at the end of 2006-07 and were entitled to seek better deals elsewhere, but Cureton and Brown were both under contract and had to make formal transfer requests. Considerable, if futile, efforts were said to have been made to persuade the two to stay.

A further blow was dealt when Williams' assistant Mick Harford left to join QPR. Harford had played an important role in the club's successful debut season in the Championship, but he claimed that all the driving from his Hertfordshire home to Colchester had aggravated an old back injury. Before long he was replaced by the out-of-work former Coventry boss Micky Adams. U's supporters were naturally dismayed as all the big names made for the door, and accusations inevitably followed that the club was lacking in ambition by allowing such an exodus. Owner Cowling was keen to repel these bad vibrations and promised that the club was at the dawn of a new era, with or without the players who were leaving:

'Accusations of a lack of ambition are misplaced – Colchester United are ambitious, of course, but we are not foolish. We know we have to work within certain limitations at our current home of Layer Road and, whilst aiming to progress we still have to retain some economic sense within that. There have been a number of clubs who have been foolhardy within their planning and many have fallen by the wayside as a result. Of course it is currently difficult for us to compete on wages with a club that attracts 25,000 fans and has a £10 million parachute payment. However, that won't always be the case and we can confirm that, in terms of money to spend, we have made available the best budget in the club's history, both in terms of transfer fees and for paying far better wages. While our current stadium provides constraints on how far we can go, the future remains bright – we have a new stadium on the agenda and, in time with continued success, we will be looking to expand that new facility. Furthermore we are currently a long way down the line in terms of securing improved training facilities.'

Cowling's determination to run the club on strict and sensible financial lines was underlined when figures were published which showed Colchester to be the only club in the Championship that had not paid a penny to players' agents during the second half of 2006-07. Promoted Birmingham and Sunderland shelled out huge sums, but this was a league table in which the U's were glad to finish bottom. Football League chairman Lord Mawhinney praised Colchester and welcomed the news that clubs outside the Premiership were apparently reducing their spending on agents and urged that the cuts continue.

During the 2007 summer recess, Cowling formally took over as chairman when Peter Heard stood down after sixteen years at Layer Road. Fulsome tributes were paid to Heard's leadership, which covered the full period of the rise from Conference to Championship. During that time he had also cut a major figure at the Football League and the Football Association, serving as a permanent FL board member and acting chairman of the FA. Heard was at the centre of many high-profile disciplinary matters at the FA, including the case involving Rio Ferdinand, his missed drugs test, and the controversial long ban. The founder and former head of London property company Churston Heard, he had been born in Colchester and was a referee in his younger days.

Heard's contribution to United's progress since 1991 was acknowledged by many sources, including the Colchester players. Skipper Karl Duguid even urged the club to name the proposed new ground, or at least one of its stands, in his name: 'He's been a massive part of what we have achieved over the last ten years or so,' Duguid told the *Gazette*. 'His relationship with the players is good and he has always made sure that he has time for every player. When I was injured for eighteen months he kept an eye on how everything was going with my injury and did all he could to help me see all of the best specialists. He's been great to work for and it's a shame to see him go.'

Peter Heard first became involved at Layer Road after an invitation from a desperate board, at a time when the U's were out of the Football League, in dire financial straits and the future looked bleak. But by the time he retired as chairman sixteen years later the club that had always been close to his heart was prospering in a whole new world.

## CHAPTER 11

Leaving Layer Road: A 35-Year Saga

OBITUARY: LAYER ROAD STADIUM (1909-2008)
Layer Road Stadium, beloved home of Colchester United FC, passed
peacefully away at the age of 99 years on Saturday April 26, after the
final home match of the 2007-08 season against Stoke City.
The deceased had been unwell for many years.
In accordance with the wishes of its nearest and dearest, some of the
remains will be dismantled into small pieces and disposed of to CUFC
supporters as souvenirs. Burial will be carried out by house-builders on
a date yet to be arranged. One minute's silence will be observed in
remembrance at the new Cuckoo Farm Community Stadium
before the start of the 2008-09 football season.
REST IN PEACE

The above death notice has been composed – a few months in
advance – in readiness for the sad event expected to occur in the late
spring of 2008. I have provided these words now, just in case the good
folk at Colchester United become too overcome with emotion to do it
themselves when the time finally comes to lay our old friend Layer Road
to rest.

The building of the new stadium at Cuckoo Farm is undoubtedly one
of the most exciting and important developments in Colchester United's
history. Yet the big move is bound to be tinged with sadness. To the regular U's supporter Layer Road has been like a second home. A place of
retreat where every emotion from joy to despair can be experienced while
the trials and tribulations of everyday existence take a back seat. For all
its shortcomings, and there are certainly many, the ground has a special
place in the affections of thousands of people. My first visit was more
than 40 years ago in 1965, and I for one am finding it very strange coming to terms with the fact that the old place will soon disappear off the
football map for good.

Colchester United directors first talked seriously about finding a new
home back in the early 1970s. The topic was occasionally mentioned even
earlier than that. For a high number of adult supporters the search has
therefore been underway for their entire lifetime. When Colchester started looking there were hardly any 'new' football stadiums operating in the
Football League. But since then, a long list of clubs have successfully

packed up and moved, beating the U's to it. In the lower divisions these have included Scunthorpe, Oxford, Chester, Shrewsbury, Darlington, Northampton, Walsall, Doncaster, Swansea, Huddersfield, Hull, Reading and Wigan. Seeing all these outfits thrive in new surroundings while the U's remained mired in red-tape and legal argument has been a frustrating situation for U's fans.

Why on earth did it take so long to find the U's a new home – particularly as the current ground has always been so clearly unsuitable for purpose? To try to answer this, let us examine the chequered history of Layer Road, along with the tortuous and meandering path that has been trodden in the name of replacing it.

The Layer Road ground's shortcomings have been well documented. According to football lore, Colchester's giant-killing tradition is largely down to the cramped surroundings of their ground and the close proximity of the fans to the pitch. Apparently a sense of claustrophobia paralyses visiting players more used to spacious surroundings. Big clubs have come, seen and failed to conquer. Colchester is Britain's oldest recorded town, and to many visitors the stadium resembles the country's oldest football ground. It is undoubtedly a relic from a bygone age, lacking in the type of facilities and freedoms the modern football fan is entitled to expect. Covenant restrictions have always meant the club could not raise revenue from bars, restaurants and other facilities most supporters nowadays take for granted. On a number of occasions the U's have gone close to going out of business, and problems pertaining to the ground have always been largely to blame.

Nevertheless, the final match at the ground will undoubtedly be a day of mixed emotions, particularly for the older supporters. For a true U's fan there is no better experience than soaking in the atmosphere at a packed Layer Road, the crumbling terraces bursting at the seams under Friday night floodlights. Such is the nature of the place that even crowds as low as 4,000 can create a stirring ambience. And the bigger they come, the more a visiting team seems to be inhibited by such surroundings. The list of clubs from higher divisions beaten in cup-ties here seems endless. Fortress Layer Road may have been rickety, but it has always remained resilient.

When closure comes in mid-2008, fans can expect to look forward to a better, brighter future – but that won't prevent many a tear being shed. However impressive Cuckoo Farm looks, I suspect there will be feelings of fond nostalgia for the old-fashioned surroundings of the Barside, or the half-time change of ends that involved squeezing into the popular terraces either side of the main stand seats. I have to confess to being old enough to recall jumping up and down on wooden terracing at the Layer Road end when this was home-fan territory. There was also a notable occasion when a friend and I arrived so early for a big match that gates and turnstiles were not yet manned, and we strolled into the empty stadium for free, gaining new insights into the old place as we surreptitiously went on our illegal tour during the long wait for kick-off.

Author and lifelong U's fan Jeff Whitehead spoke for many like-minded folk when he wrote: 'When the fans of the new century sit, cramped in their plastic seats, eating their plastic fast-food and watching play-backs on the big screen, will they spare a thought for homely Layer Road? Remember the timber terracing at the Layer Road End that flexed under foot as excited fans bounced up and down; the smell of lineament wafting from the changing room and mixing uninvitingly with the burger bar next door; running for cover from the open Clock End as the heavens opened; the choke of cigarette smoke on a calm chill night; brushing rust particles from your hair as another stray pass hits the Barside roof; and the Post Horn Gallop; the grace of Arsenal, Leeds, Manchester United and others; cup glory; relegation sorrow; championship joy and promotion dreams. Packed to the rafters or bare to the bones, Layer Road has witnessed it all.'

Like most old sporting stadia, Layer Road has enjoyed a fascinating history. The record books show that football first arrived here in 1909. This was a good year for sport: Twickenham staged its first rugby match, Indianapolis its first motor race and cricket's ICC was formed. It was the year that Colchester Town FC (which would later morph into Colchester United) descended on the present Layer Road site, having earlier played on fields in Cambridge Road, Reed Hall, Maldon Road, Albert Road and Sheepen Road.

The Town club, known as The Oysters, had at last found a home at which it could settle. The land was rented from Mr Arthur Cant, who had previously leased it to the Army, who were, and still are, based nearby. An early match report described Layer Road as a 'bleak spot on a cold and rainy day, with no cover'. A club member, Alfred Crowther, used his contacts and called favours to get a grandstand erected free of charge, designed and supervised by architect Walter Cressall. It was paid for by subscribers, one of whom was the former Colchester Town star Albert Gosnell, who later played for Spurs, Newcastle and England. The opening of the new stand was marked by a visit of an Arsenal team in April 1910.

In the early days the players' changing facilities comprised nothing more than a converted railway carriage, which housed a single tin bath. It would not be until the late 1920s that proper dressing rooms were created under the stand, and they remain in that position to this day. In early 1937, it was decided to form a professional football club in Colchester. The new outfit would use Layer Road, it was decided, sharing the ground with Colchester Town, who intended to carry on as an amateur outfit. During the same year the Charles Clark Memorial Hall was built beside the main stand and would serve as a committee room and reception area until long after the 1939-45 War. Small covered stands were created on the 'popular' side of the ground, opposite the main stand, and also at the Layer Road end. Documents reveal that at this time the land was valued at £700, the main stand itself worth £1,542, and the Memorial Hall building £293. With no offices on the site, United's administrative affairs were conducted in rooms at the nearby Salisbury Hotel in Butt Road, which still exists today.

By late 1937 Colchester Town was reeling from financial troubles and problems with the Essex FA, who would not allow one set of officials to run both the Town and United clubs. The end result was that Town disbanded and the sole occupiers of Layer Road became the six-months-old Colchester United, now members of the Southern League. Before their first SL home game, against Bath City, United's goalkeeper Ronnie Dunn – who had been a bugler in the Army – played a fanfare when the teams ran on the pitch. Ronnie chose to play the *Post Horn Gallop*, which proved so popular it would greet the teams' arrival for many years afterwards. When Ipswich Town attracted a full house two days later, the sell-out crowd was so absorbed by the 3-3 thriller that many failed to notice a fire on the popular side of the ground. It was quickly dealt with and the game continued. There was further damage to the ground that season when a gale in January 1938 saw the recently erected timber and corrugated roof at the Layer Road end blow off and clatter into the road outside. Eleven of the thirteen roof sections were dislodged and Layer Road was blocked to traffic for two days, with a number of private houses opposite sustaining damage.

By now a thriving CUFC supporters club had been created, with a membership of over 2,000, which contributed a much-needed £1,000 towards essential ground improvements. The money did not stretch to fixing every hole in the fencing, however, for a match with Bristol Rovers was held up for ten minutes when a stray dog joined the action. Strangely enough this would also happen many years later, during a televised match with Brentford in 1970. On the latter occasion the little mutt collided with visiting goalkeeper Chic Brodie who sustained a career-threatening knee injury.

The ground's first VIP guests turned up in April 1938 when Arsenal and Wolves played each other for the Colchester Challenge Cup in front of a record crowd of 18,000. These star-studded teams were fulfilling clauses in two earlier transfers, when promising U's youngsters had been sold. Before the big game, the two teams' players played golf at Frinton-on-Sea and afterwards enjoyed a civic banquet at the Town Hall.

In August 1939, following complaints from local hacks, the press box was extended from six to twelve seats. Military personnel in uniform would also be allowed admission at half-price, but no such concessions would be granted to women or the unemployed. When a local building firm became agitated about overdue payments for work at the ground after the 1938 gales, directors had to dip into their own pockets to stave off legal action. With the outbreak of war the club shut, packed all its loose property and made an inventory. The various trophies won were deposited in a local bank, contracts were suspended, and staff and players went their various ways to support the war effort.

Colchester United may have temporarily closed, but the ground continued to occasionally stage games, some featuring big names from the nearby garrison. In April 1944 the Army played an Allied Services side which included internationals from Poland, Belgium, Czechoslovakia, Holland and France. In 1945 the ground hosted a Colchester Garrison v Combined Services match which featured fourteen pre-war internationals. For most of the war, the ground was controlled by the Auxiliary Fire Services which had agreed to keep the pitch and buildings in good order, although the football club had to continue paying rental and fire insurance bills.

At the end of the war the local Romans Club provided the club with a public address system, and the Ind Coope brewery forked out £35 for permanent advertising on the main stand roof. Groundsman Jock Duncan returned to find the ground in a state of decay. As a matter of urgency he needed to distemper the dressing rooms, paint the water cisterns and scrub the bath and hand-basins. He also had to clean and oil the turnstiles and supervise an army fatigue party which was recruited to level out the top of the open end. The club awarded Jock a pay-rise of ten shillings a week and presented him with a new mower, donated by the supporters club. Before post-war football got into full swing, the stand on what is now known as the Barside was demolished and the timbers salvaged were used to strengthen the Layer Road end and main stand.

Some of the work described above, and other maintenance tasks, were carried out by a supervised party of Italian Prisoners of War from the nearby garrison. After returning to his homeland, an Italian soldier,

Guiseppe Rebuglio, wrote to the club thanking them for the hospitality and friendship received while working at Layer Road.

The ground could hold, at a push, more than 18,000 spectators, and in early 1947 it was decided that extra entrances should be created at the Gladwin Road end. Negotiations began with neighbouring residents to purchase twenty feet of their gardens, but they drove a hard bargain and the plan floundered. Ever since, it has only remained possible to enter the ground from one of the four sides. However, when Superintendent Phillibrown and Inspector Wisely of Colchester police visited in 1947, accompanied by the Borough Engineer Richardson, they found potentially dangerous areas and insisted on two more exits, one of them into Gladwin Road. They also advised that the maximum capacity be set at 16,000. This figure would be exceeded for the FA Cup giant-killings of Huddersfield and Bradford in January 1948 and later that year 19,072 somehow squeezed inside for a Cup-tie with Reading, the latter remaining the ground record.

In April 1949 there was more storm damage and the roof of the Layer Road stand again went 'awol', causing more damage to the long-suffering residents' properties opposite. This end of the ground needed urgent repairs but the post-war shortage of steel held things up. The club chairman apologised in his programme notes to fans who liked to inhabit that part of the ground. Just before Football League status was won in 1950, the club announced plans to erect floodlights, but a £500 quotation from Edison Swan Electric proved too expensive, so United lost the chance to become the first club in Division Three (South) to go under lights. Smartening up the ground for the League era proved expensive, and a proposal to asphalt the path from the main entrance to the dressing room area was also doomed when a quotation of 5s 6d (27.5p) per square yard exceeded expectations.

The wooden plank terracing at the Layer Road end, which flexed unnervingly when spectators jumped, was a worry. The wood to the left of the goal was to be replaced with concrete, but this was another delayed project thanks to shortages of cement and steel. Temporary arrangements were made in this area for the visit of Norwich, and 14,000 still managed to get in. Money was so tight that many proposals simply failed to materialise. Toilets, for example, were denied to women except in the directors' room.

Instead of concentrating on improving the ground, the directors preferred to invest in club houses, ostensibly as a means of attracting new players. By 1954 the club owned at least six freehold houses and two flats in Colchester, all free from mortgage commitments. They bought a large house in Maldon Road for £2,250 and converted it into two flats for players and their families. In those days many fans travelled to the ground by bicycle, and late arrivals, keen not to miss kick-off, would prop their cycles against exit gate. This required police intervention.

Lack of heating meant that during winter months board meetings had to be held in the town's Liberal Club, although in 1954 offices and a boardroom were built on the site of the present main offices. The supporters club often provided funding for ground improvements. By 1957 it had £5,000 available, to add to £3,000 they'd spent on the ground earlier, which funded an extension behind the main stand to accommodate hospitality facilities for directors and visitors. This scheme required the Charles Clark Memorial Hall to be demolished. Shortly afterwards a plan to extend the main stand roof over the 'spion kop' corner was approved, along with a new bar and tearoom, plus a brick wall to replace the hedge behind the main stand.

During 1958-59 a stirring FA Cup run saw Colchester watched by nearly 63,000 at Arsenal, and some of the proceeds went on installing floodlights. Four pylons were erected for £10,000 in time for the following season. The lights were first tried at a friendly with Norwich in September 1959, with the official opening ceremony at a special match with Ipswich the following month.

Although the supporters club had provided considerable cash, a dispute arose over a door at the back of their clubroom which led directly onto the terraces. This invited accusations of watching games for free and the doorway was bricked up. TV cameras came to Layer Road for the first time in October 1962 when 'Anglia' chose the 1-2 defeat by Crystal Palace as its match of the week.

The policy of buying houses rather than improve Layer Road continued well into the 1960s. For example, the family house next to the players entrance was added to the Layer Road 'portfolio' for £3,000 and used by Neil Franklin and his family, after the former Stoke and England centre-half became U's manager in December 1963. Living next door to the ground meant Franklin had no problems commuting to work, and proved useful when he was confined to bed with a back injury a few years later – he followed the progress of an FA Cup-tie with Torquay via the roars and groans of the crowd.

The floodlights were given a fresh lick of paint, a new half-time scoreboard was erected and new buffet and bar area opened as the ground was smartened up in the late 60s. The club decided to buy back the ground from the local Council in September 1969. This was made possible by a cheque for £5,800 from former player Vic Keeble's thriving fund-raising association and a £5,000 loan, payable over ten years at three per cent interest, from the Football Association. A condition of the sale was that the land could not be resold for housing.

As hooliganism spread in the 1970s 'boot boys' began infiltrating the flimsy Layer Road end. The corrugated iron at the back of the stand took a fearful hammering. Occupants of the Layer Road end could taunt opposing fans in the street through a gap in the stand, so builders were called in to close it. Low stands and fencing meant countless footballs disappeared into gardens, never to reappear, which cost the club a small fortune.

Following the cup heroics of 1971 the club erected a flag-pole, from which fluttered a blue-and-white flag bearing the legend 'Watney Cup Winners and Giant Killers Cup winners 1971'. This was followed by the installation of new floodlights, the old ones having to be sold for scrap after a non-league buyer could not be found. The new lights were unveiled at a pre-season game in 1972 against St Mirren, who included a young Gordon McQueen. The U's sported a new all-white kit and red boots.

Frustrated by their restrictive surroundings, in the early 1970s the U's board finally gave serious thought to a new stadium. Land beside the Colchester by-pass, near the River Colne, was thought to be available at £1,000 per acre, and the idea of having a new football ground within a larger sports complex here was suggested in 1973, but the idea made little progress. Instead, it was proposed to develop and modernise Layer Road. The pitch could be shifted 23 feet towards the open end, leaving space for a 5,000-capacity terrace behind the Layer Road goal. Opposite the main stand would be an all-seater stand with executive boxes, which would raise the capacity to 18,000. This would provide a stadium fit for the Second Division, but it would have set the U's back around £320,000 and the idea was still-born.

In April 1980, a supermarket chain was said to be interested in acquiring Layer Road, which might pave the way for relocation to a site between Colne Bank Avenue and North Station. This time a 25,000-capacity stadium with under-soil heating and 4,500 seats was mentioned. It would be known as the Colne River Centre and would have 3,500 parking spaces, sports halls, a showground, a 1,745-bed hotel and 200,000 square feet of retail development, which would allow the U's to move in free. It sounded too good to be true, and it was. The all-important retail aspect of the plan contravened Borough planning policy. The Council condemned the plans as 'an excuse to build a hypermarket, with a stadium thrown in as a token gesture'. There were also environmental issues, for the site formed part of a flood-plain meadow. Later in 1981 the plan was kicked out altogether by the Council, who claimed it would adversely affect their Culver Precinct proposals in the town centre.

Relations between club and Council appeared strained throughout the 1980s. The Council refused a request to lift the covenant on Layer Road, and backed local residents who opposed a plan to create a seven-days-a-week social and conference facility. The club had purchased the ground at a bargain price and the covenant was part of the bargain. In November 1983, as the U's prepared for the visit of Manchester United in the Milk Cup, a brand new stadium proposal emerged, known as the Turner Rise development. Bordered by Turner Road and North Station, it involved a 15,000-capacity stadium with other sporting and retail outlets. It would have an all-weather playing surface, more resilient and less bouncy than at QPR. This plan, too, stalled as it became entangled in red tape.

The 13,000-plus who attended the Manchester United tie (a 0-2 defeat which saw ground record receipts of £22,745), made up the last five-figure crowd to attend a match at Layer Road. In the wake of the Valley Parade and Heysel disasters, spectator safety topped the list of priorities everywhere. The timber of the main stand and Layer Road end posed fire hazards. Major refurbishment took place and visiting supporters were provided with a specifically designated 'away section'.

With plans to move to a new stadium, maintenance work had been neglected, which meant the club faced a bill of around £500,000 to comply with new national safety legislation. Lacking a safety certificate, the capacity had to be reduced to 4,900.

During the awful early months of 1988-89, with the prospect of demotion from the League looming large, a farmer from Great Horkesley laid claim to a plot of land within the proposed Turner Rise site, which effectively scuppered the project. Towards the end of the ill-fated 1989-90 season another plan, this time involving land next to the A12 at Ardleigh and called Stadium Park, was announced. The details were published in the *Mail on Sunday*, which caught the eye of local residents who rallied to object.

After United were demoted into the Conference in 1990, the ground was sold back to Colchester Borough Council for £1.2 million. By 1991-92 worried directors feared that the lease on Layer Road expired in eighteen months and still they were no nearer to securing a new ground. Once again the spectre of ground-sharing reared its head, and barrels were being scraped when it was suggested the U's could temporarily share the Broad Lane ground near Essex University, home of minor league Wivenhoe. Covetous eyes were directed at Conference rivals Wycombe

Wanderers, who had recently settled into a smart new stadium at Adams Park. Colchester had to return to the Council with cap in hand and plead for an extension to the lease on Layer Road. Fortunately this was granted and extended for a further ten years, which satisfied the immediate demands of the Football League.

To play League football the club had to meet new safety requirements. To continue using the open end they were faced with a daunting bill of £85,000, and had little choice but to close most of the terracing at that end, leaving it three-quarters derelict for four years. Layer Road was frankly becoming an embarrassment and the board erected a small all-seater stand at the eyesore open end, which caused many to fear that the directors had wearied of finding a new ground. Not so, claimed chairman Gordon Parker, who in 1997 raised the idea of yet another new site. A planned 'leisure village' at Essex University in Wivenhoe Park involved a 22-acre site at Salary Brook, off the Elmstead Road. Plans included a multiplex cinema, leisure centre, pubs, restaurants, a hotel and bowling alley. Once again, the talks would come to nothing.

Peter Heard, then vice-chairman, announced publicly in 1997 that the club had five years to sort the problem out. Premier League and National Lottery money was available to help those clubs seeking a new home and Colchester would benefit. Football Trust money previously available had not been taken up because the club 'had not got its act together' and this wouldn't be allowed to happen again.

CHAPTER 12

Going Cuckoo

1998 saw the beginning of the end of Colchester United's long search for a new home. Peter Heard, new chairman of the U's, and the chief executive of Colchester Borough Council, John Cobley, were the principal architects. Land adjacent to the A12 to the north of Colchester was revealed as the preferred location.

Council-owned, it sat close to the Boxted Road bridge that crosses the A12 by-pass and was formerly part of Cuckoo Farm. The ultimate success of the plan was said at the time to hinge on a new junction being provided on the A12, plus the securing of private finance.

The idea of creating a joint-use community centre and football stadium was helped by permission for a relief road to be built. Plans were advanced to construct a new junction off the A12 between the Boxted Road and Severalls Lane flyovers to link up with the Cuckoo Farm site. Yet another alternative – this one at Stanway – had been examined, but the land parcel at Cuckoo Farm had the advantage of being Council-owned and therefore cheaper.

Over the next several years the wheels moved agonisingly slowly and the project seemed for ever mired in red tape. By 2004 the *Evening Gazette* and the Colchester Community Stadium Action Group had launched campaigns to try to hurry things along. Further minor snags in 2005 then proceeded to push the anticipated completion date even further into the future.

By the time Colchester started their first season in the Championship the whole thing boiled down to whether or not councillors would saddle the Council with a multi-million pound loan to fund the Cuckoo Farm scheme.

With the U's now regularly hosting big clubs and live TV, the need for a new ground had never been more urgent. On Thursday, 28 June 2007 the last hurdle was cleared when approval was given for the detailed design of the 10,000-capacity stadium. The plans showed provision for a 667-space car park with room for 29 disabled motorists and 32 coaches, plus a terminal for shuttle buses taking fans to and from the town centre and railway station. Stadium shadow board chairman Dave Murthwaite explained:

'This will not just be a football stadium but a community facility. We want the stadium to be available to the public 24/7, including the pitch, and already have a lively plan for events to take place there. We have been practical and what we have here we can afford, but it offers the opportunity to be expanded too.'

The planners and architects handed the project over to builders Barr, who set the target of having the stadium ready for the start of 2008-09. The club was awarded £2 million from the Football Stadia Improvement Fund towards the costs of building work, and a ceremony to mark the builders' first cutting of the soil was carried out in July. Within a few weeks, the new stadium started to take shape. The first visible signs were the appearance on the site of foundation work, involving East Stand piling and cap cage reinforcements.

Perhaps predictably, no sooner had the builders' Portakabins appeared on site than words of caution were being issued to Colchester fans. The long-awaited stadium might not be quite as prestigious as they hoped, according to MP Bob Russell, who had seen the plans. He feared the new creation might be 'worse than those to be found at many Non-League clubs', for although it was costing more than £14 million to build, what the club will get is an inadequate shell which it would be responsible for fitting out. Russell continued:

'Let us contrast Colchester's £14 million 10,000-seater stadium with the £60 million 22,000-seater stadium which has just been built for League Two side Milton Keynes.

'This suggests that those behind MK Dons are showing more ambition than Colchester United, and it shows that the Council at Milton Keynes values a League Football Club more than Colchester Borough Council does. And let's contrast the £16 million Visual Arts Facility [proposed by CBC] with the Community Stadium. The former will have luxury facilities while the latter will have basic facilities not worthy of the 21st century, and while the former will require an annual subsidy from the public purse of £600,000 to cover operating costs the U's will be paying £300,000 every year in rent to the Council for a stadium which will be the worst new stadium in the country.'

The new ground has been such a long time coming that U's fans will hope Russell's fears are misplaced. Whatever the shortcomings of the new home, they surely won't rival some of the horrors of Layer Road. Consider the away dressing rooms, for example:

There is an often-repeated story which tells how the 'grey, dark concrete bomb shelter' which the away team are currently invited to use at Layer Road is such a draughty and depressing place that former Manchester United and England star Paul Parker quit the game altogether after having to use it.

A quick flick through the record books confirms that Paul Parker's final away match in his farewell season at Fulham was indeed the game at Colchester on an icy January night in 1997.

Guide to Seasonal Summaries

Seasons 1991-92 to 1998-99 give basic information relating to Colchester United only. Greater detail is available in our earlier book, *Colchester United: From Graham to Whitton.*

For seasons 1999-2000 to 2006-07, the following guide applies.

Col 1:   Match number (for league fixtures); Round (for cup-ties).
           e.g. 4R means 'Fourth round replay.'

Col 2:   Date of the fixture and whether Home (H), Away (A), or Neutral (N).

Col 3:   Opposition.

Col 4:   Attendances. Home gates appear in roman; Away gates in italics.
           Figures in bold indicate the largest and smallest gates, at home and away.
           Average home and away attendances appear after the final league match.

Col 5:   Respective league positions of Colchester and opponents after the game.
           Colchester's position appears on the top line in roman.
           Their opponents' position appears on the second line in italics.
           For cup-ties, the division and position of opponents is provided.
           e.g. 2:12 means the opposition are twelfth in Division 2.

Col 6:   The top line shows the result: W(in), D(raw), or L(ose).
           The second line shows Colchester's cumulative points total.

Col 7:   The match score, Colchester's given first.
           Scores in bold show Colchester's biggest league win and heaviest defeat.

Col 8:   The half-time score, Colchester's given first.

Col 9:   The top line shows Colchester's scorers and times of goals in roman.
           The second line shows opponents' scorers and times of goals in italics.
           A 'p' after the time of a goal denotes a penalty; 'og' an own-goal.
           The third line gives the name of the match referee.

Team line-ups: Colchester line-ups appear on top line, irrespective of whether
           they are home or away. Opposition teams are on the second line in *italics*.
           Players of either side who are sent off are marked !
           Colchester players making their league debuts are displayed in **bold**.

Substitutes: Names of substitutes appear only if they actually took the field.
           A player substituted is marked *
           A second player substituted is marked ^
           A third player substituted is marked "
           These marks do not indicate the sequence of substitutions.

N.B.   For clarity, all information appearing in *italics* relates to opposing teams.

GM VAUXHALL CONFERENCE

First team coach: Roy McDonough — SEASON 1991-92

No.		Date	Opponents	Att	F-A		Scorers	1	2	3	4	5	6	7	8	9	10	11	Subs (2)
1	H	17/8	MACCLESFIELD	2,233	2-0	W	Bennett, McGavin	Barrett	Donald	Grainger	Kinsella	English	Elliott	Collins	Bennett	McDonough	McGavin*	Smith	Walsh
2	A	24/8	BARROW	1,480	1-1	D	Kinsella	Barrett	Donald	Grainger	Kinsella	English	Elliott	Collins	Bennett	McDonough	McGavin	Smith	
3	A	26/8	SLOUGH	2,226	4-2	W	McDonough 4	Barrett	Donald	Grainger	Kinsella	English	Elliott^	Collins	Bennett	McDon'gh^	McGavin*	Smith	Phillips/Abrahams
4	H	31/8	BATH	2,416	5-0	W	McGavin 2, Bennett 3	Barrett	Donald	Grainger	Kinsella	English	Elliott	Collins	Bennett	McDon'gh*	McGavin	Smith	Abrahams
5	A	7/9	WITTON	1,045	2-2	D	Collins, McDonough	Barrett	Donald	Grainger*	Kinsella	English	Elliott	Collins	Bennett	McDonough	McGavin	Smith	Goodwin
6	H	10/9	FARNBOROUGH	2,954	2-3	L	McGavin, Collins	Barrett	Donald	Grainger	Kinsella	English	Elliott	Collins	Bennett	McDonough	McGavin	Smith	
7	H	13/9	YEOVIL	2,979	4-0	W	English, Bennett 2, McGavin	Barrett	Donald	Grainger	Kinsella	English	Elliott	Collins	Bennett	McDonough	McGavin	Smith	
8	A	21/9	CHELTENHAM	1,157	1-1	D	McDonough	Barrett	Donald	Grainger	Kinsella	English	Elliott	Collins	Bennett	McDonough	Gray	Smith	
9	A	28/9	WYCOMBE	5,186	2-1	W	Smith, Barrett	Barrett	Donald	Roberts	Kinsella*	English	Elliott	Collins	Bennett	McDonough	McGavin	Smith	Cook
10	H	5/10	ALTRINCHAM	2,853	3-3	D	Anderson (og), McGavin, McD'gh (p)	Barrett	Donald	Roberts	Kinsella	English	Elliott	Collins	Bennett*	McDonough	McGavin	Smith	
11	H	12/10	RUNCORN	2,617	2-1	W	Bennett, McDonough 86 (p)	Barrett	Donald	Roberts	Cook	English	Elliott*	Collins	Bennett*	McDonough	McGavin	Smith	Kinsella
12	H	19/10	TELFORD	1,109	3-0	W	McDonough 2 (1p), Smith	Barrett	Donald	Roberts	Cook*	English	Elliott	Collins	Bennett	McDon'gh*	McGavin	Smith	
13	A	30/10	YEOVIL	2,385	1-0	W	McGavin	Barrett	Donald	Roberts	Kinsella	English	Elliott	Collins	Bennett	McDonough	McGavin	Smith*	
14	H	2/11	STAFFORD	2,139	2-0	W	Smith, McDonough	Barrett	Donald^	Roberts	Kinsella	English	Elliott	Collins	Bennett	McDon'gh^	McGavin	Smith	
15	A	9/11	FARNBOROUGH	3,069	2-0	W	Bennett, Elliott	Barrett	Donald	Roberts	Kinsella	English	Elliott*	Collins	Bennett	McDon'gh*	McGavin	Smith	Restarick/Cook
16	H	16/11	WELLING	2,933	3-1	W	Bennett, Cook, English	Barrett	Donald	Roberts	Kinsella	English	Elliott^	Collins	Bennett^	McDonough	McGavin	Smith	Collins/Restarick
17	A	30/11	NORTHWICH	1,042	1-1	D	McDonough	Barrett	Donald	Roberts	Phillips	Grainger	Elliott	Collins	Cook	McDonough	McGavin	Smith*	Kinsella
18	A	3/12	STAFFORD	961	3-3	D	Bennett 2, McGavin	Barrett	Donald	Roberts	Kinsella	Cook	Elliott	Collins	Bennett	McDonough	McGavin	Smith	Cook
19	H	7/12	WYCOMBE	5,086	3-0	W	Bennett, McGavin 2	Barrett	Donald	Roberts	Kinsella	Cook	Elliott	Collins	Bennett	McDonough	McGavin	Smith	Kinsella
20	A	14/12	GATESHEAD	542	2-0	W	Bennett, McDonough	Barrett	Donald	Roberts	Kinsella*	English	Elliott	Collins	Bennett	McDonough	Restarick*	Smith	Abrahams
21	A	21/12	WITTON	2,842	3-2	W	McGavin, Bennett, English	Barrett	Donald^	Roberts	Kinsella	English	Elliott^	Collins	Bennett^	McDonough	McGavin	Smith	English/Restarick
22	A	26/12	REDBRIDGE	2,327	1-0	W	McDonough	Barrett	Donald	Roberts	Kinsella	English	Elliott*	Collins*	Bennett^	McDonough	McGavin	Smith	Collins/Restarick
23	A	28/12	RUNCORN	863	3-1	W	Bennett, Cook, McGavin	Barrett	Cook*	Roberts	Cook*	English	Cook	Collins*	Bennett^	McDonough	McGavin	Smith	Kinsella
24	H	1/1	REDBRIDGE	4,733	1-0	W	McGavin	Barrett	Donald	Roberts	Cook*	English	Elliott	Collins	Bennett^	McDonough	McGavin	Smith	Kinsella/Restarick
25	A	4/1	MERTHYR	1,032	0-2	L		Barrett	Cook*	Roberts	Cook*	English	Elliott^	Cook	Bennett*	McDon'gh*	McGavin	Smith	Restarick/Grainger
26	H	18/1	CHELTENHAM	2,643	4-0	W	McGavin 2, McDonough, Kinsella	Barrett	Cook^	Roberts*	Donald	English	Elliott	Cook	Bennett^	McDon'gh^	McGavin	Smith	Masters/Grainger
27	H	24/1	KETTERING	4,100	2-2	D	McGavin, Smith	Barrett	Donald^	Roberts	Donald	English	Elliott^	Cook*	Bennett^	McDon'gh^	McGavin	Smith	Masters
28	A	7/2	KIDDERMINSTER	1,826	2-2	D	Bennett, Smith	Barrett	Cook*	Roberts	Cook*	English	Elliott	Collins*	Bennett^	McDon'gh*	McGavin	Smith	Donald/Masters
29	H	11/2	BOSTON	3,229	1-0	W	McGavin	Barrett	Cook	Roberts	Kinsella	English	Elliott	Collins^	Bennett*	McDon'gh*	McGavin	Smith	Stewart/Donald
30	A	15/2	WELLING	1,837	1-4	L	McDonough (p)	Barrett	Cook^	Roberts	Kinsella	English	Elliott	Collins	Stewart^	McDon'gh*	McGavin	Smith	Stewart/Donald
31	H	22/2	ALTRINCHAM	905	2-1	W	McGavin, McDonough	Barrett	Donald	Roberts	Kinsella	Cook	Martin	Cook	Bennett^	McDon'gh*	McGavin^	Smith	Bennett/Masters
32	H	7/3	GATESHEAD	2,897	2-2	D	Roberts, Masters	Barrett	Donald*	Roberts	Kinsella	Cook	Martin	Cook*	Stewart^	McDon'gh*	McGavin^	Smith	Bennett/Masters
33	A	21/3	NORTHWICH	3,218	1-0	W	Smith	Barrett	Donald	Roberts	Kinsella	English	Martin*	Cook^	Bennett^	McDon'gh*	McGavin^	Smith	Collins/Stewart
34	A	24/3	BATH	1,101	0-0	D		Barrett	Donald	Roberts	Kinsella	English	Martin	Cook	Stewart	McDon'gh^	McGavin*	Smith	Martin
35	H	28/3	KIDDERMINSTER	3,073	3-0	W	English, Benton (og), Stewart	Barrett	Donald	Roberts*	Kinsella	English	Martin	Cook	Masters^	McDon'gh*	McGavin*	Smith	Collins/Masters
36	H	14/4	SLOUGH	3,197	4-0	W	McDon', Masters, Stewart, Kins'	Barrett	Donald	Roberts	Kinsella	English	Martin	Cook	Masters^	McDon'gh^	McGavin^	Smith	Masters/Bennett
37	H	18/4	TELFORD	3,964	2-0	W	McDonough 2	Barrett	Donald	Roberts	Kinsella	English	Martin	Cook	Stewart	McDon'gh*	McGavin^	Smith	Bennett/Masters
38	H	20/4	MERTHYR	4,148	2-0	W	Smith, Masters	Barrett	Donald*	Roberts	Kinsella	English	Martin	Cook	Masters	McDon'gh*	McGavin^	Smith	Bennett/Elliott
39	A	22/4	BOSTON	2,305	4-0	W	McGavin, McDon' 2 (1p), Masters	Barrett	Donald	Roberts	Kinsella	English	Martin	Cook*	Masters^	McDonough	McGavin	Smith	Elliott/Bennett
40	H	25/4	MACCLESFIELD	886	4-4	D	Kendall (og), English 2, McDonough	Barrett	Donald	Roberts	Kinsella*	English	Martin^	Cook	Masters^	McDonough	McGavin	Smith	Elliott/Bennett
41	H	28/4	KETTERING	6,303	3-1	W	McDonough 2, McGavin	Barrett	Donald	Roberts	Kinsella	English	Martin	Cook	Masters^	McDonough	McGavin	Smith	Elliott/Bennett
42	H	2/5	BARROW	7,193	5-0	W	Masters 3, Smith, McDonough	Barrett	Donald	Roberts	Kinsella*	English	Martin	Cook	Masters	McDon'gh^	Bennett	Smith	Elliott/Stewart

FA CUP

Rd	H/A	Date	Opponent	Att	Result	Score	Scorers
4Q	H	26/10	BURTON	2,147	W	5-0	McD'(p), McGavin 2 (1p), Rest', Kin'
1	H	16/11	EXETER	4,965	D	0-0	
1R	A	27/11	EXETER	4,066	D	0-0	(aet, lost 2-4 on pens)

FA Cup line-ups

Match												Sub
Burton	Barrett	Donald	Collins^	Elliott	English	Kinsella	Phillips	Bennett	McDonough*	McGavin	Smith	Restarick/Abrahams
Exeter	Barrett	Donald	Collins	Elliott	English	Kinsella	Cook	Bennett	McDonough	McGavin	Smith*	Grainger
Exeter (R)	Barrett	Donald	Collins	Goodwin*	English	Kinsella	Cook	Bennett^	McDonough	McGavin	Smith	Grainger/Restarick

League table

	Team	P	W	D	L	F	A	W	D	L	F	A	Pts
			Home					Away					
1	COLCHESTER	42	19	1	1	57	11	9	9	3	41	29	94
2	Wycombe	42	18	1	2	49	13	12	3	6	35	22	94
3	Kettering	42	12	6	3	44	23	8	7	6	28	27	73
4	Merthyr	42	14	4	3	40	24	4	10	7	19	32	68
5	Farnborough	42	8	7	6	36	27	10	5	6	32	26	66
6	Telford	42	10	4	7	32	31	9	3	9	30	35	64
7	Redbridge	42	12	4	5	42	27	6	5	10	27	29	63
8	Boston	42	10	4	7	40	35	8	5	8	31	31	63
9	Bath	42	8	6	7	27	22	8	6	8	27	29	60
10	Witton	42	11	6	4	41	26	5	4	12	22	34	58
11	Northwich	42	10	4	7	40	25	6	2	13	23	33	54
12	Welling	42	8	6	7	40	38	6	6	9	29	41	54
13	Macclesfield	42	7	7	7	25	21	6	6	9	25	29	52
14	Gateshead	42	8	5	8	22	22	4	7	10	27	35	48
15	Yeovil	42	8	6	7	22	21	3	8	10	18	28	47
16	Runcorn	42	5	11	5	26	26	6	2	13	24	37	46
17	Stafford	42	7	8	6	25	24	3	8	10	16	35	46
18	Altrincham	42	5	8	8	33	39	6	4	11	28	43	45
19	Kidderminster	42	8	6	7	35	32	4	3	14	21	45	45
20	Slough	42	7	3	11	26	39	6	3	12	30	43	45
21	Cheltenham	42	8	5	8	28	35	2	8	11	28	47	43
22	Barrow	42	6	4	8	29	23	3	6	12	23	49	38
		924	208	120	134	759	584	134	120	208	584	759	1266

Appearances and Goals

Player	Lge	Sub	FAT	Sub	FAC	Sub	Lge	FAT	FAC	Tot
							Goals			
Abrahams, Paul		3								
Barrett, Scott	42		9		3		1			1
Bennett, Gary	31	8	4	4	3		16	2		18
Collins, Eamonn	29	3	3	2	3	2	2	1		3
Cook, Jason	28	3	6		2		2	1		3
Dart (Hazel), Julian		2								
Donald, Warren	38	3	8		3					
Elliott, Shaun	32	5	5		2		1			1
English, Tony	37		9		3		6	2		8
Goodwin, James		3		1						
Grainger, Martin	8	2	2		2	2				
Gray, Simon	1									
Kinsella, Mark	37	5	8	1	3		3	1	1	5
Martin, Dave	8	1	3							
Masters, Mike	7	8	2	2	2		7	1		8
McDonough, Roy	40		7		3		26	2	1	29
McGavin, Steve	39		9		3		20	4	2	26
Phillips, Ian	1	2								
Restarick, Steve	1	6	2		2			1	1	2
Roberts, Paul	35		9							
Smith, Nicky	42		9		3		1			1
Stewart, Ian	6	4	3	1			8	3		11
Walsh, Mario		1					2	2		4
(own-goals)							3			3
23 players used	462	58	99	14	33	5	98	20	5	123

Odds & Ends

Double wins: (7) Boston, Gateshead, Runcorn, Telford, Slough, Wycombe, Yeovil.

Double defeats: (0).

Won from behind: (2) Slough (a), Runcorn (a).

Lost from in front: (2) Farnborough (h), Redbridge (a).

High spots: Regaining Football League status.
Becoming GMVC champions with a record number of points.
Reaching Wembley for first time (3-1 FA Trophy victory over Witton).
Superb home record, including a record 16 wins in succession.
Doing the 'double' over rivals Wycombe.
Goalkeeper Scott Barrett's remarkable winning goal at Wycombe.
The five-goal romp on the final day, to clinch the title and promotion.

Low spots: The first club to exit the FA Cup without conceding a goal.
When Layer Road's unsuitability looked like denying promotion.

Player of the Year: Nicky Smith.

Ever presents: (2) Scott Barrett, Nicky Smith.

Hat-tricks for: (3) Roy McDonough, Gary Bennett, Mike Masters.

Hat-tricks against: (1) Mark West (Wycombe) (in Bob Lord Trophy).

Leading scorer: (29) Roy McDonough.

BARCLAYS LEAGUE DIVISION 3 — Manager: Roy McDonough — SEASON 1992-93

#	H/A	Date	Opponents	Att	F-A	Scorers	1	2	3	4	5	6	7	8	9	10	11	Subs (2)
1	H	15/8	LINCOLN	4,131	W 2:1	McDonough, Oxbrow	Newell	Donald	Roberts	Kinsella	English	Oxbrow	Devereux*	Bennett*	McDonough	Grainger	Smith	Abrahams
2	A	21/8	BARNET	3,600	L 1:3	Kinsella	Newell	Donald	Roberts	Kinsella	English	Oxbrow	Devereux*	Bennett*	McDonough	Grainger^	Smith	Abrahams/Phillips
3	H	29/8	DARLINGTON	3,524	L 0:3		Newell	Devereux	Roberts	Kinsella	English	Oxbrow	Cook^	Bennett	McDonough	Hazel*	Smith	Abrahams/Donald
4	H	1/9	SHREWSBURY	3,530	L 0:2		Newell	Donald	Roberts	Kinsella	English	Oxbrow	Cook	Hazel*	McDon'gh !	McGavin^	Smith	Bennett
5	A	5/9	BURY	2,072	L 2:3	Bennett, McDonough	Newell	Donald	Roberts	Kinsella	English*	Oxbrow	Cook	Bennett	McDonough	McGavin^	Smith	Grainger/Abrahams
6	H	12/9	WALSALL	3,218	W 3:1	Bennett, Smith, McDonough(p)	Newell	Donald	Roberts	Kinsella	English	Oxbrow	Cook	Bennett	McDonough	Grainger	Smith	
7	A	15/9	DONCASTER	1,719	L 0:1		Newell	Donald*	Roberts	Kinsella	English	Oxbrow	Cook	Bennett	Grainger	McGavin	Smith	
8	A	19/9	YORK	3,820	L 0:2		Newell	Donald^	Roberts	Kinsella	English	Oxbrow	Cook	Bennett	Grainger	McGavin	Smith	Ball/Devereux
9	H	26/9	CHESTERFIELD	3,436	W 3:0	Bennett 2, Kinsella	Newell	Grainger	Roberts	Kinsella	English	Oxbrow	Cook	Bennett	Ball	McGavin	Smith	
10	A	10/10	HALIFAX	2,445	W 4:2	Kinsella, Oxbr'w, McDon'gh, Benn'tt	Newell	Grainger	Roberts	Kinsella	Cawley	Oxbrow	Ball^	Bennett	McDon'gh*	McGavin	Smith	Devereux/Donald
11	H	16/10	CREWE	4,524	W 3:2	Bennett, McDonough, Oxbrow	Newell	Grainger	Roberts	Kinsella	Cawley	Oxbrow	Cook^	Bennett	McDonough	Ball*	Smith	English/McGavin
12	H	24/10	SCUNTHORPE	2,473	L 1:3	McGavin	Newell	Grainger	Roberts	Kinsella	Cawley	Oxbrow	Cook*	Bennett	McDonough	McGavin	Smith	Devereux/English
13	H	30/10	WREXHAM	4,423	L 2:4	Ball, Kinsella	Newell	Grainger*	Roberts	Kinsella	Cawley	English	Cook^	Bennett	McDonough	Ball	Smith	Oxbrow/McGavin
14	H	3/11	CARLISLE	3,263	W 2:1	Roberts, Cawley	Newell	Grainger	Roberts	Kinsella	Cawley	English	Cook	Bennett	Ball*	McGavin	Smith	McDonough
15	H	7/11	CARDIFF	5,505	L 1:3	Kinsella	Green	Cook	Roberts	Kinsella*	Cawley	English	Ball	Bennett^	Sorrell	McGavin	Smith*	Oxbrow/McDon'gh
16	H	21/11	ROCHDALE	3,172	D 4:4	Cawley, Ball, Sorrell, McDonough	Green	Sorrell	Roberts	Kinsella*	Cawley	English	Ball	Bennett^	McDonough	McGavin	Smith	Cook/Oxbrow
17	A	28/11	HEREFORD	1,671	L 1:3	Oxbrow	Green	Donald	Roberts	Sorrell	Cawley	English	Ball^	Bennett	McDon'gh*	McGavin	Smith	Oxbrow/Cook
18	H	11/12	TORQUAY	2,774	W 2:0	McDonough, Smith	Emberson	Grainger*	Roberts	Kinsella	Cawley^	English	Ball^	Sorrell	McDon'gh*	McGavin	Smith	Bennett/Ball
19	A	18/12	GILLINGHAM	2,331	W 1:0	McGavin	Emberson	Grainger*	Roberts	Kinsella	Betts	English	Cook	Bennett	McDonough	McGavin	Smith	Sorrell
20	A	26/12	NORTHAMPTON	4,861	L 0:1		Emberson	Grainger	Roberts	Kinsella	Betts	English	Cook	Bennett*	McDonough	McGavin	Smith	Abrahams
21	H	29/12	SCARBOROUGH	3,640	W 1:0	McGavin	Emberson	Grainger	Roberts	Kinsella	Cawley	English	Cook	Bennett	McDonough	McGavin	Smith	
22	A	2/1	WALSALL	3,669	W 3:1	Martin, McGavin, Cawley	Emberson	Grainger	Roberts	Kinsella	Cawley	Betts	Cook	Bennett^	Martin	McGavin	Smith	Ball/Abrahams
23	A	8/1	DONCASTER	4,402	W 2:0	Grainger, McGavin	Emberson	Grainger	Roberts	Kinsella	Cawley	Betts	Cook*	Bennett^	Martin	McGavin	Smith	
24	H	16/1	CHESTERFIELD	3,016	L 0:4		Emberson	Grainger	Roberts	Kinsella	Cawley	Betts	Cook*	Bennett^	Martin	McGavin	Smith	Ball/Abrahams
25	H	22/1	YORK	4,528	D 0:0		Emberson	Grainger	Roberts	Kinsella	Cawley	English	Cook*	Bennett	Martin*	McGavin	Smith	Ball/Abrahams
26	H	29/1	BARNET	5,609	L 1:2	Bennett	Emberson	Ball	Roberts	Kinsella	Cawley	English	Betts	Bennett	Martin	McGavin	Smith	Abrahams
27	A	6/2	LINCOLN	3,380	D 1:1	Martin	Emberson	Grainger	Roberts	Kinsella	Cawley*	English	Betts	Bennett	Martin^	McGavin	Smith	
28	H	13/2	BURY	3,264	D 0:0		Emberson	Grainger	Roberts	Ball	Cawley*	English	Betts	Bennett	Martin	McGavin	Smith	Cook/Abrahams
29	A	20/2	SHREWSBURY	2,653	L 3:4	Hopkins, Grainger(p), McGavin	Emberson	Grainger	Roberts	Ball*	Cawley	English	Betts	Hopkins*	Martin	McGavin	Smith	Abrahams/Kinsella
30	H	26/2	HALIFAX	3,007	W 2:1	McGavin, Grainger	Emberson	Grainger	Roberts	Kinsella	Cawley	English	Cook	Bennett	McDon'gh*	McGavin	Smith	Abrahams
31	H	12/3	CARDIFF	4,538	L 2:4	McDonough(p), McGavin	Emberson	Betts	Roberts	Kinsella	Flowers*	Hopkins^	Cook	Bennett	McDon'gh^	McGavin	Smith	Partner/Abrahams
32	A	20/3	CARLISLE	3,003	W 2:0	Cook, Edmondson(og)	Barber	Betts	Roberts	Kinsella	Flowers	Hopkins	Cook	Bennett*	McDon'gh*	McGavin	Smith	Ball/Abrahams
33	H	23/3	HEREFORD	3,024	W 3:1	Titterton(og), McDon'gh, Abrahams	Barber	Grainger	Roberts	Hopkins	Cawley	Betts*	Cook*	Bennett^	McDonough	McGavin	Smith	English/Abrahams
34	A	27/3	ROCHDALE	1,783	L 2:5	Smith, Abrahams	Barber	Grainger	Roberts	Kinsella	Cawley	Betts^	Hopkins*	English	McDon'gh !	Abrahams	Smith	Bennett/Cook
35	H	6/4	TORQUAY	2,915	D 2:2	McGavin, Ball	Barber	Grainger	Roberts	Kinsella	Cawley	English	Ball	Hopkins*	Abrahams	McGavin	Smith	Bennett/Cook
36	A	13/4	SCARBOROUGH	1,803	W 1:0	Abrahams	Barber	Betts	Roberts	Kinsella	Cook	English	Ball	Hopkins*	Abrahams	McGavin	Smith	Bennett
37	H	16/4	GILLINGHAM	4,695	W 3:0	Clark(og), Smith, Abrahams	Barber	Betts	Roberts	Kinsella	Cook	English	Ball	Hopkins*	Abrahams^	McGavin	Smith	Bennett
38	H	20/4	NORTHAMPTON	3,519	W 2:0	Ball(p), Abrahams	Barber	Betts	Roberts	Kinsella	Cook	English	Ball*	Hopkins	Abrahams	McGavin	Smith	Grainger/Bennett
39	A	24/3	CREWE	3,250	L 1:7	English	Barber	Betts	Roberts	Kinsella	Cook*	English	Ball	Hopkins	Abrahams*	McGavin^	Smith	Bennett/Cawley
40	H	1/5	SCUNTHORPE	3,421	W 1:0	Abrahams	Barber	Betts	Roberts	Kinsella	Cook*	English	Ball	Hopkins*	Abrahams	McGavin	Smith	Grainger/McDonough
41	A	4/5	DARLINGTON	2,007	L 0:1		Barber	Grainger*	Roberts*	Betts	Cook	English	Ball	Bennett	Abrahams^	McGavin	Smith	Cawley/McDon'gh
42	A	8/5	WREXHAM	9,705	L 3:4	Hardy(og), Bennett, Kinsella	Munson	Betts	Roberts	Kinsella	Grainger	Cawley	Ball	Bennett	Abrahams^	McGavin	Smith	Flowers/Hopkins

COCA-COLA (LEAGUE) CUP

Tie		Date	Opponent	Att	Res		Scorers
1:1	H	18/8	BRIGHTON	3,814	D	1-1	English
1:2	A	26/8	BRIGHTON	4,125	L	0-1	

Line-ups:
- 1:1 — Newell, Donald, Roberts, Kinsella, English, Oxbrow, Devereux, Bennett, McDonough, Grainger, Smith, Abrahams
- 1:2 — Newell, Donald*, Roberts, Kinsella, English, Oxbrow, Cook, Bennett, McDonough, Hazel, Smith, Abrahams

FA CUP

Rd		Date	Opponent	Att	Res		Scorers
1	H	14/11	SLOUGH	3,858	W	4-0	Sorrell, Bennett 2, Ball
2	A	5/12	GILLINGHAM	5,319	D	1-1	McGavin
2R	H	16/12	GILLINGHAM	4,440	L	2-3	Ball 2

Line-ups:
- 1 — Green, Sorrell, Roberts, Kinsella, Cawley, English, Ball, Bennett, McDonough*, Grainger, Smith, Oxbrow
- 2 — Green, Grainger, Roberts, Kinsella, Cawley, English, Cook, Sorrell!, McDonough, McGavin, Smith, Oxbrow
- 2R — Green, Grainger, Roberts, Kinsella, Ball, English, Cook^, Sorrell*, McDonough, McGavin, Smith, Bennett/Betts

AUTOGLASS TROPHY

Rd		Date	Opponent	Att	Res		Scorers
1	H	1/12	NORTHAMPTON	1,454	L	1-2	Grainger (p)
1	A	21/12	BARNET	1,193	L	2-4	Ball, Cook

Line-ups:
- 1 (Northampton) — Green, Donald, Grainger, Devereux, Oxbrow, English, Hazel*, Roberts^, McDonough, Grainger, Smith, Bennett/Kinsella
- 1 (Barnet) — Monk, Betts, Phillips*, Roberts, Partner, Ball, Cook, Bennett, McDonough, Hazel, Smith, Donald

League Table

	Team	P	Home						Away						Pts
			W	D	L	F	A		W	D	L	F	A		
1	Cardiff	42	13	7	1	42	20		12	1	8	35	27		83
2	Wrexham	42	14	3	4	48	26		9	8	4	27	26		80
3	Barnet	42	16	4	1	45	19		7	6	8	21	29		79
4	York*	42	13	6	2	41	15		8	6	7	31	30		75
5	Walsall	42	11	6	4	42	31		11	1	9	34	30		73
6	Crewe	42	13	3	5	47	23		8	4	9	28	33		70
7	Bury	42	10	7	4	36	19		8	2	11	27	36		63
8	Lincoln	42	10	6	5	31	20		8	3	10	26	33		63
9	Shrewsbury	42	11	3	7	36	30		6	8	7	21	22		62
10	COLCHESTER	42	13	3	5	38	26		5	2	14	29	50		59
11	Rochdale	42	10	3	8	38	29		6	7	8	32	41		58
12	Chesterfield	42	11	3	7	32	28		4	8	9	27	35		56
13	Scarborough	42	7	7	7	32	30		8	2	11	34	41		54
14	Scunthorpe	42	8	7	6	38	25		6	5	10	19	29		54
15	Darlington	42	5	6	10	23	31		7	8	6	25	22		50
16	Doncaster	42	6	5	10	22	28		5	9	7	20	29		47
17	Hereford	42	7	9	5	31	27		3	6	12	16	33		45
18	Carlisle	42	7	5	9	29	27		4	6	11	22	38		44
19	Torquay	42	6	4	11	18	26		5	3	13	27	41		43
20	Northampton	42	6	5	10	19	28		5	3	13	29	46		41
21	Gillingham	42	9	4	8	32	28		0	9	12	16	36		40
22	Halifax	42	3	5	13	20	35		6	4	11	25	33		36
		924	209	111	142	740	571		142	111	209	571	740		1275

* promoted after play-offs

Appearances and Goals

Player	Appearances								Goals				
	Lge	Sub	LC	Sub	FAC	Sub	AT	Sub	Lge	LC	FAC	AT	Tot
Abrahams, Paul	9	14							6				6
Ball, Steve	19	5	2		2		2		4		3	1	8
Barber, Fred	10												
Bennett, Gary	30	8	2		1	1	1	1	8		2		10
Betts, Simon	23						1						
Cawley, Peter	22	2			2				2				2
Cook, Jason	30	4	2		2		2		2			1	3
Devereux, Robbie	3	3					1						
Donald, Warren	8	2	2				1	1					
Emberson, Carl	13												
English, Tony	30	3	2		3		1		2	1			3
Flowers, Paul	2	1											
Grainger, Martin	28	3	1		2		3		3			1	4
Green, Ron	4				3								
Hazel, Julian	2					1	1						
Hopkins, Robert	13	1							1				1
Kinsella, Mark	37	1	2		3		2	1	6				6
McDonough, Roy	21	4	2		3		2		9				9
McGavin, Steve	35	2			3		2		8		1		9
Martin, Dean	8	2							2				2
Munson, Nathan	1												
Monk, Alastair							1						
Newell, Paul	14		2										
Oxbrow, Darren	12	4	2		1	1		1	4				4
Partner, Andy							1						
Phillips, Ian							1						
Roberts, Paul	42		2		3		2		1				1
Smith, Nicky	42		2		3		2		4				4
Sorrell, Tony	4	1			3			1	1		1		2
(own-goals)									4				4
29 players used	462	60	22	3	33	1	22	3	67	1	7	3	78

Odds & ends

Double wins: (5) Carlisle, Gillingham, Halifax, Scarborough, Walsall.

Double defeats: (5) Barnet, Cardiff, Darlington, Shrewsbury, Wrexham.

Won from behind: (2) Lincoln (h), Halifax (h).

Lost from in front: (4) Barnet (a), Cardiff (h), Rochdale (a), Barnet (h).

High spots: Kicking off the season as a Football League club again.

Above-average goal action: 143 in the 42 League games.

The late effort to reach the play-offs, with four wins in five games.

Fred Barber's crowd-pleasing antics.

The emergence of a 'local hero' in young Paul Abrahams.

Low spots: Four defeats in the first five League games of the new era.

The controversial defeat at Darlington, which ended play-off hopes

The failure to recruit a permanent goalkeeper throughout the season.

The loss of striker Mike Masters and failure to adequately replace him.

The 1-7 thrashing by fellow play-off contenders Crewe.

Player of the Year: Paul Roberts.

Ever presents: (2) Paul Roberts, Nicky Smith.

Hat-tricks for: (0).

Hat-tricks against: (1) Tony Naylor (Crewe).

Leading scorer: Roy McDonough (9).

ENDSLEIGH LEAGUE DIVISION 3   Manager: Roy McDonough   SEASON 1993-94

		Date	Opponents	Att	F-A	Scorers	1	2	3	4	5	6	7	8	9	10	11	Subs (2)
1	H	14/8	LINCOLN	3,198	W 1-0	Kinsella	Keeley	Betts^	Roberts	Kinsella	English	Grainger	Ball	Bennett	McDon'gh^	McGavin	Smith	Abrahams/Cook J
2	A	21/8	CREWE	2,700	L 1-2	Ball	Keeley	Betts^	Roberts	Kinsella	English	Grainger	Ball	Bennett*	McDon'gh^	McGavin	Smith	Allpress/Campbell
3	H	28/8	NORTHAMPTON	2,874	W 3-2	Grainger(p), English, Kinsella	Keeley	Allpress	Roberts	Kinsella	English	Grainger	Ball	Bennett*	McDon'gh^	McGavin	Smith	Morrow/Brown S
4	H	31/8	SHREWSBURY	2,723	D 3-3	McGavin 2, Brown S	Keeley	Allpress	Roberts	Kinsella	English	Grainger	Ball	Brown S	McDonough	McGavin	Smith	
5	A	4/9	TORQUAY	2,989	D 3-3	Brown S, McGavin, Curran(og)	Keeley	Allpress^	Roberts	Kinsella	English	Cawley	Ball*	Brown S	McDon'gh*	McGavin	Smith	Grainger/Dickens
6	H	11/9	ROCHDALE	2,776	L 2-5	McDonough, Brown S	Keeley	Allpress	Roberts	Kinsella	English	Grainger	Ball*	Brown S	McDonough	McGavin	Smith	Bennett/Dickens
7	A	18/9	WYCOMBE	6,025	W 5-2	Kin', McG', McD', Grainger, Brown S	Keeley	Betts	Roberts	Kinsella*	English	Cawley	Dickens	Brown S^	McDonough	McGavin	Smith	Grainger
8	H	25/9	BURY	2,702	W 4-1	Brown S 3, McGavin	Keeley	Betts*	Roberts	Kinsella*	English	Cawley	Dickens	Brown S	McDonough	McGavin	Smith	Grainger/Richards'n
9	A	2/10	PRESTON	6,412	L 0-1		Keeley	Betts*	Roberts	Kinsella	English	Cawley	Dickens	Brown S	McDonough	McGavin	Smith	Richardson
10	H	9/10	SCUNTHORPE	3,405	W 2-1	Kinsella, Brown S	Keeley	Locke	Roberts	Kinsella*	English	Cawley	Dickens	Brown S	McDonough	McGavin	Smith	
11	H	16/10	HEREFORD	1,848	L 0-5		Keeley !	Locke	Roberts	Kinsella*	English	Cawley	Dickens	Brown S^	McDonough	McGavin	Smith	Ball/Munson !
12	A	23/10	WIGAN	2,814	W 3-1	McDonough 2, Kinsella	Keeley	Allpress	Roberts	Kinsella	English	Cawley	Dickens*	Brown S	McDonough	McGavin	Smith	Ball
13	A	30/10	GILLINGHAM	3,964	L 0-3		Desborough	Locke	Roberts	Kinsella	English	Cawley	Ball	Brown S	McDonough	McGavin*	Smith	Richardson
14	A	2/11	DARLINGTON	1,299	L 3-7	Dickens, McGavin, Kinsella	Keeley	Locke	Roberts	Kinsella	English	Cawley	Dickens	Ball*	McDonough	McGavin	Smith	Richardson
15	H	6/11	WALSALL	2,736	L 0-1		Keeley	Betts	Roberts	Kinsella	English	Cawley	Dickens	Richardson*	McDonough	McGavin	Smith	Abrahams
16	H	20/11	DONCASTER	2,034	L 1-2	McGavin	Keeley	Betts	Basham	Kinsella	English	Cawley	Dickens*	Brown S	McDonough	McGavin	Smith	Ball/Richardson
17	H	27/11	CARLISLE	2,316	W 2-1	English 2	Munson	Betts*	Roberts^	Kinsella	English	Cawley	Ball	Brown S	McDonough	McGavin*	Smith*	Abrahams/Rich'rds'n
18	A	11/12	CREWE	2,647	L 2-4	English, Brown S	Munson	Betts	Roberts	Kinsella	English	Cawley	Ball^	Brown S	McDonough	McGavin	Smith*	Dickens/Richardson
19	A	27/11	MANSFIELD	3,478	D 0-0		Sheffield	Betts	Roberts	Kinsella	English	Cawley	Ball^	Brown S	McDonough	McGavin^	Smith	Fry/Dickens
20	H	28/12	SCARBOROUGH	1,226	W 2-0	McDonough, McGavin	Sheffield	Betts	Roberts*	Kinsella	English	Cawley	Dickens	Brown S^	McDonough	Fry*	Smith	McGavin/Ball
21	H	1/1	CHESTER	3,170	D 0-0		Sheffield	Betts	Roberts*	Kinsella	English	Cawley	Dickens	Brown S	McDon'gh*	McGavin	Smith	Fry
22	A	3/1	SHREWSBURY	4,245	L 1-2	Ball	Sheffield	Betts	Roberts*	Kinsella	English	Cawley	Dickens	Brown S^	McDon'gh*	McGavin	Smith	Ball/Allpress
23	H	15/1	HEREFORD	2,439	W 1-0	Dickens	Sheffield	Betts	Allpress	Kinsella	English	Cawley	Dickens	Watts*	McDonough	Fry	Ball	Booty
24	A	22/1	SCUNTHORPE	2,854	D 1-1	Cawley	Ch'sewright	Betts	Allpress	Kinsella	English	Cawley	Dickens	Brown S^	McDonough	Fry*	Ball	Smith/Watts
25	H	29/1	GILLINGHAM	3,436	L 1-2	Watts	Ch'sewright	Betts	Smith	Kinsella	English	Cawley	Dickens	Ball*	McDonough	Fry*	Brown S*	Watts/Smith
26	A	5/2	WIGAN	1,695	W 1-0	Dickens	Ch'sewright	Betts	Smith	Kinsella	English	Cawley	Dickens	Ball	McDonough	Fry*	Watts	Campbell
27	A	12/2	CHESTERFIELD	2,783	L 0-2		Ch'sewright	Betts	Allpress	Kinsella	English	Cawley	Dickens	Ball*	McDonough	Campbell^	Watts	Fry/Smith
28	A	19/2	NORTHAMPTON	3,185	L 0-1	McDonough	Ch'sewright	Betts	Allpress	Kinsella	English	Cawley	Dickens	Brown S^	McDonough	Hyslop !	Watts*	Fry/Smith
29	H	25/2	TORQUAY	2,573	L 1-2	Betts	Ch'sewright	Betts	Allpress	Kinsella	English	Cawley	Dickens	Brown S	McDon'gh*	Hyslop	Smith	Fry
30	A	5/3	ROCHDALE	2,202	L 1-2	Watts	Ch'sewright	Hyslop	Allpress	Kinsella	English	Cawley	Dickens	Brown S	Ball*	Watts^	Fry	Betts/Smith
31	H	12/3	WYCOMBE	3,932	D 0-0		Ch'sewright	Hyslop	Allpress	Kinsella	English	Cawley	Dickens	Brown S^	Watts^	Fry*	Ball	Smith/Betts
32	H	15/3	LINCOLN	1,631	L 0-2		Ch'sewright	Betts	Allpress*	Kinsella	English	Cawley	Dickens	Brown S^	Watts	Hyslop	Ball	Smith
33	A	19/3	BURY	2,108	W 1-0	McDonough	Ch'sewright	Betts	Allpress	Kinsella	English	Hyslop	Dickens	Brown S^	McDonough	Watts*	Ball	Smith/Campbell
34	H	26/3	PRESTON	2,950	D 1-1	Brown I	Ch'sewright	Betts	Hyslop	Kinsella	English	Cawley	Dickens	Brown S^	McDonough	Ball^	Brown I	Smith
35	A	29/3	CHESTERFIELD	3,089	D 0-0		Ch'sewright	Betts	Hyslop*	Kinsella	English	Cawley	Dickens*	Whitton	McDonough	Brown I	Ball^	Smith/Brown S
36	A	2/4	MANSFIELD	2,117	L 0-1	Gray(og)	Ch'sewright	Betts	Smith	Kinsella	English	Cawley	Dickens*	Whitton	Brown S	Brown I^	Ball	McDonough/Watts
37	H	4/4	SCARBOROUGH	2,501	L 1-2	Meyer(og)	Ch'sewright	Betts	Smith	Kinsella	English	Cawley	Dickens	Whitton	McDonough	Brown I^	Ball*	Watts/Brown S
38	A	9/4	CHESTER	3,394	L 1-2	Brown S	Ch'sewright	Betts	Smith	Kinsella	English	Cawley	Allpress	Whitton	Brown S	Fry	Ball	
39	H	16/4	DARLINGTON	2,337	L 1-2	Kinsella	Ch'sewright	Betts	Allpress*	Kinsella	English	Cawley	Dickens	Whitton	Brown S	Fry	Smith	McDonough
40	A	23/4	WALSALL	2,980	W 3-1	Watkiss(og), Kinsella	Ch'sewright	Betts	Allpress	Kinsella	English	Cawley	Ball	Whitton	McDonough	Fry	Ball	
41	H	30/4	DONCASTER	2,378	W 3-1	Whitton 2, Brown S	Barada	Betts	Allpress	Kinsella	English	Cawley	Cook T*	Whitton	McDon'gh*	Fry	Smith	Gentle/Brown S
42	A	7/5	CARLISLE	9,305	L 0-2		Ch'sewright	Betts	Allpress	Kinsella	English	Cawley	Ball*	Whitton	McDon'gh^	Fry^	Brown S	Cook T/Gentle

COCA-COLA (LEAGUE CUP)

		Date	Opponents	Att	F-A	Scorers	1	2	3	4	5	6	7	8	9	10	11	Subs (2)
1:1	A	17/8	FULHAM	2,820	L 1-2	Kinsella	Keeley	Betts^	Roberts	Kinsella	English	Grainger	Ball	Bennett*	McDonough	McGavin	Smith	Abrahams/Allpress
1:2	H	24/8	FULHAM	3,360	L 1-2	McDonough	Keeley	Allpress	Roberts	Kinsella	English	Grainger	Ball	Bennett*	McDonough	McGavin	Smith	Abrahams

FA CUP

		Date	Opponent	Att	Result	Scorers
1	H	13/11	SUTTON UNITED	3,051	L 3-4	McGavin, Brown S, English

AUTOGLASS TROPHY

		Date	Opponent	Att	Result	Scorers
1	A	28/9	GILLINGHAM	1,091	D 0-0	
1	H	19/10	CAMBRIDGE U	1,489	D 2-2	Kinsella, Brown S
2	A	4/12	WREXHAM	1,860	W 1-0	McDonough
3	H	11/1	WYCOMBE	2,751	L 0-1	

Line-ups (shirt positions 1–11, with substitutes):

Match	1	2	3	4	5	6	7	8	9	10	11	Subs
Sutton United (FAC)	Keeley	Betts	Roberts	Kinsella	English	Cawley	Dickens	Brown S	McDonough	McGavin	Smith	Richardson*, McGavin
Gillingham	Keeley	Betts	Roberts	Kinsella	English	Cawley	Dickens	Brown S	McDonough	McGavin	Ball	Richardson*, McGavin
Cambridge U	Keeley	Locke*	Allpress	Kinsella	English	Cawley	Ball	Brown S	McDonough	McGavin	Smith	McDonough
Wrexham	Munson	Betts	Roberts	Kinsella	English	Cawley	Dickens	Brown S	McDonough	McGavin	Smith	Booty^
Wycombe	Ch'sewright	Betts	Allpress	Kinsella	English	Cawley	Dickens	Ball	McDonough	Booty^	Campbell*	Watts/Cook T, Ball/Richardson

League table

		P	W	D	L	F	A	W	D	L	F	A	Pts
				Home					Away				
1	Shrewsbury	42	10	8	3	28	17	12	5	4	35	22	79
2	Chester	42	13	5	3	35	18	8	6	7	34	28	74
3	Crewe	42	12	4	5	45	30	9	6	6	35	31	73
4	Wycombe *	42	11	6	4	34	21	8	7	6	33	32	70
5	Preston	42	13	5	3	46	23	5	8	8	33	37	67
6	Torquay	42	8	10	3	30	24	9	6	6	34	32	67
7	Carlisle	42	10	4	7	35	23	8	6	7	22	19	64
8	Chesterfield	42	8	8	5	32	22	8	6	7	23	26	62
9	Rochdale	42	10	5	6	38	22	6	7	8	25	29	60
10	Walsall	42	7	5	9	28	26	10	4	7	20	27	60
11	Scunthorpe	42	9	7	5	40	26	6	7	8	24	30	59
12	Mansfield	42	9	6	6	28	30	6	7	8	25	38	55
13	Bury	42	9	6	6	33	22	5	5	11	22	34	53
14	Scarborough	42	8	4	9	29	28	7	4	10	26	33	53
15	Doncaster	42	8	6	7	24	26	6	4	11	20	31	52
16	Gillingham	42	8	8	5	27	23	4	6	10	17	28	51
17	COLCHESTER	42	8	4	9	31	33	5	6	10	25	38	49
18	Lincoln	42	7	4	10	26	29	5	7	9	26	34	47
19	Wigan	42	6	7	8	33	33	5	5	11	18	37	45
20	Hereford	42	6	4	11	34	33	6	2	13	26	46	42
21	Darlington	42	7	5	9	24	28	3	6	12	18	36	41
22	Northampton	42	6	7	8	25	23	3	4	14	19	43	38
		924	193	125	144	705	560	144	125	193	560	705	1261

* promoted after play-offs

Odds & ends

Double wins: (2) Bury, Wigan.
Double defeats: (3) Crewe, Darlington, Gillingham.

Won from behind: (5) Northampton (h), Wycombe (a), Scunthorpe (h). Carlisle (h), Doncaster (h).
Lost from in front: (2) Rochdale (h), Shrewsbury (a).

High spots: New recruit Steve Brown's early form, including a hat-trick. The 5-2 win at Wycombe, one of the best 'away days' in memory.
The arrival of the first cash signing (Chris Fry) for several years.
Goals galore: 62 in a run of 12 games early in the season.
The signing, after a protracted pursuit, of experienced Steve Whitton.

Low spots: Denial, by the League, of the popular Friday home fixtures.
A home defeat in the FA Cup by non-League Sutton United.
Embarrassing defeats by Rochdale, Hereford and Darlington.
The loss of the talented Steve McGavin to balance the books.
Creating a record with two keepers sent off in one match (v Hereford).
The run of seven home games without a win from January.
The apparent lack of action over plans to acquire a new stadium.
The 0-2 home defeat by Wycombe and subsequent protest by fans.

Player of the Year: Mark Kinsella.
Ever presents: (2) Tony English, Mark Kinsella.
Hat-tricks for: (1) Steve Brown (v Bury).
Hat-tricks against: (2) Adrian Foster (Torquay), Chris Pike (Hereford).
Leading scorer: Steve Brown (13).

Appearances and Goals

Player	App Lge	Sub	LC	Sub	FAC	Sub	AT	Sub	Goals Lge	LC	FAC	AT	Tot
Abrahams, Paul	1	3											
Allpress, Tim	21	8					2						
Ball, Steve	27	5	2				3	1	2				2
Barada, Taylor	1												
Basham, Michael	1												
Bennett, Gary	3	1			2								
Betts, Simon	31	2	1				3		1				1
Booty, Justin					1		1						
Brown, Ian	4								1				1
Brown, Steve	30	4			1		3		11	1		1	13
Campbell, Sean	1	3					1						
Cawley, Peter	36				1		4		1				1
Cheesewright, John	17						1						
Cook, Jason	1		1										
Cook, Tony	1	1											
Desborough, Mike													
Dickens, Alan	28	4			1		3		3				3
English, Tony	42		2		1		4		4		1		5
Fry, Chris	12	5											
Gentle, Justin													
Grainger, Martin	5	3					2		1				1
Hyslop, Christian	8												
Keeley, John	15		2				2						
Kinsella, Mark	42		2		1		3		8		1	1	10
Locke, Adam	4						1						
McDonough, Roy	36		2		1		3		7	1			8
McGavin, Steve	20	1	2		1		3		1		1		2
Morrow, Grant							1		1				1
Munson, Nathan	2	1					1						
Richardson, John	1	7					2						
Roberts, Paul	21	2					2		2				2
Sheffield, John	6												
Smith, Nicky	29	10	2				2		1				1
Watts, Grant	8	4							2				2
Whitton, Steve	8								2				2
(own-goals)									4				4
35 players used	462	63	22	3	11	3	44	5	56	2	3	3	64

ENDSLEIGH LEAGUE DIVISION 3

Manager: George Burley ⇒ Steve Wignall

SEASON 1994-95

#	H/A	Date	Opponents	Res	F-A	Att	Scorers	1	2	3	4	5	6	7	8	9	10	11	Subs (2)
1	H	13/8	TORQUAY	L	1-3	3,175	Kinsella	Ch'sewright	**Culling**	**Dalli***	English	**Caesar**	**Dennis**	Fry	Brown	Whitton	Kinsella	Abrahams	Allpress
2	A	20/8	MANSFIELD	L	0-2	2,247		Ch'sewright	Culling	**Davis**	Allpress	Caesar	English	Dennis	Brown	Whitton	Kinsella*	Abrahams	Fry
3	A	27/8	DONCASTER	L	0-3	2,320		Ch'sewright	Burley	Davis	Allpress	Caesar	Dennis	**Putney**	Brown	Whitton	Kinsella	Abrahams	
4	A	30/8	EXETER	L	0-1	1,804		Ch'sewright	Burley	Davis	Allpress	Caesar*	Dennis	Putney	Brown	Whitton	Kinsella	Abrahams	Fry/Partner
5	A	3/9	SCARBOROUGH	W	1-0	1,494	Dennis	Ch'sewright	English	Davis	Cawley	Caesar	Dennis	Putney	Brown*	Whitton	Kinsella	Abrahams*	Fry
6	H	10/9	HARTLEPOOL	W	1-0	2,428	Whitton	Ch'sewright	Burley	English	Cawley	Caesar	Dennis	Putney	Brown	Whitton	Kinsella	Abrahams*	**Allen**
7	H	13/9	WALSALL	W	3-2	2,239	Kinsella 2, Whitton	Ch'sewright	Burley	English	Cawley	Caesar	Dennis	Putney*	Brown	Whitton	Kinsella	Abrahams*	**Betts**
8	A	17/9	TORQUAY	D	3-3	3,390	Whitton, Brown, Dennis	Ch'sewright	Betts	English	Cawley	Caesar	Dennis	Putney	Brown*	Whitton	Kinsella	Abrahams*	Burley
9	A	24/9	DARLINGTON	W	3-2	2,260	Whitton 2, Brown	Ch'sewright	Betts	English	Cawley	Caesar	Dennis	Putney	Brown*	Whitton	Kinsella	Fry^	Locke/Allen
10	H	1/10	BURY	W	2-0	3,286	Cawley	Ch'sewright	Betts	English	Cawley	Caesar	Dennis	Locke	Brown	Whitton	Kinsella	Abrahams	
11	H	8/10	CHESTERFIELD	L	0-3	3,476		Ch'sewright	Betts	English	Cawley*	Caesar	Dennis	Putney	Brown	Whitton	Kinsella	Abrahams^	Fry/Burley
12	A	15/10	CARLISLE	D	0-0	5,817		Ch'sewright	Betts	English	Cawley	Caesar	Dennis^	Putney	Brown	Whitton	Kinsella	Fry^	Abrahams/Locke
13	H	22/10	PRESTON	W	3-1	3,015	Brown 2, Whitton	Ch'sewright	Betts	English	Cawley	Caesar	Locke	Putney	Brown	Whitton	Kinsella	Fry^	Abrahams
14	H	29/10	WIGAN	W	2-1	1,621	Kinsella, Fry	Ch'sewright	Betts	English	Cawley	Caesar	Locke	Putney	Brown	Whitton	Kinsella	Fry*	Dennis/Abrahams
15	H	5/11	GILLINGHAM	D	2-2	3,817	Fry, Kinsella	Ch'sewright	Betts	English	Cawley	Caesar	Locke*	Putney	Brown	Whitton	Kinsella	Abrahams	Fry
16	H	19/11	ROCHDALE	D	0-0	1,903		Ch'sewright	Betts	English	Cawley	Caesar	Locke	Putney	Brown	Whitton	Kinsella	Abrahams	Fry
17	H	26/11	SCUNTHORPE	W	4-2	2,904	Brown, Abrahams 2, Whitton	Ch'sewright	Betts	Dennis	Cawley	Caesar	Dennis*	Putney	Brown	Whitton	Kinsella	Abrahams	
18	A	10/12	MANSFIELD	D	1-1	3,016	Fry	Ch'sewright	Betts	English	Cawley	Caesar	Locke	Fry	Brown	Whitton	Kinsella	Abrahams	
19	H	16/12	DONCASTER	W	2-1	2,460	Cawley, Brown	Ch'sewright	Burley	Betts	Dennis	Caesar^	Locke	Fry	Brown*	Whitton	Kinsella*	Dennis	Abrahams/Allpress
20	A	26/12	NORTHAMPTON	L	0-1	5,064		Ch'sewright	Betts	English	Dennis	Caesar	Locke	Putney	Brown*	Whitton	Kinsella	Abrahams	Fry
21	A	27/12	FULHAM	W	2-1	4,243	Kinsella, Blake(og)	Ch'sewright	Betts	English	Dennis	Caesar	Locke !	Putney*	Brown*	Whitton	Kinsella	Fry	Abrahams/Allpress
22	A	31/12	HEREFORD	D	2-2	3,322	Stoneman, Whitton	Ch'sewright	Betts	**Stoneman**	Cawley	Caesar	Locke	Putney*	Brown	Whitton	Kinsella	Fry*	Abrahams/Allpress
23	A	2/1	PRESTON	L	1-2	6,377	Fry	Ch'sewright^	Betts	English !	English !	Caesar	Locke	Putney	Brown	Whitton	Kinsella	Abrahams*	Fry/Emberson
24	H	14/1	BARNET	D	1-1	3,706	Putney	Emberson	Betts	Stoneman	Cawley	Caesar	Locke	Putney*	Dennis	**Thompson***	Kinsella	Abrahams	Fry
25	H	28/1	WIGAN	L	0-1	3,067		Emberson	Betts	Stoneman	Cawley	Caesar	Locke	Putney*	Dennis	Thompson^	Kinsella	Abrahams	
26	A	4/2	SCUNTHORPE	W	4-3	2,748	Locke, English, Thompson 2	Emberson	English	Betts	Cawley	Caesar	Locke*	Fry	Dennis	Whitton	Kinsella*	Brown	Thompson
27	A	11/2	ROCHDALE	D	0-0	3,080		Emberson	English	English	English	Caesar	Locke	Fry	Dennis	Whitton^	Kinsella	Thompson	Allpress/Abrahams
28	A	18/2	BARNET	W	1-0	2,242	Asaba	Emberson	Locke	Betts	English	Caesar	Dennis	Fry	Brown	Whitton^	Kinsella	Abrahams*	Allpress/Thompson
29	H	21/2	LINCOLN	L	0-2	1,969		Emberson	Locke	Betts	English	Caesar	Dennis	Fry	**Asaba**	Whitton*	Kinsella	Abrahams	Lock
30	H	25/2	BURY	L	1-4	2,484	Fry	Emberson	Locke	Betts	English	Caesar	Dennis	Fry	Asaba	Whitton*	Kinsella	Abrahams*	Allpress
31	H	4/3	DARLINGTON	W	1-0	6,055	Asaba	Emberson	Locke	Betts	Cawley*	Caesar	Dennis	Fry	Putney !	Whitton*	Kinsella	Asaba	Brown
32	A	11/3	HARTLEPOOL	L	1-3	1,371	Fry	Emberson	Betts	Betts^	Cawley^	Caesar	Dennis	Fry*	Brown^	Whitton^	Kinsella*	**Williams**	Allpress/Thompson
33	H	18/3	EXETER	W	3-1	2,375	Thompson, Betts(p), Lock	Emberson	Betts	**Gibbs**	English	**McCarthy**	Dennis	Fry	Thompson	Whitton*	Kinsella	Williams^	**Lock**
34	A	25/3	SCARBOROUGH	L	0-2	3,025		Emberson	Betts	Gibbs	English	McCarthy	Caesar	Putney*	Asaba	Whitton	Kinsella	Williams*	Thomps'n/**Cheeth'm**
35	A	1/4	WALSALL	L	0-2	3,622		Emberson	Betts	Gibbs	McCarthy	Caesar	Dennis	Cheetham	Locke	Asaba^	Kinsella	Asaba	
36	A	8/4	HEREFORD	L	0-3	1,669		Emberson	English	English	McCarthy	Caesar	Dennis	Cheetham	Putney	Whitton	Kinsella	Whitton	Fry/Thompson
37	H	11/4	GILLINGHAM	W	3-1	3,328	Betts(p), Thompson 2	Emberson	Kinsella	Betts	McCarthy	Caesar	Putney	Fry^	English	Asaba*	Cheetham	Gibbs*	**Reinelt**/Thompson
38	H	15/4	FULHAM	W	5-2	3,448	Cheetham, English, Caesar, Fry 2	Emberson	Kinsella	Betts^	McCarthy	Caesar	Putney	Fry	English	Gibbs	Cheetham	Whitton^	Reinelt/Thompson
39	A	17/4	NORTHAMPTON	D	1-1	5,011	Whitton	Emberson	Kinsella	Gibbs	McCarthy	Caesar*	Putney	Fry	English	Gibbs	Cheetham	Whitton	Asaba/Thompson
40	H	22/4	LINCOLN	L	1-2	2,654	McCarthy	Emberson	Kinsella	Betts	McCarthy	Caesar	Dennis	Fry*	English	Reinelt*	Cheetham	Whitton	Asaba/Reinelt
41	H	29/4	CARLISLE	L	0-1	3,333		Emberson	Kinsella	Betts	McCarthy	Caesar	Dennis	Putney	Fry	Reinelt	Cheetham	Whitton	Asaba
42	A	6/5	CHESTERFIELD	D	2-2	4,133	Whitton, Putney 65(p)	Emberson	Kinsella	Betts	McCarthy	Caesar	Dennis	Fry*	Putney*	Reinelt	Cheetham	Whitton	Gibbs

COCA-COLA (LEAGUE) CUP

		Date	Opponent	Att		Score	Scorers
1:1	H	16/8	BRENTFORD	2,521	L	0-2	
1:2	A	23/8	BRENTFORD	2,315	L	0-2	

FA CUP

		Date	Opponent	Att		Score	Scorers
1	A	12/11	YEADING	1,780	D	2-2	Whitton, Abrahams
1R	H	22/11	YEADING	4,016	W	7-1	Abrahams 2, Whitton 2, Brown 2, Kin'[sella]
2	A	3/12	EXETER	3,528	W	2-1	Whitton, English
3	A	7/1	WIMBLEDON	6,903	L	0-1	

AUTO WINDSCREENS SHIELD

		Date	Opponent	Att		Score	Scorers
1	H	27/9	LEYTON ORIENT	1,486	W	1-0	Abrahams
1	A	8/11	FULHAM	1,451	L	2-3	Abrahams, Kinsella

Line-ups

Match	1	2	3	4	5	6	7	8	9	10	11	Subs used
LC 1:1	Ch'sewright	Culling	Dennis	Caesar	Allpress	English	Fry*	Brown	Whitton	Kinsella	Abrahams	Roberts
LC 1:2	Emberson	English*	Dennis	Caesar	Allpress	Davis	Roberts	Brown	Whitton	Kinsella	Abrahams	Burley
FA 1	Emberson	Betts	Dennis	Caesar	Cawley	English	Locke	Brown	Whitton	Kinsella	Abrahams	Dennis/Thompson
FA 1R	Ch'sewright	Betts	Locke*	Caesar	Cawley	English	Fry	Brown^	Whitton^	Kinsella	Abrahams	Dennis/Fry
FA 2	Ch'sewright	Betts	Locke	Caesar	Cawley	English	Putney*	Brown	Whitton	Kinsella	Abrahams	Dennis
FA 3	Ch'sewright	Betts	Locke	Caesar	Cawley	English	Putney	Brown	Whitton	Kinsella	Abrahams*	
AWS 1 H	Ch'sewright	Betts	Dennis	Caesar	Cawley	English	Locke	Brown	Whitton	Kinsella	Abrahams	
AWS 1 A	Ch'sewright	Betts	Dennis	Caesar	Cawley	English	Locke	Brown*	Whitton	Kinsella	Abrahams^	Fry/Burley

League table

	Team	P		Home						Away				Pts
			W	D	L	F	A	W	D	L	F	A		
1	Carlisle	42	14	5	2	34	14	13	5	3	33	17		91
2	Walsall	42	15	3	3	42	18	8	8	4	33	22		83
3	Chesterfield*	42	11	7	3	26	10	12	5	4	36	27		81
4	Bury	42	13	7	1	39	13	10	4	7	34	23		80
5	Preston	42	13	3	5	37	17	6	7	8	21	24		67
6	Mansfield	42	10	5	6	45	27	6	6	9	39	32		65
7	Scunthorpe	42	12	2	7	40	30	6	6	9	28	33		62
8	Fulham	42	11	5	5	39	22	6	9	7	21	32		62
9	Doncaster	42	9	5	7	28	20	8	5	8	30	23		61
10	COLCHESTER	42	9	7	5	29	30	8	5	8	27	34		58
11	Barnet	42	8	7	6	37	27	7	4	10	19	36		56
12	Lincoln	42	8	7	6	34	22	5	4	12	20	33		56
13	Torquay	42	10	8	3	35	25	4	5	12	19	32		55
14	Wigan	42	7	6	8	28	30	7	4	8	25	30		52
15	Rochdale	42	8	6	7	25	23	4	8	9	19	44		50
16	Hereford	42	9	6	6	22	19	3	7	11	23	43		49
17	Northampton	42	8	5	8	25	29	5	9	10	20	38		44
18	Hartlepool	42	8	7	6	33	32	2	5	14	10	37		43
19	Gillingham	42	8	7	6	31	25	2	4	15	15	39		41
20	Darlington	42	7	5	9	25	24	4	3	14	18	33		41
21	Scarborough	42	4	7	10	25	31	6	3	11	23	39		34
22	Exeter	42	5	5	11	25	36	3	5	13	11	34		34
		924	209	121	132	705	524	132	121	209	524	705		1265

* promoted after play-offs

Odds & ends

Double wins: (3) Darlington, Fulham, Scunthorpe.

Double defeats: (0).

Won from behind: (5) Walsall (h), Fulham (a), Scunthorpe (a), Gillingham (a), Fulham (h).

Lost from in front: (1) Torquay (h).

High spots: The autumn rise up the table prior to Burley's exit.
The emphatic 7-1 win over Yeading in the FA Cup.
A fine display, and support, at Premiership Wimbledon in the FA Cup.
The remarkable comeback from 0-3 down to win at Scunthorpe.
The success of the 'free admission' experiment versus Darlington.

Low spots: Six straight defeats at the beginning of the season.
The acrimonious departure of manager Burley in December.
Failure to win any of the last four games, to miss the play-offs again.
Half-a-dozen misses from the penalty spot.

Player of the Year: Steve Whitton.
Ever presents: (1) Mark Kinsella.
Hat-tricks for: (0).
Hat-tricks against: (1) Nicky Southall (Hartlepool).
Leading scorer: Steve Whitton (13).

Appearances and Goals

Player	Appearances								Goals					
	Lge	Sub	LC	Sub	FAC	Sub	AS	Sub	Lge	Sub	LC	FAC	AS	Tot
Abrahams, Paul	20	8	2		4		2		2			3	2	7
Allen, Leighton														
Allpress, Tim	3		2											
Asaba, Carl	9								2					2
Betts, Simon	34	1			4		2		2					2
Brown, Steve	26	2	2		4		2		6			2		8
Burley, George	5	2						1						
Caesar, Gus	39		2		4		2		1					1
Cawley, Peter	23				4		2							
Cheesewright, John	23		1		3		2							
Cheetham, Michael	8	7		1					1					1
Culling, Gary	2		1											
Dalli, Jean	1													
Davis, Aaron	4	1	1											
Dennis, Tony	32	1	2	3	1	2	2		2					2
Emberson, Carl	19	1	1		1									
English, Tony	33	2	2		4	1	2		2			1		3
Fry, Chris	24	9	1	1	1	1		1	1					1
Gibbs, Paul	8	1												
Kinsella, Mark	42		2		4		2					1	1	9
Lock, Tony		3												
Locke, Adam	20	2	1		4		2							1
McCarthy, Tony	10													
Partner, Andy		1												
Putney, Trevor	28				2				2					2
Reinelt, Robbie	2	3												1
Roberts, Danny			1	1										
Stoneman, Paul	3								1					1
Thompson, Niall	5	8		1					5					5
Whitton, Steve	36		2		4		2		9			4		13
Williams, Martin	3	2							1					1
(own-goals)														1
31 players used	462	56	22	2	44	5	22	2	56	2		11	3	70

ENDSLEIGH LEAGUE DIVISION 3 Manager: Steve Wignall SEASON 1995-96

#		Date	Opponents	Att		F-A	Scorers	1	2	3	4	5	6	7	8	9	10	11	Subs (3)
1	H	12/8	PLYMOUTH	3,585	W	2-1	Betts, Locke	Emberson	Locke	Betts	McCarthy	Caesar	Cawley	Kinsella	English !	Whitton	Adcock	Cheetham*	Dennis
2	A	19/8	BARNET	1,966	D	1-1	Adcock	Emberson	Locke	Betts	McCarthy	Caesar	Cawley	Kinsella	English	Whitton	Adcock*	Cheetham	Reinelt
3	H	26/8	LINCOLN	2,939	W	3-0	Dennis 2, Mardenborough	Emberson	Locke	Betts	McCarthy	Caesar^	Cawley	Kinsella	Dennis	Whitton	Adcock	Cheetham*	Fry/**Mardenborough**
4	A	29/8	CAMBRIDGE U	3,476	L	1-3	Adcock	Emberson	Locke	Betts	McCarthy	English	Cawley !	Kinsella	Dennis^	Whitton	Adcock	Cheetham*	English/Mardenborough
5	H	2/9	GILLINGHAM	7,667	W	1-0	Adcock	Emberson	Locke	Betts	McCarthy	English	Cawley	Kinsella	Dennis	Whitton	Adcock	Cheetham*	Mardenborough
6	H	9/9	CHESTER	3,422	L	1-2	Whitton	Emberson	Locke*	Betts	McCarthy	English	Cawley	Kinsella	Dennis	Whitton	Adcock	Cheetham^	Fry/Reinelt
7	A	12/9	PRESTON	2,869	D	2-2	Fry, Whitton	Emberson	Locke*	Betts	McCarthy	English	Fry	Kinsella	Dennis^	Whitton*	Adcock	Cheetham	Reinelt
8	A	16/9	DARLINGTON	1,695	D	2-2	Dennis, Cheetham	Emberson	Fry	Betts	McCarthy	English	Cawley	Kinsella	Dennis	Whitton*	Adcock	Cheetham	Mardenborough/Gibbs
9	H	23/9	HEREFORD	2,596	W	2-0	Reinelt 2	Emberson	Locke*	Betts	McCarthy	English	Cawley	Kinsella	Fry^	Reinelt*	Adcock	Cheetham^	Mardenborough/Gibbs
10	A	30/9	SCUNTHORPE	2,051	L	0-1		Emberson	Locke"	Betts	McCarthy	English	Cawley	Kinsella	Fry^	Reinelt*	Adcock	Cheetham	Mardenborough/Gibbs/Ball
11	H	7/10	HARTLEPOOL	2,618	W	4-1	Locke 2, Adcock, Reinelt	Emberson	Locke"	Betts	McCarthy	English	Cawley	Kinsella^	Fry	Reinelt	Adcock	Cheetham*	Mardenborough/Gibbs/Dennis
12	A	14/10	ROCHDALE	2,193	D	1-1	Reinelt	Emberson	Locke"	Betts	McCarthy	English	Cawley	Kinsella^	Fry !	Reinelt	Adcock	Cheetham*	Dennis
13	H	21/10	NORTHAMPTON	3,823	W	1-0	Kinsella	Emberson	Fry	Betts	McCarthy	Caesar*	Cawley	Kinsella	English	Reinelt	Adcock	Cheetham	Gibbs/**Boyce**
14	A	28/10	CARDIFF	3,207	W	2-1	Adcock 2	Emberson	English	Betts	McCarthy	Caesar	Cawley	Kinsella*	Dennis	Mardenboro'^	Adcock	Cheetham*	Lewis
15	H	31/10	FULHAM	2,870	D	1-1	Mardenborough	Emberson	Betts	Gibbs	McCarthy	English	Cawley	Kinsella	Dennis !	Mardenboro'^	Adcock	Cheetham	Reinelt
16	H	4/11	EXETER	3,377	D	1-1	Kinsella	Emberson	Fry	Betts	McCarthy	Caesar	Cawley	Kinsella	English	Mardenboro'*	Adcock	Cheetham*	Boyce
17	A	18/11	DONCASTER	1,603	L	2-3	Cheetham, Adcock	Emberson	Fry	Betts	McCarthy	Caesar	Cawley	Kinsella	English	Reinelt^	Adcock	Cheetham*	Gibbs/Mardenborough
18	A	25/11	MANSFIELD	2,819	L	1-3	Adcock(p)	Emberson	Fry	Betts*	McCarthy	Greene	Cawley	Kinsella	English	Reinelt^	Adcock	Cheetham*	**Duguid**
19	H	9/12	HEREFORD	3,324	D	1-1	Betts	Emberson	Fry	Betts	McCarthy	Greene	Cawley	Kinsella	English	Ball*	Adcock	Cheetham	Dennis
20	H	16/12	SCUNTHORPE	2,138	W	2-1	Ball, Kinsella	Emberson	Fry	Betts	McCarthy	Greene	Cawley	Kinsella	English	Ball*	Adcock	Cheetham^	Dennis
21	A	23/12	BURY	3,559	D	0-0		Emberson	Fry	Betts	McCarthy	Greene	Cawley	Kinsella	English	Ball*	Adcock	Cheetham	Dennis
22	H	26/12	LEYTON ORIENT	4,965	D	0-0		Emberson	Fry	Betts	McCarthy	Greene	Cawley	Kinsella	English	Fry	Adcock	Cheetham^	Dennis/Locke
23	A	1/1	TORQUAY	2,425	W	3-2	Kinsella, Duguid, Betts	Emberson	Dennis*	Betts	McCarthy	Greene	Cawley	Kinsella	English	Fry	Adcock	Abrahams	Duguid
24	H	13/1	BARNET	3,252	W	3-2	Betts(p), Abrahams 2	Emberson	Fry	Betts	McCarthy	Greene	Cawley	Kinsella	Locke^	Abrahams*	Adcock	Cheetham	Duguid/Dennis
25	A	20/1	PLYMOUTH	5,800	D	1-1	Greene	Emberson	Fry	Betts	McCarthy	Greene	Cawley	Kinsella	Dennis	Abrahams	Adcock	Gregory*	Duguid
26	A	30/1	WIGAN	2,101	L	0-2		Emberson	Fry*	Betts	McCarthy	Greene	Cawley	Kinsella	Dennis^	Abrahams	Adcock	Gregory	Cheetham/Duguid
27	A	3/2	LINCOLN	2,531	D	0-0		Emberson	Locke	Betts	McCarthy	Caesar	Cawley	Kinsella	Ball*	Abrahams	Adcock	Gregory	Fry
28	H	6/2	SCARBOROUGH	2,299	D	1-1	Cawley	Emberson	Locke	Betts	McCarthy	Caesar	Cawley	Kinsella	Cheetham*	Abrahams	Adcock	Gregory^	Reinelt/Ball
29	H	10/2	WIGAN	3,082	L	1-2	Adcock	Emberson	Locke	Betts	McCarthy	Caesar	Cawley	Kinsella	Cheetham*	Abrahams	Adcock	Gregory^	Cheetham/Duguid/Gibbs
30	A	17/2	PRESTON	9,335	L	0-2		Emberson	Fry	Betts*	Caesar	McCarthy	Ball"	Kinsella	Dennis	Abrahams	Adcock	Gregory^	**McGleish**
31	H	24/2	DARLINGTON	2,653	D	1-1	Adcock	Emberson	Fry	Betts	Caesar	McCarthy	Locke*	Kinsella	Dennis	Duguid	Adcock	Gibbs	Cheetham
32	H	27/2	CHESTER	2,001	D	1-1	Gibbs	Emberson	Fry	Betts	McCarthy	Caesar	Cawley	Kinsella	Dennis	Duguid	Adcock	Gibbs*	McGleish/Gregory
33	A	2/3	LEYTON ORIENT	4,049	W	1-0	Adcock(p)	Emberson	Fry^	Betts	McCarthy	Caesar	Cawley	Kinsella	Dennis	Duguid	Adcock	Gibbs^	McGleish/Gregory
34	H	9/3	BURY	2,832	W	1-0	Caesar	Petterson	Fry	Betts	McCarthy	Caesar	Cawley	Kinsella	Dennis"	Duguid*	Adcock	Gibbs^	McGleish/Reinelt
35	A	16/3	SCARBOROUGH	1,201	D	0-0		Petterson	Fry	Betts	McCarthy	Caesar	Cawley	Kinsella	Dennis"	Duguid^	Adcock	Gibbs*	McGleish/Reinelt/Gregory
36	H	19/3	CAMBRIDGE U	2,995	D	2-1	Adcock, McGleish	Petterson	Fry	Betts	McCarthy	Caesar	Cawley	Kinsella !	Locke	Duguid*	Adcock	Gibbs^	McGleish/Gregory
37	A	23/3	TORQUAY	2,888	W	3-1	Fry, McGleish, Betts(p)	Petterson	Fry	Betts	McCarthy	Caesar	Cawley	Kinsella	Locke	McGleish	Adcock^	Gibbs*	Duguid/Whitton
38	A	30/3	HARTLEPOOL	1,364	L	1-2	Gibbs	Emberson	Fry	Betts	McCarthy	Caesar	Cawley	Kinsella	Locke !	McGleish*	Whitton"	Gibbs^	Reinelt/Duguid/**Dunne**
39	H	2/4	ROCHDALE	3,021	W	1-0	Reinelt	Emberson	Fry	Betts	McCarthy	Caesar	Cawley	Kinsella	Locke	McGleish	Whitton"	Gibbs	Reinelt
40	H	6/4	CARDIFF	3,345	W	1-0	Kinsella	Emberson	Fry	Betts	McCarthy	Caesar	Cawley	Kinsella	Locke*	McGleish^	Adcock^	Gibbs*	Gibbs/Dennis/Dunne
41	A	8/4	NORTHAMPTON	5,021	L	1-2	Reinelt	Emberson	Dunne	Betts	McCarthy	Caesar	Cawley"	Kinsella	Fry	McGleish*	Adcock	Reinelt	Reinelt
42	H	13/4	FULHAM	3,795	D	2-2	McGleish 2	Emberson	Fry^	Gibbs	McCarthy	Caesar*	Dennis	Kinsella	Dennis	McGleish	Adcock !	Gibbs	Gibbs
43	H	16/4	GILLINGHAM	4,952	D	1-1	McGleish	Emberson	Fry^	Betts	McCarthy	Caesar*	Cawley	Kinsella	English	McGleish	Adcock*	Reinelt	Dunne/Gibbs/Duguid
44	A	20/4	EXETER	2,788	D	2-2	Caesar, McGleish	Emberson	Fry	Betts	McCarthy	Dunne	Cawley	Kinsella	Dennis	McGleish	Reinelt	Duguid^	Locke/Gibbs
45	A	27/4	MANSFIELD	2,073	W	2-1	Reinelt, Dunne	Emberson	Fry*	Betts	McCarthy	Caesar*	Cawley	Kinsella	Dennis	McGleish	Reinelt	Duguid^	Locke/Gibbs
46	H	4/5	DONCASTER	5,038	W	1-0	Gibbs	Emberson	Fry	Betts	McCarthy	Caesar*	Cawley	Kinsella	Dennis	McGleish	Reinelt*	Gibbs	Locke/Whitton

DIVISION THREE PLAY-OFFS

		Date	Opponent	Att		Score	Scorers
S:1	H	12/5	PLYMOUTH	6,511	W	1-0	Kinsella
S:2	A	15/5	PLYMOUTH	14,525	L	1-3	Kinsella (lost 2-3 on aggregate)

COCA-COLA (LEAGUE) CUP

		Date	Opponent	Att		Score	Scorers
1:1	H	15/8	BRISTOL CITY	2,831	W	2-1	Adcock, Kinsella
1:2	A	22/8	BRISTOL CITY	3,648	L	1-2	Cheetham (aet; lost on penalties)

FA CUP

		Date	Opponent	Att		Score
3	A	11/11	GRAVESEND	3,218	L	0-2

AUTO WINDSCREENS SHIELD

		Date	Opponent	Att		Score	Scorers
1	H	26/9	TORQUAY	1,121	W	5-2	Adcock 3, Reinelt, Cawley
1	A	8/11	SWINDON	6,222	L	0-2	
2	A	28/11	OXFORD	1,943	W	2-1	Adcock, Betts(p)
3	A	9/1	PETERBOROUGH	2,460	L	2-3	Betts, Kinsella

Line-ups (subs marked *, ^, ")

Match	1	2	3	4	5	6	7	8	9	10	11	Subs
S:1	Emberson	Fry	Betts	McCarthy	Caesar"	Cawley	Kinsella	Dennis	McGleish	Reinelt^	Gibbs*	Locke/Whitton
S:2	Emberson	Fry	Betts	McCarthy	Caesar"	Cawley	Kinsella	Dennis	McGleish	Reinelt*	Gibbs^	Adcock/Whitton/Locke
1:1	Emberson	Locke	Betts	McCarthy	Caesar	Cawley	Kinsella	English	Whitton	Adcock	Cheetham	
1:2	Emberson	Locke	Betts	McCarthy	Caesar	Cawley	Kinsella	English	Whitton	Adcock*	Cheetham^	Reinelt/Fry
FA 3	Emberson	Fry	Betts	McCarthy	Caesar*	Cawley	Kinsella	English	Adcock	Cheetham		
AWS 1H	Emberson	Locke*	Betts	McCarthy	English	Cawley	Kinsella	Fry	Adcock	Cheetham	Ball*	
AWS 1A	Emberson	Betts	Gibbs	McCarthy	Lewis	Caesar*	Kinsella	Dennis	Mardenboro'/Adcock	Mardenboro'/Fry	Ball*	
AWS 2	Emberson	Fry	Betts	McCarthy	Greene	Cawley	Kinsella	English	Adcock	Abrahams*	Fry	
AWS 3	Emberson	Locke	Betts	McCarthy	Greene	Cawley	Kinsella	English	Adcock	Duguid	Fry	

League table — Division Three

		P	Home W	D	L	F	A	Away W	D	L	F	A	Pts
1	Preston	46	11	8	4	44	22	12	9	2	34	16	86
2	Gillingham	46	16	6	1	33	6	6	11	6	16	14	83
3	Bury	46	11	7	5	33	21	11	6	6	33	27	79
4	Plymouth*	46	14	5	4	41	20	8	7	8	27	29	78
5	Darlington	46	10	6	7	30	21	10	12	1	30	21	78
6	Hereford	46	13	5	5	40	22	7	9	7	25	25	74
7	COLCHESTER	46	13	7	3	37	22	5	11	7	24	29	72
8	Chester	46	11	9	3	45	22	7	7	9	27	31	70
9	Barnet	46	13	6	4	40	19	5	10	8	25	26	70
10	Wigan	46	15	3	5	36	21	5	7	11	26	35	70
11	Northampton	46	9	10	4	32	22	9	3	11	19	22	67
12	Scunthorpe	46	8	8	7	36	30	7	7	9	31	31	60
13	Doncaster	46	11	6	6	25	19	5	5	13	24	41	59
14	Exeter	46	9	9	5	25	22	4	9	10	21	31	57
15	Rochdale	46	7	8	8	32	33	7	5	11	25	28	55
16	Cambridge	46	8	8	7	34	30	6	4	13	27	41	54
17	Fulham	46	10	7	6	32	26	2	10	11	25	37	53
18	Lincoln	46	6	9	8	32	26	7	5	11	25	47	53
19	Mansfield	46	5	10	8	30	24	6	10	7	24	40	53
20	Hartlepool	46	8	9	6	30	24	4	4	15	11	41	49
21	Leyton Orient	46	11	7	5	27	24	1	4	18	17	39	47
22	Cardiff	46	8	6	9	24	22	3	6	14	17	42	45
23	Scarborough	46	5	4	14	22	28	6	3	14	17	41	40
24	Torquay	46	4	9	10	17	36	1	5	17	13	48	29
		1104	239	175	138	781	565	138	175	239	565	781	1481

* promoted after play-offs

Appearances & Goals

Player	Lge	Sub	LC	Sub	FAC	Sub	AS	Sub	G:Lge	LC	FAC	AS	Tot
Abrahams, Paul	8							1	2				2
Adcock, Tony	41	2	2		1		3		12	1		4	17
Ball, Steve	6	2				1	1		1				1
Betts, Simon	45		2		1		4		5			2	7
Boyce, Robert		2											
Caesar, Gus	23		2		1		1		2				2
Caldwell, Grant							1						
Cawley, Peter	42		2		1		3		1			1	2
Cheetham, Michael	25	3	2		1	1	3		1	1		1	3
Dennis, Tony	24	8	1				3		3				3
Duguid, Karl	7	9					1		1				1
Dunne, Joe	2	3											
Emberson, Carl	41		2		1		3						
English, Tony	20	1	2		1		3		1				1
Fry, Chris	35	3		1	1		3	1					
Gibbs, Paul	13	11					2		1			1	2
Greene, David	14						2		3				3
Gregory, David	7	3							1				1
Kinsella, Mark	45		2		1		4		5	1		1	7
Lewis, Ben	1	1											
Locke, Adam	22	1	2			1	2		3				3
Mardenboro', Steve	4	8			1		1		2				2
McCarthy, Tony	44		2		1		4						
McGleish, Scott	10	5					2		6				6
Petterson, Andy	5												
Reinelt, Robbie	12	10		1			1		7			1	8
Whitton, Stevo	10	2	2				2		2				2
27 players used	506	74	22	2	11	1	44	4	61	3	0	9	73

Odds & Ends

Double wins: (2) Cardiff, Torquay.

Double defeats (1) Wigan.

Won from behind: (2) Mansfield (a). Torquay (a).

Lost from in front: (1) Wigan (h).

High spots: Squeezing into the play-offs on the final day of the season.

A run of just two defeats in the last 16 League games.

The Auto Windscreens Shield victory away at Division Two Oxford.

Mark Kinsella's spectacular long-range goals.

Low spots: Plymouth's late play-off goal preventing a Wembley date.

A run of eight league games without a win from January 20.

The high number of suspensions and injuries.

The loss of the influential Steve Whitton to a serious injury.

Losing a Coca-Cola Cup penalty shoot-out at Bristol City.

FA Cup defeat at Beazer Homes Leaguers Gravesend & Northfleet.

Player of the Year: Mark Kinsella.

Ever presents: (0).

Hat-tricks: (1). Tony Adcock (v Torquay, AWS).

Hat-tricks against: (0).

Leading scorer: (17) Tony Adcock.

NATIONWIDE LEAGUE DIVISION 3   Manager: Steve Wignall   SEASON 1996-97

		Date	Opponents	Att		F-A	Scorers	1	2	3	4	5	6	7	8	9	10	11	Subs (3)
1	H	17/8	HARTLEPOOL	2,942	L	0-2		Caldwell	Betts	**Barnes**	McCarthy !	Greene	Cawley	Kinsella	Locke	Whitton	Adcock	Fry*	Reinelt
2	A	24/8	ROCHDALE	1,816	D	0-0		Caldwell	Dunne	Barnes	McCarthy	Greene	Cawley	Kinsella	Locke	Whitton	Adcock	Reinelt*	Fry
3	A	27/8	DARLINGTON	2,906	D	1-1	Locke	Caldwell	Dunne	Barnes	McCarthy	Greene	Cawley	Kinsella	Locke	Whitton	Adcock*	Wilkins	Reinelt
4	H	31/8	HEREFORD	2,723	D	1-1	Reinelt	Caldwell	Dunne	Betts	Gregory	Greene^	Cawley	Kinsella	Locke*	Whitton"	Reinelt	Wilkins	Reinelt/Fry
5	A	7/9	FULHAM	5,189	L	1-3	Whitton	Emberson	Dunne	Betts	Gregory^	Greene	Cawley	Kinsella	Locke*	Fry	Reinelt	Wilkins	Fry/Duguid/Adcock
6	H	10/9	BRIGHTON	2,540	W	2-0	Kinsella, Reinelt	Emberson	Dunne	Betts	McCarthy	Greene	Cawley	Kinsella	Reinelt	Fry	Adcock	Wilkins	Wilkins
7	H	14/9	HULL	3,073	D	1-1	Kinsella	Emberson	Dunne	Betts	McCarthy	Greene*	Cawley	Kinsella	Reinelt	Fry	Adcock	Wilkins	Wilkins
8	A	21/9	LEYTON ORIENT	5,264	D	1-1	Fry	Emberson	Dunne	Betts	McCarthy	Greene*	Cawley !	Locke	Reinelt*	Fry^	Adcock^	Wilkins*	Duguid
9	H	28/9	DONCASTER	2,672	D	2-2	Cawley, Adcock	Emberson	Dunne	Barnes"	McCarthy	Greene	Cawley	Locke	Reinelt*	Fry^	Adcock^	Wilkins*	Duguid/Gregory
10	A	1/10	CARLISLE	4,089	L	0-3		Emberson	Dunne	Barnes"	McCarthy	Greene	Cawley	Locke	Reinelt*	Fry"	Adcock^	Wilkins*	Whitton/Duguid/Gregory
11	A	4/10	SWANSEA	2,531	D	1-1	Greene	Emberson	Dunne	Barnes	Gregory	Greene	Cawley	Locke	Fry*	Whitton	Duguid	Wilkins	Reinelt
12	H	12/10	WIGAN	2,700	W	3-1	Adcock, Gregory, Duguid	Emberson	Dunne"	Betts	McCarthy	Greene	Gregory	Locke	Kelly*	Whitton	Duguid^	Wilkins	Adcock/Reinelt/Fry
13	H	15/10	BARNET	2,732	W	1-0	Fry	Emberson	Dunne	Betts	McCarthy	Greene	Cawley	Gregory	Kelly"	Whitton	Duguid^	Wilkins	Reinelt/Fry
14	A	19/10	NORTHAMPTON	4,119	L	1-2	Fry	Emberson	Dunne	Betts	McCarthy^	Greene^	Cawley	Gregory	Fry"	Whitton"	Duguid^	Wilkins	Adcock/Reinelt/Kelly
15	A	26/10	LINCOLN	2,769	L	2-3	Betts(p), Duguid(p)	Emberson	Dunne	Betts*	McCarthy	Greene^	Gregory	Fry	Wilkins	Whitton !	Duguid	Abrahams	Locke/Reinelt
16	H	29/10	EXETER	2,384	W	1-0	Myers(og)	Emberson	Dunne	Gibbs	McCarthy	Greene	Locke	Fry	Wilkins	Whitton	Duguid	Abrahams	
17	H	2/11	CARDIFF	3,226	D	1-1	Duguid	Emberson	Dunne	Gibbs	McCarthy"	Greene	Locke	Fry	Wilkins"	Whitton"	Duguid	Abrahams*	Adcock/Reinelt/Gregory
18	A	9/11	TORQUAY	2,251	W	2-0	Reinelt, Abrahams	Emberson	Gregory	Gibbs	Locke	Greene	Locke	Fry	Wilkins	Reinelt	Taylor	Abrahams	Locke/Dunne
19	H	19/11	SCUNTHORPE	1,842	D	1-1	Sertori(og)	Emberson	Dunne	Barnes	Gregory	Greene	Cawley	Abrahams	Wilkins	Taylor	Adcock^	Duguid*	Fry/Reinelt
20	A	22/11	CHESTER	2,028	W	2-1	Taylor 2	Emberson	Gregory	Barnes	Locke	Greene	Cawley	Fry	Wilkins	Whitton*	Taylor	Abrahams*	Gibbs
21	H	30/11	LINCOLN	2,738	W	7-1	Ab', Taylor(2p), Whit'n, Adcock, Fry 2	Emberson	Gregory	Barnes	Locke	Greene	Cawley	Fry*	Wilkins	Whitton*	Taylor	Abrahams	Adcock
22	A	3/12	SCARBOROUGH	1,605	D	1-1	Locke	Emberson	Gregory	Barnes	Locke	Greene	Buckle	Fry*	Wilkins	Whitton	Taylor	Abrahams	Dunne
23	H	14/12	MANSFIELD	1,653	D	1-1	Abrahams	Emberson	Gregory	Barnes	**Buckle**	Greene*	Cawley	Fry	Wilkins	Whitton*	Taylor	Abrahams^	Dunne
24	H	20/12	CAMBRIDGE U	3,707	D	2-2	Taylor, Adcock	Emberson	Gregory	Gibbs*	Buckle	Greene"	Cawley"	Fry	Wilkins	Whitton*	Taylor*	Abrahams^	Adcock/Duguid/Dunne
25	A	26/12	BRIGHTON	4,839	L	1-1	Whitton	Emberson	Gregory	Gibbs^	McCarthy	Greene	Buckle	Fry	Wilkins	Whitton"	Taylor*	Duguid"	Adcock/Dunne/Reinelt
26	A	1/1	DONCASTER	1,458	D	0-0		Emberson	Gregory	Gibbs^	McCarthy	Greene	Buckle	Fry	Wilkins	Whitton	Adcock	Abrahams^	Locke/Dunne
27	H	14/1	FULHAM	3,820	W	2-1	Abrahams, Fry	Emberson	Gregory	Gibbs	McCarthy	Greene !	Buckle	Fry	Wilkins	Whitton	Adcock	Abrahams	Locke
28	H	18/1	CARLISLE	3,588	D	1-1	Adcock(p)	Emberson	Gregory	Gibbs	McCarthy	Greene	Buckle	Fry	Wilkins	Whitton	Adcock	Abrahams*	Locke/Reinelt !
29	A	25/1	EXETER	2,666	W	3-0	Abrahams, Locke 2	Emberson	Gregory	Gibbs	McCarthy	Greene	Buckle	Fry	Wilkins	Locke	Adcock	Abrahams^	Lock/Dunne
30	H	31/1	TORQUAY	3,895	W	2-0	Adcock 2	Caldwell	Gregory	Gibbs	McCarthy	Cawley^	Buckle	Locke*	Wilkins	Whitton	Adcock	Abrahams	Reinelt/Dunne
31	H	4/2	LEYTON ORIENT	3,689	W	2-1	Wilkins 2	Vaughan	Gregory	Gibbs	McCarthy	Cawley	Buckle	Locke*	Wilkins	Whitton"	Adcock*	Abrahams^	Fry
32	A	8/2	CARDIFF	3,912	W	2-1	Adcock, Whitton	Vaughan	Gregory	Gibbs	McCarthy	Greene	Buckle	Fry*	Wilkins	Whitton	Adcock*	Abrahams^	Lock/Locke
33	A	14/2	CHESTER	3,855	D	0-0		Vaughan	Gregory	Gibbs*	McCarthy	Greene	Buckle	Fry*	Wilkins	Whitton	Adcock	Abrahams^	Lock/Locke
34	H	22/2	SCUNTHORPE	2,738	L	1-2	Whitton	Vaughan	Gregory	Gibbs*	McCarthy	Greene	Buckle	Fry	Wilkins	Locke	Adcock"	Abrahams^	Dunne/Lock/Whitton
35	A	28/2	SCARBOROUGH	3,719	L	1-3	Adcock	Vaughan	Gregory	Gibbs*	McCarthy	Greene	Buckle	Fry	Wilkins^	Whitton	Adcock"	Abrahams^	Duguid/Locke
36	H	7/3	CAMBRIDGE U	3,495	L	0-1		Emberson	Gregory	Dunne	McCarthy	Greene	Buckle	Fry*	Wilkins	Whitton	Adcock	Abrahams	Abrahams
37	H	14/3	MANSFIELD	3,064	W	2-1	Greene, Adcock	Emberson	Gregory*	Gibbs	McCarthy	Greene*	Buckle"	Fry*	Wilkins	Whitton"	Adcock	Sale	Dunne/**Pitcher**/Locke
38	A	21/3	ROCHDALE	3,211	W	1-0	Abrahams	Emberson	Gregory	Gibbs	McCarthy	Greene"	Buckle	Fry"	Wilkins	Whitton"	Adcock*	Sale	Abrahams/Duguid/D'nne
39	A	29/3	HARTLEPOOL	2,725	L	0-1		Emberson	Gregory	Gibbs^	McCarthy !	Greene	Buckle	Fry*	Wilkins*	Whitton*	Adcock*	Abrahams"	Adcock/**Stamps**/Dune
40	H	31/3	DARLINGTON	3,604	L	0-3		Emberson	Gregory	Stamps	McCarthy	Greene	Buckle	Fry"	Wilkins	Whitton*	Adcock	Sale	Abrahams/Gibbs
41	A	5/4	HEREFORD	2,535	L	0-1		Emberson	Dunne	Stamps	McCarthy	Greene"	Cawley"	Buckle	Wilkins	Whitton	Sale*	Sale	Adcock^/Dunne/Fry
42	H	8/4	WIGAN	4,571	L	0-1		Emberson	Dunne	Stamps	McCarthy	Greene	Cawley	Buckle	Duguid^	Whitton	Sale*	Abrahams"	Adcock^/Fry/Gregory
43	H	11/4	SWANSEA	3,162	W	3-1	Whitton, Sale, Abrahams	Emberson	Dunne	Stamps	McCarthy	Greene	Cawley	Buckle	Sale	Whitton	Adcock*	Abrahams"	Fry/Duguid
44	A	15/4	HULL	2,035	W	2-1	Adcock, Sale	Emberson	Dunne	Stamps	McCarthy	Greene	Cawley	Buckle	Sale	Whitton	Adcock*	Abrahams"	Locke/Fry
45	H	26/4	NORTHAMPTON	5,956	D	0-0		Emberson	Dunne^	Stamps	McCarthy*	Greene	Cawley	Wilkins	Sale	Whitton	Buckle	Abrahams"	Locke/Gregory/Lock
46	A	3/5	BARNET	1,909	W	4-2	Lock, Sale, Forbes, Haydon	Emberson	Dunne	Stamps	**Forbes***	Greene	Cawley	Wilkins	Sale	Locke^	Buckle	Lock	McCarthy/**Haydon**

COCA-COLA (LEAGUE) CUP

		Date	Opponent	Res		Att	Scorers
1:1	H	20/8	WEST BROM	L	2-3	2,466	Kinsella, Fry
1:2	A	3/9	WEST BROM	W	3-1	(lost 4-5 on agg.) 9,809	Reinelt 2, Dunne
2:1	A	17/9	HUDDERSFIELD	D	1-1	5,112	Adcock
2:2	H	24/9	HUDDERSFIELD	L	0-2	(lost 1-3 on aggregate) 4,095	Wilkins

FA CUP

		Date	Opponent	Res		Att	Scorers
1	H	16/11	WYCOMBE	L	1-2	4,376	Wilkins

AUTO WINDSCREENS SHIELD

		Date	Opponent	Res		Att	Scorers
1	A	10/12	CAMBRIDGE U	W	1-0	1,108	Whitton
2	A	7/1	MILLWALL	W	3-2	2,759	Adcock 2, Buckle
3	A	28/1	BRENTFORD	W	1-0	2,253	Abrahams
4	H	18/2	NORTHAMPTON	W	2-1	3,978	Greene, Buckle
S1	A	11/3	PETERBOROUGH	L	0-2	4,556	
S2	H	18/3	PETERBOROUGH	W	3-0	5,000	Fry, Buc', Ab' (won on 'golden goal')
F	N	20/4	CARLISLE	D	0-0	45,077	(at Wembley) (lost 3-4 on penalties)

Line-ups (read left to right)

Match	Starting XI / substitutes
Cola 1:1	Whitton, Adcock, Reinelt, Locke, Kinsella, Cawley, McCarthy, Betts*, Caldwell … Fry; sub Fry
Cola 1:2	Whitton, Reinelt*, Locke, Kinsella, Cawley, Gregory, Dunne, Caldwell*, Fry*; sub Adcock/Fry
Cola 2:1	Fry*, Adcock^, Wilkins, Reinelt, Kinsella, Cawley, McCarthy, Dunne, Emberson; sub Locke/Duguid
Cola 2:2	Fry, Adcock^, Wilkins, Reinelt, Locke, Cawley, McCarthy, Dunne", Emberson; sub Whitton/Duguid/Gregory
FA 1	Wilkins, Locke, Abrahams, Gibbs, Greene, McCarthy, Dunne, Emberson, Reinelt^, Cawley, Fry
AWS 1	Whitton, Taylor, Abrahams, Wilkins, Greene, McCarthy, Gregory, Emberson, Betts, Buckle, Cawley
AWS 2	Whitton, Adcock, Abrahams, Wilkins, Fry*, Greene, Gregory, Emberson, Gibbs, Buckle, Cawley; sub Cawley/Lock
AWS 3	Locke, Adcock, Abrahams, Wilkins, Fry*, Cawley, McCarthy, Gregory, Emberson, Buckle; sub Sale/Gibbs
AWS 4	Locke, Adcock, Abrahams^, Fry*, Greene, McCarthy, Gregory, Emberson, Dunne, Gibbs*, Buckle; sub Abrahams/Locke
AWS S1	Whitton, Adcock, Duguid^, Sale, Fry*, Greene, McCarthy, Gregory, Emberson, Gibbs*, Buckle; sub Fry/Locke/Duguid
AWS S2	Whitton*, Adcock, Sale, Fry, Greene, McCarthy, Gregory, Emberson, Dunne, Gibbs*, Cawley
AWS F	Whitton, Adcock^, Abrahams", Sale, Wilkins, Greene, Gregory^, Dunne, Emberson, Gibbs*, Cawley; sub Adcock/Duguid

League table

		P	W	D	L	F	A	W	D	L	F	A	Pts
1	Wigan	46	17	3	3	53	21	9	6	8	31	30	87
2	Fulham	46	13	5	5	41	20	12	7	4	31	18	87
3	Carlisle	46	16	3	4	41	21	8	9	6	26	23	84
4	Northampton*	46	14	4	5	43	17	6	8	9	24	27	72
5	Swansea	46	13	5	5	37	20	8	3	12	25	38	71
6	Chester	46	11	8	4	30	16	7	8	8	25	27	70
7	Cardiff	46	11	4	8	30	23	9	5	9	26	31	69
8	COLCHESTER	46	11	9	3	35	23	8	4	11	26	28	68
9	Lincoln	46	10	8	5	35	25	8	4	11	35	44	66
10	Cambridge	46	11	5	7	30	27	7	6	10	23	32	65
11	Mansfield	46	9	8	6	21	17	7	8	8	26	28	64
12	Scarborough	46	9	5	9	36	31	7	6	10	29	37	63
13	Scunthorpe	46	11	3	9	36	33	7	6	10	23	29	63
14	Rochdale	46	10	6	7	34	24	4	10	9	24	34	58
15	Barnet	46	9	9	5	32	23	5	7	11	14	28	58
16	Leyton Orient	46	11	6	6	28	20	4	6	13	22	28	57
17	Hull	46	9	8	6	29	26	4	10	9	15	24	57
18	Darlington	46	11	5	7	37	28	3	5	15	27	50	52
19	Doncaster	46	9	7	7	29	23	5	3	15	23	43	52
20	Hartlepool	46	8	6	9	33	32	6	3	14	20	34	51
21	Torquay	46	9	4	10	24	24	4	7	12	22	38	50
22	Exeter	46	9	6	9	25	30	6	3	14	23	43	48
23	Brighton**	46	12	6	5	41	27	6	3	14	12	43	47
24	Hereford	46	6	8	9	26	25	5	6	12	24	40	47
		1104	256	148	148	807	576	148	148	256	576	807	1506

* promoted after play-offs
** 2 points deducted

Odds & Ends

Won from behind: (3) Wigan (h), Hull (a), Barnet (a).
Lost from in front: (3) Northampton (a), Lincoln (a), Scarborough (h).
High spots: Reaching Wembley to contest the AW Shield final.
Fine cup performances against four clubs from higher divisions.
The excellent 7-1 Layer Road victory over Lincoln.
Just one defeat in 22 League and cup games from 4 October.
Low spots: Failure to reach the play-offs by just one point.
The run of four straight defeats after qualifying for the Wembley final.
Losing at Wembley to Carlisle in a penalty shoot-out.
The bad start: only one win from the first 11 League games.
Picking up eight red cards in all competitions.

Player of the Year: Chris Fry
Ever presents: (0).
Hat-tricks for: (0).
Hat-tricks against: (1) Glenn Naylor (Darlington).
Leading scorer: Tony Adcock (14).

Appearances and Goals

	Appearances								Goals				
	Lge	Sub	LC	Sub	FAC	Sub	AS	Sub	Lge	LC	FAC	AS	Tot
Abrahams, Paul	27	7	3	1			5	1	7			2	9
Adcock, Tony	26	2	3	1	1		6	1	11			3	14
Barnes, David	11						1						
Betts, Simon	10		4						1				1
Buckle, Paul	24						2					3	3
Caldwell, Garrett	6		2										
Cawley, Peter	28	4			1		3		1				1
Duguid, Karl	10	10				1	1		3				3
Dunne, Joe	23	12	3		1		2			1			1
Emberson, Carl	35		2		1		6						
Forbes, Steve	1								1				1
Fry, Chris	31	11	2	2	1		6	1	6	1		1	8
Gibbs, Paul	18	2					5	1					
Greene, David	44		4		1		6		2			1	3
Gregory, David	32	6	1	1	1		7		1				1
Haydon, Nicky	2	1											
Kelly, Tony	7								1				1
Kinsella, Mark	1	5							1	1			2
Lock, Tony	22	10					4	3	1				1
Locke, Adam	34	1	3	1	1		5		4				4
McCarthy, Tony	8	13											
Pitcher, Geoff		1											
Reinelt, Robbie	10		4		1		2	1	3	2			5
Sale, Mark	7	1					3		3				3
Stamps, Scott	8												
Taylor, John	5						1		5				5
Vaughan, John	5						1						
Whitton, Steve	36	3	2	1			6		6			1	7
Wilkins, Richard	40	3	3		1		6		1	1	1		3
(own-goals)									2				2
29 players used	506	89	44	8	11	2	77	11	62				78

NATIONWIDE LEAGUE DIVISION 3 — Manager: Steve Wignall — SEASON 1997-98

No		Date	Opponents	Att	F-A	Scorers	1	2	3	4	5	6	7	8	9	10	11	Subs (3)
1	H	9/8	DARLINGTON	2,958	W 2:1	Abrahams, Buckle(p)	Emberson	Gregory D	Stamps	Skelton^	Greene	Cawley	Wilkins	Buckle	Sale*	Abrahams	**Hathaway**	Adcock/Forbes
2	A	16/8	HARTLEPOOL	2,174	L 2:3	Buckle(p), Abrahams	Emberson	Gregory D	Stamps	Skelton"	Greene	Cawley*	Wilkins	Buckle	Sale*	Abrahams	Hathaway^	Adcock/Lock/Forbes
3	H	22/8	BARNET	3,286	D 1:1	Wilkins	Emberson	Gregory D	Stamps	Skelton^	Greene	Cawley*	Wilkins	Buckle	Sale	Abrahams	Hathaway^	Adcock/Lock/Forbes
4	A	30/8	TORQUAY	2,081	D 1:1	Wilkins	Emberson	Gregory D	Stamps	Forbes	Greene	Cawley	Wilkins	Buckle^	Sale	Abrahams	Hathaway	Abrahams
5	A	2/9	CAMBRIDGE U	3,264	L 1:4	Gregory D	Emberson	Gregory D	Stamps	Forbes"	Greene	Cawley	Wilkins	Buckle^	Sale	Adcock*	Abrahams	Lock/Haydon/Whitton
6	H	8/9	BRIGHTON	3,081	W 3:1	Greene 2, Abrahams	Emberson	Gregory D	Stamps	Forbes^	Greene	Cawley	Wilkins	Buckle	Sale	Adcock*	Abrahams	Lock/Haydon
7	A	12/9	SCARBOROUGH	2,756	W 1:0	Lock	Emberson	Gregory D	Stamps	Forbes"	Greene	Cawley	Wilkins	Buckle	Sale	Adcock*	Abrahams	Lock/Hathaway
8	A	20/9	SWANSEA	2,414	W 1:0	Greene	Emberson	Gregory D	Stamps	Skelton*	Greene	Cawley	Wilkins	Buckle	Sale	Adcock^	Abrahams	Lock/Whitton
9	H	27/9	EXETER	3,175	L 1:2	Abrahams	Emberson	Gregory D	Stamps	Skelton^	Greene	Cawley	Wilkins	Buckle	Sale^	Adcock*	Abrahams	Adcock/Lock
10	A	4/10	MANSFIELD	2,341	D 1:1	Greene	Emberson	Gregory D	Stamps	Skelton	Greene	Cawley	Wilkins*	Buckle	Sale	**Rankin**	Abrahams	Adcock/Lock
11	A	11/10	PETERBOROUGH	6,277	L 2:3	Rankin, Adcock	Emberson	Gregory D	Stamps	Skelton	Greene	Cawley	Wilkins	Buckle*	Sale^	Adcock	Rankin	Abrahams/Duguid
12	H	18/10	SHREWSBURY	2,977	D 1:1	Skelton	Emberson	Haydon	Stamps	Skelton	Whitton*	Cawley	Buckle	Forbes"	Sale^	Adcock	Rankin	Brown/Abrahams/Duguid
13	H	21/10	DONCASTER	2,588	W 2:1	Sale, Skelton	Emberson	Gregory D*	Stamps	Skelton	Haydon	Cawley	Buckle	Forbes	Sale	Adcock	Abrahams	Duguid
14	A	25/10	LEYTON ORIENT	4,592	W 2:0	Adcock, Forbes	Emberson	Gregory D	Stamps	Skelton	Greene	Cawley	Buckle	Forbes	Sale	Adcock*	Lock^	Haydon/Abrahams
15	H	31/10	SCUNTHORPE	3,134	D 3:3	Rankin, Buckle, Sale	Emberson	Gregory D	Stamps	Skelton	Greene	Cawley^	Whitton	Forbes	Sale	Adcock*	Rankin	Lock/Brown/Whitton
16	A	4/11	MACCLESFIELD	1,577	D 0:0		Emberson	Gregory D	Stamps	Skelton	Greene	Cawley	Whitton	Forbes	Sale	Adcock*	Rankin^	Buckle/Duguid
17	H	8/11	ROCHDALE	1,702	L 1:2	Duguid	Emberson	Gregory D*	Stamps"	Skelton*	Greene	Cawley	Whitton	Forbes	Sale	Adcock^	Duguid"	Buckle/Lock
18	H	18/11	NOTTS COUNTY	2,643	W 2:0	Sale, Rankin	Emberson	Dunne	Stamps^	Skelton	Greene	Cawley	Abrahams	Rankin	Sale	Whitton	Duguid^	Hathaway/Forbes
19	H	22/11	LINCOLN	2,932	L 0:1		Emberson	Dunne	Betts*	Gregory D	Greene	Cawley!	Abrahams	Rankin	Sale	Whitton	Duguid*	Adcock/Hathaway
20	A	29/11	ROTHERHAM	3,259	L 2:3	Skelton, Sale	Emberson	Dunne	Betts	Gregory D	Greene	Cawley	Hathaway	Skelton*	Sale	Whitton	Duguid	Rankin
21	A	13/12	HULL	3,895	L 1:3	Adcock	Emberson	Dunne	Gregory D	Skelton	Greene	Cawley	Wilkins*	Haydon	Forbes^	Adcock	Stamps"	Lock/Buckle/Hathaway
22	H	19/12	CHESTER	1,867	W 2:0	Adcock, Duguid	Emberson	Dunne*	Gregory D	Skelton	Greene	Cawley	Wilkins	Rankin	Forbes	Adcock	Stamps	Duguid/Buckle
23	A	26/12	BRIGHTON	2,647	D 4:4	Rankin 2, Adcock, Stamps	Emberson	Gregory D*	Gregory D^	Skelton^	Greene	Cawley	Wilkins	Rankin	Forbes"	Adcock	Stamps	Lock/Haydon
24	H	29/12	CAMBRIDGE U	4,518	W 3:2	Wilkins 2, Skelton	Emberson	Gregory D	Stamps*	Skelton	Greene	Cawley	Wilkins	Whitton"	Sale^	Adcock	Duguid*	Lock/Haydon
25	H	3/1	HARTLEPOOL	2,885	L 1:2	Buckle	Emberson	Dunne	Gregory D	Skelton*	Greene	Cawley	Wilkins	Whitton"	Sale*	Adcock	Buckle	Gregory D/Lock/Forbes
26	A	10/1	DARLINGTON	2,170	L 2:4	Lock	Emberson	Haydon	Gregory D"	Skelton^	Greene	Cawley	Wilkins	Forbes	Gregory N	Sale	Buckle	Gregory D/Lock/Forbes
27	H	16/1	TORQUAY	2,776	W 1:0	Lock	Emberson	Gregory D	Stamps^	Skelton	Greene	Cawley*	Wilkins	Forbes	Gregory N	Sale	Buckle	Gregory D/Lock
28	H	20/1	CARDIFF	1,929	W 2:1	Gregory N, Buckle	Emberson	Gregory D	Gregory D	Skelton	Greene*	Gregory D	Wilkins	Forbes	Gregory N	Sale	Buckle	Dunne/Lock/Whitton
29	A	24/1	BARNET	2,471	L 2:3	Skelton, Wilkins	Emberson	Gregory D	Gregory D^	Skelton	Branston	Gregory D	Wilkins	Forbes^	Gregory N	Sale	Buckle"	Haydon/Lock/Whitton
30	A	31/1	SCARBOROUGH	2,219	D 1:1	Whitton	Emberson	Dunne	Haydon	Skelton	Branston	Gregory D	Wilkins	Forbes^	Gregory N	Sale	Whitton	
31	A	6/2	SWANSEA	2,789	L 1:2	Gregory N	Emberson	Dunne	Haydon"	Skelton	Greene*	Gregory D	Wilkins	Forbes	Gregory N	Sale^	Whitton*	Buckle/Lock/Duguid
32	H	13/2	MANSFIELD	2,320	W 2:0	Lock, Gregory D	Emberson	Gregory D	Betts	**Branston**	Greene*	Buckle	Wilkins	Forbes^	Gregory N	Sale^	Whitton	Duguid/Skelton
33	A	21/2	EXETER	3,346	W 1:0	Lock	Emberson	Dunne	Betts	Skelton	Branston	Buckle	Wilkins	Forbes	Gregory N	Sale^	Whitton	
34	A	24/2	SHREWSBURY	1,972	W 2:0	Gregory N, Gregory D	Emberson	Gregory D	Betts	Skelton	Branston	Buckle	Wilkins	Forbes	Gregory N	Lock*	Stamps	Adcock
35	H	27/2	PETERBOROUGH	4,117	W 2:0	Branston	Emberson	Dunne	Betts	Skelton"	Branston	Buckle	Wilkins	Forbes	Adcock	Lock*	Whitton	Duguid/Dunne
36	H	3/3	ROCHDALE	2,112	D 0:0		Emberson	Dunne	Betts	Skelton	Greene	Buckle	Wilkins	Forbes	Adcock	Lock	Whitton	Sale*
37	H	7/3	SCUNTHORPE	2,143	L 0:1		Emberson	Dunne	Betts	Skelton	Branston	Buckle	Wilkins	Forbes	Sale	Lock*	Gregory D*	Sale/Hathaway
38	A	14/3	MACCLESFIELD	2,760	W 5:1	Sale 2, Skelton, Abrahams, Lock	Emberson	Dunne	Betts	Skelton*	Branston	Buckle	Wilkins	Haydon	Sale	Lock*	Duguid*	Haydon/Abrahams/Hathaway
39	A	21/3	NOTTS COUNTY	6,264	D 0:0		Emberson	Dunne	Betts	Skelton*	Greene*	Gregory D	Wilkins	Buckle	Sale*	Lock^	Abrahams^	Forbes/Duguid/Haydon
40	H	28/3	LINCOLN	4,040	W 1:0	Dunne	Emberson	Dunne	Betts	Skelton	Greene	Branston	Wilkins	Buckle	Sale*	Lock^	Gregory D	Forbes/Abrahams
41	A	3/4	ROTHERHAM	3,824	W 2:1	Skelton, Sale	Emberson	Dunne*	Betts	Skelton"	Greene	Branston	Wilkins	Buckle	Sale*	Lock^	Gregory D	Gregory N/Abrahams
42	H	11/4	CARDIFF	2,809	W 2:0	Abrahams, Gregory D	Emberson	Dunne	Betts	Skelton	Greene	Branston"	Wilkins	Buckle	Sale^	Lock^	Gregory D	Gregory N/Duguid/Abrahams
43	H	13/4	HULL	4,700	W 4:3	Gregory D, Lock, Dunne, Duguid	Emberson	Dunne	Betts	Skelton*	Greene	Branston	Wilkins	Buckle	Sale*	Lock^	Gregory D*	Gregory N/Duguid/Abrahams
44	A	18/4	CHESTER	1,780	L 1:3	Abrahams	Emberson	Dunne	Betts	Skelton^	Greene*	Branston	Wilkins	Buckle"	Sale*	Lock	Gregory D"	Forbes/Duguid/Abrahams
45	A	25/4	LEYTON ORIENT	6,220	W 1:0	Gregory N	Emberson	Dunne	Betts	Gregory D	Greene*	Skelton	Wilkins	Buckle	Sale*	Gregory N	Abrahams^	Skelton/Duguid/Forbes
46	A	2/5	DONCASTER	3,572	W 1:0	Gregory N	Emberson	Dunne	Betts	Gregory D	Greene	Skelton	Wilkins"	Buckle	Sale*	Gregory N	Abrahams^	Lock/Duguid/Forbes

DIVISION THREE PLAY-OFFS

						Lineup
S1	A	10/5	BARNET	3,858	L 0-1	Emberson, Dunne, Betts, Skelton, Greene, Branston!, Forbes, Gregory N*, Gregory D, Sale, Buckle, Lock
S2	H	13/5	BARNET	5,863	W 3-1 Gregory D 2 (1p), Greene (aet)	Emberson, Dunne, Betts, Forbes*, Greene, Gregory D, Wilkins, Gregory N*, Abrahams", Sale, Buckle, Skelton/Duguid/Lock
F	N	22/5	TORQUAY	19,486	W 1-0 Gregory D (p) (at Wembley)	Emberson, Dunne, Betts, Skelton*, Greene, Gregory D, Wilkins, Gregory N*, Forbes, Sale, Buckle, Duguid/Lock

COCA-COLA (LEAGUE) CUP

						Lineup
1:1	H	12/8	LUTON	2,840	L 0-1	Emberson, Gregory D, Stamps, Skelton", Greene, Cawley, Wilkins, Abrahams*, Hathaway, Sale^, Buckle, Adcock/Lock/Forbes
1:2	A	26/8	LUTON	2,816	D 1-1 Hathaway (lost 1-2 on aggregate)	Emberson, Gregory D, Stamps, Forbes, Greene, Cawley, Wilkins, Abrahams*, Hathaway^, Sale, Buckle, Adcock/Lock

FA CUP

						Lineup
1	H	15/11	BRENTFORD	2,899	D 2-2 Sale, Gregory D	Emberson, Gregory D, Stamps, Skelton", Greene, Cawley, Wilkins^, Forbes*, Whitton, Sale, Duguid, Adcock/Dunne/Abrahams
1R	H	25/11	BRENTFORD	3,694	D 0-0 (aet, won 4-2 on penalties)	Emberson, Gregory D, Betts, Gregory D, Greene, Cawley, Abrahams^, Adcock*, Whitton", Sale, Duguid, Lock/Hathaway/Skelton
2	H	6/12	HEREFORD	3,558	D 1-1 Gregory D	Emberson, Dunne, Betts, Gregory D, Greene", Skelton, Duguid, Buckle, Adcock*, Sale, Buckle, Lock/Stamps/Haydon
2R	A	16/12	HEREFORD	3,752	D 1-1 Forbes (aet, lost 4-5 on penalties)	Emberson, Dunne, Gregory D, Skelton, Greene, Cawley, Wilkins*, Haydon", Stamps", Forbes, Haydon^, Lock/Duguid/Betts

AUTO WINDSCREENS SHIELD

						Lineup
1	A	9/12	LEYTON ORIENT	933	L 0-1	Emberson, Dunne, Betts, Gregory D, Greene, Skelton, Duguid, Buckle, Adcock*, Sale, Stamps, Gregory D

League Table

Pos	Team	P	Home W	D	L	F	A	Away W	D	L	F	A	Pts
1	Notts Co	46	14	7	2	41	20	15	5	3	41	23	99
2	Macclesfield	46	19	4	0	40	11	4	9	10	23	33	82
3	Lincoln	46	11	7	5	32	24	9	8	6	28	27	75
4	COLCHESTER*	46	12	7	4	41	24	7	6	10	31	36	74
5	Torquay	46	14	4	5	39	22	7	7	9	29	37	74
6	Scarborough	46	14	6	3	44	23	6	6	11	23	35	72
7	Barnet	46	10	8	5	35	22	10	7	6	26	29	70
8	Scunthorpe	46	11	5	7	30	24	8	7	8	26	28	69
9	Rotherham	46	10	9	4	41	24	6	10	7	26	31	67
10	Peterborough	46	13	6	4	37	16	5	7	11	26	35	67
11	Leyt' Orient**	46	14	5	4	40	20	5	7	11	22	27	66
12	Mansfield	46	11	9	3	42	26	5	8	10	22	29	65
13	Shrewsbury	46	9	7	7	35	28	8	4	11	26	34	61
14	Chester	46	12	7	4	34	15	3	5	15	15	46	61
15	Exeter	46	10	8	5	39	25	5	7	11	29	38	60
16	Cambridge	46	11	8	4	39	27	3	10	10	24	30	60
17	Hartlepool	46	10	12	1	40	22	5	2	16	21	31	59
18	Rochdale	46	15	3	5	43	15	2	4	17	13	40	58
19	Darlington	46	13	6	4	43	28	3	1	19	13	44	54
20	Swansea	46	8	8	7	24	16	5	3	15	25	46	50
21	Cardiff	46	5	13	5	27	22	9	1	13	21	30	50
22	Hull	46	10	6	7	36	32	1	2	20	20	51	41
23	Brighton	46	3	10	10	21	34	3	7	13	17	32	35
24	Doncaster	46	3	3	17	14	48	1	5	17	16	65	20
		1104	267	164	121	857	574	121	164	267	574	857	1489

* promoted after play-offs
** 2 pts deducted

Odds & Ends

Double wins: (2) Cardiff, Doncaster.
Double defeats: (1) Hartlepool.

Won from behind: (2) Cambridge (h), Hull (h).
Lost from in front: (4) Peterborough (a), Barnet (a), Swansea (h), Rotherham (a).

High spots: Promotion to Division Two achieved at last.
The club's third Wembley appearance in six years.
Rising from mid-table with 10 wins from the final 15 League games.
The arrival of Guy Branston to shore up an inconsistent defence.
Aaron Skelton's spectacular long-range goals.
The mauling of Macclesfield and draw at leaders Notts Co.

Low spots: The low Wembley crowd, due largely to a change of date.
Conceding three-goal leads against Scunthorpe and Brighton.
Bowing out of the FA Cup to a non-League outfit again.

Player of the Year: Richard Wilkins.
Ever presents: (1) Carl Emberson.
Hat-tricks for: (0).
Hat-tricks against: (1) Paul Emblen (Brighton).
Leading scorers: Mark Sale and Neil Gregory (8).

Appearances and Goals

Player	Lge	Sub	LC	Sub	FAC	Sub	AS	Sub	Lge	LC	FAC	AS	Tot
Abrahams, Paul	16	9	2		1	1			7				7
Adcock, Tony	19	6	2		3	1	1		5				5
Betts, Simon	17		2		2		1						
Branston, Guy	12								1				1
Brown, Wayne		2											
Buckle, Paul	33	5	2		1	1	1		5				5
Cawley, Peter	27	2	2		3								
Duguid, Karl	6	15			3	1	1	1	3				3
Dunne, Joe	22	3			3	1	1		2				2
Emberson, Carl	46		2		4		1						
Forbes, Steve	25	10	1	1	2				1		1		2
Greene, David	38	2			4				4				4
Gregory, David	42	2	2		4		1		5		2		7
Gregory, Neil	12	3							8				8
Hathaway, Ian	5	7	2		1					1			1
Haydon, Nicky	9	8			1	1	1						
Lock, Tony	14	18	2	3	1	1			6				6
Rankin, Isiah	10	1							4				4
Sale, Mark	38	1	2		3		1		7		1		8
Skelton, Aaron	37	2	1		3	1			7				7
Stamps, Scott	26	2	2		2	1			1				1
Whitton, Steve	15	6			2				4				4
Wilkins, Richard	37	2			5				2				2
23 players used	506	98	22	5	44	12	11	3	72	1	4		77

NATIONWIDE LEAGUE DIVISION 2

Manager: Steve Wignall ⇔ Mick Wadsworth

SEASON 1998-99

#		Date	Opponents	Att		F-A	Scorers	1	2	3	4	5	6	7	8	9	10	11	Subs (3)
1	H	8/8	CHESTERFIELD	4,042	W	1-0	Sale	Emberson	Betts	Stamps	Williams	Greene	Buckle	Wilkins*	Gregory D*	Sale	Lock*	Abrahams	Duguid/Dunne/Gregory N
2	A	15/8	WREXHAM	4,157	W	4-2	Abrahams, Haydon, Gregory N	Emberson	Betts	Stamps	Williams	Greene	Buckle	Haydon^	Gregory D	Sale	Gregory N*	Abrahams"	Adcock/Dunne/Wiles
3	H	22/8	FULHAM	6,377	L	0-1		Emberson	Dunne*	Stamps	Williams	Greene	Buckle	Wilkins	Gregory D	Sale^	Gregory N*	Abrahams"	Haydon/Adcock/Forbes
4	A	29/8	LUTON	5,005	L	0-2		Emberson	Dunne"	Stamps*	Williams	Greene	Buckle^	Wilkins	Gregory D	Sale	Gregory N^	Abrahams	Haydon/Duguid/Forbes
5	H	31/8	STOKE	4,726	L	0-1		Emberson	Haydon	Betts	Williams	Greene	Buckle	Wilkins	Gregory D	Sale	Gregory N*	Duguid*	Abrahams/Forbes
6	H	5/9	YORK	2,699	W	2-1	Gregory N, Forbes	Emberson	Haydon*	Stamps	Williams	Greene	Buckle	Wilkins"	Gregory D	Sale	Gregory N*	Lock*	Forbes/Rainford/Betts
7	A	8/9	WIGAN	2,784	D	1-1	Sale	Emberson	Haydon*	Stamps*	Williams	Greene	Buckle	Forbes	Gregory D	Sale	Gregory N	Lock	Betts/Dunne
8	H	12/9	GILLINGHAM	4,612	D	1-1	Gregory N	Emberson	Dunne	Stamps*	Williams	Greene	Buckle	Forbes^	Gregory D	Sale	Gregory N	Lock	Haydon/Duguid
9	A	19/9	READING	9,058	D	1-1	Duguid	Emberson	Dunne	Betts	Williams	Greene	Buckle	Forbes"	Gregory D	Sale	Gregory N*	Lock*	Adcock/Duguid/Betts
10	H	26/9	WYCOMBE	4,205	W	2-1	Forbes, Gregory D(p)	Emberson	Dunne	Stamps	Williams	Greene	Buckle	Forbes	Gregory D	Sale	Gregory N*	Lock^	Adcock/Duguid
11	A	3/10	OLDHAM	4,231	L	0-1		Emberson	Dunne	Stamps	Williams	Greene	Buckle"	Forbes	Gregory D	Sale	Gregory N*	Lock^	Skelton/Duguid/Branston
12	H	9/10	BURNLEY	5,532	L	0-4		Emberson	Dunne	Betts^	Williams^	Greene	Buckle	Forbes*	Gregory D	Sale"	Gregory N	Abrahams	Lock/Duguid/Skelton
13	A	17/10	PRESTON	10,483	L	0-2		Emberson	Dunne	Stamps	Williams"	Greene	Buckle	Forbes*	Gregory D	Sale^	Gregory N	Abrahams^	Dozzell/Duguid/Betts
14	A	20/10	WALSALL	3,319	D	1-1	Lock	Emberson	Dunne	Stamps	Williams	Greene	Buckle	Dozzell*	Gregory D	Sale	Gregory N	Forbes	Forbes/Lock
15	H	31/10	MANCHESTER CITY	24,820	L	1-2	Dozzell	Emberson	Dunne	Stamps	Williams	Greene	Buckle	Dozzell	Gregory D	Sale	Gregory N*	Duguid^	Sale/Abrahams
16	H	6/11	MACCLESFIELD	3,925	D	1-1	Greene	Emberson	Haydon	Haydon	Williams	Greene	Buckle	Dozzell	Gregory D	Lock	Gregory N*	Duguid^	Sale/Forbes/Adcock
17	A	10/11	NORTHAMPTON	3,598	L	1-2	Greene	Emberson	Dunne	Stamps	Williams*	Greene	Buckle	Dozzell	Gregory D	Lock	Gregory N"	Forbes"	Gregory N/Haydon
18	A	21/11	NOTTS COUNTY	4,598	W	3-1	Greene 2, Gregory D	Emberson	Dunne	Betts	Williams	Greene	Buckle	Dublin	Gregory D	Sale^	Lock*	Duguid^	Dozzell/Gregory N
19	H	28/11	MILLWALL	4,476	D	0-0		Emberson	Dunne	Betts	Williams	Greene	Buckle	Dublin	Gregory D	Sale"	Lock"	Duguid^	Abrahams/Dozzell
20	H	12/12	LINCOLN	4,513	D	0-0		Emberson	Dunne	Betts*	Williams	Greene	Buckle	Wilkins	Gregory D	Sale*	Lock"	Stamps	Sale/Lock
21	A	19/12	BLACKPOOL	3,228	D	2-2	Greene, Gregory D	Emberson	Dunne	Betts	Williams	Greene	Abrahams*	Wilkins	Gregory D	Sale	Duguid^	Stamps*	Gregory N/Lock/Sale
22	A	26/12	FULHAM	11,939	L	0-2		Emberson !	Dunne !	Betts	Williams	Greene	Buckle	Wilkins	Gregory D	Dozzell"	Gregory N^	Stamps*	Gregory N/Lock/Abrahams
23	H	28/12	BRISTOL ROVERS	4,609	L	0-3		Emberson	Dunne^	Betts	Williams	Greene	Buckle"	Wilkins	Gregory D	Sale*	Abrahams^	Lock	Sale/Haydon/Abrahams
24	H	2/1	LUTON	4,694	D	2-2	Gregory D(p), Abrahams	Fernandes	Haydon	Betts	Williams*	Greene	Buckle	Wilkins	Gregory D*	Sale*	Gregory N"	Duguid^	Gregory N/Lock/Haydon
25	A	9/1	CHESTERFIELD	3,761	L	1-3	Lua-Lua	Fernandes	Dunne	Haydon	Williams	Greene	Buckle	Wilkins	Gregory D	Sale	Abrahams	Duguid	Lock/Lua-Lua
26	H	15/1	WREXHAM	3,491	L	1-3	Wilkins	Fernandes	Dunne	Haydon	Williams	Greene	Lock*	Wilkins	Gregory D	Sale	Abrahams	Duguid	Lua-Lua
27	A	23/1	STOKE	12,507	D	3-3	Betts, Gregory D, Dozzell	Emberson	Dunne	Pounewat'	Aspinall	Greene	Buckle	Wilkins*	Gregory D*	Skelton	Abrahams	Duguid*	Abrahams/Dozzell
28	A	30/1	BRISTOL ROVERS	6,249	D	1-1	Gregory D(p)	Emberson	Dunne	Betts	Williams*	Greene	Buckle	Wilkins	Gregory D	Skelton	Gregory N*	Duguid"	Dozzell/Lua-Lua/Abrahams
29	H	5/2	YORK	3,982	W	2-1	Betts, Greene	Emberson	Dunne	Aspinall	Williams"	Greene	Skelton	Wilkins	Gregory D	Dozzell	Gregory N*	Duguid"	Lua-Lua
30	H	12/2	WIGAN	3,934	W	2-1	Wilkins, Gregory D	Emberson	Dunne	Betts	Williams^	Greene	Skelton	Wilkins	Gregory D	Dozzell"	Gregory N*	Duguid"	Lua-Lua/Buckle
31	A	20/2	GILLINGHAM	7,276	D	1-1	Duguid	Emberson	Dunne	Duguid	Aspinall	Greene !	Skelton	Aspinall	Buckle	Dozzell"	Buckle	Duguid	Gregory N/Abrahams/Sale
32	A	27/2	READING	4,696	D	1-1	Gregory N	Emberson	Dunne	Betts	Williams^	Greene	Skelton*	Aspinall	Gregory D	Dozzell	Gregory N*	Allen^	Forbes/Abrahams/Sale
33	H	6/3	WYCOMBE	4,670	D	2-2	Dozzell, Gregory D(p)	Emberson	Dunne	Richard*	Williams	Betts	P'newatchy	Aspinall	Gregory D	Allen^	Gregory N*	Dozzell"	Buckle/Abrahams/Sale
34	H	9/3	OLDHAM	3,616	D	2-2	Allen, Gregory D(p)	Emberson	Dunne	Wilkins"	Williams"	P'newatchy	P'newatchy	Aspinall"	Gregory D	Allen	Gregory N*	Dozzell"	Lua-Lua/Abrahams/Sale
35	A	13/3	MACCLESFIELD	2,796	L	0-2		Emberson	Abrahams	Duguid	Williams"	Greene	Buckle	Wilkins	Gregory D*	Allen^	Gregory N	Dozzell"	Dozzell/Dunne/Williams
36	A	20/3	MANCHESTER CITY	6,544	L	0-1		Emberson	Dunne	Duguid	P'newatchy	Greene	Buckle	Aspinall	Gregory D	Launders	Gregory N*	Williams	Sale^/Stamps
37	A	27/3	BOURNEMOUTH	6,442	W	1-0	Greene	Emberson	Dunne	Richard*	Williams	Greene	Buckle"	Aspinall	Gregory D	Dozzell"	Gregory N^	P'newatchy	Betts/Abrahams/Lua-Lua
38	H	2/4	PRESTON	5,644	W	1-0	Aspinall	Emberson	Richard	Dunne"	Williams"	Greene	Buckle	Aspinall"	Gregory D	Dozzell	Lua-Lua !	Duguid	Gregory N/Germain/Buckle
39	A	5/4	BURNLEY	10,747	L	1-3	Gregory D	Emberson	Richard	Wilkins"	Williams"	Greene	P'newatchy	Aspinall"	Gregory D	Dozzell	Lua-Lua	Duguid	Buckle/Germain/Betts
40	H	10/4	WALSALL	4,082	W	1-0	Greene	Emberson	Richard	Dunne"	Williams"	Greene	P'newatchy	Buckle	Gregory D	Dozzell	Lua-Lua	Aspinall	Wilkins/Abrahams
41	H	14/4	MILLWALL	4,686	L	0-2		Fernandes	Richard	P'newatchy	Williams"	Greene	Buckle	Wilkins	Gregory D	Dozzell	Lua-Lua	Aspinall	Gregory N/Duguid*/'Abra'ms
42	H	16/4	NOTTS COUNTY	4,215	D	3-3	Buckle 37, Aspinall 86p, Duguid 71	Fernandes	Richard	P'newatchy	Betts	Stamps	Buckle	Wilkins	Aspinall	Dozzell*	Gregory N*	Lua-Lua	Abrahams
43	A	24/4	NORTHAMPTON	6,136	D	3-3	Buckle 3, Aspinall 47p, Dozzell	Fernandes	Richard	P'newatchy	Betts*	Greene	Buckle	Wilkins	Aspinall	Dozzell"	Abrahams^	Abrahams"	Gregory D/Germain/Duguid
44	H	27/4	BOURNEMOUTH	4,168	W	2-1	Hayter(og), Dozzell	Fernandes	Richard	P'newatchy	Betts	Greene	Buckle	Wilkins	Aspinall	Dozzell^	Duguid^	Duguid"	Stamps/Germain/Lock
45	A	1/5	LINCOLN	4,613	L	1-2	Duguid	Fernandes	Richard	Stamps	Betts*	Greene	Buckle	Wilkins"	Gregory D"	Dozzell"	Aspinall	Duguid	Lock/Germain
46	A	8/5	BLACKPOOL	4,866	L	1-2	Pounewatchy	Walker	Richard	Duguid	Duguid	Greene	Buckle	Wilkins	Gregory D*	Germain"	Aspinall	Lua Lua	**Okafor/Opara**

WORTHINGTON (LEAGUE) CUP

		Date	Opponent	Att	Result	Score	Scorers
1:1	A	11/8	BOURNEMOUTH	3,745	L	0-2	(lost 2-3 on aggregate)
1:2	H	18/8	BOURNEMOUTH	2,550	W	3-2	Gregory D(2p), Abrahams

Line-ups:
- 1:1 — Emberson, Betts^, Stamps, Williams, Greene, Buckle, Haydon, Gregory D, Sale, Gregory N*, Abrahams^ · subs Duguid/Adcock
- 1:2 — Emberson, Betts^, Stamps, Williams, Greene, Buckle, Haydon, Gregory D, Sale, Gregory N*, Abrahams · subs Forbes/Dunne

FA CUP

		Date	Opponent	Att	Result	Score	Scorers
1	A	14/11	BEDLINGTON TERR.	2,027	L	1-4	Adcock

Line-up:
- Emberson, Dunne, Stamps^, Williams, Greene, Buckle, Dozzell, Gregory D, Sale", Lock, Forbes* · subs Adcock/Duguid/Haydon

AUTO WINDSCREENS SHIELD

		Date	Opponent	Att	Result	Score	Scorers
1	H	5/12	GILLINGHAM	1,742	L	1-5	Gregory D(p)

Line-up:
- Emberson, Dunne, Betts, Williams, Greene, Buckle, Forbes", Gregory D, Sale*, Lock, Gregory N*, Abrahams · subs Dozzell/Lock/Stamps

League Table

		P	W	D	L	F	A	W	D	L	F	A	Pts
				Home						Away			
1	Fulham	46	19	3	1	50	12	12	5	6	29	20	101
2	Walsall	46	13	7	3	37	23	13	2	8	26	24	87
3	Man City*	46	13	6	4	38	14	9	10	4	31	19	82
4	Gillingham	46	15	5	3	45	17	7	9	7	30	27	80
5	Preston	46	12	6	5	46	23	10	7	6	32	27	79
6	Wigan	46	14	5	4	44	17	8	5	10	31	31	76
7	Bournemouth	46	12	2	9	37	11	7	6	10	26	30	76
8	Stoke	46	10	4	9	32	32	11	2	10	27	31	69
9	Chesterfield	46	14	5	4	34	16	3	8	12	12	28	64
10	Millwall	46	9	8	6	33	24	8	3	12	19	35	62
11	Reading	46	10	6	7	29	26	6	6	11	26	37	61
12	Luton	46	10	6	7	25	26	6	6	11	26	34	58
13	Bristol Rov	46	8	9	6	35	28	5	8	10	30	28	56
14	Blackpool	46	7	8	8	24	24	7	6	10	20	30	56
15	Burnley	46	8	7	8	23	33	5	9	9	31	40	55
16	Notts Co	46	8	6	9	29	27	6	8	11	23	34	54
17	Wrexham	46	8	6	9	21	28	5	8	10	22	34	53
18	COLCHESTER	46	9	7	7	25	30	3	9	11	27	40	52
19	Wycombe	46	8	5	10	31	26	5	7	11	21	32	51
20	Oldham	46	8	4	11	26	31	6	5	12	22	35	51
21	York	46	6	8	9	28	33	7	3	13	28	47	50
22	Northampton	46	4	12	7	26	31	6	6	11	17	26	48
23	Lincoln	46	9	4	10	27	27	4	3	16	15	47	46
24	Macclesfield	46	7	4	12	24	30	4	6	13	19	33	43
		1104	243	146	163	769	589	163	146	243	589	769	1510

* promoted
after play-offs

Appearances and Goals

Player	Lge	Sub	LC	Sub	FAC	Sub	AS	Sub	Lge	LC	FAC	Tot
Abrahams, Paul	13	14	2					1	2	1		3
Allen, Bradley	4								1			1
Aspinall, Warren	15								3			3
Adcock, Tony		6		1		1					1	1
Betts, Simon	22	6	2				1		2			2
Branston, Guy		1										
Buckle, Paul	39	4	2		1		1		2			2
Dozzell, Jason	23	6			1			1	4			4
Dublin, Keith	2											
Duguid, Karl	23	10		1		1			4			4
Dunne, Joe	32	4		1	1		1					
Emberson, Carl	37		2		1		1					
Fernades, Tamar	8											
Forbes, Steve	8	7		1	1		1		2			2
Fumaca	1											
Germain, Steve		5										
Greene, David	42		2		1		1		8			8
Gregory, David	43	1	2		1		1		11	2	1	14
Gregory, Neil	29	9	2				1		4			4
Haydon, Nicky	7	6	2			1						
Launders, Brian	1											
Lock, Tony	14	9			1		1		1			1
Lua-Lua, Lom' Tresor	6	7							1			1
Okafor, Sam		1										
Opara, KK		1										
Pounewatchy, Steph'	15								1			1
Rainford, David		1										
Richard, Fabrice	10											
Sale, Mark	21	10	2		1		1		2			2
Skelton, Aaron	7	2										
Stamps, Scott	19	2	2		1			1				
Walker, Andy	1											
Wiles, Ian		1										
Wilkins, Richard	25	1							2			2
Williams, Geraint	38	1	2		1		1		1			1
(own-goals)									1			1
35 players used	506	115	22	4	11	3	11	3	52	3	1	57

Odds & Ends

Double wins: (1) York.
Double defeats: (3) Burnley, Fulham, Manchester City.
Won from behind: (1) Wycombe (h).
Lost from in front: (2) Bournemouth (a), Burnley (a).
High spots: Retaining the hard-won Division Two status.
Two tussles with 'fallen giants' Manchester City.
The instigation of a brand new project to create a new stadium.
The rise in gates to the highest average (4,479) for 11 seasons.
The interest created by an influx of foreign signings.
The vastly improved home form after the change of management.
The emergence of exciting young talent Lomana Tresor Lua-Lua.
A record number of penalties given for a season, 11 of 13 were scored.
Low spots: The FA Cup humiliation by minnows Bedlington Terriers.
Defeat in all three cup competitions at the first hurdle.
The poor strike-rate by the forward line throughout the season.
The departure of popular manager Steve Wignall.
Heavy home defeats by Burnley, Bristol Rovers and Gillingham.

Player of the Year: David Greene.
Ever presents: (0).
Hat-tricks for: (0).
Hat-tricks against: (0).
Leading scorer: (14) David Gregory.

NATIONWIDE DIVISION 2

Manager: Mick Wadsworth ⇨ Steve Whitton — SEASON 1999-2000

No	Date	Att	Pos	Pt	F-A	H-T	Scorers, Times, and Referees
1	A CHESTERFIELD 7/8	2,930	7 / 22	W 3	1-0	0-0	Dozzell 74. Ref: G Laws
2	H NOTTS CO 14/8	3,986	18 / 3	L 3	0-3	0-2	Hughes 5, Stallard 35, Blackmore 79. Ref: B Knight
3	A BOURNEMOUTH 21/8	4,508	20 / 7	L 3	0-4	0-1	Stein 15, Jorg'n 58, Fletcher 80, 89. Ref: M Fletcher
4	H READING 28/8	3,443	12 / 21	W 6	3-2	1-1	Aspinall 45, 88p, Duguid 78; Forster 22, Williams 64. Ref: P Rejer
5	A BURY 30/8	3,360	14 / 7	L 6	2-5	1-2	Wilkins 40, Lua-Lua 82 (Preece 74); Lawson 12, 57, 68, Littlejohn 15. Ref: M Pike
6	H SCUNTHORPE 11/9	3,280	20 / 17	L 6	0-1	0-0	Hodges 49. Ref: K Leach
7	A BURNLEY 18/9	10,090	23 / 1	L 6	0-3	0-2	Payton 9, 38p, 51. Ref: P Robinson
8	A MILLWALL 25/9	7,161	23 / 14	L 6	0-1	0-0	Ifill 83. Ref: A Leake
9	H WREXHAM 1/10	3,315	22 / 12	D 7	2-2	0-0	Duguid 79, Wilkins 90; Owen 56, Morrell 85. Ref: P Danson
10	A CAMBRIDGE 15/10	5,039	24 / 19	L 7	2-5	1-2	Dozzell 17, 54 (Benjamin 74); Butler 29, 85, 88, Greene 37 (og). Ref: G Poll
11	A BRISTOL CITY 19/10	7,777	23 / 15	D 8	1-1	0-1	Duguid 58; Tinnion 34. Ref: M Warren

Squad Numbers In Use / subs used

No	Line-up	subs used
1	Brown, Duguid, Keith, Burton, Greene, Aspinall, Wilkins, Gregory, Lua-Lua, Launders*, Dozzell*	Germain^, Opara*
1	Leaning, Hewitt, Woods, Curtis, Payne, Breckin, Baumont, Holland, Reeves, Ebdon^, Bettney^	Lomas, Willis
2	Brown, Duguid, Keith, Burton, Greene, Aspinall, Wilkins, Gregory, Lua-Lua, Launders, Dozzell	Opara^, Pinault
2	Ward, Holmes, Blackmore, Warren, Redmile, Richardson, Owers, Ramage^, Stallard*, Hughes, Darby*	Dyer, Robson, Rapley
3	Brown, Duguid, Keith, Burton!, Greene, Aspinall, Wilkins, Gregory, Lua-Lua, Launders^, Dozzell^	Pinault, Richard
3	Ovendale, Young, Warren, Howe, Cox, Mean*, Jorgensen^, Robinson, Stein, Fletcher S, Hughes	Hayter, Huck
4	Brown, Duguid, Keith, Burton, Greene, Aspinall, Wilkins, Gregory, Lua-Lua, Launders, Moralee*	Forbes
4	Howie, Bernal, Gray, Grant, Hunter, Casper, Smith, Caskey, Williams, Forster*, Haddow^	Scott, Evers, McIntyre
5	Brown, Duguid, Keith, Burton, Greene, Aspinall, Wilkins, Gregory, Lua-Lua, Launders, Moralee	Forbes
5	Kenny, Billy, Collins, Daws, Swailes, Richardson, Littlejohn, Preece^, Reid, Lawson^, James	Redmond, Avdiu, Rocha
6	Brown, Duguid, Keith, Richard, Greene, Aspinall, Wilkins, Gregory, Lua-Lua, Launders^, Moralee^	Opara, Germain, Farley
6	Evans, Harsley, Dawson, Fickling, Wilcox, Hope, Shelton*, Hodges, Ipoua^, Humphreys, Calvo-Garcia	Sparrow, Guinan
7	Brown, Duguid, Keith, Richard, Greene, Aspinall, Wilkins, Gregory, Lua-Lua, Moralee*, Germain^	Opara, Farley
7	Crichton, West, Smith, Mellon*, Davis, Thomas, Little^, Cook, Payton, Branch, Armstrong	Johnrose, Mullin
8	Brown, Duguid, Keith, Richard, Greene, Farley, Wilkins, Gregory, Arnott, Moralee*, Dozzell^	Neill
8	Warner, Bircham, Stuart, Cahill, Nethercott, Fitzgerald, Reid, Newman, Harris*, Shaw^, Ifill	Ifill, Sadlier
9	Brown, Farley, Keith, Burton, Greene, Arnott, Wilkins, Gregory, Moralee*, Duguid, Dozzell	Lua-Lua, Lock
9	Dearden, McGregor, Hardy, Owen, Carey, Ridley, Chalk, Stevens^, Russell, Ferguson, Faulcbridge*	Lowe, Morrell
10	Brown, Farley*, Keith, Burton^, Greene, Arnott, Wilkins, Gregory, Lua-Lua, Duguid, Dozzell	McGavin, Skelton
10	V Heusden, Ashbee, Wilson, Mackenzie, Eustace*, Duncan, Mustoe, Paterson", Benjamin, Butler, Kyd^	Joseph, Taylor, Preece
11	Brown, Farley, Keith, Skelton*, Greene, Arnott^, Wilkins, Gregory, Lua-Lua, Duguid, Dozzell	Moralee, McGavin
11	Phillips, Lavin, Brennan, Mortimer, Taylor, Sebok^, Goodridge^, Hutchings, Jones, Beadle*, Tinnion	Murray, Thorpe, Brown

Match notes

1. A mazy run from Lua-Lua and a 25-yard free-kick from Launders both nearly result in an opener for United. Andy Leaning is kept busy but can do nothing about Dozzell's tap-in for the winner, which is the climax of a fine move involving Lua-Lua, Launders and the lively Duguid.

2. Andy Hughes stabs in a Duane Darby cross and Mark Stallard doubles the lead with a carbon-copy goal. The U's work hard but get nowhere, and Clayton Blackmore seals the away victory with an angled free-kick. A depressing afternoon against Sam Allardyce's workmanlike outfit.

3. Experienced Mark Stein opens the scoring with a low drive. Burton is then sent off for two yellow card offences and the U's begin to crumble. Claus Jorgensen stabs a second goal and Steve Fletcher rubs salt into the U's wounds, snapping up two late chances for Mel Machin's outfit.

4. Nicky Forster heads in but Aspinall levels with a rasper. Martin Williams lofts a shot over Brown to regain the lead. Lua-Lua's mazy run ends with Duguid stabbing in. Near the end Keith Scott handles and Aspinall scores from the spot, giving Whitton an exciting winning start as boss.

5. Ian Lawson opens the scoring from a free header. Adrian Littlejohn lobs the second after keeper Brown is left stranded out of his goal. Wilkins sends a marvellous 30-yarder into the Bury net, but the U's then collapse to three strikes in 17 minutes. Lua-Lua heads in a consolation effort.

6. Aspinall goes close and then Lua-Lua misses with a free header and sends an overhead kick over the bar. Brian Laws' outfit take the lead just after the break with a strike by new signing Lee Hodges. Duguid goes close from long range and Hodges forces Brown into a fine double save.

7. Experienced Clarets are too strong for a youthful U's. Andy Payton heads in from close range and then grabs his second from the penalty spot. This was hotly disputed as Payton appeared to dive and the incident looked outside the box. Payton completes a hat-trick with a 12-yard drive.

8. Arnott arrives on loan from Brighton and plays his part in a solid defensive performance. Lock returns, having been released months earlier. All the good work comes to nothing when Keith Stephens' men grab a late winner, sub Paul Ifill ending a fine run with an unstoppable drive.

9. Gareth Owen's heavily deflected 30-yarder finds the U's net. Lua-Lua's shot is spilled by Kevin Dearden and Duguid nets the loose ball. Andy Morrell dives to head a late goal, but the U's hit back in style. Wilkins, reinstated as skipper after Aspinall's departure, heads in a Keith cross.

10. U's start brightly and Dozzell nets Duguid's pass. Martin Butler levels, then Greene slices the ball into his own net. Dozzell scores again from a Lua-Lua assist, but Roy McFarland's outfit finish the match strongly. Butler completes a fine hat-trick, the third opponent to do this season.

11. The troubled U's put on a vastly improved display with Lua-Lua the star performer. A hopeful cross is accidentally diverted by Greene into Brian Tinnion's path and he makes no mistake. Arnott feeds Lua-Lua who skilfully finds the waiting Duguid, who raps in a deserved equaliser.

Colchester United — Match-by-Match Record (matches 12–23)

12 H MILLWALL 23/10 — L 1–2
Att: 3,392 · Pts: 8 · Positions: U's 24th, Millwall 13th
McGavin 17 / Moody 33, Ifill 82 · Ref: R Harris
Colchester: Brown, Farley, Skelton^, Keith, Greene, Duguid, Wilkins, Gregory, Lua-Lua, McGavin*, Dozzell. Subs: Opara, Moralee
Millwall: Warner, Birchall, Cahill, Ryan, Nethercott, Fitzgerald, Ifill, Reid", Moody^, Shaw*, Neill. Subs: Harris, Sadler, Bowry
McGavin crowns his first home start in six years by helping home Gregory's goalbound effort. Paul Moody then equalises for the Lions with a header that is deflected in after a corner. The Londoners grab both points with a late Paul Ifill winner, the goal set up by Essex boy Neil Harris.

13 H WIGAN 26/10 — D 2–2
Att: 2,915 · Pts: 9 · Positions: U's 24th, Wigan 4th
McGavin 7, Duguid 38 / Barlow 12, Liddell 90 · Ref: F Stretton
Colchester: Brown, Farley, Skelton, Keith, Greene, Duguid, Wilkins, Gregory, Lua-Lua, McGavin*, Dozzell. Subs: Moralee, Lock
Wigan: Stillie, Green, McGibbon, Kilford, Balmer, DeZeeuw, O'Neill, Sheridan, Martinez, Liddell, Barlow. Subs: Mathie, Gunlaugsson
Against the run of play McGavin converts Duguid's cross. Ian Kilford's defence-splitting pass sets up Stuart Barlow for an equaliser. McGavin cushions a Skelton pass into the path of Duguid who rifles in. The U's hang on until the last minute when Andy Liddell glances home a header.

14 A OXFORD 2/11 — D 1–1
Att: 4,444 · Pts: 10 · Positions: U's 24th, Oxford 21st
McGavin 23 / Lambert 1 · Ref: P Rejer
Colchester: Brown, Farley, Richard, Keith, Greene, Skelton^, Wilkins, Duguid, Lua-Lua, McGavin, Dozzell.
Oxford: Arendse, Robinson, Powell, Fear, Watson, Whelan, Lilley*, Lambert*, Murphy, Folland, Beauchamp. Subs: Cook, Abbey
From the U's kicking off, the ball runs through to keeper Andre Arendse who smashes it upfield, where Jamie Lambert latches on to it and nets after 17 seconds. From a corner Richard's header is helped in by McGavin. The U's hang on as Matt Murphy blasts a penalty against the bar.

15 H PRESTON 6/11 — D 2–2
Att: 3,818 · Pts: 11 · Positions: U's 24th, Preston 3rd
Skelton 16, Lua-Lua 68 / Mathie 61, Nogan 85 · Ref: M Messias
Colchester: Brown, Duguid, Richard, Keith, Greene, Skelton, Wilkins, Gregory, Lua-Lua^, McGavin*, Dozzell. Subs: Moralee, Lock
Preston: Moilanen, Alexander, Edwards, Murdock, Jackson, Gregan, Cartwright^, Rankine, Nogan, Macken, Diaf*.
Skelton's 25-yard free-kick eludes everyone and ends up in the bottom corner of the net. Brown parries a drive but Alex Mathie swoops and equalises. Lua-Lua puts United ahead with a screamer that goes in off the underside of the crossbar. Kurt Nogan pounces for a late equaliser.

16 A OLDHAM 14/11 — W 2–1
Att: 5,147 · Pts: 14 · Positions: U's 22nd, Oldham 15th
Lua-Lua 45, Greene 63p / Dudley 46 · Ref: D Laws
Colchester: Vaughan, Richard^, Keith, Duguid*, Greene, Skelton, Wilkins, Gregory, Lua-Lua*, McGavin, Dozzell. Subs: Farley, Lock, Johnson G
Oldham: Kelly, McNiven, Holt, Hotte, Rickers, Dudbury, Adams*, Sheridan, Allott, Dudley, Futcher. Subs: Tipton, Whitehall
This Sunday game sees Lua-Lua net a superb shot on the stroke of half-time after a Skelton free-kick. Craig Dudley heads an equaliser just 40 seconds after the restart. Lua-Lua is impeded as he attempts to reach a rebound off the goalkeeper and Greene drives home a penalty winner.

17 H BRENTFORD 19/11 — L 0–3
Att: 3,464 · Pts: 14 · Positions: U's 22nd, Brentford 4th
Partridge 60, Owusu 65, Rowlands 90 / Ref: M Jones
Colchester: Vaughan, Richard, Keith", Opara^, Greene, Skelton, Wilkins, Gregory, Lua-Lua, McGavin*, Dozzell. Subs: Moralee, Lock, Johnson G
Brentford: Woodman, Boxall, Anderson*, Quinn, Marshall, Rowlands, Ingimarsson, Owusu, Partridge, Scott^. Subs: Jenkins, Agyemang*, Warner
For an hour United dominate proceedings, but fail to kill off the Bees. Scott Partridge then breaks away to score and the rot sets in. Another counter-attack ends with Lloyd Owusu making it two. Martin Rowlands scores in injury time to complete a thoroughly miserable afternoon.

18 H CARDIFF 23/11 — L 0–3
Att: 2,557 · Pts: 14 · Positions: U's 22nd, Cardiff 14th
Humphreys 37, 75, Brazier 51 / Ref: P Alcock
Colchester: Vaughan, Richard", Keith, Skelton^, Greene, Duguid, Wilkins, Gregory, Lua-Lua", McGavin, Dozzell. Subs: Lock, Opara, Farley
Cardiff: Hallworth, Faerber, Legg, Perrett, Eckhardt, Vaughan, Bonner*, Carpenter, Brazier, Humphreys. Subs: Boland, Roberts
Another promising opening comes to nothing. The course of the game changes direction after Andy Legg's 25-yard free-kick is blocked by Vaughan, only for Richie Humphreys to pounce. Matt Brazier's deflected shot beats Vaughan and Humphries bags his second to sink the U's.

19 A STOKE 27/11 — D 1–1
Att: 14,183 · Pts: 15 · Positions: U's 23rd, Stoke 7th
Skelton 71 / Lightbourne 82 · Ref: G Frankland
Colchester: Vaughan, Richard, Keith, Skelton^, Greene, White, Wilkins, Duguid*, Gregory, McGavin, Dozzell. Subs: Lock, Farley
Stoke: Ward, Robinson, Clarke*, Mohan, Jacobsen^, O'Connor, Danielsson, Keen, Thorne, Kavanagh, Lightbourne. Subs: Petty, Crowe
A big crowd welcomes Stoke's new Icelandic management team at an appropriately chilly Britannia Stadium. A slick U's move culminates in Skelton netting the first headed goal of his career from Duguid's well-placed cross. Kyle Lightbourne equalises after a free-kick by Kevin Keen.

20 H CHESTERFIELD 3/12 — W 1–0
Att: 3,027 · Pts: 18 · Positions: U's 20th, Chesterfield 24th
Lua-Lua 52 / Ref: M Halsey
Colchester: Vaughan, Richard, Keith, Skelton^, Greene, White, Johnson G, Duguid, Gregory, Moralee*, Dozzell. Subs: Lua-Lua
Chesterfield: Gayle, Pearce, Hewitt*, Blatherwick, Payne, Howard, Beaumont, Williams, Reeves, D'Auria, Galloway. Subs: Agogo
John Duncan's men dominate the first half, but find Vaughan in fine form. United bring on sub Lua-Lua and once again he manages to enliven proceedings. In typical style he jinks past two men before firing a powerful drive into the net. Junior Agogo sees his header pushed onto a post.

21 A BRISTOL ROV 11/12 — L 1–2
Att: 7,023 · Pts: 18 · Positions: U's 20th, Bristol Rov 3rd
Lua-Lua 66 / Roberts 31, 54 · Ref: S Tomlin
Colchester: Vaughan, Richard, Keith, Skelton^, Greene, White, Johnson G, Duguid, Gregory, Moralee^, Dozzell. Subs: Lua-Lua, Wignall
Bristol Rovers: Jones, Prichard, Foster, Thomson, Tilson, Vaughan, Mauge, Bryant*, Reeves, Cureton, Roberts. Subs: Challis, Ellington
Jamie Cureton has a fine game, setting up Jason Roberts twice to net for Ian Holloway's men. Lua-Lua, carrying an injury, comes off the bench and the U's press forward. Lua-Lua's deflected shot pulls one back, and near the end he goes close, forcing a spectacular save from Lee Jones.

22 H LUTON 17/12 — W 3–0
Att: 3,049 · Pts: 21 · Positions: U's 18th, Luton 11th
McGavin 48, 54, Dozzell 74 / Ref: L Cable
Colchester: Brown, Richard, Keith, Skelton, Greene, White, Johnson G, Gregory, Lua-Lua, McGavin, Dozzell.
Luton: Abbey, Fraser, Taylor, Spring, Watts, Johnson, Sodje!, Locke, Thorpe, Doherty, George*. Subs: McLaren
Lua-Lua's shot hits Efe Sodje, who is harshly red-carded for handball, but Greene strikes the crossbar with the penalty. Lennie Lawrence's ten men keep the U's at bay until Gregory sets up McGavin for a double strike. It's United's first two-goal lead for over a year.

23 A GILLINGHAM 26/12 — L 1–2
Att: 7,338 · Pts: 21 · Positions: U's 20th, Gillingham 5th
McGavin 89 / Rowe 13, Southall 42 · Ref: L Arnott
Colchester: Brown, Dunne, Keith, Richard, Greene, Skelton, White!, Gregory, Lua-Lua, McGavin, Dozzell. Subs: Lock, Arnott
Gillingham: Bartram, Pennock, Edge, Smith, Butters, Ashby, Southall, Hessenthaler, Rowe^, Saunders. Subs: Nosworthy*, Thunsun, Hudge
Rodney Rowe hits a post but minutes later shoots past Brown. Loanee White, in his final game before returning to Luton, is sent off for a late tackle. Nicky Southall buries a powerful drive into the roof of the net for 2–0. McGavin pulls a goal back late on to unsettle the nervous Gills.

NATIONWIDE DIVISION 2   Manager: Mick Wadsworth ⇒ Steve Whitton   SEASON 1999-2000

No	Date	Opponent	Att	Pos	Pt	Res	F-A	H-T	Scorers, Times, and Referees	Squad numbers used	subs used
24	3/1	A BLACKPOOL	3,462	20 / 22	22	D	1:1	0-1	Duguid 52 / Bent 21 / Ref: D Crick	Brown, Keith, Dunne^, Bramble, Greene, Johnson G, Duguid, Gregory, Dozzell*, McGavin, Skelton *Caig, Bardsley, Shuttlew'th, Bushell, Carlisle, Forsyth, Matthews, Clarkson, Murphy, Bent*, Beesley* Rob Matthews beats four U's defenders on a long mazy run before setting up Junior Bent, who shoots home the opening goal from ten yards. McGavin crosses to Moralee, whose first time volley is clawed away by Tony Caig, but only to Duguid who volleys it into the roof of the net.	Moralee/Arnott *Coid*
25	8/1	H BRISTOL ROV	4,482	16 / 3	25	W	5-4	1-1	McGav' 36, 62, Duguid 80, 82, Lua' 89 / Roberts 12, 46, Cureton 59p, Ellington 86 / Ref: A Butler	Brown, Keith, Dunne, Bramble", Greene, Johnson G, Duguid, Gregory, Dozzell*, McGavin^, Skelton *Byrne^, Prichard, Foster, Trought, White*, Challis, Hillier, Walters, Cureton, Roberts* U's looked doomed at 1-3, after two clinical Jason Roberts strikes and a Jamie Cureton penalty. McGavin pulls one back before Duguid nicks two in two minutes. Cureton misses his second penalty but Nathan Ellington equalises. The drama continues and Lua-Lua wins it at the death.	Lua-Lua/Opara/Arnott *Pethick/Ellington*
26	15/1	A NOTTS CO	4,931	16 / 7	28	W	2:1	2-0	McGavin 30, 45, Stallard 65 / Ref: M Ryan	Brown, Keith, Johnson R, Greene, Johnson G, Opara", Gregory, Moralee, McGavin, Dozzell *Ward, Holmes", Liburd, Warren, Redmile^, Richardson, Owers, Ramage, Stallard, Rapley, Boland** The reshuffled U's win a penalty when Opara is pulled back. McGavin converts the kick. Opara's near-post cross is flicked in by McGavin to crown an excellent first-half's work. County pull a goal back when Dunne's clearance hits Kevin Rapley's foot and balloons high into the net.	Lua-Lua *Hughes/Murray/Tierney*
27	18/1	H WYCOMBE	4,075	16 / 10	31	W	1-0	0-0	Lua-Lua 81 / Ref: K Hill	Brown, Keith, Johnson R, Greene, Johnson G, Duguid, Gregory*, Moralee, McGavin, Dozzell *Taylor, Lawrence, Vinnicombe, Ryan, Cousins, Bates*, Simpson!, Brown!, Devine^, Baird* Michael Simpson is sent off after two yellow cards, and Lawrie Sanchez's reshuffle leads to the game becoming a dull affair. Sub Lua-Lua is hauled down by Steve Brown who also departs. The nine men finally succumb when Lua-Lua plays a one-two and fires home a fierce drive.	Lua-Lua *McCarthy/Senda/Bulman*
28	22/1	H BOURNEMOUTH	3,767	15 / 12	34	W	3-1	1-1	Moralee 33, Lua-Lua 63, 83 / Robinson 35 / Ref: D Pugh	Walker, Keith, Johnson R, Greene, Johnson G, Duguid, Gregory, Moralee^, McGavin^, Dozzell *Ovendale, Young*, Broadhurst, Hayter, Cox, Mean", O'Shea, Stein, Fletcher C^, Hughes* Moralee heads his first league goal for the U's from Dunne's cross. Steve Robinson soon levels with a ten-yard volley. Super-sub Lua-Lua takes a Dozzell pass to hammer United ahead, and then jinks through for a brilliant third goal. He departs injured to a lengthy standing ovation.	Wilkins/Lua-Lua"/Opara *Jorgensen/O'Neill/Stock*
29	29/1	A READING	7,304	15 / 20	34	L	0:2	0-1	Caskey 22, 78 / Ref: B Knight	Brown, Keith, Johnson R, Greene, Wilkins", Duguid, Gregory, Moralee^, McGavin^, Dozzell *Howie, Gurney, Robinson, Hunter, Primus, Nicholls^, Grant, Caskey, McIntyre*, Forster, Parkinson* Nicky Forster cuts inside to set up Darren Caskey for the Royals' first goal. Gregory hits the post and Duguid has an effort disallowed for offside. The U's generally look below par and Caskey seals things with a 20-yarder. Midfielder Phil Parkinson shines for Alan Pardew's side.	Lua-Lua/Opara/Skelton *Hodges/Scott*
30	5/2	H BURY	3,915	16 / 15	34	L	1:3	1-1	Duguid 16 / Swailes D 23, James 53, Barnes 58 / Ref: P Walton	Walker, Richard^, Keith, Johnson R, Greene*, Wilkins, Duguid, Gregory, Lua-Lua, Dozzell *Kenny, Barrass, Williams, Daws, Redmond, Bullock, Swailes D, Barnes^, Lawson", Reid, James** Paddy Kenny saves a fine Duguid effort but can do nothing when Duguid converts Richard's cross superbly. Unmarked Danny Swailes swoops to equalise from a corner. Lutel James and Paul Barnes also benefit from space to add further goals, despite some heroics from young Walker.	Opara/Moralee/Skelton *Littlejohn/Preece/Billy*
31	12/2	A WIGAN	6,022	16 / 3	37	W	1:0	1-0	McGavin 38 / Ref: P Danson	Brown, Keith, Johnson R, Greene*, Johnson G", Wilkins, Duguid, Gregory, Moralee*, Dozzell *Carroll, Bradshaw, Sharp*, Martinez, Balmer, DeZeeuw, O'Neill, McLoughlin^Haworth, Liddell, Barlow* Gavin Johnson exchanges passes with McGavin, whose fine pass finds Dozzell in a shooting position. His effort is saved by Roy Carroll's legs but falls to Moralee who crosses for McGavin to dive bravely and head a splendid goal. This unexpected win gets a standing ovation at the end.	Lock/Skelton *Sheridan/McGibbon*
32	19/2	H STOKE	4,364	14 / 6	40	W	1:0	0-0	McGavin 87 / Ref: A Hall	Brown, Keith, Johnson R, Greene*, Johnson G, Wilkins, Duguid^, Gregory, Moralee^, Dozzell *Ward, Hanssen, Clarke*, Petty, Kippe, O'Connor^, Gunnarsson, Jacobsen, Connor, Lightbourne Kavanagh* Sub Lua-Lua comes on as sub for Moralee after an hour and the U's immediately seize the initiative. Lua-Lua's pinpoint cross is headed home by McGavin in the closing minutes. For the second week running promotion-chasers are beaten and the U's reach a season's highest position.	Lua-Lua/Lock *Gislason/Thorne*
33	26/2	H BURNLEY	6,194	15 / 5	40	L	1:2	1-2	McGavin 19 / Davis 17, 38 / Ref: R Styles	Brown, Keith, Johnson R, Greene^, Johnson G, Duguid, Gregory, Moralee*, McGavin, Dozzell *Crichton, Johnrose, Thomas, Cox, Davis, Little, Cooke, Branch, Wright, Mullin** Ian Wright's second game for Burnley after signing from Celtic pulls in a big crowd, and the striker is booked after a clash with Duguid. Steve Davis stabs past Brown, only for McGavin to equalise when Paul Crichton gifts him the ball. Davis wins the points, heading in a corner-kick.	Lua-Lua/Lock/Skelton *Jepson*
34	4/3	A SCUNTHORPE	4,253	15 / 19	41	D	0:0	0-0	Ref: M Brandwood	Brown, Keith, Johnson R, Greene^, Johnson G, Duguid, Gregory, Moralee*, Lock, Dozzell *Evans, Dunne, Stanton, Logan, Fickling", Hope, Walker, Housham^, Ipoua", Quailey, Harsley* The U's create a number of chances and go closest via Skelton's free-kick. The run of 52 matches without a goalless draw comes to an end. Wilkins, 34, aggravates an old neck injury and afterwards bows to the inevitable and has to retire after a long career (437 league games in all).	Lua-Lua/Skelton *Sheldon/Sparrow/Bull*

Match-by-Match Record (Games 35–46)

35 — A PRESTON — 7/3
Att: 11,323 | Pos: 2 | Pts: 44 | Game 14 | W 3-2 (1-0)
Keith 14, Lua-Lua 57, Duguid 87; Angell 71, 82. Ref: T Heilbron
United: Brown, Dunne*, Keith, Johnson R, Johnson G, Skelton, Duguid, Gregory, Moralee, Lock^, Dozzell; subs/opp: Moilanen, Alexander^, Edwards, Murdock, Jackson, Kidd, Cartwright, Rankine, Basham", Macken, Anderson*, Eyres/Gunlaugsson/Angell; Lua-Lua/Arnott
Dunne's cross is headed home by Keith. Lua-Lua jinks past two defenders to score a tremendous second on the break. Loanee sub Brett Angell scrambles one back and then heads an equaliser. With the U's hanging on, Arnott then chips cleverly to Duguid who volleys in a shock winner.

36 — H OXFORD — 11/3
Att: 4,058 | Pos: 21 | Pts: 44 | Game 14 | L 1-2 (0-1)
Skelton 63; Weatherstone 22, Whelan 90. Ref: A Leake
United: Brown, Duguid, Keith, Johnson R, Johnson G, Skelton, Lua-Lua, Gregory, Moralee*, Lock^, Dozzell; opp: Lundin, Robinson, Powell, Edwards, Watson, Whelan, Lilley", Tait, Murphy, Jemson^, Weath'st'ne^, Anthrobus/Cook/Russell; Opara/Arnott
Simon Weatherstone capitalises on an error to stride forward and crack a fine goal. Skelton stabs in a Keith corner. The U's look eager to nail a winner, but their efforts come to nothing thanks to a late, freakish winner. Defenders fail to clear and Phil Whelan scores from a prone position.

37 — A CARDIFF — 17/3
Att: 5,174 | Pos: 22 | Pts: 44 | Game 14 | L 2-3 (1-1)
Dozzell 43, Lua-Lua 51; Bowen 34, 70, Nugent 83. Ref: M Fletcher
United: Brown, Duguid, Keith, Johnson R, Johnson G, Skelton, Lua-Lua, Gregory, Moralee^, Lock*, Dozzell; opp: Hallworth, Brayson", Legg, Perrett, Young, Ford, Fowler", Bonner, Bowen, Nugent, Brazier^, Carpenter/Hill/Low; Opara/McGavin
Jason Bowen picks up Brown's poor clearance to shoot Billy Ayre's men ahead. After hitting a post Jason Dozzell nets the equaliser. Lua-Lua cuts in to bury a low drive. Bowen levels after a mix-up and then Kevin Nugent rifles a superb winner past Brown to climax a pulsating game.

38 — H OLDHAM — 21/3
Att: 3,282 | Pos: 14 | Pts: 44 | Game 16 | L 0-1 (0-1)
Holt 22. Ref: S Bennett
United: Brown, Duguid^, Keith, Lock, Johnson R*, Skelton, Lua-Lua, Gregory, Moralee, McGavin, Dozzell; opp: Kelly, McNiven, Holt, Garnett, Rickers^, Duxbury, Jones, Dudley, Sheridan, Whitehall*, Hotte, Allott/Innes; Farley/Arnott
With the ten-man U's still reorganising after Duguid departed with a foot injury, Andy Holt ventures forward unchallenged and rifles home a 30-yard drive. United create a host of chances but fail to take them, including a penalty blazed over by McGavin following a foul on Lua-Lua.

39 — H GILLINGHAM — 25/3
Att: 4,337 | Pos: 6 | Pts: 47 | Game 14 | W 2-1 (0-0)
McGavin 60, Lock 66; Rowe 79. Ref: A Kaye
United: Brown, Duguid, Keith, Johnson R, Sodje, Skelton, Johnson G, Gregory*, McGavin^, Lock, Dozzell*; opp: Bartram, Bass, Edge*, Smith, Butters, Ashby, Southall, Nosworthy, Rowe, Onuora", Lewis^, McGlinchey/Pinnock/Butler; Lua-Lua/Moralee/Arnott
McGavin scrambles the ball in after a Keith corner. Lock takes on two defenders and slips an angled drive under Vince Bartram. A Lock solo effort nearly makes it three. Rodney Rowe pulls one back for Peter Taylor's play-off hopefuls. Sodje, signed from Luton, gives a fine display.

40 — A LUTON — 1/4
Att: 5,125 | Pos: 10 | Pts: 47 | Game 18 | L 2-3 (0-1)
McGavin 52, Lock 59; Watts 10, Doherty 76, Taylor 82. Ref: G Barber
United: Brown, Duguid, Keith, Johnson R, Sodje*, Skelton, Johnson G^, Gregory", McGavin, Lock, Dozzell; opp: Roberts, White, Watts, Johnson, Boyce, McLaren, Spring, George, Doherty, Gray, Taylor; Lua-Lua/Arnott/Dunne
Julian Watts heads Luton in front and they miss more chances before McGavin fires past Ben Roberts. Lock exploits poor defending shortly after Emerson Boyce hit a post. Gary Doherty slides in to level, then Matthew Taylor cracks in the winner with the U's screaming for offside.

41 — H BLACKPOOL — 8/4
Att: 3,351 | Pos: 22 | Pts: 48 | Game 17 | L 1-1 (1-0)
Duguid 1; Thomas 66. Ref: M Messias
United: Brown, Dunne, Keith, Johnson R, Johnson G, Skelton, Duguid, Gregory, Moralee*, Lock, Ferguson; opp: Caig, Bardsley, Jaszczun, Richardson, Carlisle, Hughes, Coid*, Wellens, Murphy, Thomas, Gill, Newell
United score at 2.59pm! The match kicks off a minute or two early and within seconds Dunne's smart through pass is volleyed home by the alert Duguid. The U's fail to grab the crucial second goal and Steve McMahon's men level when James Thomas's header creeps in off a post.

42 — A WYCOMBE — 15/4
Att: 4,558 | Pos: 11 | Pts: 48 | Game 18 | L 0-3 (0-0)
Ryan 62, 67, Brown 90. Ref: P Joslin
United: Brown, Taylor, Keith, Johnson R, Sodje, Skelton, Johnson G, Gregory^, McGavin^, Lock*, Ferguson; opp: Taylor, Ryan, Vinnicombe, McCarthy, Bates, Rogers, Carroll", Simpson, Brown, Devine, Baird, McSporran; Dozzell/Lua-Lua/Keeble
Injury-hit United are woeful. Keith Ryan is left unmarked to head home a free-kick. Five minutes later he slots home from a similar position. Sub Lua-Lua misses an open goal and the U's are out for the count when Steve Brown finds the net with a long-distance effort in injury-time.

43 — H CAMBRIDGE — 22/4
Att: 4,902 | Pos: 19 | Pts: 51 | Game 18 | W 3-1 (2-0)
Duguid 17, McGavin 22, Keeble 57; Benjamin 54. Ref: K Leach
United: Brown, Dunne, Keith, Johnson R, Johnson G, Skelton, Lock, Gregory, Dozzell*, McGavin^, Ferguson; opp: Perez, Kavanagh, Joseph, Ashbee*, McNeill, Wanless, Wilson, Mustoe*, Benjamin, Taylor, Youngs^, Hunt/Abbey/Hansen; Farley/Keeble
Safety is ensured. McGavin flicks on Brown's long kick and Duguid tucks the ball home. Dozzell's handball is missed and he initiates a move that ends with McGavin poaching the second. Keeble clinches the points with a brave diving header – a goal very reminiscent of his father Vic!

44 — A WREXHAM — 24/4
Att: 2,460 | Pos: 14 | Pts: 51 | Game 18 | L 0-1 (0-1)
Hardy 26p. Ref: F Stretton
United: Brown, Dunne, Keith, Pinault*, Johnson G, Skelton, Keeble, Gregory, Lua-Lua, McGavin^, Ferguson; opp: Rogers, McGregor, Hardy^, Warren^, Carey, Ridler, Williams", Connolly, Morrell, Ferguson^, Gibson, Faulc'bridge/Roberts/Thomas; Duguid/McGavin
Dunne tangles with Andy Morrell and, to many observers' surprise, ref Stretton awards a penalty. Phil Hardy converts for his first Wrexham goal. Pinault gets his first start but is replaced at the interval. Kristian Rogers pulls off some fine saves, including one from a Dunne 20-yarder.

45 — H BRISTOL CITY — 29/4
Att: 4,013 | Pos: 9 | Pts: 51 | Game 18 | L 3-4 (2-1)
Lua-Lua 12, Skelton 29p, Duguid 46; Mur' 39, Mee' 63, Ferg' 71(og), Bell 84. Phillips; Ref: C Foy
United: Brown, Dunne, Keith, Duguid*, Johnson G, Skelton, Ferguson, Gregory, Lua-lua", Lock*, Dozzell; opp: Phillips, Burnell, Bell, Jordan, Millen, Holland, Murray, Brown*, Meechan, Hulbert^, Tinnion, Burns/Odejayi; Lock/Johnson R/Keeble
Lua-Lua sweeps in a Keith corner and United go further ahead when Andrew Jordan handles and Skelton nets from the spot. Scott Murray then gives City new hope. Dozzell squares for unmarked Duguid to make it 3-1, but tricky Murray hasn't finished yet and inspires a great fightback.

46 — A BRENTFORD — 6/5
Att: 5,297 | Pos: 17 | Pts: 52 | Game 18 | D 0-0 (0-0)
Ref: W Jordan
United: Brown, Dunne, Keith, Lock*, Johnson R, Skelton", Gregory^, Lua-Lua, McGavin, Dozzell; opp: Glass, Rowlands^, Anderson, Quinn, Marshall, Powell, Evans, O'Connor*, Owusu, Partridge, Scott", Folan/Graham/Tuanwuite; Opara/Johnson G/Ferguson
Both sides are clear of relegation and have little to play for, resulting in a drab, end-of-season affair. Ron Noades' side haven't won any of their last 12 games and lack confidence. United go closest when sub Ferguson beats Jimmy Glass, but sees his goalbound header cleared off the line.

Home Average 3,782 — Away 6,040

NATIONWIDE DIVISION 2 (CUP-TIES) Manager: Mick Wadsworth ⇨ Steve Whitton SEASON 1999-2000

Column key: bold = Colchester United (U's) line-up / squad numbers in use; *italic* = opponents' line-up and scorers.

Worthington Cup

1:1 H CRYSTAL PALACE D 2:2 H-T 1-0 10/8 Att 4,242

Scorers, Times, and Referees: Dozzell 36, Lua-Lua 63 · *Smith 62, Rizzo 90* · Ref: W Jordan

SQUAD NUMBERS IN USE											subs used
Brown !	Duguid	Keith	Burton	Greene	Aspinall	Wilkins*	Gregory	Lua-Lua	Launders	Dozzell	Walker/Richard
Digby	*Smith*	*Frampton^*	*Austin*	*Tuttle*	*Woozley*	*Mullins"*	*Rodger*	*Bradbury*	*Morrison*	*Thomson**	*Harris/Rizzo/Evans*

Brown is sent off for handling outside his area. Ten-man U's take the lead with Dozzell's neat shot. Hayden Mills hits the bar but Jamie Smith nets the rebound. Lua-Lua cracks a spectacular goal and performs an equally fine celebration. Nicky Rizzo slams in the dramatic late equaliser.

1:2 A CRYSTAL PALACE 20 L 1:3 H-T 0-2 24/8 Att 5,470 1:11

Scorers, Times, and Referees: Keith 75 · *Smith 18, Morrison 37, Rizzo 87* · Ref: R Olivier
(U's lose 3-5 on aggregate)

SQUAD NUMBERS IN USE											subs used
Walker	Duguid	Keith	Burton	Greene	Aspinall	Wilkins	Gregory	Lua-Lua*	Launders	Dozzell^	Pinault/Moralee
Digby	*Smith*	*Frampton*	*Austin*	*Harris*	*Woozley*	*Svensson^*	*Rodger**	*Bradbury*	*Morrison*	*Thomson*	*Rizzo/Carlisle*

A poor first-half display puts paid to the U's. They impose themselves better when 0-2 down, but by then it's too late. The following day Mick Wadsworth quits, blaming the pressures of long-distance travel to and from his home in the North. Assistant Steve Whitton gets the vacant job.

FA Cup

1 A SWANSEA 24 L 1:2 H-T 0-0 30/10 Att 3,622 3:14

Scorers, Times, and Referees: Lua-Lua 52 · *Cusack 83, Watkin 89* · Ref: R Furnandiz

SQUAD NUMBERS IN USE											subs used
Brown	Duguid	Keith	Skelton	Greene	Farley	Richard	Gregory*	Lua-Lua	McGavin	Dozzell	Lock
Freestone	*Cusack*	*Howard*	*Price*	*Smith*	*Bound*	*Keegan"*	*Appleby*	*Boyd"*	*Alsop*	*O'Leary^*	*Casey/Lacey/Watkin*

At a very soggy Vetch Field, Lua-Lua shoots a spectacular opening goal from well outside the area. Seven minutes from time a corner-kick is converted by Nick Cusack. With time almost up, Steve Watkins then pounces to fire in a superb volley to send United tumbling out of the Cup.

Auto Windscreens Shield

1 A SWANSEA 20 L 1:3 H-T 0-2 7/12 Att 1,222 3:8

Scorers, Times, and Referees: Moralee 56 · *Mutton 16, Thomas 19, Watkin 75* · Ref: A Bates

SQUAD NUMBERS IN USE											subs used
Brown	Farley	Keith	Skelton	White*	Lock^	Moralee	Gregory	Lua-Lua	McGavin	Dozzell	Wignall/Opara
Freestone	*Jones S*	*Appleby*	*Thomas*	*Smith*	*Bound*	*Keegan"*	*Jenkins**	*Mutton'*	*Alsop*	*Casey*	*Roberts/Watkin/Coates*

Tommy Mutton scores with ease and then Martin Thomas heads a second for John Hollins' men. Moralee nets his first goal for United in an improved second-half display. Sub Steve Watkin settles things with an 18-yard drive. Jack Wignall, the son of former manager Steve, debuts.

League Table

#	Team	P	Home W	Home D	Home L	Home F	Home A	Away W	Away D	Away L	Away F	Away A	Pts
1	Preston	46	15	4	4	37	23	13	7	3	37	14	95
2	Burnley	46	16	3	4	42	23	9	10	4	27	24	88
3	Gillingham*	46	16	3	4	46	21	9	7	7	33	27	85
4	Wigan	46	15	3	5	37	14	7	14	2	35	24	83
5	Millwall	46	14	7	2	41	18	9	6	8	35	32	82
6	Stoke	46	13	7	3	37	18	10	6	7	31	24	82
7	Bristol Rovers	46	13	7	3	34	19	10	4	9	35	26	80
8	Notts Co	46	9	6	8	32	27	9	5	9	29	28	65
9	Bristol City	46	7	14	2	31	18	5	10	8	28	39	64
10	Reading	46	10	9	4	28	18	8	5	10	29	45	62
11	Wrexham	46	9	6	8	23	24	8	5	10	29	37	62
12	Wycombe	46	11	4	8	32	24	5	9	9	24	29	61
13	Luton	46	10	7	6	41	35	7	3	13	20	30	61
14	Oldham	46	8	5	10	27	28	8	7	8	23	27	60
15	Bury	46	8	10	5	38	33	5	8	10	23	31	57
16	Bournemouth	46	11	6	6	37	19	5	5	13	22	43	57
17	Brentford	46	8	6	9	27	31	5	7	11	20	30	52
18	COLCHESTER	46	9	4	10	36	40	5	6	12	23	42	52
19	Cambridge	46	8	6	9	38	33	4	6	13	26	32	48
20	Oxford	46	6	5	12	24	38	6	4	13	19	35	45
21	Cardiff	46	5	10	8	23	34	4	7	12	22	33	44
22	Blackpool	46	4	10	9	26	37	7	7	12	23	40	41
23	Scunthorpe	46	6	13	4	16	34	5	6	12	24	40	39
24	Chesterfield	46	5	7	11	17	25	2	8	13	17	38	36
		1104	234	155	163	770	634	163	155	234	634	770	1501

* promoted after play-offs

Appearances and Goals

Player	Lge	Sub	LC	Sub	FAC	Sub	AW	Sub	G Lge	G LC	G FAC	G AW	G Tot
Arnott, Andy	4	8											
Aspinall, Warren	7		2						2				2
Bramble, Titus	2												
Brown, Simon	38				1								
Burton, Sagi	9		2										
Dozzell, Jason	38	1	2		1				5	1			6
Duguid, Karl	40	1	2		2				12				12
Dunne, Joe	19	1											
Farley, Craig	8	6	1										
Ferguson, Barry	5	1											
Forbes, Steve		2											
Germain, Steve	1	2							1				1
Greene, David	29		2		1				1				1
Gregory, David	45		2		1								
Johnson, Gavin	24	3											
Johnson, Ross	17	1											
Keeble, Chris	2	3							1				1
Keith, Joe	45		2		1				1	1			2
Launders, Brian	6		2										
Lock, Tony	12	12	2				1		2				2
Lua-Lua, Lomana	24	17	2		1		1		12	1	1		14
McGavin, Steve	30	4	1		1		1		16				16
Moralee, Jamie	20	7	1									1	1
Opara, Kelechi ('KK')	2	14											
Pinault, Thomas	1	3	1		1								
Richard, Fabrice	13	1			1								
Sodje, Efe	3												
Skelton, Aaron	27	6	1		1				4				4
Vaughan, John	6												
Walker, Andy	2		1										
White, Alan	4						1						
Wignall, Jack		1											
Wilkins, Richard	23	1	2						2				2
33 players used	506	95	22	4	11	1	11	2	59	3	1	1	64

Odds & ends

Double wins: (1) Chesterfield.

Double losses: (4) Burnley, Bury, Cardiff, Millwall.

Won from behind: (2) Reading (H), Bristol Rovers (H).

Lost from in front: (7) Bristol C (H), Bury (H), Cambridge (A), Cardiff (A).

Luton (A), Millwall (H), Swansea (FAC) (A).

High spots: The series of spectacular goals by Lua-Lua.

The improvement after 'Y2K' started, meaning relegation was avoided.

Surprise wins over promotion-chasers Preston, Wigan and Stoke.

Classic entertainment in a 5-4 win over high-flying Bristol Rovers.

Low spots: The run of 11 without a win, dropping the U's to 24th spot.

A 15% drop in gates, to the second-lowest average in Division Two.

The enforced retirement of Richard Wilkins after 279 League games.

The disruption caused in August when manager Wadsworth resigned.

The legal row following the dismissal of midfielder Brian Launders.

Note: Even after the wholesale changes of the previous season, a further 16 players made their debuts in 1999-2000.

Player of the Year: David Greene.

Ever-presents: (0).

Hat-tricks for: (0).

Hat-tricks against: (3) Ian Lawson (v Bury, A), Andy Payton (v Burnley, A), Martin Butler (v Cambridge, A).

Leading scorer: (16) Steve McGavin.

NATIONWIDE DIVISION 2

Manager: Steve Whitton — SEASON 2000-01

No	Date	Venue	Opponent	Att	Pos (U's / opp)	Pt	F-A	H-T	Scorers, Times	Referee
1	12/8	A	SWINDON	7,296	– / –	D (1)	0-0	0-0		S Dunn
2	18/8	H	ROTHERHAM	3,807	18 / 8	L (1)	0-1	0-1	Robins 34	P Walton
3	26/8	A	SWANSEA	6,247	10 / 22	W (4)	2-0	1-0	Lua-Lua 15, 83	P Rejer
4	29/8	H	OLDHAM	3,675	12 / 17	D (5)	1-1	1-0	Duguid 37 / Holt 52	K Hill
5	2/9	H	BOURNEMOUTH	3,459	5 / 22	W (8)	3-1	2-1	Skelton 4, 40, Stockwell 62 / Jorgensen 44	R Beeby
6	9/9	A	WIGAN	5,782	10 / 6	L (8)	1-3	1-2	Duguid 30 / Haworth 12, 42, 50	M Pike
7	12/9	A	BURY	2,577	12 / 2	D (9)	0-0	0-0		A Kaye
8	16/9	H	WREXHAM	3,724	14 / 18	D (10)	1-1	0-1	Lock 63 / Sam 12	P Joslin
9	23/9	A	BRISTOL CITY	7,411	12 / 23	D (11)	1-1	1-1	Lock 2 / Thorpe 20	M Warren
10	30/9	H	STOKE	3,758	12 / 8	L (11)	0-1	0-1	Thorne 14	I Cable
11	6/10	H	WALSALL	3,428	13 / 1	L (11)	0-2	0-2	Angell 20, Leitao 43	R Halsey

Squad numbers in use (U's listed first, opponents in italics)

1. SWINDON (A)
- U's: Brown, Dunne, Keith, Skelton, White, Clark, Duguid*, Gregory, Lua-Lua, Stockwell^, Dozzell^
- Swindon: *Griemink, Robinson, Davis, O'Halloran, Reeves, Willis, Invincible, Hewlett, Alexander, Grazioli*, Duke^*
- Subs used: Lock / Pinault / McGavin | *Cowe / Howe*
- A lively affair ends goalless with the U's new-look defence looking impressive. New skipper Simon Clark, signed from Leyton Orient, partners Alan White, previously on loan. Lua-Lua hits a post soon after the break. U's fans do well to reach the match with chaotic scenes on the M25.

2. ROTHERHAM (H)
- U's: Brown, Dunne, Keith, Skelton, White*, Clark, Duguid, Gregory*, Lua-Lua, Stockwell, Dozzell
- Rotherham: *Gray, Bryan, Beech, Scott, Garner, Branston, Watson, Robins, Fortune-West, Warne, Talbot*
- Subs used: McGavin / Johnson G | *Talbot / Berry*
- Poacher Mark Robins strikes for Ronnie Moore's men against the run of play. United fail to cash in on their superiority and after the break the visitors pack their defence and hold on. New recruit Adam Tanner is on the U's bench, given a chance after off-the-field problems at Ipswich.

3. SWANSEA (A)
- U's: Brown, Dunne, Keith, Skelton, White, Clark, Duguid^, Gregory, Lua-Lua, Stockwell, Dozzell
- Swansea: *Freestone, Jones, Howard^, Cusack, Smith, Bound, Jenkins, Price, Mutton^, Watkin, Coates^*
- Subs used: Gregory / Lock | *Thomas / Casey / Roberts*
- Dozzell's dazzling run leads to Lua-Lua firing firmly home. Lua-Lua hits the bar with a spectacular effort and Lock hits a post before Lua-Lua makes the points safe with a 20-yarder. Home fans invade the pitch to protest, but the U's celebrate a wonderful individual display by Lua-Lua.

4. OLDHAM (H)
- U's: Brown, Dunne, Keith*, Skelton, White, Clark, Duguid*, McGavin, Lua-Lua, Stockwell, Dozzell
- Oldham: *Kelly, Jones, Holt, Garnett, Ricketts, Duxbury, McNiven, Boshell*, Allott^, Corazzin, Dudley*
- Subs used: Lock / Johnson G | *Innes / Tipton / Whitehall*
- United have more possession and things look good when Duguid steals in to put them ahead at Boundary Park. Their luck is out after the break and a defensive error allows Andy Ritchie's side back on terms through defender Andy Holt. Steve McGavin completes his 250th league game.

5. BOURNEMOUTH (H)
- U's: Brown, Gregory, Johnson G*, Skelton, White, Clark, Duguid, McGavin, Lua-Lua*, Stockwell, Dozzell
- Bournemouth: *Memetier, Angus, Purches, Fenton, Tindall, Grant*, Jorgensen, Fletcher, Eribenne^, Huck^, ...*
- Subs used: Keith / Lock | *Day / Smith / I/O'Connor*
- Sean O'Driscoll's winless Cherries succumb to a double strike from Skelton, his second direct from a 20-yard free-kick. The visitors claim he was allowed to take it too quickly and their wild protests lead to an FA charge. Claus Jorgensen and Danny Smith are both red-carded later on.

6. WIGAN (A)
- U's: Brown, Gregory, Green*, Skelton, White, Clark, Duguid, McGavin*, Lua-Lua, Stockwell^, Dozzell^
- Wigan: *Carroll, Sharp, McGibbon, Balmer, De Zeeuw, Kilford, Haworth, Liddell, Martinez^, Nicholls*
- Subs used: Lock / Keeble | *McLaughlin / Nicholls*
- After the fine cup win at QPR, United look disjointed and Whitton is angered at 'our worst display so far'. Simon Haworth converts Andy Liddell's cross, before Duguid levels with a deflected drive. Lethal Haworth is set up twice more by Liddell and has a fourth goal disallowed.

7. BURY (A)
- U's: Brown, Gregory, Kenny, Skelton^, White, Clark, Duguid, McGavin, Lua-Lua*, Stockwell*, Dozzell^
- Bury: *Barrass*, Collins, Dawes, Swailes, Redmond, Billy, Reid, Preece^, Bullock*, Littlejohn*
- Subs used: Lock / Tanner | *James / Crowe / Forrest*
- Gritty United bounce back from the Wigan loss and prevent Andy Preece's men going top of the table with a hard-working display. A national fuel shortage affects the size of the crowd, but scouts are here in force to watch Lua-Lua and the speculation mounts over when he will be sold.

8. WREXHAM (H)
- U's: Brown, Gregory^, Dearden, Skelton, White, Clark, Duguid, Sam?, McGavin, Stockwell*, Dozzell
- Wrexham: *Barrass*, Roche, Barrett, Tanner*, Carey, Rider, Ferguson, Reid, Preece^, Edwards^*
- Subs used: Keith / Keeble | *Faulconbridge / Gibson / Roberts*
- United start slowly and Wrexham's recent recruit, Trinidadian Hector Sam, notches his sixth goal in five matches. Brian Flynn's men are less potent after the break as the U's begin to knock the ball around better. Lock brings things level and they go close to clinching all three points.

9. BRISTOL CITY (A)
- U's: Brown, Phillips, Amankwaah, Skelton^, White*, Clark, Duguid, Murray, Lock, McGavin^, Dozzell^
- Bristol City: *Bell, Goodridge*, Millen, Carey, Dunning, Beadle, Thorpe, Tinnion*
- Subs used: Keith / Keeble / Opara | *Testimitanu / Brown*
- After Lock's early strike is cancelled out by crafty striker Tony Thorpe, Brown has a stormer to keep Danny Wilson's side at bay. White tackles Moldovan sub Testimitanu and is carried off injured. His condition is not helped when the stretcher-bearers stumble and tip him off!

10. STOKE (H)
- U's: Brown, Ward, Hansson, Skelton, White, Clark, Duguid, Gunnarsson, Lock^, McGavin*, Dozzell*
- Stoke: *Dorigo, Thomas, Mohan, Gudjonsson, Kavanagh, Lightb'urne*, Thorne^, O'Connor*
- Subs used: Tanner / Opara / Arnott | *Petty / Thordarson*
- Experienced goalfighter Peter Thorne strikes for Gudjon Thordarson's side after some slack U's defending. United's build-up play is good but the first-half loss of both strikers, McGavin and Lock, proves a serious blow. Injury-hit Whitton signs Chelsea striker Mark Nicholls on loan.

11. WALSALL (H)
- U's: Brown, Walker, Brightwell, Skelton, White*, Clark, Duguid*, Keeble, Nicholls, Stockwell*, Dozzell
- Walsall: *Aranalde, Tillson, Barras, Bukran", Hall, Bennett, Angell*, Leitao^, Matias*
- Subs used: Lock / Tanner | *Roper / Byfield / Keates*
- Ray Graydon's table-toppers make life hard for United with a hard-working display. Mark Nicholls debuts but injury-hit United struggle for any rhythm and Whitton says he is 'frustrated and disappointed' by the outcome. Portuguese Jorge Leitao's sixth of the season proves decisive.

12 — A PORT VALE · 14/10
Pos 17 · L 1-3 (0-1) · Att 3,192 · 18 · 11
Scorers: Scott 63 | Tankard 4, Naylor 68, 76 · Ref: D Pugh
U's: Brown, Dunne, Johnson G, Skelton^, White !, Keeble, Duguid, Nicholls*, Scott, Stockwell*, Keith/Lock/McGavin
Opp: Goodlad, Tankard, Carragher, Brammer, Walsh, Widdington, Bridge, Wilk'n Cummins, Gray*, Naylor, Vijanen

Allen Tankard heads home after the U's fail to deal with a long throw. Debutant Scott levels with a cracking shot on the turn. Tony Naylor evades a static defence to regain the lead. Lively Naylor reacts first to head in Alex Smith's cross. White is red-carded for a 'professional foul'.

13 — A BRENTFORD · 17/10
Pos 21 · L 0-1 (0-0) · Att 3,595 · 11 · 11
Scorers: — | Scott 89 · Ref: S Mathieson
U's: Brown, Gregory, Keith, Skelton, White, Johnson G, Duguid, Nicholls*, Scott, Stockwell*, Dozzell
Opp: Gottskalks'nCrowe^, Tankard, Theobald, Mahon, Quinn, Marshall, Ingimarsson, Evans, Scott, Rowlands*, Partridge, Folan/Williams

United revert to a three-man central defence and Gregory returns to midfield. Brown does well to save from Paul Evans and Gavin Mahon. Scott and McGavin go close, the latter hitting the bar. A point looks likely until Evans floats in a free-kick and Andy Scott nets from six yards.

14 — H CAMBRIDGE · 21/10
Pos 18 · W 2-0 (1-0) · Att 3,761 · 8 · 14
Scorers: McGavin 39, 63p · Ref: P Dowd
U's: Brown, Gregory, Johnson G, Fitzgerald, White*, Clark, Duguid, McGavin, Scott, Stockwell, Skelton
Opp: Perez, Ashbee, Cowan!, McAnespie, Dreyer, Wanless, Slade, Abbey", Russell*, Youngs, Taylor/Axeldal/Mustoe

Tom Cowan is sent off early on for apparently kicking Duguid in the face. Roy McFarland's ten men try to reorganise but an excellent move down the left involving one-touch passing leads to McGavin finishing nicely with a low drive. The same player's penalty clinches three points.

15 — H BRISTOL ROV · 24/10
Pos 17 · W 2-1 (1-0) · Att 2,987 · 11 · 17
Scorers: Gregory 36, Duguid 62 | Ellis 87 · Ref: S Tomlin
U's: Brown, Gregory, Johnson G, Skelton, White!, Clark, Duguid, McGavin, Scott*, Stockwell, Dozzell
Opp: Culkin, Walters*, Challis, Foster, Andreasson, Jones, Astafjevs, Evans, Allsopp, Hogg^, Bryant, Pethick/Ellis

Scott's knock-down is latched on to by Gregory, who nets his first goal of the season with a smart finish. A fine move involving Dozzell and Johnson down the left allows Duguid to make it two. Clinton Ellis bags a late consolation but the U's are delighted with six points in four days.

16 — A PETERBOROUGH · 28/10
Pos 17 · L 1-3 (0-0) · Att 5,469 · 12 · 17
Scorers: Duguid 48 | McKenzie 56, Lee 87, Clarke 89 · Ref: R Pearson
U's: Brown, Gregory, Johnson G, Skelton, Fitzgerald, Clark !, Duguid, McGavin, Scott*, Stockwell, Nicholls
Opp: Tyler, Hooper", Drury, Forsyth, Rea, Edwards, Farrell, Oldfield, Clarke, Lee*, MacKenzie, Shields/Green/Gill

McGavin picks out Duguid inside the area and a simple tap-in does the rest. Mark Tyler makes some fine saves after Posh hit back with an equaliser and then United suffer two crucial setbacks as loanee Scott suffers a serious knee injury and Clark is sent off after two yellow cards.

17 — H NORTHAMPTON · 4/11
Pos 19 · L 0-2 (0-1) · Att 3,352 · 6 · 17
Scorers: — | Forrester 39, Howard 60 · Ref: M North
U's: Brown, Arnott, Johnson G, Skelton^, Fitzgerald, Clark, Duguid*, McGavin, Scott*, Stockwell, Dozzell, Lock/Morgan
Opp: Welch, Savage, Hughes, Sampson, Hope, Hunt, Hodge, Howard, Forrester, Gabbiadini, Hargreaves

Kevin Wilson's men work hard for their win in a match where there was little to choose between the sides, apart from the finishing of Jamie Forrester and his big partner Steve Howard. 'KK' Opara leaves the U's for disciplinary reasons. Marie Partner is promoted to Chief Executive.

18 — A READING · 11/11
Pos 17 · W 1-0 (1-0) · Att 11,549 · 5 · 20
Scorers: Johnson G 38 · Ref: M Messais
U's: Woodman, Gregory^, Johnson G, Skelton^, White!, Fitzgerald, Duguid, McGavin^, Conlon, Stockwell, Dunne/Lock
Opp: Whitehead, Gurney^, Newman, Viveash, Mackie, Parkinson, Hodges, Caskey^, Cureton, Butler*, Jones, MacIntyre/Rougier/Igoe

Emergency signing Woodman links up with the squad just hours before kick-off. Gavin Johnson becomes the 250th different player to score a league goal for the U's with a wonder strike from a free-kick. Conlon has a fine debut in attack. Ricky Newman hits the bar as the U's hang on.

19 — H WYCOMBE · 25/11
Pos 17 · D 0-0 (0-0) · Att 3,646 · 7 · 21
Scorers: — · Ref: R Furnandiz
U's: Woodman, Dunne^, Stockwell, Skelton, White, Clark, Duguid, Gregory, Conlon, McGavin^, Keeble, Lock !
Opp: Taylor, Rogers, Beeton, Bulman, Cousins, Bates, Ryan, Simpson, McSporran, Rammell, Thompson^, Parkin

After the Yeovil debacle, United show plenty of fight. Keeper Martin Taylor keeps Lawrie Sanchez's side on terms on a number of occasions. sub Lock is red-carded for a wild tackle near the touchline.

20 — H NOTTS CO · 2/12
Pos 13 · W 2-0 (1-0) · Att 3,280 · 15 · 24
Scorers: Keeble 43, Conlon 78 · Ref: P Armstrong
U's: Woodman, Dunne, Fitzgerald, Skelton, White, Keeble, Duguid, Gregory, Conlon, Stockwell*, Keeble*/Arnott
Opp: Gibson, McDermott, Pearce, Fenton, Richardson, Jacobsen, Owers, Stallard, Bolland*, Hamilton^, Hughes/Newton

Conlon and Stockwell break fast in a move down the right and Keeble gets in position to put United ahead. The improving Conlon uses his strength to latch on to a through pass and finish expertly. Clark is missing again, still recovering from shock following a fatal road accident.

21 — A LUTON · 16/12
Pos 12 · W 3-0 (1-0) · Att 4,791 · 23 · 27
Scorers: Conlon 28, Gregory 48, Pinault 76 · Ref: M Pike
U's: Woodman, Dunne*, Johnson G, Skelton, Fitzgerald, Keeble, Duguid, McLaren, Conlon, Stockwell*, Clark/McGavin/Pinault
Opp: Abbey, Helin, Watts, Whitbread, Johnson, Spring, Locke*, Taylor, George, Nogan, Fotiadis

Lil Fuccillo's side lack punch and miss chances. Dunne is carried off with a dreadful facial injury that needs 40 stitches. U's dominate midfield and take their chances on the counter-attack. Pinault gets his first goal, and Whitton admits 3-0 is a little flattering given the nature of the game.

22 — H OXFORD · 22/12
Pos 8 · W 3-2 (2-0) · Att 3,695 · 24 · 30
Scorers: Conlon 27, Stockwell 35, 89 | Gray 56, Beauchamp 57 · Ref: P Alcock
U's: Woodman, Gregory, Fitzgerald, Skelton, White, Clark, Duguid, Keeble, Conlon, Stockwell*, Dozzell*/McGavin/Johnson R
Opp: Cutler, Hartswell, Jarman, Fear, Linighan, Richardson*, Anthrobus, Gray, Murphy, Hackett, Beauchamp, Powell

Confident United cruise to a 2-0 half-time lead but are shocked when David Kemp's men, bottom of the table since September, battle back to level the scores. The experienced Stockwell calms matters by notching the winner. Loanee keeper Woodman becomes a permanent signing.

23 — A MILLWALL · 26/12
Pos 12 · L 1-6 (0-2) · Att 11,156 · 1 · 30
Scorers: Ryan 87 (og) | Harris 18,76,90p, Moody 26, 62, Ifill 88 · Ref: M Cooper
U's: Woodman, Gregory, Fitzgerald, Skelton, White, Clark, Duguid, Keeble*, Conlon, Stockwell*, McGavin/Johnson G
Opp: Warner, Lawrence*, Ryan, Cahill, Dyche, Dolan, Livermore, Moody^, Harris, Ifill, Kinet, Reid/Sadlier

Mark McGhee's side outclasses the U's. Neil Harris fires a hat-trick including a penalty after Fitzgerald handles. The only consolation comes as Robbie Ryan diverts a McGavin cross into his own goal. But for Woodman's heroics it could have been ten. It's the worst defeat in 11 years.

NATIONWIDE DIVISION 2

Manager: Steve Whitton — SEASON 2000-01

No			Date	Att	Pos	Pt	F-A	H-T	Scorers, Times, and Referees
24	A	OLDHAM	13/1	4,076	15 / 16	31	D 1-1	0-0	Stockwell 59 / Tipton 90 / Ref: G Cain
25	A	OXFORD	27/1	5,064	15 / 24	34	W 1-0	1-0	Dunne 45 / Ref: C Webster
26	A	BOURNEMOUTH	3/2	4,407	15 / 10	35	D 2-2	2-0	McGleish 22, Stockwell 28 / Hughes 63p, Fletcher C 86 / Ref: S Baines
27	H	MILLWALL	6/2	4,523	15 / 1	35	L 0-1	0-1	Ifill 21 / Ref: T Leake
28	H	WIGAN	10/2	3,275	15 / 2	35	L 0-2	0-1	Bidstrup 3, Liddell 77 / Ref: B Curson
29	A	WREXHAM	17/2	2,492	17 / 14	35	L 0-1	0-1	McGregor 36 / Ref: H Webb
30	H	BURY	20/2	2,725	17 / 14	36	D 1-1	0-0	Skelton 59p / Preece 82 / Ref: F Stretton
31	H	BRISTOL CITY	24/2	3,430	17 / 7	39	W 4-0	2-0	Gregory 7, Keith 42, Stockwell 57, [Conlon 69] / Ref: T Parkes
32	A	ROTHERHAM	27/2	5,864	17 / 2	39	L 2-3	1-0	Johnson G 35, Keith 74 / Robins 48, Artell 50, Hurst 84 / Ref: A Butler
33	A	STOKE	3/3	11,714	17 / 6	39	L 1-3	1-2	Skelton 4p / Thorne 9, 40, Kavanagh 88 / Ref: M Cowburn
34	H	PORT VALE	7/3	2,579	17 / 18	39	L 0-1	0-0	Brammer 54 / Ref: J Robinson

Squad numbers in use — subs used

24 OLDHAM — Woodman, Dunne, Johnson G, Fitzgerald, Johnson R, Clark, Skelton, Gregory, Conlon, Stockwell*, McGavin^ — subs used: Keeble/McGleish
(Opposition: Kelly, McNiven, Innes, Garnett, Ricketts, Hotte*, Carss, Sheridan, Tipton, Corazzin^, Eyres — Holt/Alliott)
Striker McGleish returns for his second spell at Layer Road. A big punt by Woodman is misjudged and Stockwell gets clear on goal, finishing expertly. The Latics pile men forward and are rewarded in the dying seconds when John Sheridan's cross is cracked home by Matthew Tipton.

25 OXFORD — Woodman, Dunne*, Johnson R, Skelton, Clark, Johnson G, Gregory, Conlon, Stockwell*, McGleish^ — subs used: Duguid/McGavin
(Opposition: Cutler, Hartswell, Robertson, Jarman*, Quinn, Monk, Scott, Gray, Murphy, Hackett, Beauchamp — Fear)
An even first half ends with G Johnson, Conlon and Stockwell combining on the left, with Stockwell crossing for Dunne to head a rare goal in off a post. Sub Duguid causes problems for the home side, one shot striking the crossbar. Dunne gets top honours for a fine all-round display.

26 BOURNEMOUTH — Woodman, Dunne, Johnson G, Skelton, Clark, Fitzgerald, Gregory, Conlon, Stockwell*, McGleish^ — subs used: Duguid/McGavin
(Opposition: Stewart, Ford*, Bernard*, Howe, Tindal, Fletcher C, Jorgensen, Elliott^, Defoe, Hughes, Hayter/Smith/O'Connor)
Conlon's header is parried to McGleish, who makes no mistake. A long-ranger by Stockwell crosses the line via the crossbar with the keeper in a muddle. A Dunne tackle is controversially deemed a foul and Richard Hughes nets the penalty. Carl Fletcher's powerful drive levels matters.

27 MILLWALL — Woodman, Dunne, Johnson R, Fitzgerald, Clark, Skelton, Gregory, Conlon, Stockwell*, McGleish* — subs used: Duguid/McGavin
(Opposition: Gueret, Lawrence, Ryan, Cahill, Dyche, Nethercott, Livermore^, Moody, Harris, Ifill, Neill^ — Reid/Bircham)
On a tricky pitch, United put up a great fight against the leaders but end up with nothing to show for it. Lions boss Mark McGhee says it was the most intense sustained pressure his men had faced all season. Keeper Willy Gueret is their saviour after Paul Ifill gives them an early lead.

28 WIGAN — Woodman, Dunne*, Johnson G^, Fitzgerald, Clark, Skelton*, Gregory, Conlon, Stockwell*, McGleish/Keeble — subs used: Duguid/McGavin/Keeble
(Opposition: Stillie, Green, Sharp, Bidstrup, McGibbon, De Zeeuw, Martinez^, McLaughlin*, Haworth, Roberts, Liddell — Griffiths/Balmer)
Norwegian Stefan Bidstrup delivers a decisive blow early on and although United rally well, they are forced to chase the game dangerously. Bruce Rioch's promotion-chasers exploit the gaps at the back with a breakaway goal from Andy Liddell. Arnott quits the club due to injury.

29 WREXHAM — Woodman, Dunne^, Keith, Johnson R*, Fitzgerald, Clark, Skelton, Gregory, McGavin, Stockwell*, Edwards* — subs used: White/Duguid/Keeble
(Opposition: Dearden, McGregor, Roche, Owen^, Carey, Rider, Barrett, Ferguson, Russell, Edwards*, Faulc'bridge" — Gibson/Blackwood/Trundle)
Against the run of play, full-back Mark McGregor thrashes home a pot-shot from 30 yards. The returning Keith runs on to a Dunne cross and hits the bar from 20 yards. McGleish gets clean through but his effort is saved. Highly rated youngster Lee Trundle debuts and nearly scores.

30 BURY — Woodman, Dunne*, Keith, Johnson R, Fitzgerald, Clark, Skelton, Gregory, Conlon, Stockwell, McGleish — subs used: —
(Opposition: Kenny, Billy, Armstrong, Collins, Swailes, Redmond*, Dawes, Reid, Newby, Cramb^, Forrest* — Preece/Littlejohn/Jarrett)
The U's look nervous and edgy in the first half, but the prospect of the first win in 2001 looks rosier when Skelton strokes home a penalty. Andy Preece's hard-up side, who could not afford a hotel and had a five-hour bus trip, save a point with a late goal from their player-manager.

31 BRISTOL CITY — Woodman, Dunne*, Keith, Johnson R, Fitzgerald, Clark, Skelton, Gregory^, Conlon, Stockwell*, Duguid* — subs used: McGavin/Johns'n G/McG'ish
(Opposition: Phillips, Amankw'h^, Woodman, Clist*, Millen, Carey, Murray, Brown, Beadle, Peacock, Tinnion — Thorpe/Hill)
After much bad weather, fans help drain the pitch and are rewarded by a fine display. The passing is slick and four chances are put away with precision. City's heaviest defeat of the season so far dents their promotion bid and manager Danny Wilson says his men 'need to get tougher'.

32 ROTHERHAM — Woodman, Dunne, Keith, Fitzgerald, Clark, Johnson G, Gregory^, Conlon, Stockwell*, Duguid — subs used: White
(Opposition: Pettinger, Garner, Hurst, Scott, Artell, Branston, Watson, Robins*, Brown, Barker^, Warne — Talbot, Sedgwick/Lee)
Skelton's free-kick is headed in by G Johnson at the near post. Mark Robins levels and David Artell heads in a long throw. The U's complain about the home side using towels to aid their throw-ins. Keith equalises with a header but Paul Hurst beats Woodman in the air for the winner.

33 STOKE — Woodman, Dunne, Keith, Fitzgerald, White, Johnson R*, Johnson G, Conlon*, Skelton, Stockwell, Duguid — subs used: McGavin/McGleish
(Opposition: Kristinsson, Hansson, Dorigo, Thomas, Mohan, Kippe, Gudjonsson*, Risom, Cooke^, Thorne, Gunnars or^ — Kavanagh/Petty/Goodfellow)
G Johnson is brought down and Skelton powers in the penalty. Poor marking allows Tony Dorigo's free-kick to find Peter Thorne, who fires past Woodman. Another Dorigo free-kick is headed in from close range by Thorne. Graham Kavanagh heads in off a post to finish things off.

34 PORT VALE — Woodman, Dunne, Keith, Fitzgerald, Johnson R, Skelton*, Gregory, Conlon, Stockwell, Duguid^ — subs used: McGavin/McGleish
(Opposition: Goodlad, Burton, Carragher, Brammer, Walsh, Brisco, Cummins, Bridge-Wilk'n/Naylor, Smith)
Gregory is hampered by what turns out to be a broken foot, but this is no excuse for a very poor team display. Whitton calls a team meeting later in the week to clear the air. Fears of relegation are increasing. Lua-Lua attends this game, but fans are told he won't be returning on loan.

Match 35 — WALSALL (A) 10/3

4,553 · 17 · 4 · W · 1-0 · 42

Scorer: Conlon 56 · Ref: P Dowd

U's: Woodman, Dunne, Keith, Johnson R, White, Fitzgerald, Skelton, Johnson G, Conlon^, Stockwell*, Duguid / McGavin/McGleish

Walsall: Walker, Marsh, Aranalde, Tilson, Roper, Barras", Keates, Bennett, Byfield*, Leitao^, Simpson / Bukran/Hall/Angell

Whitton's team meeting seems to have done the trick as the U's look transformed. The reorganised defence looks outstanding. Duguid goes on a good run and finds Dunne, whose pinpoint cross is powerfully headed home by Conlon. Woodman plays superbly as the U's hang on grimly.

Match 36 — BRENTFORD (H) 16/3

3,423 · 14 · 13 · W · 3-1 · 45

Scorers: Keith 41, Stockwell 51, Duguid 74 / Owusu 9 · Ref: D Laws

U's: Woodman, Dunne, Keith, Johnson R, White, Fitzgerald, Skelton, Johnson G, Conlon, Stockwell*, Duguid^ / McGavin/McGleish

Brentford: Gottskalksson'n Dobson, Lovett*, Mahan, Powell, Marshall, Ingimarsson Evans, Owusu, O'Connor Partridge^, Folan/Williams

Lloyd Owusu buries a thundering header early on. Keith, now raiding from midfield, volleys the equaliser. Keith creates an opportunity for Stockwell, who sweeps the ball home. Duguid goes on a long run and finishes clinically, to cap a good win and an impressive personal display.

Match 37 — SWINDON (H) 20/3

2,736 · 15 · 18 · L · 0-1 · 45

Scorer: Reddy 28 · Ref: W Burns

U's: Woodman, Dunne, Keith, Johnson R, White, Fitzgerald, Skelton*, Johnson G, Conlon^, Stockwell, Duguid* / McGavin/McGleish/Scott

Swindon: Mitenhall Robinson, Davis, Haywood, Reeves, Robinson, Invincible, Hewett, Alexander, Graziol*, Reddy, Van der Linden

A defensive mix-up leads to Andy King's outfit taking the lead through Michael Reddy. Relegation certainties a few weeks ago, the visitors are filled with confidence and keep the U's at bay. A series of second-half chances go begging and United remain part of the relegation dogfight.

Match 38 — LUTON (H) 31/3

4,271 · 14 · 22 · W · 3-1 · 48

Scorers: Stockwell 17, 37, Skelton 43p / Howard 83p · Ref: P Warren

U's: Woodman, Duguid, Keith*, Fitzgerald, White, Clark, Skelton, Johnson G, Scott^, Stockwell*, McGleish / McGavin/Conlon/Izzet

Luton: Abbey, Helin, Dryden, Boyce, Mansell, McLaren, Spring, Rowland^, Taylor, Howard, George, Douglas

Lethal Stockwell pounces twice, leaving Hatters boss Joe Kinnear furious with his men's poor marking. The game is over by the interval when Skelton nets from the spot. Luton improve in the second half, but only beat Woodman once, new signing Steve Howard converting a penalty.

Match 39 — SWANSEA (H) 3/4

2,886 · 12 · 23 · W · 3-0 · 51

Scorers: Conlon 20, 86, McGleish 64 · Ref: S Tomlin

U's: Woodman, Duguid, Clark*, Skelton, White, Fitzgerald, Izzet, Johnson G, Conlon^, Stockwell*, McGleish / Dunne/McGavin/Morgan

Swansea: Freestone Lacey*, Howard^, Cusack, O'Leary", Bound, Price, Romo, Savarese, Watkin, Fabiano, Roberts/Jenkins/Phillips

Kemi Izzet, a pre-deadline signing, is impressive against John Hollins' doomed outfit. Johnson's corner is powerfully headed home by Conlon. McGleish settles it when heading in another Johnson cross. Roger Freestone's poor clearance is intercepted and Conlon grabs his second goal.

Match 40 — BRISTOL ROV (A) 14/4

6,551 · 17 · 21 · L · 0-2 · 51

Scorers: Astafjevs 85, Ellington 90 · Ref: J Brandwood

U's: Woodman, Duguid, Keith*, Fitzgerald, White, Clark, Skelton, Izzet, Scott^, Stockwell*, McGleish^ / Dunne/McGavin/Conlon

Bristol Rov: Culkin, Astafjevs, Wilson, Foster, Thomson, Jones, Mauge, Hogg, Cameron*, Gall, Bryant", Ellington/Owusu

Rovers pile on the first-half pressure with no reward. After the break the ref turns down a strong penalty claim when Izzet hauls down Lewis Hogg. Justice is done when Latvian Vitalijs Astafjevs beats Woodman with a low shot. In injury time a fine drive by Owusu adds the second.

Match 41 — PETERBOROUGH (H) 17/4

4,336 · 17 · 11 · D · 2-2 · 52

Scorers: Stockwell 18, Izzet 77 / Lee 11, Oldfield 53 · Ref: C Foy

U's: Woodman, Duguid, Fitzgerald, White, Fitzgerald, Skelton, Johnson G, Scott^, Stockwell*, Izzet / McGavin/Conlon

Peterborough: Tyler, Hooper", Drury, Forsyth, Rea, Farrell, Oldfield, Clarke, Lee*, McKenzie^, Shields/Green/Gill

Jason Lee puts Barry Fry's side ahead but minutes later a superbly taken equaliser by Stockwell cancels it out. David Oldfield restores the lead after the interval, but the U's bounce back again, Izzet grabbing the first league goal of his career. Loanee Izzet has now signed permanently.

Match 42 — NORTHAMPTON (A) 21/4

5,012 · 17 · 12 · L · 0-2 · 52

Scorers: Savage 35p, Forrester 81 · Ref: A Hall

U's: Woodman, Duguid^, Johnson R, Fitzgerald, White, Skelton, Johnson G, Conlon, Scott*, Stockwell, Johnson G* / Keith/McGleish

Northampton: Sollitt, Frain, Dempsey, Sampson, Hope, Lopes^, Hodge*, Savage, Forrester, Gabbiadini", Whitley, Hunter/Lowe/Howey

United pin the Cobblers in their own half for 25 minutes, but a controversial penalty changes the pattern of the game. Dave Savage puts away a kick that should have been an indirect free-kick, claims Whitton. Jamie Forrester makes the points safe with a shot deflected past Woodman.

Match 43 — READING (H) 28/4

5,010 · 16 · 3 · W · 2-1 · 55

Scorers: Conlon 34, Skelton 43p / Cureton 24 · Ref: P Danson

U's: Woodman, Dunne, Keith*, Johnson R, Fitzgerald, Clark, Skelton, Johnson G, Conlon^, Stockwell, Duguid* / White/McGleish

Reading: Whitehead Murty, Robinson^, Viveash, Whitbread, Parkinson, McIntyre", Harper*, Cureton, Butler, Igoe, Caskey/Rougier/Forster

Alan Pardew's promotion-chasing side get a right royal chasing in an exciting first period. Jamie Cureton turns the game upside down. The drop is now highly unlikely.

Match 44 — CAMBRIDGE (A) 1/5

5,317 · 16 · 20 · L · 1-2 · 55

Scorers: McGleish 81 / Richardson 48, Cowan 56 · Ref: P Jones

U's: Woodman, Dunne, Keith, Skelton*, White, Fitzgerald, Skelton, Johnson G, Conlon^, Stockwell, Duguid / McGavin/McGleish

Cambridge: Perez, Fleming, Hanson, Duncan, Joseph, Wanless, Pilu*, Kitson, Revell^, Cowan, Riza/Richardson

John Beck's substitutions do the trick and steer the home side towards safety from the drop. Marcus Richardson needs just two minutes to steer a shot in. Paul Wanless lays the ball off and Tom Cowan smashes a spectacular second. McGleish leaps high to convert a cross by McGavin.

Match 45 — NOTTS CO (A) 3/5

2,860 · 17 · 9 · D · 2-2 · 56

Scorers: Stockwell 9, McGleish 89 / Stallard 41, Jacobsen 60 · Ref: T Jones

U's: Brown, Dunne, Keith, Skelton, Johnson R, Clark, Pinault, McGavin, Scott^, Stockwell*, McGleish / Morgan

Notts Co: Ward, McDermott, Nicholson, Newton, Richardson, Jacobsen, Owers, Allsop, Bolland, Nicholson

Anders Jacobsen's attempted clearance ricochets into goal off the shins of Stockwell. Mark Stallard produces a clever lob to equalise for Jocky Scott's side. Jacobsen blasts home after a corner, but McGleish conjures up a trademark leap and bullet header to save a late point for the U's.

Match 46 — WYCOMBE (A) 5/5

7,516 · 17 · 13 · D · 1-1 · 57

Scorers: McGleish 51 / Ryan 70 · Ref: B Knight

U's: Woodman, Dunne, Keeble*, Johnson R, White, Clark, Pinault, Johnson G, McGavin^, Stockwell*, McGleish / Keith/Duguid/Morgan

Wycombe: Taylor, Marsh, Vinnicombe, Bulman, Senda, Bates, Ryan, Simpson, Whittingham Essandoh, Brown", Clegg"/Harkin

Due to fixture rescheduling, this is the U's fifth game in eight days. Wycombe's biggest crowd of the season creates a real party atmosphere. McGleish heads in after a free-kick to open the scoring, but home skipper Keith Ryan nets a powerful header from Chris Vinnicombe's cross.

Home 3,555 · Away 5,596 · Average 5,596

NATIONWIDE DIVISION 2 (CUP-TIES) Manager: Steve Whitton SEASON 2000-01

		Att	F-A	H-T	Scorers, Times, and Referees
Worthington Cup					
1:1 H QP RANGERS 23/8	18 L	3,916 1:14	0-1	0-1	Kiwomya 27 — Ref: R Fletcher
1:2 A QP RANGERS 6/9	5 W	4,042 1:13	4-1	2-1	Lua-Lua 11, 18, 86, McGavin 56 / Kiwomya 45 — Ref: D Gallagher — (U's win 4-2 on aggregate)
2:1 A SHEFFIELD UTD 19/9	14 L	3,531 1:10	0-3	0-1	Devlin 18, Clark 80 (og), Kelly 83 — Ref: P Danson
2:2 H SHEFFIELD UTD 27/9	12 L	1,981 1:7	0-1	0-0	Devlin 59 — Ref: D Elleray — (U's lose 0-4 on aggregate)
FA Cup					
1 A YEOVIL 18/11	17 L	4,552 NL	1-5	0-0	Duguid 69 / (Skiverton 57, Way 80p), Patmore 50, 85, Belgrave 53 — Ref: W Burns
LDV Vans Trophy					
1 A CAMBRIDGE 5/12	13 L	1,555 12	0-2	0-2	Dreyer 3, Axeldal 18 — Ref: S Baines

SQUAD NUMBERS IN USE / subs used

1:1 H QP RANGERS
- Brown, Dunne, White, Keith, Skelton, McGavin, Clark, Dozzell, Stockwell*, Duguid, Lua-Lua
- *Harper, Perry, Baraclough, Carlisle, Morrow, Langley, Ready, Peacock*, Crouch^, Wardley, Kiwomya*
- subs used: Johnson G / Koejoe/Heinola

Just like five days earlier against Rotherham, the U's are the more inventive side, but fall behind when Chris Kiwomya pounces. Lua-Lua gives Karl Ready a torrid time. QPR boss Gerry Francis admits his side were poor and the better team lost. Gavin Peacock exits with a broken nose.

1:2 A QP RANGERS
- Brown, Gregory, White, Johnson G, Skelton, McGavin, Clark, Dozzell, Stockwell, Duguid, Lua-Lua
- *Harper, Perry, Breacker, Rose, Morrow, Langley, Carlisle, Darlington, Koejoe, Connolly*, Kiwomya*
- subs used: Lua-Lua / Crouch/Bruce

Lua-Lua strikes twice early, his second sees him jink past three men before slotting home. Chris Kiwomya nods Rangers back into the contest, but in-form Lua-Lua sets up McGavin for the U's third. Near the end Lua-Lua dances round the goalkeeper to net in front of delirious U's fans.

2:1 A SHEFFIELD UTD
- Brown, Dunne, White, Johnson G, Tanner^, McGavin, Clark^, Dozzell*, Stockwell, Duguid, Lock
- *Tracey, Uhlenbeek, Woodh'se^, Murphy, Sandford, Devlin, Brown, Bent*, Kelly, Ford*
- subs used: Keeble/Keith / Smith/Cryan

During a week of negotiations with Newcastle over Lua-Lua's transfer, United put up a brave performance at Bramall Lane, but are undone by two late strikes. Clark's unlucky own-goal is a major blow after playing some good football. Lua-Lua finally heads north for a club record fee.

2:2 H SHEFFIELD UTD
- Brown, Dunne, White, Johnson G, Skelton^, McGavin, Clark^, Dozzell, Stockwell, Duguid, Lock
- *Tracey, Uhlenbeek, Quinn, Jagielka, Sandford, Devlin, Sandford, Brown, Bent*, Ford^*
- subs used: Arnott/Tanner/Keith / Smith/Cryan

Injury-hit United welcome back Arnott following his broken arm. Layer Road has its first sub-2,000 crowd for three years, a reflection on the state of the tie. Neil Warnock's negative Blades cruise into the third round, any lingering U's hopes ended by Paul Devlin's breakaway strike.

FA Cup 1 A YEOVIL
- Brown, Gregory, Johnson G*, Skelton^, Fitzgerald, Duguid, White, Dozzell", Stockwell, Conlon, Clark
- *Pennock, Piper, Tonkin, Skiverton, White, Belgrave, Way, Smith, Patmore^, Lindegaard*, Crittenden*
- subs used: Clark/Lock/Dunne / Lindegaard* O'Brien/Bent

Warren Patmore sets the ball rolling after a Brown blunder. Barrington Belgrave makes it two after a melee. Skiverton converts a header, but the U's hit back through a Duguid header. Way's penalty and Patmore's header complete the humiliation by Colin Addison's non-Leaguers.

LDV Vans Trophy 1 A CAMBRIDGE
- Woodman, Dunne, Gregory, Skelton, Fitzgerald, Arnott, Keeble*, Conlon, Stockwell, Duguid, Dozzell
- *Perez, Joseph, Ashbee, Oakes", Duncan, McAnespie, Dreyer, Mustoe, Axeldal*, Hansen^, Abbey*
- subs used: McGavin / Taylor/Preece/Guttridge

United's last chance of cup glory this season vanishes within 20 minutes. After a foul on Jonas Axeldal, the free-kick is headed in by veteran defender John Dreyer from close range. Dunne loses possession and Ian Ashbee sets up Axeldal, who lets fly with a tremendous left-foot drive.

Final League Table

Pos	Team	P	Home W	Home D	Home L	Home F	Home A	Away W	Away D	Away L	Away F	Away A	Pts
1	Millwall	46	17	2	4	49	26	11	7	5	40	27	93
2	Rotherham	46	16	4	3	50	26	11	6	6	29	29	91
3	Reading	46	15	5	3	58	26	10	6	7	28	26	86
4	Walsall*	46	15	5	3	51	23	8	8	7	28	27	81
5	Stoke	46	12	6	5	39	21	8	8	7	35	28	77
6	Wigan	46	12	9	2	29	18	7	9	7	24	24	75
7	Bournemouth	46	11	6	6	37	23	9	7	7	42	32	73
8	Notts Co	46	10	6	7	37	33	9	6	8	25	33	69
9	Bristol City	46	11	6	6	47	29	7	8	8	23	27	68
10	Wrexham	46	10	6	7	33	28	8	6	10	32	43	63
11	Port Vale	46	9	8	6	35	22	7	6	10	20	27	62
12	Peterborough	46	12	6	5	38	27	7	8	8	23	39	59
13	Wycombe	46	8	7	8	24	23	7	7	9	22	30	59
14	Brentford	46	9	10	4	34	30	5	11	7	22	40	59
15	Oldham	46	11	5	7	35	26	4	8	11	18	39	58
16	Bury	46	10	6	7	25	22	6	4	13	20	36	58
17	COLCHESTER	46	10	5	8	32	23	5	7	11	23	31	57
18	Northampton	46	9	6	8	26	28	6	6	11	20	31	57
19	Cambridge	46	8	6	9	32	31	5	5	12	29	46	53
20	Swindon	46	8	6	9	30	35	7	5	11	17	30	52
21	Bristol Rov	46	6	10	7	28	26	6	5	12	25	31	51
22	Luton	46	5	6	12	24	35	4	7	12	28	45	40
23	Swansea	46	5	9	9	26	24	3	4	16	21	49	37
24	Oxford	46	5	4	14	23	34	2	2	19	30	66	27
		1104	242	151	159	842	624	159	151	242	624	842	1505

* promoted after play-offs

Odds & ends

Double wins: (4) Luton, Oxford, Reading, Swansea.

Double losses: (6) Millwall, Northampton, Port Vale, Rotherham, Stoke, Wigan.

Won from behind: (2) Brentford (H), Reading (H).

Lost from in front: (3) Peterborough (A), Rotherham (A), Stoke (A).

High spots: Shock wins over promotion-chasers Reading and Walsall. The stunning individual display at QPR by Lua-Lua, the club's first hat-trick scorer in seven years. The huge 2.25 million profit made on Lua-Lua. Astute signings by Steve Whitton in his first full season as boss.

Low spots: The second-half FA Cup collapse at non-League Yeovil. The six-goal Boxing Day mauling by Millwall. The dreadful home display against Port Vale in March.

Player of the Year: Mick Stockwell.

Ever-presents: (1) Mick Stockwell.

Hat-tricks for: (1) Lomana Tresor Lua-Lua (v QPR, A, LC).

Hat-tricks against: (2) Simon Haworth (v Wigan, A), Neil Harris (v Millwall, A).

Leading scorer: (11) Mick Stockwell.

Appearances and Goals

Player	App Lge	Sub	LC	Sub	FAC	Sub	LDV	Sub	Goals Lge	Sub	LCFAC	LDV	Tot
Arnott, Andy	1	2						1					
Brown, Simon	18		4		1		1						
Clark, Simon	33	1	4		1		1						
Conlon, Barry	23	3							8				8
Dozzell, Jason	22		4		1		1						
Duguid, Karl	34	7	3		1		1		5	1			6
Dunne, Joe	31	3	3		1		1		1				1
Fitzgerald, Scott	30				1		1						
Gregory, David	27	1	1		1		1		3				3
Izzet, Kem	5	1					1		1				1
Johnson, Gavin	33	4	3		1		1		2				2
Johnson, Ross	17	1	1		1								
Keeble, Chris	10	6	1		1		1		1				1
Keith, Joe	21	6	1		2			1	3				3
Lock, Tony	3	11				1			2				2
Lua-Lua, Lomana	7	22	2						2		3		5
McGavin, Steve	19	3	2		3	1			2		1		3
McGleish, Scott	11	10	3		1				5				5
Morgan, Dean		4											
Nicholls, Mark	3												
Opara, Kelechi ('KK')		2											
Pinault, Thomas	3	2							1				1
Scott, Keith	8	1	1						1				1
Skelton, Aaron	43	1	3		1		1		6				6
Stockwell, Mick	46		4		1		1		11				11
Tanner, Adam	1	3	1		1								
White, Alan	29	3	4		1								
Woodman, Andy	28						1						
(own-goals)												1	1
28 players used	506	95	44	6	11	3	11	1	55	1	4	1	60

No			Date	Att	Pos	Pt	F-A	H-T
1	A	CHESTERFIELD	11/8	3,939		3	W 6-3	3-1
2	H	TRANMERE	18/8	3,618	2	6	W 2-1	0-0
3	A	WREXHAM	25/8	2,952	16	7	D 1-1	1-0
4	H	PORT VALE	27/8	3,611	11	10	W 2-0	1-0
5	A	SWINDON	1/9	4,889	11	10	L 0-1	0-0
6	H	NORTHAMPTON	8/9	3,705	23	13	W 3-1	3-0
7	A	BRISTOL CITY	15/9	9,992	2	13	L 1-3	1-1
8	H	OLDHAM	18/9	2,991	5	16	W 2-1	2-0
9	H	NOTTS CO	22/9	3,796	13	16	L 0-1	0-0
10	A	STOKE	26/9	9,515	6	16	L 0-3	0-1
11	A	BRENTFORD	29/9	5,179	4	16	L 1-4	1-2

Match details

1. A CHESTERFIELD 11/8 — W 6-3 (H-T 3-1)
Scorers, Times: Dun'9, B'y29 (og), St'37, Rap'48, McG'62,78 / Willis 10, Beckett 47, Payne 55. Ref: G Cain
Squad: Woodman, Dunne, Johnson G*, Pinault^, Fitzgerald, Clark, Izzet, Gregory, Stockwell^, Rapley
Chesterfield: Abbey, Booty, Edwards, Breckin, Blatherw'k*, Payne, Williams, Ebdon, Willis*, Beckett
Subs used: Keith, Bowry/Duguid / Rowland, Reeves/Ingledow/Rushbury
Dunne's right-foot shot and Jason Booty's close-range own-goal set the U's up for their best ever opening-day result. Nicky Laws' men are shell-shocked, and debutant keeper Nathan Abbey has a nightmare. At 3–4 the Spireites look dangerous, but lively McGleish finishes them off.

2. H TRANMERE 18/8 — W 2-1 (H-T 0-0)
Scorers: Rapley 84, McGleish 89 / Barlow 90p. Ref: P Prosser
Squad: Woodman, Dunne, Keith, Pinault*, Fitzgerald, Clark, Izzet, Gregory, Stockwell, Rapley^
Tranmere: Murphy, Hazell!, Roberts, Henry^, Challinor, Hill, Flynn, Parkinson, Barlow, Allison^, Mellon
Subs used: Bowry/Morgan / Hume/N'Diaye
A fine team display and in a late flurry Gareth Roberts blasts a clearance against Rapley and it flies into goal. Reuben Hazell pulls Stockwell back and is red-carded. Woodman makes two crucial saves before McGleish's shot on the turn goes in. Woodman's foul concedes a penalty.

3. A WREXHAM 25/8 — D 1-1 (H-T 1-0)
Scorers: Stockwell 20 / Edwards 73. Ref: M Cowburn
Squad: Woodman, Dunne, Keith, Pinault, Fitzgerald, Clark^, Izzet^, Gregory, Stockwell*, Rapley
Wrexham: Rogers, Holmes, Edwards, Blackwood^, Carey, Lawrence, Chalk!, Ferguson!, Russell, Faulconbridge/Thomas*
Subs used: Bowry/Morgan/White / Barrett/Gibson
Stockwell gives United the lead from close range and a win looks likely as Martyn Chalk and Darren Ferguson are both sent off for two yellow card offences apiece. But the nine men rally and Carlos Edwards cracks home a 20-yard rocket. Kristian Rogers makes a series of fine saves.

4. H PORT VALE 27/8 — W 2-0 (H-T 1-0)
Scorers: Keith 21, McGleish 46. Ref: P Armstrong
Squad: Woodman, Dunne*, Keith, Pinault, Fitzgerald, White, Izzet^, Gregory, Stockwell*, Rapley, McGleish^
Port Vale: Goodlad, Cummins, Ingram, Carragher, Walsh, Burton, Gurney, O'Callagh'n*/Brisco, Brooker, McPhee, Hardy
Subs used: Duguid/Bowry/Morgan / McPhee, Hardy, Dodd
Keith nets the first with a 'Beckhamesque' effort from a free-kick. McGleish pounces straight after the interval to sink Brian Horton's outfit. It's the club's best start to a season in 52 years. There is much gnashing of teeth when Whitton misses out on the Manager of the Month award.

5. A SWINDON 1/9 — L 0-1 (H-T 0-0)
Scorers: / Ruddock 53. Ref: R Harris
Squad: Woodman, Duguid, Keith, Pinault, White, Clark, Izzet*, Gregory, Rapley^, Stockwell*, McGleish*
Swindon: Griemink, Duke*, Davis, Heywood, Ruddock, Gurney, O'Halloran, Howe, Sabin*, Osei-Kuffr*/Hewlett
Subs used: Bowry/Morgan / Invincible/Robinson/Davies
Swindon's new management team of Roy Evans and Neil Ruddock bring the U's great start to a halt. Complete with specially made outsize shorts, big 'Razor' hammers home a 25-yard free-kick and soon after saves his keeper's blushes by clearing a Pinault effort off the goalline.

6. H NORTHAMPTON 8/9 — W 3-1 (H-T 3-0)
Scorers: Rapley 7, McGleish 8p, Hope 42 (og) / Hargreaves 78. Ref: P Rejer
Squad: Woodman, Duguid, Keith, Pinault, Clark, Fitzgerald, Izzet!, Gregory!, Rapley^, Stockwell*, McGleish*
Northampton: Sollitt, Marsh, Hunter, Frain^, Evatt, Hope, Carey, Hunt*, McGregor, Forrester, Gabbiadini*
Subs used: Dunne/Bowry/Morgan / Wolfston/Asamoah/Carruth's
Rapley sidefoots home for a great start and moments later McGleish nets a penalty after Rapley is upended. Richard Hope turns a cross past his own keeper Adam Sollitt. Gregory gets his marching orders but Kevin Wilson's men only respond with a single Chris Hargreaves consolation.

7. A BRISTOL CITY 15/9 — L 1-3 (H-T 1-1)
Scorers: Rapley 45 / Murray 40, Jones 47, Clist 89. Ref: R Olivier
Squad: Woodman, Duguid, Keith, Fitzgerald, Clark*, Izzet, Gregory*, Rapley, Stockwell, McGleish^
Bristol City: Stowell, Murray, Bell, Hill, Lever, Carey, Doherty*, Brown, Jones, Thorpe*, Timnion
Subs used: Izzet/Morgan/White / Clist/Matthews
Brian Tinnion's astute pass is converted by Scott Murray. Rapley chips a clever equaliser just before half-time. Steve Jones heads in a Louis Carey's cross and the U's go close when a Keith free-kick is deflected onto the bar. An even game is decided as sub Simon Clist nets a beauty.

8. H OLDHAM 18/9 — W 2-1 (H-T 2-0)
Scorers: Izzet 10, McGleish 27 / Eyres 81. Ref: P Alcock
Squad: Woodman, Duguid, Keith, Fitzgerald*, White, Clark, Izzet, Johnson G, Rapley, Stockwell^, McGleish*
Oldham: Kelly, McNiven, Sheridan D, Garnet^, Balmer, Durbury, Rickers*, Sheridan J, Allott*, Eyre, Eyres
Subs used: Corrazin/Prenderville/Dudley / Eyres
At kick-off Andy Ritchie's side are top, but Izzet shows scant respect with an early strike, followed soon after by McGleish heading decisively home. A dazzling U's first half is followed by a more even second period. Jason Dozzell quits the game through injury after a 16-year career.

9. H NOTTS CO 22/9 — L 0-1 (H-T 0-0)
Scorers: / Allsopp 62. Ref: S Tomlin
Squad: Woodman, Duguid, Keith, Fitzgerald*, White, Johnson G, Izzet, Cas, Rapley, Stallard*, McGleish
Notts Co: Mildenhall, Fenton, Barraclough, Caskey^, Richardson, Grayson, Owers, Cas, Allsopp*, Hamilton
Subs used: Dunne/Clark/Morgan / Hackworth/Jorgensen
A McGleish effort brings a super save from Steve Mildenhall and within seconds struggling County take the lead. Australian Danny Allsopp nets a fine volley to ease the pressure on manager Jocky Scott. Gary Owers and Simon Grayson both strike wood on a dismal day for the U's.

10. A STOKE 26/9 — L 0-3 (H-T 0-1)
Scorers: / Van Deurzen 45, Thordarson 57, 90. Ref: R Pearson
Squad: Woodman, Duguid, Johnson G, Pinault*, White, Izzet, Clark, Fitzgerald^, Rapley, Stockwell^, McGleish
Stoke: Cutler, Thomas, Clarke, Handyside, Shtanyuk, Gunnarson*, Gudjonsson, O'Connor, Cooke, Van Deurzen, Thordarson, Henry
Subs used: Izzet/Morgan/White / Henry
A frustrating day against Gudjon Thordarson's cosmopolitan side. Belgian Juergen Van Deurzen breaks the deadlock at a crucial time and the U's toil in vain. Fouls on Pinault go unpunished and the French midfielder shows his frustration and is cautioned, meaning he now faces a ban.

11. A BRENTFORD 29/9 — L 1-4 (H-T 1-2)
Scorers: McGleish 17 / Evans 5p, 62, Burgess 34, Owusu 83. Ref: W Jordan
Squad: Woodman, Duguid, Johnson G, Pinault, White, Izzet, Clark, Fitzgerald, Rapley*, Stockwell, McGleish
Brentford: Gottskalks'n/Dobson, Anderson, Ingimarsson, Powell, Price^, Evans, Mahon, Owusu*, Burgess, Gibbs
Subs used: Bowry/Morgan / Williams/Rowlands
Bees skipper Paul Evans cracks home a penalty, but McGleish responds with a cracking goal. U's fans get soaked, but during this 20-minute rainstorm the U's play their best football. On-loan Ben Burgess marks his farewell game by regaining the lead. McGleish misses a late penalty.

Matches 12–23

#		Date	Opponent	Att	Pos		Pts	Res	FT	HT	Ref
12	H	5/10	READING	3,691	7	11	19	W	2-0	2-0	K Hill
13	A	13/10	BLACKPOOL	5,546	11	13	19	L	1-2	0-0	M Clattenburg
14	H	20/10	CAMBRIDGE	4,684	8	20	22	W	3-1	2-1	R Dowd
15	H	23/10	WYCOMBE	5,186	6	8	23	D	2-2	2-2	T Parkes
16	A	27/10	BRIGHTON	6,531	9	2	23	L	0-1	0-1	M Messias
17	H	3/11	BOURNEMOUTH	4,369	13	16	23	L	1-2	1-2	M Warren
18	A	9/11	WIGAN	5,735	9	20	26	W	3-2	2-0	G Laws
19	A	20/11	CARDIFF	8,013	9	8	27	D	1-1	0-1	C Wilkes
20	H	24/11	BURY	3,534	13	20	27	L	0-1	0-0	J Ross
21	A	1/12	QP RANGERS	11,158	12	10	28	D	2-2	2-1	P Armstrong
22	H	15/12	PETERBOROUGH	3,480	11	15	31	W	2-1	1-1	P Jones
23	H	22/12	HUDDERSFIELD	3,543	12	10	32	D	3-3	2-1	L Cable

---

12 — READING (H) 2-0
Goals: Rapley 8, McGleish 26

Colchester: Woodman, Duguid, Johnson G^, Pinault, Johnson R, Clark, Izzet*, Gregory, Rapley, Bowry, McGleish. Subs: Stockwell, Keith.
Reading: Whitehead, Murty, Robinson^, Whitbread, Williams, Parkinson^, Jones*, Harper*, Rougier, Butler, Smith. Subs: Forster, Henderson, Igoe.

Ross Johnson returns after long-term injury and the consistent Stockwell is given a rest. In a lively opening, Alan Pardew's expensively assembled squad are stream-rollered aside. Applications go in for planning permission for a new stadium on a 250-acre site north of the town.

13 — BLACKPOOL (A) 1-2
Goals: Izzet 86 / Ormerod 50, 90

Colchester: Woodman, Duguid, Johnson G, Pinault, Johnson R, Clark, Izzet, Gregory*, Rapley, Bowry, McGleish*. Subs: Stockwell*, White, Morgan, Opara.
Blackpool: Pullen, Parkinson, Coid, O'Kane, Caldwell, Reid, Milligan, Simpson, Ormerod, Fenton*, Bullock^. Subs: Murphy, Thompson.

Blackpool's Steve McMahon gives his men a half-time ear-bashing and United feel the heat. Brett Ormerod heads home from Jamie Milligan's cross. Izzet levels but Ormerod has the last laugh two minutes into stoppage time, finishing a three-man move with a powerful 15-yard drive.

14 — CAMBRIDGE (H) 3-1
Goals: McGleish 37, 87, Johnson G 42 / One 14

Colchester: Woodman, Duguid, Johnson G, Pinault, Johnson R, Clark, Izzet, Bowry, Rapley, Stockwell, McGleish. Subs: Keith.
Cambridge: Perez, Fleming, Goodhind, Walling, Angus, Ashbee, Wanless, Prokas, Kitson, One, Youngs.

A superb strike by giant French teenager Armand One gives Cambridge a surprise lead. United turn on the power, McGleish levels and Gavin Johnson nets his first in over a year with a cracking shot. The U's dominate and McGleish buries a stunning late 20-yard shot from an angle.

15 — WYCOMBE (H) 2-2
Goals: Stockwell 13, Rapley 28 / Brown 14, Currie 45

Colchester: Woodman, Duguid, Johnson G, Pinault, Johnson R, Clark, Izzet, Bowry, Rapley, Stockwell, McGleish. Subs: Keith, Morgan.
Wycombe: Taylor, Senda, Vinnicombe, Bulman, Rogers, McCarthy, Walker^, Simpson, Currie^, Brown^, Mayo. Subs: Ryan, Holligan, Roberts.

A tremendous atmosphere under the Layer Road lights and there's no sign the 10-year rivalry between these clubs is on the wane, for they go hammer and tongs at each other. Steve Brown and Darren Currie equalise early goals in an entertaining contest that ebbs and flows throughout.

16 — BRIGHTON (A) 0-1
Goals: — / Zamora 16

Colchester: Woodman, Duguid, Johnson G^, Pinault*, Johnson R, Clark, Izzet, Bowry, Rapley^, Stockwell, McGleish. Subs: Keith, Morgan.
Brighton: Kuipers, Watson, Mayo, Morgan^, Wicks, Carpenter, Hart, Oatway, Steele^, Zamora, Jones. Subs: Brooker, Crosby.

Bobby Zamora pounces for his 11th goal of the season, but first at home for seven weeks, after former Seagull Johnson fails to deal with a free-kick from Paul Watson. Whitton is left exasperated as United outplay Peter Taylor's outfit for long periods but fail to take opportunities.

17 — BOURNEMOUTH (H) 1-2
Goals: Duguid 25 / Feeney 13, Howe 20

Colchester: Woodman, Duguid, Johnson G^, Pinault*, Johnson R, Clark, Izzet, Bowry, Rapley^, Stockwell, McGleish. Subs: Pinault, Keith, Morgan.
Bournemouth: Stewart, Broadhurst, Elliott, Purches, Tindall, Fletcher C^, Howe, Hayter, Feeney !, Stock^, Holmes*. Subs: Erbanne, Hughes, Bernard.

The U's look poor in the first half and fall behind to a Warren Feeney header. Skipper Eddie Howe stretches the lead with another powerful header. A stunning 30-yard free-kick by Duguid narrows the gap. A flare-up involving Chris Feeney sees him red-carded, but the Cherries hang on.

18 — WIGAN (A) 3-2
Goals: Stockwell 13, 19, Johnson R 77 / Fitzgerald 52 (og), Liddell 56

Colchester: Woodman, Johnson G^, Keith, White, Fitzgerald, Johnson R, Izzet, Bowry, Stockwell^, Duguid, McGleish*. Subs: Pinault, Rapley, Morgan.
Wigan: Stillie, Green, Kenna, Dinning, Jackson, DeZeeuw, Dalglish, Liddell, Kennedy*, McCulloch, Bramall. Subs: Liddell, McCulloch.

Whitton makes tactical changes aiming to tighten things up and hit Wigan on the break and it works a treat. After a night at Wigan chairman Whelan's hotel, the luck goes U's way with R Johnson's long-range winner taking a wicked deflection, not long after the home side hit the bar.

19 — CARDIFF (A) 1-1
Goals: Dunne 87 / Collins 33

Colchester: Woodman, Dunne^, Keith*, Pinault, Fitzgerald, Johnson R, Clark, Izzet, Bowry, Duguid, McGleish. Subs: Alexander, Gabbidon, Legg.
Cardiff: Alexander, Gabbidon, Legg, Young, Prior, Boland, Kavanagh*, Collins, Earnshaw, Hamilton, Maxwell. Subs: Bonner, Maxwell.

Andy Legg's corner causes panic and late teenage call-up James Collins pounces for Alan Cork's men. United soak up heavy pressure and in a rare late attack a mistake by Scott Young allows Dunne to volley home an equaliser against the run of play. Cardiff are jeered off by their fans.

20 — BURY (H) 0-1
Goals: — / Newby 82

Colchester: Woodman, Dunne^, Keith*, Pinault, Fitzgerald, Johnson R, Clark, Izzet, Bowry, Duguid, McGleish. Subs: Kenny, Unsworth, Stuart.
Bury: Kenny, Barry, Unsworth, Stuart, Nelson, Redmond, Forrest*, Jarrett, Newby, Lawson, Barley. Subs: Clegg, Connell.

United are below par early on but are transformed after the interval and apply plenty of pressure on Paddy Kenny's goal. Kenny has an inspired match with brilliant saves from Pinault and Stockwell. Dunne picks up a nasty knee injury. Near the end Jon Newby grabs an unlikely winner.

21 — QP RANGERS (A) 2-2
Goals: Stockwell 29, Keith 39 / Gallen 22, 54

Colchester: Woodman, White*, Keith, Warren*, Fitzgerald, Johnson R, Clark, Izzet, Bowry, Rapley^, McGleish. Subs: Digby, Forbes.
QP Rangers: White, Warren, Rose, Shittu, Bignott, Gallen, Bonnot, Palmer, Nelson, Thomson, Barley. Subs: Gallen, Connolly, Doudou.

Ian Holloway's men welcome back former hero Kevin Gallen on a 'free' from Barnsley and he gives them a lead which is soon cancelled out by Stockwell and Keith. Gallen strikes again with a 15-yard drive to leave Whitton moaning that a draw didn't do the United's efforts justice.

22 — PETERBOROUGH (H) 2-1
Goals: Duguid 8, White 70 / Edwards 7

Colchester: Woodman, Duguid, Keith, White, Fitzgerald, Clark, Pinault, Izzet, Bowry, Rapley*, McGleish. Subs: Tyler, Joseph, Jelleyman, Cullen*.
Peterborough: Tyler, Joseph, Jelleyman, Rea, Edwards, Bullard, Oldfield", Clarke A, Fenton*, Farrell, Clarke L. Subs: Barrett, Williams, Shields.

Andy Edwards' early goal is cancelled out within seconds by a fine Duguid strike. Patience pays off with a late winner after White combines with Pinault. Strikers Adrian Coote and Graham Barrett join the club. Four London-based U's players escape from a nasty pile-up on the M25.

23 — HUDDERSFIELD (H) 3-3
Goals: Duguid 9, Stockwell 23, McGleish 74 / Booth 40, 61, Schofield 59

Colchester: Woodman, Duguid, Keith*, Clark, Fitzgerald^, Pinault, Izzet, Bowry, Rapley, Barrett", McGleish. Subs: Margetson, Jenkins !, Evans.
Huddersfield: Margetson, Jenkins !, Irons, Moses, Gray, Baldry", Knight, Booth, Schofield, Mattis, Wijnhard. Subs: Clarke, R Coote.

McGleish and Stockwell fire United into a strong position but Andy Booth heads Lou Macari's men back into the game. Two goals in as many minutes from Danny Schofield and Booth turn things upside down before McGleish levels. Skipper Steve Jenkins departs for a foul on Bowry.

NATIONWIDE DIVISION 2 — Manager: Steve Whitton — SEASON 2001-02

No	Venue	Opponent	Date	Att	Pos	Opp Pos	Pt	F-A	H-T	Res
24	A	NORTHAMPTON	26/12	4,740	12	24	35	3-2	1-1	W
25	A	PORT VALE	29/12	4,444	12	16	35	1-3	0-2	L
26	H	WREXHAM	5/1	2,835	12	22	38	2-1	1-1	W
27	A	TRANMERE	12/1	8,387	10	7	39	0-0	0-0	D
28	H	CHESTERFIELD	19/1	4,060	12	16	39	1-2	0-1	L
29	A	HUDDERSFIELD	22/1	7,179	12	10	39	1-2	0-2	L
30	A	READING	26/1	12,743	12	1	39	0-3	0-1	L
31	H	SWINDON	30/1	3,132	13	14	39	1-3	1-0	L
32	H	BRENTFORD	2/2	3,657	14	5	40	1-1	0-1	D
33	A	CAMBRIDGE	9/2	3,954	13	24	43	2-1	0-1	W
34	H	BLACKPOOL	16/2	3,553	13	17	44	1-1	0-1	D

24 — A NORTHAMPTON (26/12)
Scorers/Times: Sampson 45 (og), Barrett 50, 66 / Hope 36, Forrester 80. **Ref:** A Bates
United: Woodman, Duguid, Keith, White, Johnson R, Clark, Pinault*, Bowry, Barrett, Stockwell^, McGleish^ — subs: Izzet/Rapley/Coote
Northampton: Sollitt, Frain, Spedding^, Sampson, Burgess, Hope", Hunter, Parkin, Forrester, McGregor*, Hargreaves — subs: Asamoah/Hodge/Dempsey

The Cobblers pile on the pressure in the first half, going close before Richard Hope heads them in front. United hit back via an Ian Sampson own goal, before the lively loanee Barrett pounces for two well-taken goals. Jamie Forrester's late strike creates a nervous ending for the U's.

25 — A PORT VALE (29/12)
Scorers/Times: Duguid 90 / Armstrong 35, Rowland 39, Brooker 69. **Ref:** D Crick
United: Woodman, Duguid!, Keith, Pinault, Clark, Izzet, Bowry^, Barrett, Stockwell^, McGleish^ — subs: Rapley/Johnson R/Coote
Port Vale: Goodlad, Cummins, Rowland, Carragher, Walsh, McClare, Durnin, Brooker, McPhee, Armstrong^, Webber

Vale's potent first-half display is rewarded by two fine goals. Ian Armstrong swerves a 20-yarder home, then Stephen Rowland cracks in a half volley for his first league goal. Stephen Brooker nets a third for Brian Horton's men before Duguid's gives disappointing United a consolation.

26 — H WREXHAM (5/1)
Scorers/Times: Stockwell 12, Bowry 78 / Thomas 29. **Ref:** K Hill
United: Woodman, Duguid, Johnson R, Pinault^, White, Clark, Izzet, Bowry, Barrett, Stockwell^, McGleish — subs: Fitzgerald/Coote
Wrexham: Rogers, Whitley, Holmes, Thomas*, Roberts, Lawrence, Ferguson, Phillips, Morrell, Sam, Blackwood — sub: Evans

Stockwell bags his ninth goal of the season before Steve Thomas drills home a 30-yard equaliser. Bowry pounces to register his first goal for United and secure a rather fortunate three-point haul. Whitton's verdict: 'We were terrible. Definitely our worst performance of the season.'

27 — A TRANMERE (12/1)
Ref: M Pike
United: Brown, Duguid, Keith^, White, Fitzgerald, Clark, Izzet, Bowry^, Barrett, Stockwell, McGleish — subs: Pinault/Morgan
Tranmere: Achterberg, Hinds, Yates, Henry, Allen!, Hill, Flynn, Mellon^, Price, Allison*, Koumas — subs: Parkinson/Sharp

Graham Allen becomes Rovers' fourth dismissal of the season for a professional foul on Keith. United work hard but have to settle for a point. John Halls (Arsenal) joins on loan as cover.

28 — H CHESTERFIELD (19/1)
Scorers/Times: Barrett 49 / Burt 17, Hurst 75. **Ref:** P Danson
United: Brown, Duguid!, Keith, White, Fitzgerald, Halls, Pinault, Izzet, Barrett, Stockwell^, McGleish^ — subs: Morgan/Coote
Chesterfield: Abbey, Booty^, Edwards, Parrish, Breckin, Payne, Hurst, Williams, Allott*, Burt, Innes — subs: Willis/Richardson/Howard

Angry Whitton slams ref Danson for dishing out bookings galore and Duguid's first ever sending-off, for two yellow cards. Jamie Burt hits a deserved opener but the impressive Barrett levels. Debutant Hall does well but makes one glaring error and Glyn Hurst nicks the winning goal.

29 — A HUDDERSFIELD (22/1)
Scorers/Times: White 83 / Schofield 5, 25. **Ref:** M Cooper
United: Brown, Duguid, Keith, White, Fitzgerald, Halls, Pinault, Izzet, Barrett, Stockwell^, McGleish^ — subs: Morgan/Coote
Huddersfield: Margetson, Jenkins, Evans, Irons, Clark, Gray, Knight, Holland, Booth*, Schofield, Hay^ — subs: Armstrong/Wijnhard

White has a good game to keep lethal Andy Booth quiet, but generally the U's play second fiddle in the first half. Danny Schofield sets the McAlpine Stadium alight with two goals and the U's are left chasing the game. They improve greatly later on but only pull one back via White.

30 — A READING (26/1)
Scorers/Times: Forster 38p, 69, Hughes 48. **Ref:** J Taylor
United: Brown, Keith^, White, Fitzgerald, Halls, Izzet, Bowry^, Barrett, Stockwell, McGleish, Johnson G — subs: Pinault
Reading: Roberts, Murty, Sharey, Williams, Parkinson^, Igoe, Hughes, Rougier", Forster*, Salako — subs: Henderson/Jones/Cureton

Nicky Forster puts the table-toppers ahead from the spot after John Salako's first effort but is adjudged to have moved off his line. The upset Brown then helps a long-range effort from Andy Hughes into his own net and allows Forster's shot through his legs for the third.

31 — H SWINDON (30/1)
Scorers/Times: Keith 41p / Gurney 62p, 74, Sabin 63. **Ref:** W Jordan
United: Brown, Duguid, Keith, White, Fitzgerald, Halls, Izzet, Bowry, Coote, Stockwell*, McGleish* — subs: Rapley/Morgan
Swindon: Griemink, Robinson, Davis, Heywood, Willis, Gurney, Howe^, Invincible, Sabin, Hewlett*, Grazioli" — subs: Duke/McAreavey/Foley

Record signing Coote gets his first start, and the U's look good going forward, Keith giving them a lead from the spot. The fragile confidence is evident at the break, however, and they collapse over a 15-minute period to their fourth successive loss, and are plummeting down the table.

32 — H BRENTFORD (2/2)
Scorers/Times: Coote 66 / Owusu 25. **Ref:** M Fletcher
United: Brown, Johnson G, White, Fitzgerald, Halls, Izzet, Coote^, Bowry, Barrett, Stockwell*, McGleish — subs: Hunt/O'Connor
Brentford: Smith, Dobson, Gibbs, Ingimarsson, Powell, Sidwell, Evans, Mahon, Owusu, Burgess, Hunt, O'Connor

Steve Coppell's men dominate the first half and go ahead through Lloyd Owusu's 12th of the season after Brown fails to hang on to an effort from loanee Steve Sidwell. Paul Evans' free-kick then strikes the woodwork. Hard-working U's deservedly level via Coote's first for the club.

33 — A CAMBRIDGE (9/2)
Scorers/Times: Coote 68, Rapley 85 / Youngs 1. **Ref:** P Alcock
United: Brown, Duguid, Keith, White, Fitzgerald, Halls, Coote, Bowry, Barrett, Stockwell*, McGleish* — subs: Rapley/Morgan
Cambridge: Marshall, Fleming, Murray, Tann, Angus, Guttridge!, Austin, Tudor, Gurney, Revell^, Youngs" — subs: Goodhind/One/Scully

Tom Youngs fires relegation-bound Cambridge ahead on only 18 seconds, but their chances of a shock win suffer when Luke Guttridge is sent off just before the break for a second yellow card. Coote rams in a Keith corner to level and Rapley's header ensures a first U's win in seven.

34 — H BLACKPOOL (16/2)
Scorers/Times: Keith 72p / Walker 41. **Ref:** P Joslin
United: Brown, Duguid, Keith, White, Fitzgerald, Halls", Coote", Johnson G*, Barrett, Stockwell, McGleish — subs: Pinault/Izzet/Rapley
Blackpool: Barnes, Collins, Jaszczun, O'Kane, Marshall, Reid, Wellens, Walker^, Ormerod, Murphy, Taylor — sub: Bullock

Blackpool lead after a raid down the left flank sees the ball pulled back for Richard Walker to beat Brown from six yards. The U's lift their game after the interval and deservedly equalise when danger-man Barrett is pushed over by Tommy Jaszczun and Keith converts the spot-kick.

Colchester United 2001–02 season — match-by-match log (games 35–46)

Results

#	Venue	Date	Opponent	Att	Pos	Res	HT	Opp Pos	FT	Pts
35	H	23/2	BRISTOL CITY	3,558	14	D	0-0	4	0-0	45
36	A	26/2	NOTTS CO	3,140	15	D	1-0	23	1-1	46
37	A	2/3	OLDHAM	5,457	15	L	1-2	6	1-4	46
38	H	5/3	STOKE	3,866	15	L	0-2	3	1-3	46
39	A	9/3	PETERBOROUGH	4,625	16	L	0-2	17	1-3	46
40	H	16/3	QP RANGERS	4,903	16	W	1-0	10	3-1	49
41	A	23/3	WYCOMBE	6,737	16	D	0-0	11	0-0	50
42	H	30/3	BRIGHTON	4,881	17	L	0-3	2	1-4	50
43	A	2/4	BOURNEMOUTH	5,908	16	W	1-0	22	1-0	53
44	H	6/4	CARDIFF	3,970	16	L	0-1	5	0-1	53
45	A	13/4	BURY	5,014	16	W	3-1	22	1-0	56
46	H	20/4	WIGAN	3,672	15	D	2-2	10	2-0	59

Average: Home 3,822 — Away 6,338

Match details

35 BRISTOL CITY (H) 0-0 — Ref: A Butler
Danny Wilson's promotion hopefuls fail to break down a determined U's in a largely dour game. The best chance sees Keith force a fine save from Steve Phillips. In the closing stages Tony Thorpe's clever lob goes narrowly wide and Lee Peacock's fierce drive is well saved by Brown.
Colchester: Brown, Duguid, Keith, Pinault, Fitzgerald, White, Izzet, Rapley^, Barrett, Stockwell*, McGleish^. Subs: Bowry/Coote.
Bristol City: Phillips, Amankwaah, Bell, Hill, Lever, Carey, Doherty, Brown, Peacock, Thorpe, Tinnion. Sub: Nicholson.

36 NOTTS CO (A) 1-1 — White 36; Allsopp 51. Ref: G Salisbury
Under new boss Billy Dearden, County look disjointed and destined for the drop. Sadly, United lack a killer instinct and drop two points. Man-of-the-match White gives the midweek travelling fans something to cheer, but the superiority counts for nothing after Danny Allsopp equalises.
Colchester: Brown, Duguid, Keith, Pinault, Fitzgerald, White, Izzet, Rapley^, Barrett, Stockwell*, McGleish. Subs: Bowry/Coote.
Notts Co: Holmes, Fenton, Barraclough, Caskey, Richardson, Ireland, Owers*, Cas, Heffernan, Allsopp, Liburd. Sub: Nicholson.

37 OLDHAM (A) 1-4 — Izzet 12 [Corazzin 90]; Smart 24, Murray 44, Eyres 77. Ref: H Webb
U's take an early lead as Stockwell tees up Izzet. The Latics hit back with Allan Smart's fourth in three games and then lead via a superb 35-yarder from Paul Murray. Goals from David Eyres and Carlo Corazzin put a smile on the face of Oldham's former U's boss Mick Wadsworth.
Colchester: Brown, Gregory, Keith, Pinault, Fitzgerald, White, Izzet, Bowry^, Barrett, Stockwell, McGleish*. Subs: Rapley/Coote.
Oldham: Kelly, Clegg, Armstrong, Beharall, Balmer, Murray, Colusso^, Smart", Corazzin, Eyres.

38 STOKE (H) 1-3 — Duguid 54; Gudjonsson 42, Burton 45, 80. Ref: D Crick
A decent display by the U's who are unlucky to be two-down by the break. Duguid stretches to slot in soon after the restart, but a comeback is derailed by a disputed Stoke third from Deon Burton. The officials come in for heavy criticism and it is agreed a draw would have been fairer.
Colchester: Brown, Duguid, Johnson R, Pinault, Fitzgerald, White, Izzet, Bowry^, Barrett, Stockwell, McGleish*. Subs: Gregory/Morgan.
Stoke: Cutler, Thomas, Clarke^, Handyside, Shtanyuk, Van Deurzen, Gudjonsson, O'Connor, Burton, Gunlaugs'n*, Iwelumo".

39 PETERBOROUGH (A) 1-3 — Barrett 87; Farrell 26, Green 39, McKenzie 77. Ref: S Tomlin
The same result as versus Stoke, but this display was dreadful. 'The worst in my two years in charge,' says furious Whitton. David Farrell and Leon McKenzie do the damage before Barrett poaches a meaningless consolation goal. Australian central defender Con Blatsis joins the club.
Colchester: Brown, Johnson R, Pinault, Fitzgerald, White", Izzet, Bowry", Barrett, Stockwell, McGleish". Subs: Rapley/Keith/Morgan.
Peterborough: Tyler, Joseph, Williams, Shields*, Gill, Edwards, Bullard, Oldfield, McKenzie, Green, Farrell. Sub: Danielsson.

40 QP RANGERS (H) 3-1 — Rapley 12, 85, McGleish 53, Dodou 90. Ref: L Cable
Rapley eases relegation worries with an early goal that visibly boosts confidence. McGleish makes it two after the first raid of the second half and Rapley makes the three points safe with a left-foot volley late on. The U's are well on top and sub Dodou's late strike is purely academic.
Colchester: Gregory, Keith, Pinault, Fitzgerald, Blatsis, Izzet, Rapley, Barrett, Stockwell*, McGleish. Subs: Duguid, Warren/Dodou.
QP Rangers: Evans, Forbes, Murphy^, Palmer, Bignott, Shittu, Langley, Peacock, Gallen, Thomson, Daly".

41 WYCOMBE (A) 0-0 — Ref: S Mathieson
Despite the intense fans' rivalry, this is a limp, goalless bore. Sean Devine's 25-yard lob drops the wrong side of the bar and Devine and Andy Rammell both blast efforts wide. The U's go close when Keith forces Martin Taylor into a fine save. Coote scores but is pulled up for offside.
Colchester: Gregory, Keith, Pinault, Fitzgerald, Blatsis, Izzet, Rapley, Barrett*, Stockwell*, McGleish*. Subs: Duguid/White/Coote.
Wycombe: Taylor, Senda, Vinnicombe, Bulman, Rogers, McCarthy, Currie, Simpson, Devine, Rammell, Brown". Sub: McSparran.

42 BRIGHTON (H) 1-4 — Stockwell 88; Carpenter 23, 90, Gray 27, Brooker 29. Ref: P Jones
Without star striker Bobby Zamora, title-chasing Albion crush the U's with three goals in six minutes. Richard Carpenter grabs the first after a free-kick. Wayne Gray caps his debut with a goal then Paul Brooker squeezes in the third. In the dying moments Carpenter buries a free-kick.
Colchester: Brown, Duguid, Keith, White", Fitzgerald, Blatsis, Izzet, Pinault, Rapley^, Stockwell, McGleish^. Subs: Morgan/Coote/MacDonald.
Brighton: Kuipers, Watson, Mayo, Morgan, Cullip, Carpenter, Hart", Lewis^, Webb, Gray", Brooker. Subs: Jones/Oatway/Pethick.

43 BOURNEMOUTH (A) 1-0 — Maher 62 (og). Ref: T Parkes
After coming in for criticism for his display against Brighton, keeper Brown puts in a great performance to keep the Cherries out. The game is no classic and is decided by a piece of good fortune when Shaun Maher put through his own goal. Sean O'Driscoll's men are relegation-bound.
Colchester: Brown, Duguid, Keith, Pinault, Fitzgerald, Blatsis, Izzet, Rapley, Barrett*, Stockwell*, McGleish^. Subs: White/Coote.
Bournemouth: Stewart, Young*, Elliott, Maher", Purches, Tindall, Feeney, Holmes, Hayter, Fletcher C, Hughes^. Subs: Foyewa/Cooke/Thomas.

44 CARDIFF (H) 0-1 — Prior 20. Ref: P Danson
City take a giant stride towards the play-offs after defender Spencer Prior nets the only goal, smacking the ball in from close range after Danny Gabbidon's curling shot hits the post. The U's, safe from the drop, go close through Coote, and Izzet has a shot well saved by Neil Alexander.
Colchester: Brown, Duguid, Keith, Pinault, Fitzgerald, Blatsis, Izzet, Rapley^, MacDonald*, Stockwell^, Coote*. Subs: McGl'sh/Chambers/Canham.
Cardiff: Alexander, Weston, Croft, Bonner, Collins, Unsworth, Boland, Gabbidon^, Kavanagh, Campbell, Fort'ne-West/Boland. Sub: Earnshaw.

45 BURY (A) 3-1 — McGleish 45, Coote 72, 87; Billy 74. Ref: R Olivier
Andy Preece's side are condemned to the drop by this defeat. Needing reinvestment, the Shakers face an uncertain future after Coote hits two late goals. On a dreadful pitch Morgan impresses in his first start of the season and debutant keeper Knight deals well with Bury's long throws.
Colchester: Knight, White, Keith, Pinault, Fitzgerald, Blatsis, Izzet, Bowry", McGleish^, Stockwell*, Morgan". Subs: Johnson R/Coote/MacDon'd.
Bury: Kenny, Connel^, Barrass*, Clarkson, Collins, Forrest, Billy, Newby, Clegg, Lawson, Hayter. Subs: Seddon/Nugent.

46 WIGAN (H) 2-2 — McGleish 42, MacDonald 45; Roberts 60, 86. Ref: S Baines
McGleish sets the ball rolling on the season's final day with a superb 35-yard strike and MacDonald, on loan from Charlton, then rams home a rebound. The U's squander their lead as sub Neil Roberts spoils the party atmosphere with a second-half brace to leave home fans frustrated.
Colchester: Brown, White, Keith, Pinault, Fitzgerald, Blatsis, Izzet, Bowry, MacDonald*, Stockwell*, McGleish^. Subs: Duguid/Morgan/Coote.
Wigan: Filan, Jackson, Pendlebury, Mitchell^, DeLos, Teale", Jarrett, DeZeeuw, Liddell, Ellington, McMillan. Subs: Kilford/Roberts.

NATIONWIDE DIVISION 2 (CUP-TIES)

Manager: Steve Whitton — SEASON 2001-02

Worthington Cup

1 A PORTSMOUTH 21/8 — Att 7,078 1:19 — 2 W — F-A 2:1 — H-T 0:0
Scorers, Times and Referees: Stockwell 53, Izzet 82 / Crouch 77 — Ref: P Taylor

Squad numbers in use:
Woodman	Dunne*	Keith	Pinault	Fitzgerald	Clark	Gregory	Izzet	Rapley	Stockwell^	McGleish
Beasant	Panopoulos* Vincent^	Hiley	Moore*	Zamperini	O'Neil	Prosinecki	Crouch	Quashie	Pitt	Migliorani/Harper/Bradbury

Subs used: White/Bowry; Migliorani/Harper/Bradbury

Hit by the recent death of keeper Aaron Flahavan, Pompey give ex-Real Madrid star Robert Prosinecki a full debut and parade new signing Peter Crouch. They apply bags of pressure but U's counter superbly. Woodman performs heroics and Izzet pounces to cap a fine night's work.

2 H BARNSLEY 11/9 — Att 3,442 1:17 — 2 L — F-A 1:3 — H-T 0-1
Scorers, Times and Referees: Keith 72 / Dyer 27, 90, Jones 88 — Ref: D Crick

Squad numbers in use:
Woodman	Duguid	Keith	Pinault	Fitzgerald	Clark	Gregory	Izzet*	Rapley	Stockwell	McGleish
Miller	Regan	Barker	Morgan	Crooks	Ward	Neill	Sheron*	Garre^	Dyer	Barnard	Jones/Donovan

Subs used: Bowry; Jones/Donovan

The visitors are quick off the blocks and only denied by heroics from Woodman. But he can do little when a wicked deflection leaves Bruce Dyer free to fire home. Keith curls an inch-perfect free-kick but Nigel Spackman's men bounce back with late goals by Lee Jones and Dyer.

FA Cup

1 H YORK 17/11 — Att 3,350 3:12 — 10 D — F-A 0:0 — H-T 0-0
Ref: S Baines

Squad numbers in use:
Woodman	Duguid	Keith	Pinault	Fitzgerald	Johnson R	Johnson G	Izzet^	Rapley	Stockwell*	McGleish
Fettis	Hocking	Potter	Smith	Hobson	Brass	Bullock	Nogan	Proctor	Cooper	Morgan/Dunne	Richardson

Subs used: Morgan/Dunne; Richardson

Stockwell and McGleish both hit the York bar with headers, but Terry Dolan's battlers almost snatch victory in the closing minutes when on-loan Sunderland man Michael Proctor shoots just wide. A frustrating afternoon and some home fans jeer the players as they leave the pitch.

1R A YORK 27/11 — Att 2,014 3:18 — 12 D — F-A 2:2 aet — H-T 0-1
Scorers, Times and Referees: McGleish 81, Duguid 90 / Brass 8, Potter 84 — Ref: S Baines (U's lost 2-3 on penalties)

Squad numbers in use:
Woodman	Duguid	Keith*	Pinault	Fitzgerald	Johnson R	Johnson G	Bowry	Rapley^	Stockwell^	McGleish
Fettis	Edmondson/Potter	Smith	Hocking	Cooper	Brass	Stamp^	Nogan^	Proctor	Richardson	Maley/Mathie*/Bullock

Subs used: Morgan/White/Opara; Maley/Mathie*/Bullock

United dominate for much of the game, having 25 corners and 26 attempts on goal, but it takes a late scrambled effort by Duguid to take the tie into extra-time and then a shoot-out. Fitzgerald and Morgan score, but G Johnson skies his over and McGleish and Duguid have theirs saved.

LDV Vans Trophy

1 H SWINDON 16/10 — Att 1,521 10 — 11 W — F-A 1-0 — H-T 0-0
Scorers, Times and Referees: Izzet 49 — Ref: G Hegley

Squad numbers in use:
Brown	Duguid	Johnson G	Pinault	Johnson R	Clark	Bowry^	Izzet	Rapley	Stockwell*	McGleish
Griemink	Edwards N* Duke	Heywood	Reeves^	Gurney	Edwards P	McAreavey	Ose*Kuffour Grazioli*	Howe	Morgan/Keith	Brayley/Ruddock/Halliday

Subs used: Morgan/Keith; Brayley/Ruddock/Halliday

Whitton promises the U's won't be taking this competition lightly. Revenge is gained over Roy Evans' men for the earlier defeat, Izzet's strike just after the break doing the trick. Off the field, important planning applications are submitted to the local council regarding the new stadium.

2 A READING 30/10 — Att 2,725 11 — 9 L — F-A 1:2 — H-T 0-1
Scorers, Times and Referees: Stockwell 77 / Smith N 45, Henderson 72 — Ref: A Hall

Squad numbers in use:
Brown	Keith	Johnson G	Pinault*	Fitzgerald	Clark	Gregory^	Izzet	Bowry*	Morgan	McGleish
Ashdown	Murty	Sharey	Viveash	Mackie	Gamble	Hughes^	Smith N*	Forster	Henderson	Smith A*	Rougier/Igoe/Harper

Subs used: Stockwell/Opara/Hadrava; Rougier/Igoe/Harper

Alan Pardew's promotion favourites have made a mediocre start to the season, but Neil Smith and Darius Henderson are on target to punish the injury-hit U's. Whitton is full of praise for Morgan and young subs Hadrava and Opara, who grab rare opportunities to show what they can do.

League Table

		P	Home					Away					Pts
			W	D	L	F	A	W	D	L	F	A	
1	Brighton	46	17	5	1	42	16	8	10	5	24	26	90
2	Reading	46	12	7	4	36	20	11	8	4	34	23	84
3	Brentford	46	17	5	1	48	12	7	6	10	29	31	83
4	Cardiff	46	12	8	3	39	25	11	6	6	36	25	83
5	Stoke *	46	16	4	3	43	12	7	7	9	24	28	80
6	Huddersfield	46	13	7	3	35	19	8	8	7	30	28	78
7	Bristol City	46	13	6	4	38	21	8	4	11	30	32	73
8	QP Rangers	46	11	10	2	35	18	8	4	11	25	31	71
9	Oldham	46	14	6	3	47	27	4	10	9	30	38	70
10	Wigan	46	9	6	8	36	23	7	10	6	30	28	64
11	Wycombe	46	13	5	5	38	26	4	8	11	20	38	64
12	Tranmere	46	10	9	4	39	19	6	6	11	24	41	63
13	Swindon	46	10	7	6	26	21	5	7	11	20	35	59
14	Port Vale	46	11	6	6	35	24	5	4	14	16	38	58
15	COLCHESTER	46	9	6	8	35	33	6	6	11	30	43	57
16	Blackpool	46	9	9	6	39	31	6	5	12	27	38	56
17	Peterborough	46	11	5	7	46	26	4	5	14	18	33	55
18	Chesterfield	46	9	3	11	35	36	4	10	9	18	29	52
19	Notts Co	46	8	7	8	28	29	5	5	14	31	42	50
20	Northampton	46	9	4	10	30	33	5	3	15	24	46	49
21	Bournemouth	46	9	4	10	36	33	1	10	12	20	38	44
22	Bury	46	6	9	8	26	32	5	2	16	17	43	44
23	Wrexham	46	7	7	9	29	32	4	3	16	27	57	43
24	Cambridge	46	7	7	9	29	34	0	6	17	18	59	34
		1104	261	152	139	870	602	139	152	261	602	870	1504

* promoted after play-offs

Odds & ends

Double wins: (2) Cambridge, Northampton.

Double losses: (3) Brighton, Stoke, Swindon.

Won from behind: (4) Cambridge (H & A), Northampton (A), Peterborough (H).

Lost from in front: (2) Oldham (A), Swindon (H).

High spots: After five games, the best-ever start to a League season.

The club's first-ever opening-day haul of six goals.

The consistency of veteran Mick Stockwell.

Low spots: Skipper Simon Clark's shock exit 'for personal reasons'.

The death of a long-standing U's fan during the home game with Bury.

The FA Cup exit at the hands of Division Three strugglers York.

Player of the Year: Karl Duguid.

Ever-presents: (0).

Hat-tricks for: (0).

Hat-tricks against: (0).

Leading scorer: (16) Scott McGleish.

Appearances and Goals

	Appearances								Goals				
	Lge	Sub	LC	Sub	FAC	Sub	LDV	Sub	Lge	LC	FAC	LDV	Tot
Barrett, Graham	19	1							4				4
Blatsis, Con	7												
Bowry, Bobby	27	9	2	1				2	1				1
Brown, Simon	19							2					
Canham, Marc		1											
Chambers, Triston		1											
Coote, Adrian	5	14							4				4
Clark, Simon	19	2	2					2	4				4
Duguid, Karl	36	5	1		2		1		4	1			5
Dunne, Joe	6	2	1		1			1	2				2
Fitzgerald, Scott	36	1	2		1								
Gregory, David	15	1	2		1								
Hadrava, David		1											
Halls, John	6												
Izzet, Kem	36	4	2		1		2		3	1			4
Johnson, Gavin	19	1	2		2				1				1
Johnson, Ross	13	3	2		1				1				1
Keith, Joe	33	8	2		2				4		1		5
Knight, Richard	1												
MacDonald, Charlie	2	2							1				1
McGleish, Scott	44	2	2		2		2		15			1	16
Morgan, Dean	1	29					2	1					
Opara, Lloyd		1						1					
Pinault, Thomas	37	5	2		2								
Rapley, Kevin	26	9	2		2		1		9				9
Stockwell, Mick	45	1	2		2		1	1	9	1			10
White, Alan	28	5	1		1				3				3
Woodman, Andy	26		2		2								
(own-goals)									4				4
28 players used	506	107	22	3	22	5	22	4	65	3	2	2	72

NATIONWIDE DIVISION 2

Manager: Steve Whitton ⇨ Phil Parkinson

SEASON 2002-03

No	Date	Venue / Team	Att	Pos	Pt	F-A	H-T	Scorers, Times, and Referees
1	10/8	H STOCKPORT	3,300		W 3	1-0	0-0	Pinault 58 — Ref: P Danson
2	13/8	A TRANMERE	7,499	8 / 5	D 4	1-1	0-1	Keith 53 / Koumas 15 — Ref: M Pike
3	17/8	A CREWE	5,138	15 / 14	L 4	0-2	0-1	Hulse 9, Bell 81 — Ref: G Salisbury
4	24/8	H BRENTFORD	3,135	19 / 2	L 4	0-1	0-1	Hunt 45p — Ref: P Taylor
5	26/8	A PETERBOROUGH	4,203	12 / 21	W 7	1-0	0-0	Keith 80 — Ref: P Armstrong
6	31/8	H WIGAN	2,721	8 / 3	W 10	1-0	1-0	Morgan 41 — Ref: K Hill
7	7/9	H CHELTENHAM	2,845	11 / 23	D 11	1-1	0-1	Keith 59p / Naylor 45 — Ref: B Curson
8	14/9	A PORT VALE	3,328	14 / 11	L 11	0-1	0-0	Collins 47 — Ref: M Ryan
9	17/9	A NORTHAMPTON	3,663	6 / 14	L 11	1-4	1-3	Sampson(og) 39 / Gabbiadini 15, 45, 69, One 23 — Ref: G Cain
10	21/9	H OLDHAM	3,021	16 / 3	L 11	0-1	0-0	Andrews 64 — Ref: G Hegley
11	28/9	A QP RANGERS	12,906	20 / 2	L 11	0-2	0-1	Connolly 39, Gallen 72 — Ref: S Tomlin

Squad numbers in use / subs used

1. STOCKPORT — McKinney, Warren, Keith, Pinault, Johnson, White, Duguid, Bowry, Rapley*, McGleish^, Stockwell; subs: Morgan/Coote/Izzet
Jones, Lescott, Clare, Challinor, Palmer, Clark, McLachlan / Lambert*, Daly*, Beckett, Pemberton; subs: Gibbs/Briggs/Burgess*

2. TRANMERE — McKinney, Warren, Keith, Pinault, Johnson, White, Duguid*, Bowry, Rapley^, McGleish, Stockwell; subs: Izzet/Morgan/Brown
Feuer, Allen, Nicholson, Sharps^, McGibbon, Gray, Navarro, Mellon, Haworth, Price*, Koumas; subs: Harrison/Hume/Barlow*

3. CREWE — McKinney, Warren, Keith, Pinault, Johnson, White, Izzet, Bowry*, Morgan, McGleish^, Stockwell; subs: Rapley/Coote
Ince, Wright, Sodje, Brammer, Foster, Vaughan, Burton, Hulse, Lunt^, Ashton, Sorvel*; subs: Bell/Jones/Miles*

4. BRENTFORD — McKinney, Warren*, Keith, Pinault, Johnson, White, Izzet, Bowry, Morgan, McGleish^, Stockwell^; subs: Rapley/Steele/Opara
Smith P, Dobson, Sonko, Ragot, Hutchinson, Smith J, O'Connor, Vine, McCammon^, Hunt, Constantine*

5. PETERBOROUGH — McKinney, Warren!, Keith, Pinault*, Johnson, White, Izzet, Bowry, Morgan^, Coote*, Stockwell; subs: Rapley/McGleish/Odunsi
Tyler, Gill, McDonald, Forsyth, Joseph, Edwards, Bullard, Danielsson, Willis^, Green*, Newton; subs: Rea/Clarke/Fenn*

6. WIGAN — McKinney, Warren, Keith, Pinault, Johnson, White, Izzet, Bowry, Morgan^, Coote*, Stockwell; subs: McGleish/Opara
Filan, Jackson, McMillan^, Dinning!, DeVos, Breckin, Green, Flynn^, Ellington, Liddell, McCulloch; subs: Teale/Jarrett/Roberts*

7. CHELTENHAM — McKinney, Warren, Keith, Pinault, Johnson, White, Izzet, Bowry, Morgan^, Coote*, Stockwell*; subs: Rapley/Opara/Stockley
Book, Howarth, Victory, McAuley, Walker, Duff, Milton, Brayson, Alsop, Naylor*, Yates; subs: Williams/Devaney*

8. PORT VALE — McKinney, Warren, Keith, Pinault, Johnson, White, Izzet, Bowry, Morgan^, Odunsi*, Stockwell*; subs: Rapley/Baldwin"/Morgan
Goodlad, Cummins, Brightwell, Carragher, Collins, Rowland, McCarthy, Brisco, McPhee, Angell, Bridge-Wilk'n/McClare*

9. NORTHAMPTON — McKinney, Stockley, Keith, Pinault, Johnson, White, Izzet, Bowry, Morgan, McGleish^, Stockwell*; subs: Opara
Harper, Gill, Carruthers, Sampson, Burgess", Harsley, McGregor, Trollope, One^, Gabbiadini', Hagreaves; subs: Forrester/Asamoah/Rickers

10. OLDHAM — Brown, Stockley, Warren!, Pinault, Steele, White, Izzet, Bowry, Morgan, McGleish^, Stockwell*; subs: Rapley/Coote
Pogliacomi, Low, Eyres^, Beharall, Hall, Hill!, Carss, Sheridan, Corazzin*, Wijnhard, Eyre; subs: Baudet/Andrews/Holden*

11. QP RANGERS — Brown, Stockley, Warren, Pinault, Steele, White, Izzet, Bowry, Morgan, McGleish^, Rapley"; subs: Coote/Morgan/Opara
Royce, Forbes, Williams, Palmer, Carlisle, Shittu, Rose, Langley, Gallen, Connolly, Oli; subs: Furlong*

Match reports

1 STOCKPORT: Fraser McLachlan is sent off after a second yellow card early in the second half and County are punished when Pinault strikes a powerful right-foot shot from the edge of the box. Subs Coote and Morgan miss good chances, but the visitors go closest as Luke Beckett hits a post late on.

2 TRANMERE: Jason Koumas rounds McKinney after a brilliant solo run to put Rovers ahead. McKinney is replaced at half-time. Keith, the smallest man on the pitch, heads home Stockwell's cross to level. Debutant Ian Feuer produces stunning saves to deny Keith and McGleish in the later stages.

3 CREWE: Whitton accuses his strikers of looking jaded after just three games, after the U's play pretty football but lack a cutting edge. Goals from Rob Hulse and sub Lee Bell prove enough for Dario Gradi's men. United's best chance sees McGleish's thundering header saved by Clayton Ince.

4 BRENTFORD: U's dominate the first half and teenager Morgan is unlucky, foiled by excellent saves by Paul Smith. Sub Steele is controversially penalised for a challenge on Mark McCammon and Stephen Hunt fires in the spot-kick. McKinney does well to push a header from Lee Roget over the bar.

5 PETERBOROUGH: Millwall midfielder Leke Odunsi arrives on loan from Millwall. Barry Fry's side have lost three in a row without scoring before today and look low on confidence. Keith breaks the deadlock in the closing stages and United hang on, despite only having ten men after Warren is dismissed.

6 WIGAN: Morgan nets a spectacular left-foot rocket in the dying minutes of the first half, his first ever league goal. Nathan Ellington goes close with three second-half efforts, and Liddell hits the post near the end. Tony Dinning is dismissed for a late foul on Keith as the U's hang on bravely.

7 CHELTENHAM: Steve Cotterill's winless side take the lead in first-half stoppage time when the slippery Tony Naylor darts in at the near post to prod home. The second half belongs to Colchester, whose only success arrives when Keith drills home a penalty kick after a Richard Walker foul on Pinault.

8 PORT VALE: A Stockwell shot strikes a post before Sam Collins heads over from a Marc Bridge-Wilkinson free-kick. A corner sees Collins soar to bury a powerful header, his first goal for Vale. McGleish comes closest to an equaliser when his injury-time header from Joe Keith's cross curls wide.

9 NORTHAMPTON: Veteran Marco Gabbiadini charges down a goal-kick and hooks in from 18 yards. Jerry Gill crosses and Armand One heads in at the near post. Ian Sampson turns a Stockwell cross into his own net. Gabbiadini nets a close-range header and completes his hat-trick with a right-foot drive.

10 OLDHAM: In a heated few moments Clint Hill is sent off for a two-footed tackle and then after a melee Warren exits for punching Clyde Wijnhard, who is booked for his part in the incident. Minutes later sub Wayne Andrews rifles home a real beauty to give Iain Dowie's men a lead they cling to.

11 QP RANGERS: Man-of-the-match Karl Connolly opens the scoring with a low drive from 15 yards after United fail to clear their lines. He helps seal the points when his clever through ball sends Kevin Gallen clear to score in emphatic fashion. Ian Holloway's outfit celebrate their fifth victory in a row.

No	Venue	Opponent	Date	Att	Pos	Res	Opp Pos	Pts	FT	HT
12	H	WYCOMBE	5/10	3,252	20	L	15	11	0-1	0-1
13	A	SWINDON	12/10	4,152	21	D	22	12	2-2	1-0
14	H	CHESTERFIELD	18/10	3,211	17	W	7	15	2-0	0-0
15	A	HUDDERSFIELD	26/10	8,912	19	D	16	16	1-1	1-0
16	H	BARNSLEY	29/10	3,096	18	D	19	17	1-1	1-1
17	A	MANSFIELD	1/11	3,414	18	L	23	17	2-4	2-3
18	H	BRISTOL CITY	9/11	3,338	21	D	4	18	2-2	0-1
19	A	NOTTS CO	23/11	4,626	19	W	20	21	3-2	2-2
20	H	PLYMOUTH	30/11	3,714	19	D	13	22	0-0	0-0
21	A	LUTON	14/12	5,890	15	W	7	25	2-1	1-1
22	H	CARDIFF	20/12	3,096	16	L	2	25	1-2	0-1
23	H	PETERBOROUGH	26/12	3,760	17	D	22	26	1-1	1-0

12 — WYCOMBE (H)
Scorers: Brown 4p — Ref: D Pugh
U's: Brown / Stockley / Keith / Pinault* / Steele / White / Izzet / Bowry / Rapley / McGleish / Stockwell / Morgan
Opp: Taylor / Senda / Vinnicombe / Ryan / Thomson / McCarthy / Bulman / Simpson / Faulc'bridge* / Rammell / Brown^ / Harris/Johnson
Steve Brown nets an early penalty after Stockwell pulls down Michael Simpson. The U's produce a series of chances and dominate for a spell but Rapley in particular has a nightmare in front of goal. The alarm bells are ringing at Layer Road after this frustrating fifth successive defeat.

13 — SWINDON (A)
Scorers: McGleish 3, Pinault 49 — Gurney 66, Sabin 68 — Ref: M Warren
U's: Brown / Stockley / Keith / Pinault / Steele / White / Izzet / Bowry / Rapley^ / McGleish* / Stockwell / Morgan / Coote
Opp: Griemink / Gurney / Duke / Heywood / Reeves / Jackson / Davis / Robinson / Sabin / Invincible / Hewlett
A blunder by Bart Griemink allows a free-kick from Keith to squirm past for McGleish to run the ball in. Griemink then flaps at Izzet's cross to allow Pinault in. Home fans call for manager Andy King's head until Andy Gurney and Eric Sabin pounce to complete an unlikely comeback.

14 — CHESTERFIELD (H)
Scorers: Izzet 58, 73 — Ref: T Parkes
U's: Brown / Stockley / Keith / Pinault / Steele / White / Izzet / Bowry / Rapley / McGleish / Stockwell / Morgan
Opp: Muggleton / Booty / Edwards / Hudson / Blatherwick / Howson / Brandon / Ebdon / Reeves / Burt* / Rushbury^ / Allott/O'Hara
Relief at last for Whitton at this Friday-night success, following seven league games without a win. Dave Rushbury's side is sunk by second-half Izzet strikes, his first for months. Record signing Coote is farmed out on loan to Bristol Rovers with Justin Richards coming the other way.

15 — HUDDERSFIELD (A)
Scorers: Rapley 11 — Stead 90 — Ref: P Joslin
U's: Brown / Stockley^ / Keith / Pinault / Steele / White / Izzet / Bowry / Rapley* / McGleish* / Stockwell / Morgan/Odunsi/Richards
Opp: Bevan / Sharp / Jenkins / Brown^ / Moses / Holland / Baldry* / Mattis / Stead / Smith* / Thorington McDonald/Schofield/Dyson
United outplay Mick Wadsworth's side for 80 minutes after an early Rapley goal. Lanky Jon Stead poaches an unexpected last-minute leveller with his side's only chance of the second half. Whitton is furious at the injustice, while Wadsworth attacks home fans for barracking his team.

16 — BARNSLEY (H)
Scorers: Stockley 10 — Dyer 15 — Ref: C Penton
U's: Brown / Stockley^ / Keith / Pinault^ / Steele ! / White / Izzet / Bowry / Rapley* / McGleish / Stockwell / Morgan / Odunsi/Baldwin
Opp: Marriott / Mulligan* / Gibbs / Morgan / O'Callaghan Neill / Lumsdon / Betsy / Fallon / Dyer / Gorre / Ward
Izzet coolly supplies Stockley, who slots the ball past Andy Marriott. Bruce Dyer soon levels, finding space to volley home. Steele hauls Dyer down and is sent off on 17 minutes. The visitors dominate but cannot force a winning goal and at the whistle vent their anger at the officials.

17 — MANSFIELD (A)
Scorers: Keith 25p, Rapley 31 — Christie 19, 25, 29, 64 — Ref: H Webb
U's: Brown / Odunsi^ / Keith / Pinault / Baldwin ! / White ! / Izzet / Bowry / Rapley* / McGleish^ / Stockwell / Morgan/Richards
Opp: Pilkington / Lawrence / Vaughan" / Lever / Moore / Williamson / Corden / Disley / Christie / Little / Sellars* / MacKenzie/Bacon/Clarke
Mansfield had waited 300 minutes for a home goal when Iyseden Christie glances in a cross-shot. Keith nets a penalty for a push on McGleish. Christie nets a looping header before Rapley races clear to score. Christie completes a hat-trick with a penalty for a corner. White is sent off for a late foul.

18 — BRISTOL CITY (H)
Scorers: Pinault 55, Bowry 66 — Peacock 42, 58 — Ref: J Ross
U's: Brown / Stockley / Keith / Pinault / Baldwin / White / Izzet / Bowry / Rapley* / McGleish / Stockwell* / Morgan
Opp: Phillips / Coles / Bell / Burnell / Butler / Hill / Murray / Doherty / Peacock / Roberts^ / Tinnion* / Brown/Rosenior
Lee Peacock slots home after a good run by skipper Tom Doherty. Battling United deservedly equalise through a stunning strike from Pinault. Peacock restores the lead with a fine diving header, but Bowry swoops to fire in from close range after a White header is only partially cleared.

19 — NOTTS CO (A)
Scorers: Morgan 7, 35, McGleish 83 — Allsopp 16, Brough 18 — Ref: A Leake
U's: Brown / Stockley / Keith / Baldwin / Warren / White / Izzet / Bowry / Rapley* / Morgan^ / Stockwell* / Pinault/Coote/McGleish
Opp: Garden / Ramsden* / Jupp^ / Caskey / Fenton / Ashton / Brough / Whitley / Heffernan / Allsopp / Barraclough / Cas/Stallard
Morgan cuts in from the left and beats two men before firing calmly home. Danny Allsopp brings County level with a neat shot on the turn and Michael Brough scores off a post 90 seconds later. Morgan levels and the U's banish recent FA Cup misery via a late winner by sub McGleish.

20 — PLYMOUTH (H)
Scorers: — Ref: C Boyeson
U's: Brown / Stockley* / Keith / Warren / Baldwin / White / Izzet / Bowry / Rapley / Pinault / Stockwell* / Morgan/McGleish/Keeble
Opp: Larrieu / Worrell / Hodges / Barras / Wotton / Coughlan / Norris / Keith / Evans / Stonebridge / Adams
Without a League win at Layer Road since 1958, Argyle spurn first-half chances. Brown foils Micky Evans twice and Ian Stonebridge misses a real sitter. Near the end United are hanging on at the post and then Brown deny goals to Evans, David Norris, Marino Keith and Steve Adams.

21 — LUTON (A)
Scorers: Duguid 45, Morgan 58 — Fotiadis 35 — Ref: M Cowburn
U's: Brown / Duguid / Keith / Warren^ / Fitzgerald / White / Izzet / Bowry / Rapley* / Morgan / Stockwell^ / Pinault/Coote/Baldwin
Opp: Ovendale / Boyce / Neilson / Coyne / Kimble / Robinson / Nicholls / Spring* / Brkovic / Crowe / Fotiadis / Hughes
Andy Fotiadis cracks Joe Kinnear's side ahead from 18 yards. A fine free-kick from Duguid levels matters just before the break. Morgan nets a header to set up the U's second successive away win. Without suspended striker Steve Howard, Luton take the chance to move into the top six.

22 — CARDIFF (H)
Scorers: Stockwell 52 — Earnshaw 45, 77 — Ref: U Rennie
U's: Brown / Duguid / Keith / Warren / Fitzgerald / White / Izzet / Bowry / Rapley ! / Morgan* / Stockwell* / Pinault/Coote/Atangana
Opp: Alexander / Weston / Zhiyi ! / Prior / Boland / Campbell* / Kavanagh / Earnshaw^ / Thorne / Legg / Croft/Fortune-West
Rob Earnshaw controls a pass from Willie Boland and shoots home. U's level as Stockwell punishes a slip by Spencer Prior. Neil Alexander's huge kick forward finds Rob Earnshaw, who lobs neatly over Brown. Rapley and Chinese defender Fan Zhiyi see red after a second-half clash.

23 — PETERBOROUGH (H)
Scorers: Izzet 45 — Clarke 82 — Ref: G Stretton
U's: Brown / Duguid / Keith / Baldwin / Fitzgerald / White / Izzet / Bowry / Atangana^ / McGleish / Stockwell* / Pinault/Rapley
Opp: Harrison / Gill / Jellyman^ / Arber / Rea" / Edwards / Burton^ / Bullard / Clarke / Lee / Shields / Newton/Farrell/MacKenzie
A corner is only half-cleared to Izzet, who volleys home sweetly from the edge of the box. Stockwell misses a glorious chance before ex-Posh man McGleish rattles a post. Barry Fry gambles by playing four in attack and is rewarded when Andy Clarke fires home a Dave Farrell centre.

NATIONWIDE DIVISION 2

Manager: Steve Whitton ⇨ Phil Parkinson — SEASON 2002-03

No	Date	Att	Pos	Pt	F-A	H-T	Scorers, Times, and Referees	SQUAD NUMBERS IN USE	subs used
24	A BLACKPOOL 28/12	6,040	18/9	L 26	1-3	0-2	Izzet 71 — Walker 34, Grayson 45, Murphy 59 — Ref: A Kaye. Richard Walker nets a fierce diagonal shot with Steve McMahon's side well on top. Baldwin is booked for hauling down Danny Coid, and from the free-kick Richie Wellens cross is slotted in by Simon Grayson. Wellens also supplies the pass for John Murphy to head the third goal.	Brown, Duguid, Keith, Baldwin, Fitzgerald, White, Izzet, Bowry, Morgan^, McGleish, Stockley* / Barnes, Richardson, Coid, Southern, Grayson, Henry", Wellens, Bullock*, Murphy, Walker, Taylor	Pinault/Stockwell/Coote · Hills/O'Kane/Hughes
25	H TRANMERE 4/1	2,846	17/7	D 27	2-2	1-1	McGleish 12, Keith 69p — Haworth 38, Mellon 60 — Ref: L Cable. The Board warns Whitton about the serious drop in gates and a more attacking display results. Izzet's low header is turned in by McGleish, but Haworth turns and fires Rovers level. Micky Mellon curls in a free-kick. A foul on Coote sees Keith scuff his penalty, but it still finds the net.	Brown, Duguid, Keith, Baldwin, Fitzgerald, Warren, Izzet, Bowry*, McGleish, Coote, Stockwell* / Achterberg, Connelly, Jackson, Loran, Roberts, Hay, Jones, Mellon, Hume, Barlow*, Haworth	Pinault/Keeble · Robinson
26	H CREWE 11/1	2,949	19/3	L 27	1-2	1-0	Stockwell 41 — Jones 56, 62 — Ref: K Hill. Stockwell expertly finishes a nice move with an angled shot. Promotion-chasing Crewe hit back through Steve Jones, deputising for Dean Ashton. He curls in the equaliser and then benefits from a blunder by Baldwin. Keith is hauled down but his penalty is saved by Clayton Ince.	Brown, Duguid, Keith, Baldwin^, Fitzgerald, Warren, Izzet, Bowry*, McGleish, Coote, Stockwell* / Ince, Wright, Tierney, Brammer, Foster, Walton, Rix^, Hulse, Lunt", Jones", Sorvel	Pinault/Morgan/Keeble · Sodje/Vaughan/Bell
27	A WIGAN 18/1	5,792	21/1	L 27	1-2	0-1	Keith 90p — DeVos 44, Liddell 74p — Ref: A Penn. Chances go begging at both ends before the deadlock is broken when Gary Teale's corner is headed in by Jason DeVos. McGleish's foul leads to Andy Liddell netting a penalty. John Filan hauls down Atangana and Keith scores from the spot in the dying seconds to create a tense finish.	Brown, Duguid, Keith, Warren, Fitzgerald, White, Izzet, Bowry, Williams^, McGleish, Stockwell* / Filan, Eden, Kennedy, Dinning, DeVos, Jackson, Teale, Mitchell, Ellington^, Liddell, McCulloch	Morgan/Atangana · Roberts
28	H BLACKPOOL 25/1	3,305	22/8	L 27	0-2	0-0	— Murphy 52, Coid 70 — Ref: C Webster. John Murphy hustles the ball over the line and then Danny Coid fires in a blistering drive. Duguid departs for two bookings in his 250th game. It's now nine home games without a win and four days later Whitton leaves his post 'by mutual consent' after nearly four years as U's boss.	Brown, Duguid!, Keith, Warren^, Fitzgerald, Chilvers, Izzet, Bowry, Williams, Coote", Stockwell* / Barnes, Richardson, Coid*, Southern, Grayson, Flynn, Wellens", Evans, Murphy, Walker, Taylor	McGleish/Baldwin/Atangana · Jaszcun/Dalglish
29	A STOCKPORT 1/2	4,011	21/18	D 28	1-1	0-1	Keith 88 — Beckett 36 — Ref: J Ross. Coach Geraint Williams takes over as caretaker boss. Luke Beckett puts Stockport ahead but misses two glorious chances to extend the lead. There is jubilation in the U's camp near the end when Keith gets on the end of a McGleish knock-down to poke an equaliser past Ola Tidman.	Brown, Pinault, Keith, Chilvers, Fitzgerald, White, Izzet, Morgan*, Williams, McGleish, Coote" / Tidman, Lescott, Tonkin, Challinor, Clare, MacLachlan, Gibb, Lambert, Daly", Beckett, Ellis"	Stockwell/Coote/Atangana · Pemberton/Wilbraham
30	A BRISTOL CITY 8/2	11,107	20/5	W 31	2-1	1-0	McGleish 12, Pinault 69 — Fagan 51 — Ref: A Hall. Craig Fagan cancels out McGleish's first-half goal, but the U's pull off a shock win after a late 30-yard strike from Pinault bounces over keeper Steve Phillips. Williams' chances of becoming U's full-time manager are enhanced. Home boss Danny Wilson calls the result a temporary blip.	Brown, Pinault, Keith, Chilvers, Fitzgerald, White, Izzet, Morgan^, Coote, McGleish, Bowry / Phillips, Carey, Bell, Burnell, Fortune, Hill, Murray, Doherty^, Fagan, Beadle*, Tinnion	Stockwell/Williams · Peacock/Roberts
31	H MANSFIELD 14/2	3,247	16/9	W 34	1-0	0-0	McGleish 88 — Ref: I Williamson. McGleish hits the woodwork with a ferocious first-half drive. Player-manager Keith Curle marshals his side effectively and a goalless draw looks likely until Williams boldly runs at the Stags defence, has his shot blocked by Keith Welch but McGleish is on hand to nod the winner.	Brown, Pinault, Keith, Chilvers, Fitzgerald, White, Lawrence*, Morgan^, Williams, McGleish, Stockwell* / Welch, Doane, Eaton, Day, Gadsby", Curtis, Williamson, Mendes, White^, Corden	Stockwell/Williams · Disley/Christie/Curle
32	A CHELTENHAM 22/2	3,607	18/24	D 35	1-1	1-1	Williams 44 — Alsop 2 — Ref: S Baines. Julian Alsop gives Bobby Gould's men the lead after just 88 seconds, looping a header into the far corner after Michael Duff heads a corner back across goal. The U's spirited reply pays dividends when Williams drills in an equaliser set up by Keith. Brown makes some crucial saves.	Brown, Stockley*, Keith, Chilvers, Fitzgerald, White, Izzet, Pinault, Williams, McGleish, Coote / Book, Jones, Victory, McAuley", Duff S, Duff M, Yates, Devaney^, Naylor^, Alsop, McCann	Stockwell/Morgan · Spencer/Brown/Bird
33	H PORT VALE 1/3	3,581	17/20	W 38	4-1	2-0	Williams 7, 36, 72, Keith 53 — Bridge-Wilkinson 55 — Ref: S Mathieson. Reading coach Phil Parkinson is appointed United manager. Williams nets a volley and just before the break heads in McGleish's cross. After Keith is on target, Marc Bridge-Wilkinson's stunning free-kick reduces the lead. Williams had the last word with a shot into the roof of the net.	Brown, Stockley, Keith, Chilvers^, Fitzgerald, White, Izzet, Pinault, Williams, McGleish, Coote / Delany, Carragher, Rowland, Collins, Clarke, Armstrong, Boyd, Brisco*, McPhee, Brooker	Bowry/Stockwell · Bridge-Wilk'n/Paynter
34	H NORTHAMPTON 4/3	3,408	15/23	W 41	2-0	1-0	Williams 28, McGleish 76 — Ref: D Crick. Daryl Burgess miskicks and Williams allows the ball to bounce before blasting a left-footer into the roof of the net. Brown catches a corner from John Frain and quickly produces a long throw to Williams, who goes on a run before squaring for McGleish to find the back of the net.	Brown, Stockley, Keith, Baldwin, Fitzgerald, White, Izzet, Pinault, Williams, McGleish, Coote / Harper, Gill, Frain, Reid, Burgess", Harsley^, Johnson, Trollope, McGregor, Gabbiadini*, Hargreaves	Duguid · Stamp/Asamoah/Sampson

35	A	OLDHAM		17	L	0-2	0-2		Brown"	Stockley	Keith	Baldwin	Fitzgerald	White !	Izzet	Pinault	Williams*	McGleish^	Duguid	Morgan/Atangana/McKinney
8/3			*5,223*	*4*	41			*Eyre 13, Eyres 19*	*Pogliacomi*	*Carss^*	*Eyres*	*Armstrong*	*Hall*	*Haining*	*Murray*	*Appleby**	*Wijnhard*	*Corazzin*	*Eyre*	*Duxbury/Andrews*
								Ref: P Danson	Iain Dowie's lively Latics end United's unbeaten run as John Eyre cracks in a powerful shot and veteran David Eyres takes his season's tally to 11 soon after. The U's are hit again before the break when White is sent off for pulling down Clyde Wijnhard. Keeper Brown goes off injured.											
36	A	BRENTFORD		16	D	1-1	0-1	Keith 84p	McKinney	Stockley	**Jackson**	Izzet	Fitzgerald	White	Duguid	Bowry*	Morgan^	McGleish	Keith	Pinault/Stockwell
11/3			*3,990*	*12*	42			*McCammon 37*	*Smith P*	*Dobson*	*Somner*	*Frampton*	*Marshall*	*Fieldwick*	*Antoine-Cur'*	*O'Connor*	*McCam'on^*	*Vine**	*Rowlands*	*Smith J/Peters*
								Ref: P Crossley	Bees' new loan signing Mickael Antoine-Curier helps set up Mark McCammon's first-half strike, which looks like being decisive until United win a late spot-kick, converted by reliable Keith. Home boss Wally Downes complains that his side are tired after eight games in four weeks.											
37	H	HUDDERSFIELD		15	W	2-0	0-0	Izzet 74, McGleish 81	McKinney	Stockley	Jackson	Pinault	Fitzgerald	White	Duguid	Izzet	Morgan*	McGleish	Keith	Stockwell
15/3			3,835	*23*	45				*Ashcroft*	*Moses*	*Sharp !*	*Brown*	*Gavin*	*Holland*	*Worthington*	*Mattis*	*Booth*	*Stead**	*Schofield*	*Scott*
								Ref: P Armstrong	Kevin Sharp is sent off in the first half for dissent but his relegation-haunted colleagues battle hard for a point, only crumbling late in the day. Izzet forces the ball in after Duguid hits the bar. A win is assured when McGleish heads home from close range following a Stockley free-kick.											
38	A	CHESTERFIELD		12	W	**4-0**	1-0	Izzet 43, Williams 48, Payne (og) 68, [Morgan 81]	McKinney	Stockley	Jackson	Pinault	Fitzgerald	White	Duguid	Izzet	Williams^	McGleish*	Keith	Stockwell/Morgan
18/3			***3,226***	*17*	48				*Williams*	*O'Hara**	*Close*	*Dawson"*	*Blatherwick*	*Payne*	*Brandon*	*Allott*	*Reeves*	*Folan^*	*Rushbury*	*Hurst/Innes/Davies*
								Ref: N Barry	Izzet heads in a Keith free-kick and Williams punishes slack marking to drive in a rising shot. The home side look deflated and Stockley drives in a low cross that Steve Payne turns into his own net. Sub Morgan scores 20 seconds after coming on, following a dreadful defensive mix-up.											
39	A	BARNSLEY		13	D	1-1	1-1	McGleish 38	McKinney	Stockley	Jackson	Pinault	Fitzgerald	Baldwin	Izzet	Bowry*	Duguid	McGleish	Keith	Stockwell
22/3			*9,154*	*14*	49			*Dyer 36*	*Ghent*	*Donovan*	*Mulligan**	*Morgan*	*Austin*	*Kay*	*Betsy*	*Jones^*	*Sheron*	*Dyer*	*Neil*	*Gorre//Crooks*
								Ref: E Evans	Bruce Dyer scores his 17th of the season after Mike Sheron's fierce shot is parried by McKinney. Matt Ghent fumbles a Duguid free-kick and McGleish taps home the equaliser. Later McGleish strikes the bar with a header and Dyer misses a sitter. United now look safe from relegation.											
40	H	SWINDON		11	W	1-0	0-0	Izzet 57	McKinney	Stockley	Jackson	Pinault	Fitzgerald	Baldwin	Duguid	Izzet	**May**	McGleish	Keith*	Stockwell
29/3			3,787	*12*	52				*Griemink*	*Ifil**	*Duke*	*Miglioranzi*	*Heywood*	*Gurney*	*Lewis*	*Parkin*	*Sabin"*	*Invincible^*	*Hewlett*	*Reeves/Young Dykes*
								Ref: G Poll	Big striker Ben May debuts after signing on loan from Millwall. Izzet nets a fine header after ex-Swindon man Jackson nods on a corner. The nearest the visitors come to scoring is late on when a Jerel Ifil header is cleared off the line by Keith. The U's rise into the top half of the table.											
41	A	PLYMOUTH		11	D	0-0	0-0		McKinney	Stockley	**Edwards**	Canham	Fitzgerald*	White	Duguid	Izzet	May	McGleish"	Jackson^	Pinault/Stockwell/Morgan
5/4			*7,122*	*9*	53				*Larrieu*	*Worrell*	*Hodges*	*Friio^*	*Wotton*	*Aljofree*	*Lopes*	*Bent*	*Stonebridge**	*Keith*	*Smith"*	*Evans/Norris/McAnespie*
								Ref: P Taylor	McKinney has his best game yet, defying Argyle time and again. He saves a Paul Wotton penalty and denes Ian Stonebridge and Marino Keith with spectacular stops. McGleish goes closest for the U's. Five are booked in this repeat of the Layer Road goalless draw between these sides.											
42	H	NOTTS CO		11	D	1-1	1-1	Duguid 2	McKinney	Stockley	Jackson	Pinault	Fitzgerald	White	Duguid	Izzet	May	McGleish*	Morgan	Edwards
12/4			3,435	*12*	54			*Stallard 45*	*Deeney*	*McCarthy*	*Nicholson*	*Richardson*	*Fenton*	*Ireland*	*Liburd*	*Bolland**	*Stallard*	*Heffernan*	*Baraclough*	*Allsopp*
								Ref: M Warren	Duguid latches on to a bad back-pass to open the scoring early. Mark Stallard equalises in first-half injury time, making the most of a rare lapse in the home defence, netting after Paul Heffernan's effort was blocked by McKinney. *The Daily Mirror* reporter calls the match a 'snore-fest'.											
43	A	CARDIFF		10	W	3-0	1-0	Duguid 4, Izzet 61, Morgan 73	McKinney	Stockley	Jackson"	Pinault	Fitzgerald	White	Izzet^	Bowry	Morgan	McGleish*	Duguid	May/Canham/Edwards
19/4			*12,623*	*3*	57				*Margetson*	*Weston**	*Legg*	*Gabbidon*	*Barker*	*Mahon^*	*Ainsworth"*	*Kavanagh*	*Earnshaw*	*Thorne*	*Boland*	*Croft/Whalley/Gordon*
								Ref: S Tomlin	Peter Thorne hits the U's bar, but seconds later a blunder by Chris Barker allows Duguid to chip in. Barker is robbed in a move that sees Izzet rifle home. Morgan finds space to net a fierce 25-yarder. Duguid hits a post and the angry home fans call for manager Lennie Lawrence's head.											
44	H	LUTON		10	L	**0-5**	0-4	*[Nicholls 43p]*	McKinney	**Halford^**	Edwards	Canham*	Fitzgerald	White	Duguid	Izzet	May	McGleish	Morgan	Pinault/Baldwin
21/4			3,967	*8*	57			*Howard 14, 45, 90, Griffiths 21,*	*Beckwith*	*Boyce**	*Neilson*	*Wilmot*	*Davis*	*Hughes*	*Nicholls*	*Spring^*	*Holmes*	*Griffiths"*	*Howard*	*Bayliss/Skelton/Judge*
								Ref: C Penton	Steve Howard is too hot for the U's to handle and grabs a hat-trick. Carl Griffiths neatly tucks in Luton's second. McKinney has a nightmare match and pulls down Carl Griffiths for Kevin Nicholls to knock home a penalty. The U's worst home defeat since an FA Cup-tie 19 years ago.											
45	A	WYCOMBE		10	D	0-0	0-0		McKinney	Stockley	Edwards*	Pinault	Fitzgerald	White	Izzet	Bowry	Morgan	McGleish	Duguid	Baldwin
26/4			*6,283*	*17*	58				*Talia*	*Senda*	*Vinnicombe*	*Bulman*	*Thomson*	*Johnson*	*Currie**	*Simpson*	*Harris"*	*Dixon*	*Ryan^*	*Roberts/Cook/Simpemba*
								Ref: B Curson	United survive early pressure and McKinney produces a stunning save from Danny Senda. Frank Talia then shows his worth, saving from Morgan and Duguid. Parkinson is relieved to get over the Luton thrashing: 'After that defeat, today required character and bravery,' he says.											
46	H	QP RANGERS		12	L	0-1	0-0		McKinney	Stockley	Baldwin	Pinault	Fitzgerald	White	Izzet	Bowry*	Morgan	McGleish^	Duguid	Stockwell/May
3/5			**5,047**	*3*	58			*Furlong 52*	*Day*	*Kelly^*	*Padula*	*Palmer*	*Shittu*	*Rose*	*Bircham*	*Langley**	*Furlong*	*Gallen*	*McLeod*	*Pacquette/Plummer*
		Home	Away					Ref: P Durkin	Paul Furlong heads a Stephen Kelly cross against the post then sweeps in the rebound. United nearly salvage a point, but McGleish and sub May squander good chances. The win puts Rangers in the play-offs. U's fans show appreciation for the Parkinson/Williams-inspired recovery.											
Average		3,387	6,170																	

NATIONWIDE DIVISION 2 (CUP-TIES) Manager: Steve Whitton ⇨ Phil Parkinson SEASON 2002-03

Worthington Cup

			Att	F-A	H-T	Scorers, Times, and Referees
1	A	COVENTRY	6,075 1:8	0-3	0-2	McSheffrey 1, McAllister 15, Mills 83
		11/9		11	L	Ref: R Olivier

SQUAD NUMBERS IN USE — subs used

McKinney	Baldwin	Keith	Pinault^	Johnson	White	Izzet	Bowry	Morgan*	McGleish	Stockwell^	Opara/Rapley/Odunis
Debec	Caldwell	Gordon	Eustace	Konjic	Shaw	Delorge*	McAllister	Mills	McSheffrey^	Chippo"	Pipe/Borthroyd/Normann

Straight from kick-off Dean Gordon's cross is stroked in by McSheffrey after just 12 seconds. United are being completely overrun and Gary McAllister doubles the lead direct from a free-kick following Baldwin's foul. Mills powers home David Pipe's centre with a perfect header.

FA Cup

			Att	F-A	H-T	Scorers, Times, and Referees
1	H	CHESTER	2,901 NL	0-1	0-0	Tate 83
		16/11		21	L	Ref: S Tomlin

SQUAD NUMBERS IN USE — subs used

Brown	Baldwin	Keith	Pinault	Stockley*	Warren	Izzet^	Bowry	Rapley	McGleish	Stockwell	Morgan/Atangana
Brown W	Brady"	McIntyre	Guyett	Bolland	Hatswell	Carey	Clare*	Tate^	Carden	Davies	Blackburn/Ruffer/Brown M

Conference side Chester hold their own and Brown makes a series of saves. Near the end Chris Tate, on loan from Orient, fires in following a flick-on by Scott Guyett. This loss adds to the list of recent cup embarrassments against Gravesend, Sutton, Bedlington, Hereford and Yeovil.

LDV Vans Trophy

			Att	F-A	H-T	Scorers, Times, and Referees
1	A	CHELTENHAM	1,369 24	1-4	0-1	McGleish 57
		22/10		17	L	Brayson 45p,78, McCann 63, Alsop 68
						Ref: P Danson

SQUAD NUMBERS IN USE — subs used

McKinney!	Stockley	Keith	Pinault	Steele	White	Izzet	Bowry"	Rapley*	McGleish	Stockwell^	Richards/Brown/Odunsi
Howarth	Book	Victory	Forsyth	Walker"	Duff	Coates*	Devaney	Alsop^	Brayson	McCann	Yates/Griffin/Spencer

McKinney brings down Paul Brayson and is sent off. Brayson gets up to convert the penalty. McGleish heads U's level from a Keith cross, but Cheltenham regain the lead with a fine Grant McCann free-kick. Julian Alsop taps home a rebound, and Brayson rounds Brown for the fourth.

League Table

	P	W	D	L	F	A	W	D	L	F	A	Pts
		Home					Away					
1 Wigan	46	14	7	2	37	18	15	6	2	31	9	100
2 Crewe	46	11	5	7	29	19	14	6	3	47	21	86
3 Bristol City	46	15	5	3	43	15	9	6	8	36	33	83
4 QP Rangers	46	14	4	5	38	19	10	7	6	31	26	83
5 Oldham	46	11	6	6	39	18	11	10	2	29	20	82
6 Cardiff *	46	12	6	5	33	20	11	6	6	35	23	81
7 Tranmere	46	14	5	4	38	23	9	6	8	28	34	80
8 Plymouth	46	11	6	6	39	24	6	8	9	24	28	65
9 Luton	46	8	8	7	32	26	9	6	8	35	34	65
10 Swindon	46	10	5	8	34	27	6	7	10	25	36	60
11 Peterborough	46	8	7	8	25	20	6	9	8	26	32	58
12 COLCHESTER	46	8	7	8	24	24	6	9	8	28	32	58
13 Blackpool	46	10	8	5	35	25	5	5	13	21	39	58
14 Stockport	46	8	7	8	39	38	7	2	14	26	32	55
15 Notts Co	46	10	7	6	37	32	3	9	11	25	38	55
16 Brentford	46	8	8	7	28	21	6	4	13	19	35	54
17 Port Vale	46	9	5	9	34	31	5	6	12	20	39	53
18 Wycombe	46	8	7	8	39	38	5	6	12	20	28	52
19 Barnsley	46	7	8	8	27	31	6	5	12	24	33	52
20 Chesterfield	46	11	4	8	29	28	3	4	16	14	45	50
21 Cheltenham	46	6	9	8	26	31	4	9	10	27	37	48
22 Huddersfield	46	7	9	7	27	24	4	3	16	12	37	45
23 Mansfield	46	9	2	12	38	45	3	6	14	28	52	44
24 Northampton	46	7	4	12	23	31	3	5	15	17	48	39
	1104	236	150	166	793	628	166	150	236	628	793	1506

* promoted after play-offs

Appearances and Goals

	Appearances								Goals					
	Lge	Sub	LC	Sub	FAC	Sub	LDV	Sub	Lge	Sub	LC	FAC	LDV	Tot
Atangana, Simon	1	5												
Baldwin, Pat	13	6	1		1			1						1
Bowry, Bobby	33	2	1		1				1					1
Brown, Simon	26	1	1		1					1				
Canham, Marc	2	1												
Chilvers, Liam	6													
Coote, Adrian	7	9												
Duguid, Karl	26	1					3		3					3
Edwards, Mike	3	2												
Fitzgerald, Scott	26													
Halford, Greg	1													
Izzet, Kem	43	2	1		1		1		8					8
Jackson, Johnnie	8													
Johnson, Gavin	8				1									
Keeble, Chris		3						3						
Keith, Joe	36	1	1		1				9					9
May, Ben	4	2												
McGleish, Scott	38	5	1		1		1		8				1	9
McKinney, Richard	20	1	1				1							
Morgan, Dean	22	15	1			1			6					6
Odunsi, Leke	3	3		1						1				
Opara, Lloyd		5		1										
Pinault, Thomas	32	10	1		1				4					4
Rapley, Kevin	14	7				1	1		2					2
Richards, Justin		2								1				
Steele, Daniel	6	2												
Stockley, Sam	31	2	1		1				1					1
Stockwell, Mick	30	10	1		1				2					2
Warren, Mark	20				1									
White, Alan	41		1		1									
Williams, Gareth	6	2							6					6
(own-goals)									2					2
31 players used	506	98	11	3	11	2	11	3	52		0	0	1	53

Odds & ends

Double wins: (1) Chesterfield.

Double losses: (4) Blackpool, Crewe, Oldham, QP Rangers.

Won from behind: (2) Luton (A), Notts County (A).

Lost from in front: (1) Crewe (H).

High spots: The improvement in results after a change of manager.
Surprise victories away to promotion-chasing Cardiff and Bristol City.
Dean Morgan's stunning winner in the gritty win over Wigan.

Low spots: The FA Cup defeat at home to non-League Chester City.
The 0-5 home hammering by Luton – the worst in 19 years.
The failure of record signing Adrian Coote to make an impact.
The 12% drop in gates, to the lowest of any club in the division.
The poor disciplinary record (eight U's men sent off during the season).

Player of the Year: Simon Brown.

Ever-presents: (0).

Hat-tricks for: (1) Gareth Williams (v Port Vale, H).

Hat-tricks against: (3) Steve Howard (v Luton, H), Marco Gabbiadini (v Northampton, A); Iyseden Christie (v Mansfield, A).

Leading scorers: (9) Joe Keith and Scott McGleish.

NATIONWIDE DIVISION 2 — Manager: Phil Parkinson — SEASON 2003-04

Column headings: **No | Date | Att | Pos | Pt | F-A | H-T | Scorers, Times, and Referees | SQUAD NUMBERS IN USE | subs used**

---

1 A BARNSLEY 9/8
Att 8,450 · Pos — · L · 0 pts · F-A 0-1 · H-T 0-0
Scorers: Gorre 47p · Ref: C Webster

- Colchester: Brown S · Myers · Keith · Stockley · Fitzgerald · White · Pinault^ · Izzet · Duguid · Fagan · McGleish
- Barnsley: Ilic · Ireland · O'Callaghan · Milligan* · Gallimore · Handyside · Gorre^ · Hayward · Kay · Betsy · Fallon^
- Subs used: Vine/Bowry · Gibbs/Lumsdon/Rankin

Under new ownership, Gudjon Thordarson's side start brightly and Fitzgerald saves a Rory Fallon effort which beats Brown. Debutant Fagan goes close with a 20-yard curler. Fitzgerald pulls back Fallon and Dean Gorre nets the spot-kick. Keith skies a U's penalty given for handball.

---

2 H SWINDON 15/8
Att 3,339 · Pos 21 (11) · L · 0 pts · F-A 0-1 · H-T 0-0
Scorers: Mooney 87 · Ref: P Crossley

- Colchester: Brown S · Myers · Keith^ · Stockley · Fitzgerald · White · Pinault · Izzet · Duguid · Fagan · Vine*
- Swindon: Griemink · Viveash · Robinson · Gurney · Heywood · Igoe · Hewlett · Mooney · Duke · Miglioranzi · Parkin
- Subs used: McGleish/**Hadland** · Parkin

Portsmouth loanee Vine makes his full debut and goes close with a first-minute long-range effort. Fagan's pass sends Keith clean through, but with only Bart Griemink to beat, he sweeps his shot wide. Andy King's side deservedly take the points late on when Tommy Mooney blasts in.

---

3 A PORT VALE 23/8
Att 5,133 · Pos 21 (1) · L · 0 pts · F-A 3-4 · H-T 2:1
Scorers: McG'sh 26,38, Andrews 88 [McPhee 73] / Collins 34, Paynter 58, Armstrong 71 · Ref: T Parkes

- Colchester: Brown · Keith · Stockley · Fitzgerald · White^ · Pinault^ · Izzet · Duguid · McGleish · Fagan^ · Andrews
- Port Vale: Delaney · Pilkington · Walsh · Cummins · Brown · Bridge-Wilk*/McPhee · Collins · Lipa · Brooker^ · Littlejohn
- Subs used: Baldwin/Bowry/Andrews · Paynter/Armstrong

McGleish nets after the keeper parries a shot. Sam Collins heads a corner home but McGleish hits back with a superb finish. Sub Billy Paynter loops the ball over Brown, then Ian Armstrong converts a cross and Stephen McPhee's diving header makes it four. Andrews buries a rebound.

---

4 H BRISTOL CITY 26/8
Att 3,079 · Pos 19 (14) · W · 3 pts · F-A 2-1 · H-T 0-0
Scorers: McGleish 47, 55 / Peacock 66 · Ref: M Cooper

- Colchester: Brown S · Keith^ · Stockley · Fitzgerald · White · Pinault · Izzet · Duguid · McGleish · Fagan · Andrews^
- Bristol City: Phillips · Butler · Bell^ · Coles · Hill · Burnell · Carey · Wilkshire* · Doherty · Miller^ · Peacock
- Subs used: Fagan · Roberts/Tinnion/Matthews

McGleish scores his 100th League goal with a brilliant overhead kick following a corner. Soon after he ghosts in at the near post to head home Duguid's free-kick. After a triple substitution by Danny Wilson, City hit back when Peacock heads in a free-kick. Peacock later strikes a post.

---

5 A TRANMERE 30/8
Att 6,745 · Pos 19 (14) · D · 4 pts · F-A 1-1 · H-T 1-1
Scorers: Andrews 30 / Jones 14 · Ref: E Evans

- Colchester: Brown S · Myers* · Chilvers · Stockley · Fitzgerald · Pinault · Izzet · Andrews · McGleish · Vine · Baldwin
- Tranmere: Achterberg · Sharps · Connelly · Allen · Nicholson^ · Roberts · Melton* · Haworth · Dadi! · Hume · Navarro
- Subs used: Baldwin · Navarro/Hay

Graham Allen's header is hooked off the line but Gary Jones forces the ball home. John Achterberg saves from Vine but can do nothing about Andrews' spectacular effort. Jones hits a post, but the U's hold on for a well-earned point. Eugene Dadi is sent off for kicking out at a U's man.

---

6 H QP RANGERS 6/9
Att 3,835 · Pos 18 (4) · D · 5 pts · F-A 2-2 · H-T 1-0
Scorers: Vine 10, McGleish 75p / Furlong 49, 66 · Ref: P Armstrong

- Colchester: Brown S · Myers* · Chilvers · Stockley · Fitzgerald · Pinault · Izzet · Andrews · McGleish · Vine · Duguid
- QP Rangers: Day · Shittu · Gnohere · Palmer · Williams^ · McLeod · Rowlands · Furlong · Gallen · Thorpe^ · Oli
- Subs used: Edghill/Bean/Oli · Thorpe^

Duguid's cross is converted at the far post by Vine. Furlong nets after a lay-off from Kevin McLeod and then finishes off a breakaway raid with a powerful drive. The equaliser in this pulsating contest comes when Andrews is tugged back and the penalty is crashed in by McGleish.

---

7 H BRIGHTON 13/9
Att 4,169 · Pos 15 (8) · W · 8 pts · F-A 1-0 · H-T 0-0
Scorers: Andrews 67 · Ref: M Messias

- Colchester: Brown S · Myers* · Chilvers · Stockley · Fitzgerald · Pinault^ · Izzet · Andrews^ · McGleish · Vine · Duguid
- Brighton: Roberts · Cullip · Butters · Hinshelwood/Rodger^ · Harding^ · Mayo · Oatway^ · Henderson · Knight · Hart
- Subs used: Baldwin/Bowry/Fagan · Pethick/Piercey/Carpenter

A scrappy stalemate is decided when Andrews lets fly from out on the touchline and the ball screams into the net. 'If he meant that, he'd be a Premiership player,' observes Albion boss Steve Coppell. Andrews confesses it wasn't an intended shot. Gary Hart hits the post for Albion.

---

8 A WYCOMBE 16/9
Att 4,401 · Pos 13 (22) · W · 11 pts · F-A 2-1 · H-T 2-0
Scorers: Andrews 25, Vine 27 / Currie 51p · Ref: M Ryan

- Colchester: Brown S · Stockley · Fitzgerald · Pinault* · Izzet · Duguid · Vine · Andrews^ · McGleish · Harris^ · Onuora
- Wycombe: Talia · Senda · Vinnicombe · Bulman · Johnson · Rogers* · Harris^ · Simpson · Currie · Mayo · Onuora
- Subs used: Andrews^/McGleish/Bowry/Fagan · Roberts/Holligan/Ryan

After seven league meetings with the Chairboys without a win, the U's travelling fans celebrate long and loud when Andrews and Vine beat Frank Talia in seconds of each other. Darren Currie's spot-kick sparks the home side to greater effort, but the lead narrowly remains intact.

---

9 A PETERBOROUGH 20/9
Att 4,690 · Pos 11 (19) · W · 14 pts · F-A 2-1 · H-T 1-0
Scorers: Fagan 36, Keith 90 / Wood 57 · Ref: M Jones

- Colchester: Brown S · Myers* · Stockley · Fitzgerald · Chilvers · Izzet · Duguid · Pinault · Vine · Andrews · Fagan · Keith
- Peterborough: Tyler · Legg · Arber · Rea! · Shields* · Newton* · Gill^ · Clarke · McKenzie · Farrell
- Subs used: Andrews/Fagan/Keith · Burton/Thomson/Wood

Neil Wood's smart free-kick cancels out Craig Fagan's opener. Simon Rea is sent off on 67 minutes and Posh are punished at the death when Keith pounces for the winner. Manger Barry Fry raves: 'Simon has a screw loose. It came when we were dominating and it was such a shame.'

---

10 H BOURNEMOUTH 27/9
Att 3,602 · Pos 6 (10) · W · 17 pts · F-A 1-0 · H-T 0-0
Scorers: Duguid 75 · Ref: F Stretton

- Colchester: Brown S · Myers^ · Stockley · Fitzgerald · Chilvers · Izzet · Duguid · Pinault · Vine · Andrews^ · McGleish
- Bournemouth: Moss · Broadhurst · Cummings! · Browning^ · Fletcher C · Maher^ · Elliott · Purches · Feeney · Fletcher S · O'Connor
- Subs used: Andrews^/McGleish · Keith/Fagan · Hayter/Stock/Holmes

Duguid twice goes close, sending a long-range shot wide and then having a 20-yard free-kick saved. Warren Cummings then appears to stamp on him and is sent off. Duguid climaxes his eventful match by latching on to Keith's pass and curling his shot past Neil Moss for the winner.

---

11 H BRENTFORD 30/9
Att 3,343 · Pos 6 (18) · D · 18 pts · F-A 1-1 · H-T 0-1
Scorers: Vine 76 / Rougier 36 · Ref: M Fletcher

- Colchester: Brown S · Duguid · Chilvers · Fitzgerald · Stockley · Fagan · Pinault · Izzet · Andrews · McGleish · Vine
- Brentford: Smith P · Kitamirike · Dobson · Sonko · O'Connor · Wright · Hutchinson · Sommer · May^ · Hunt · Rougier^
- Subs used: McGleish/Vine · Smith J/Harrold

Duguid's attempted clearance rebounds off Tony Rougier and rolls the 20 yards into an unguarded net to give Wally Downes' outfit a rather lucky lead. Andrews hits the post before Vine beats Paul Smith with a cracking drive from 20 yards after a Duguid corner is only half-cleared.

Match 12 — A NOTTS CO, 4/10 — Att. 4,187

League: 10 — L — 0-1 — 21 / 18

Scorers: Heffernan 23, 86, Riley 76 — Ref: S Mathieson

Colchester	Mildenhall	Riley^	Jenkins^	Barras	Fenton	Richardson	Baraclough	Baldry*	Stallard	Heffernan	Brough/Nicholson/McFaul
Brown S	Duguid	Chilvers	Stockley	Fitzgerald	Pinault	Fagan	Andrews*	McGleish*	Vine	Keith	

Paul Heffernan darts in to lob over Brown. Local lad Paul Riley, a late call-up, nets a spectacular effort, his first goal for County. The U's look better after the break but things refuse to go their way and Heffernan takes a flick from Mark Stallard and flashes an angled drive into the net.

Match 13 — H BLACKPOOL, 11/10 — Att. 3,265

League: 13 — D — 1-1 — 17 / 19

Scorers: Andrews 2, Taylor 53 — Ref: I Williamson

Brown S	Duguid	Myers	Stockley^	Fitzgerald	White	Pinault	Izzet*	Fagan	Andrews	Bowry/McGleish
Jones	Grayson	Davis	Coid	Bullock	Hilton	Douglas	Wellens^	Southern*	Taylor	Clarke/Richardson

Fagan lays the ball off and Andrews sweeps a shot home on 82 seconds. A 40-yard lofted shot by Richie Wellens beats Brown but hits the bar. United fail to get the all-important second goal and Steve McMahon's side battle level, Scott Taylor hooking home a Martin Bullock centre.

Match 14 — A GRIMSBY, 18/10 — Att. 5,021

League: 13 — L — 0-2 — 17 / 19

Scorers: Onuora 41, Boulding 84 — Ref: P Joslin

Brown S	Duguid	Chilvers	Stockley^	Fitzgerald	Myers	Pinault	Izzet	Andrews*	McGleish	Vine	Keith/Halford
Davison	Edwards*	McDermott	Hamilton	Crane	Daws	Campbell	Barnard	Onuora	Anderson^	Boulding	Ford/Cas

Darren Barnard's cross catches keeper Brown out of position and big Iffy Onuora is able to head home. With United pressing forward for an equaliser, the Mariners launch a late breakaway raid which sees Onuora play Michael Boulding through and his effort is helped in by Brown.

Match 15 — A STOCKPORT, 21/10 — Att. 3,683

League: 10 — W — 3-1 — 21 / 22

Scorers: Fagan 26, Andrews 34, Vine 47; Goodwin 58p — Ref: K Friend

Brown S	Duguid	Chilvers	Stockley	Fitzgerald	Myers	Pinault	Izzet	Andrews^	Fagan	Vine*	Keith/McGleish
Colgan	Pemberton	Clare	Goodwin	Gibb*	Challinor	Hardiker	Lambert	Wilbraham	Barlow"	Ellison^	Morrison/Welsh/Williams

Fagan unleashes a tremendous shot into the net from 20 yards. Stockley delivers a precise cross for Andrews to head the second. Nick Colgan spills the ball and Vine pokes home an easy third. New boss Sammy McIlroy is aghast at what he sees. Myers' foul hands County a penalty.

Match 16 — H CHESTERFIELD, 25/10 — Att. 3,115

League: 8 — W — 1-0 — 24 / 25

Scorers: Andrews 10 — Ref: C Penton

Brown S	Duguid	Myers	Stockley^	Fitzgerald	Chilvers"	Pinault	Izzet	Andrews*	Fagan	Vine*	Keith/McGleish/White
Muggleton	O'Hare	Uhlenbeek / Payne	Davies*	Brandon	Evatt	Hudson	Cade	Allott	Robinson	Hurst	

Brown's long downfield punt is allowed to bounce and Ian Evatt and Carl Muggleton get in a muddle dealing with it, allowing Andrews to sweep the ball home. A cross by Myers and a Steve Payne long-shot both hit the bar. Gus Uhlenbeek is dismissed for two bookable offences.

Match 17 — A WREXHAM, 31/10 — Att. 4,269

League: 3 — W — 1-0 — 10 / 28

Scorers: Andrews 35 — Ref: P Prosser

Brown S	Duguid	Myers	Stockley^	Fitzgerald	White	Pinault	Izzet	Andrews*	Fagan	Vine*	Keith/McGleish
Dibble	Roberts	Holmes	Carey	Lawrence^	Ferguson	Whitley	Edwards	Sam	Jones L	Llewellyn*	Armstrong/Thomas

Izzet heads over and Fagan shoots wide before Andrews rounds veteran keeper Andy Dibble to score from six yards. Myers hits the bar with a drive and Andrews misses a good chance for a second. Brown has a fine second half, keeping out all that Denis Smith's men can throw at him.

Match 18 — H SHEFFIELD WED, 15/11 — Att. 5,018

League: 4 — W — 3-1 — 14 / 31

Scorers: McGleish 27, Andrews 81, Fagan 90; Bramby 58 — Ref: P Danson

Brown S	Duguid	Myers^	Stockley^	Fitzgerald	Chilvers	Pinault	Bowry	McGleish*	Fagan	Andrews/White
Pressman	Lee	Smith	Barry-M/phy*/Bramby	Geary	Mustoe	McLaren	Reddy	Owusu	Proudlock^	Haslam/Holt

Vine whips over a good cross for McGleish to head home. Lloyd Owusu's shot on the turn hits a post and Leigh Bromby rams in the rebound. Sub Andrews regains the lead from a Duguid lay-off. Fagan clinches the sixth successive victory, blasting home the third from a pass by Vine.

Match 19 — A RUSHDEN & D, 22/11 — Att. 4,149

League: 5 — L — 0-4 — 12 / 31

Scorers: Lowe 4, Gray 39, Burgess 58, Bignot 81 — Ref: A Hall

Brown S	Duguid	Chilvers	Stockley	Fitzgerald	Pinault*	Izzet	Bowry	Andrews^	Vine	Izzet/McGleish
Ashdown	Bignot	Edwards^	Underwood / Gray	Dempster	Burgess	Hanlon	Benjamin	Jack	Lowe*	Managu/Okuonghae

Brian Talbot's men stun United as Onandi Lowe fires home early. Fagan is red-carded after an off-the-ball incident. Stuart Gray grabs a second after Lowe's effort is blocked. Gray's corner finds Andy Burgess who nets from close range. Marcus Bignot adds to U's woes with a volley.

Match 20 — H PLYMOUTH, 29/11 — Att. 4,332

League: 8 — L — 0-2 — 2 / 31

Scorers: Capaldi 4, Keith 11 — Ref: K Wright

Brown S	Stockley	Myers	Duguid	Fitzgerald*	Chilvers	Pinault	Izzet	Andrews	Keith	Vine
McCormick	Aljofree	Connolly	Wotton	Capaldi	Coughlan	Norris	Lowndes*	Keith	Norris	Evans

A nightmare start gifts the points to Paul Sturrock's men - Argyle's first win in 45 years. First Tony Capaldi's shot slips through Brown's legs and trickles in, then Brown fails to clear properly and Keith swoops to net. Paul Wotton and Duguid both see efforts strike wood.

Match 21 — H OLDHAM, 13/12 — Att. 2,897

League: 5 — W — 2-1 — 19 / 34

Scorers: Duguid 48, Vine 72; Eyres 66 — Ref: P Robinson

Brown S	Duguid	Johnson	Myers	Fitzgerald	White	Pinault	Izzet	Andrews^	McGleish	Cade
Pogliacomi	Clegg	Haining	Cooksey	Hall	Boshell^	Johnson	Murray	Eyre*	Zola	Vernon/Eyres

Izzet wins a firm challenge in midfield to set up Duguid, who nets a magnificent drive. Struggling Latics level via newly arrived sub David Eyres, who curls a free-kick around the U's wall. United respond quickly and Vine powers a shot home after a corner is only partially cleared.

Match 22 — A HARTLEPOOL, 20/12 — Att. 4,135

League: 5 — D — 0-0 — 8 / 35

Ref: T Leake

Brown S	Stockley	Myers	Duguid	White	Chilvers	Pinault	Izzet	Andrews^	McGleish^	Vine^	Fitzgerald/Fagan/Johnson
Provett	Nelson	Barron	Webster	Robson^	Tinkler	Strachan	Shuker	Williams	Humphreys	Porter^	Robinson/Wilkinson

The U's have to battle it out with ten men after White is sent off after just two minutes for a professional foul on Eifion Williams. Fitzgerald comes on as they reorganise. Neale Cooper's team eagerly lay siege to the U's goal, but a determined team performance keeps them at bay.

Match 23 — H LUTON, 28/12 — Att. 5,083

League: 6 — D — 1-1 — 9 / 36

Scorers: McGleish 12; Mansell 28 — Ref: J Ross

Brown S	Stockley	Myers	Pinault	White	Chilvers	Fagan	Izzet	Andrews	McGleish*	Vine	Cade
Beresford	Foley	Boyce	Coyne	Davis	Mansell*	Robinson	Spring	Brkovic	Forbes	Howard	Holmes

McGleish dives to bury a spectacular opening goal, but Mike Newell's men hit back when a Matthew Spring 25-yarder is deflected into the path of Lee Mansell, who finishes clinically. Marlon Beresford makes fine saves from Andrews and Chilvers in a disappointing second half.

NATIONWIDE DIVISION 2 — Manager: Phil Parkinson — SEASON 2003-04

No	V	Date	Att	(pos)	Pos	Pt	Res	F-A	H-T	Scorers, Times, and Referees
24	A	28/12	15,720	2	9	36	L	0-2	0-1	Gallen 12, Thorpe 57 — Ref: E Evans
25	H	10/1	3,507	4	10	37	D	1-1	1-0	Andrews 25 / Betsy 78 — Ref: C Penton
26	A	17/1	6,014	6	11	37	L	0-2	0-1	Parkin 15, Mooney 46 — Ref: S Tomlin
27	A	27/1	10,733	3	13	37	L	0-1	0-1	Goodfellow 45 — Ref: F Stretton
28	H	31/1	3,099	16	14	38	D	1-1	0-1	Izzet 89 / Dadi 27 — Ref: A Penn
29	A	7/2	5,662	10	14	38	L	0-1	0-0	Showunmi 52 — Ref: E Ilderton
30	H	21/2	2,922	20	14	41	W	2-0	0-0	Fagan 65, Izzet 90 — Ref: M Fletcher
31	A	24/2	2,539	5	15	41	L	1-4	1-3	McGleish 10p (Bridge-Wilkinson 73) / Brooker 13, Brown 24(og), Cummins 27 — Ref: P Danson
32	H	2/3	2,513	23	14	44	W	2-1	0-0	Vine 50, Andrews 60 / Lambert 46 — Ref: A Butler
33	H	6/3	3,348	5	15	44	L	1-2	1-1	Halford 35 / Nelson 17, Istead 78 — Ref: T Kettle
34	A	13/3	5,937	19	13	45	D	0-0	0-0	— Ref: M Jones

Squad numbers in use (lineups, subs used)

24 — QP RANGERS
Colchester: Brown S, Stockley, Myers, Johnson, White^, Chilvers, Duguid!, Izzet, Fagan, McGleish*, Vine — subs: Andrews / Cade
QPR: Day, Padula, Shittu^, Forbes, Carlisle, Bircham, Bean, McLeod, Rowlands, Gallen, Thorpe — subs: Rose / Palmer*
Danny Shittu storms down the left flank and crosses for Kevin Gallen to convert from close range. Duguid is red-carded for stamping on Marc Bircham. McGleish's head injury is another setback. White misjudges a clearance and Tony Thorpe nips in to clinch a comfortable victory.

25 — BARNSLEY
Colchester: Brown S, Stockley, Keith, Fitzgerald, Bowry^, Chilvers*, Duguid!, Izzet, Fagan, McGleish, Andrews^ — subs: White / Halford / Vine
Barnsley: Ilic, Monk, Ireland, O'Callaghan, Austin, Warhurst, Burns, Kay, Carson^, Betsy, Rankin^ — subs: Walters / Neil / Crooks*
Sasa Ilic rushes out of goal to intercept a ball from Fitzgerald but misses it and Andrews has a simple chance to end his personal goal drought. McGleish misses a good chance before Kevin Betsy turns and fires an equaliser. Duguid is sent off again, this for a professional foul late on.

26 — SWINDON
Colchester: Brown S, Stockley, Keith, Fitzgerald, White*, Chilvers, Pinault, Halford, Fagan, McGleish, Andrews — subs: Cade
Swindon: Evans, Nicholas, Robinson, Ifil, Heywood, Igoe, Hewlett, Duke, Howard, Mooney, Parkin*
Andy King's men look good in the first half, Sam Parkin nipping between Brown and White to convert a hopeful ball by Brian Howard. Parkin has another effort disallowed before Tommy Mooney increases the lead, heading in Howard's cross. Keith's late free-kick bounces off a post.

27 — BRISTOL CITY
Colchester: McKinney, Stockley, Keith, White, Pinault, Chilvers, Duguid, Izzet^, Fagan!, McGleish, Andrews* — subs: Cade / Halford
Bristol City: Phillips, Carey, Hill, Coles, Doherty^, Brown, Woodman, Tinnion, Miller, Goodfellow^, Peacock — subs: Lita / Roberts / Bell*
Lee Peacock's header is parried by McKinney and new City signing Marc Goodfellow misses a real sitter from the rebound. He makes up for the blunder by volleying home just before the interval. Fagan is sent off near the end after two more yellow cards takes his season's tally to 11.

28 — TRANMERE
Colchester: McKinney, Stockley, Keith, White, Pinault, Chilvers, Duguid, Izzet, Tierney^, McGleish, Andrews* — subs: Fagan / Vine
Tranmere: Achterberg, Connelly, Roberts, Taylor, Allen, Mellon!, Harrison, Beresford", Jones, Dadi", Hume — subs: Linwood / Hay / Navarro*
A precision cross by Gareth Roberts is headed home by Frenchman Eugene Dadi. Micky Mellon departs on 44 minutes for his second bookable offence. John Achterberg makes a string of good saves and just when it looks like the U's will never score, Izzet flicks in Pinault's driven cross.

29 — LUTON
Colchester: Brown S, Stockley*, Keith, White, Pinault*, Chilvers, Duguid, Izzet^, Tierney, Fagan, Vine — subs: McGleish / Cade / Andrews
Luton: Hydegaard, Foley, Boyce, Coyne, Davis, Nicholls, Robinson, Spring, Holmes, Showunmi, Howard — subs: Crowe*
Izzet hits the bar and Chilvers go close, but Mike Newell's men lead when Enoch Showunmi turns and cracks home a fine drive from a Peter Holmes pass. It is the first career goal for Showunmi, recently plucked from junior football, and who missed two sitters earlier on in the match.

30 — GRIMSBY
Colchester: Brown S, Stockley, Brown W, White, Cade*, Chilvers, Duguid, Izzet, Fagan, Vine^, Pinault — subs: Keith / McGleish
Grimsby: Davison, Edwards, Ford, Hamilton, Crane, Campbell", Barnard, Thorpe, Anderson, Rankin — subs: Mansaram / Jevons*
A low crowd and a dour opening, but Fagan cheers things up heading Vine's cross in at the near post. Darren Barnard goes close as his long-range shot is superbly saved by Brown. Paul Groves' struggling side are finally subdued in the dying seconds as Izzet nods in McGleish's pass.

31 — PORT VALE
Colchester: Brown S, Stockley*, Keith, Brown W, White, Bowry^, Duguid, Izzet, Fagan, Andrews, McGleish — subs: Vine / Pinault
Port Vale: Brain, Boyd, Brown, Rowland, Pilkington, Cummins, Bridge-Wilkinson", McPhee, Collins, Paynter, Brooker^ — subs: Brisol / Littlejohn*
Andrews is brought down and McGleish tucks in the penalty. An awful mix-up in defence gifts Steve Brooker the equaliser. A shot by Michael Cummins flies in off Brown's body. Cummins heads in a free-kick to make it three. Marc Bridge-Wilkinson's drive completes the U's misery.

32 — STOCKPORT
Colchester: McKinney, Halford, White, Chilvers, Pinault, Duguid*, Izzet, Cartwright, Vine, Andrews, McGleish^ — subs: Johnson / Bowry
Stockport: Williams, Clare, Walton, Griffin, McLachlan^, Jackman, Lambert, Robertson, Welsh^, Daly — subs: Goodwin / Wilbraham / Ellison*
Just 25 seconds after the restart Ricky Lambert cashes in on hesitancy to give Sammy McIlroy's men the lead. Duguid finds Vine, who powers in a spectacular equaliser. McGleish's cross-shot is parried and Andrews swoops to score. Duguid is stretchered off with a serious knee injury.

33 — HARTLEPOOL
Colchester: McKinney, Halford, Brown W, Chilvers, White, Bowry", Izzet, Johnson*, Vine, Andrews, McGleish — subs: Keith / Pinault
Hartlepool: Provett, Nelson, Barron, Westwood, Robson^, Shuker^, Robertson, Tinkler, Humphreys, Williams", Porter — subs: Carson / Istead / Clarke
Joel Porter's effort is only partially cleared and Michael Nelson sweeps the ball home. Halford heads his career-first goal from a Johnson corner. Manager Neale Cooper's double substitution pays off when teenager Steven Istead sends in a cross-shot which sails over McKinney.

34 — OLDHAM
Colchester: McKinney, Halford*, Brown W, White, Chilvers, Bowry, Izzet, Stockley, Vine, Andrews^, McGleish — subs: Cade / Fagan
Oldham: Pagliacomi, Clegg, Griffin, Holden, Owen, Eyre, Eyres, Sheridan^, Murray, Zola, Killen — subs: Vernon / Boshell*
McKinney does well to keep out efforts by veteran David Eyres and Calvin Zola. Johnson fires a rare U's opportunity wide of the target. It's the first game in charge for Brian Talbot, who left Rushden for Oldham a few days earlier. He admits his side rarely looked like scoring today.

35 H 16/3 — WYCOMBE — 1-1 (1-1) D — Pos 14 — Att 3,092 — Opp pos 24 — Pts 46
Fagan 8p / Simpson 38 — Ref: L Mason
U's: Brown S, Stockley, White, Brown W, Chilvers, Johnson^, Bowry*, Izzet, Cade", Vine — subs Andrews/Pinault/Keith
Opp: Williams, Senda, Vinnicombe, Johnson, Nethercott, Currie, Simpson, Bloomfield, Tyson, Faulk'bridge, McSparran
Three points are expected against Tony Adams' relegation-bound side. Roger Johnson trips Fagan and the U's net an early penalty. Instead of the anticipated goalfest, the match turns into a rather drab affair after Danny Senda's cross is headed in by Michael Simpson to level things up.

36 A 20/3 — BRIGHTON — 1-2 (Izzet 69; Iwelumo 30, Knight 87) L — Pos 14 — Att 6,156 — Opp pos 4 — Pts 46
Ref: P Dowd
U's: Brown S, Halford, White, Brown W!, Stockley, Pinault, Bowry*, Izzet, Cade*, Vine" — subs Andrews/Keith/Johnson
Opp: Roberts, Cullip*, Virgo, Butters, Harding, Jones", Hart, Carpenter, Oatway, Knight, Iwelumo, El-Abd/Piercy
Chris Iwelumo, a recent free transfer from Stoke, back-heads Mark McGhee's men ahead. Vine sets up Izzet to head the equaliser. Richard Carpenter's free-kick is headed across goal by Iwelumo for Leon Knight to dive and head a late winner McGhee admits they didn't deserve.

37 A 23/3 — CHESTERFIELD — 2-1 (Halford 31, Andrews 82; Hurst 39) W — Pos 12 — Att 3,787 — Opp pos 18 — Pts 49
Ref: R Pearson
U's: Brown S, Halford, White, Brown W, Stockley, Pinault*, Bowry, Izzet, Cade, Vine^ — subs Andrews/Johnson
Opp: Muggleton, O'Hare, Uhlenbeek, Blatherwick, Davies*, Brandon, Niven, Evatt, Allott, Hurst, Innes/Reeves
A 30-yard rocket from Halford flies past Carl Muggleton. Roy McFarland's side level when top scorer Glynn Hurst is left unmarked to head in Chris Brandon's looping cross. With time running out, a close-range Fagan effort is palmed into the air and Andrews pounces for the winner.

38 H 27/3 — PETERBOROUGH — 0-0 D — Pos 13 — Att 3,754 — Opp pos 19 — Pts 50
Ref: D Crick
U's: Brown S, Halford, White^, Brown W, Stockley, Pinault, Johnson, Izzet, Cade*, Andrews! — subs Williams/Chilvers
Opp: Tyler, Legg, Branston, Arber, Rea, Woodhouse, Newton, Williams^, Willcock, Platt, Farrell, Thomson
Barry Fry's side make a number of chances and Brown has to be alert. Andrews is sent off on 63 minutes for what appears to be a retaliatory kick at Mark Arber. The U's have a penalty appeal turned own when Johnson is felled in the area. Parkinson praises the attitude of his 10 men.

39 A 30/3 — BLACKPOOL — 0-0 D — Pos 13 — Att 5,473 — Opp pos 14 — Pts 51
Ref: C Boyeson
U's: Brown S, Halford, White, Brown W, Stockley, Keith, Johnson, Izzet, Bowry*, Andrews — sub Chilvers
Opp: Barnes, Grayson, Flynn, Elliott, Coid!, Bullock, Matias^, Donnelly, Wellens^, Murphy, Sheron", Hessey/Southern/Blinkhorn
A dour, mistake-ridden game. Fagan heads two chances wide. The game's talking point comes as Coid is red-carded for a challenge on Bowry, who is jeered for over-reacting. Blackpool boss Steve McMahon is sent to the stands for dissent and Parkinson is seen arguing with home fans.

40 A 3/4 — BOURNEMOUTH — 1-1 (Halford 35; Hayter 86) D — Pos 12 — Att 6,896 — Opp pos 6 — Pts 52
Ref: M Cooper
U's: Brown S, Halford, White, Chilvers, Stockley, Keith, Johnson, Izzet, Bowry, Andrews^ — sub Pinault
Opp: Moss, Burton, Cummings, Maher^, Purches, Jorgensen, Stack", Fletcher C, Hayter, Fletcher S, Feeney", Holmes/O'Connor/Browning
Johnson's corner is headed in by Halford, who misses another good chance soon after. Sean O'Driscoll's side improve after the interval and loanee Claus Jorgensen brings a fine save from Brown. James Hayter levels with an overhead kick near the end, then Carl Fletcher goes close.

41 H 10/4 — NOTTS CO — 4-1 (2-0) (Fagan 9, 17, 53, Williams 78; Richardson 87) W — Pos 12 — Att 3,782 — Opp pos 23 — Pts 55
Ref: L Cable
U's: Brown S, Halford, White, Keith^, Stockley, Johnson, Izzet, Bowry^, Williams — subs Cade/Chilvers/Pinault
Opp: Garden, Richardson, Barras, Fenton, Baldry, Oakes, Pipe, McHugh^, Scully", Scoffham*, Heffernan, Parkinson/Bolland/McGold'k
Fagan, now signed after a loan spell, nets a fine solo goal and then a clever chip. His first hat-trick is completed with a close-range header. Williams, loaned from Palace, ends a good move by slotting the fourth. Gary Mills' strugglers pull one back through Ian Richardson's header.

42 A 12/4 — BRENTFORD — 2-3 (White 53, Fagan 80; Tabb 45, Sonko 58, Harrold 78) L — Pos 13 — Att 5,017 — Opp pos 20 — Pts 55
Ref: J Ross
U's: Gerken, Chilvers*, White, Keith*, Stockley, Brown W, Johnson, Izzet, Bowry*, Andrews^ — subs Cade/Vine/Pinault
Opp: Nelson, Bull, Frampton", Dobson, Sonko, Talbot, Tabb", Hunt, Hutchinson, Harrold, Wright", May/O'Connor/Sonner
Jay Tabb beats young debutant Gerken after a long-throw. White drills an equaliser, but Ibrahim Sonko stabs the Bees in front. Matt Harrold punishes a Brown error to make it three. Fagan's chip creates a tense ending. Home boss Martin Allen is red-carded for delaying a U's throw.

43 A 17/4 — WREXHAM — 3-1 (Williams 16, Halford 45, McGleish 82; Sam 18) W — Pos 13 — Att 3,077 — Opp pos 14 — Pts 58
Ref: A Marriner
U's: Brown S, Halford, White, Chilvers*, Stockley, Keith, Brown W, Izzet, Johnson^, Williams* — subs McGleish/Pinault
Opp: Ingham, Roberts, Holmes, Morgan, Lawrence, Thomas, Crowell", Sam, Armstrong^, Llewellyn, Jones M/Jones L
Izzet's shot falls for Williams to crack into the roof of the net. Hector Sam heads an equaliser from Dennis Lawrence's cross. Keith's cross is headed in by Halford from close range before the break. The three points are made safe when McGleish fires home his 16th goal of the season.

44 A 24/4 — SHEFFIELD WED — 1-0 (Keith 48) W — Pos 11 — Att 20,464 — Opp pos 16 — Pts 61
Ref: N Miller
U's: Brown S, Halford, White, Keith, Stockley, Brown W, Johnson^, Izzet, Bowry, Williams* — subs Andrews/Pinault
Opp: Pressman, Wood, Smith, Barry, Murphy, Geary, McLaren, Brunt, McMahon, Quinn, Robins", Proudlock^, Shaw/Cooke/Mustoe
Johnson has a header cleared off the line and minutes later a comical defensive mix-up nearly lets the U's in but Richard Wood boots clear. Brown pulls off several crucial saves before Keith sends a dipping shot into the net from 18 yards. Angry home fans call for their Board to quit.

45 H 1/5 — RUSHDEN & D — 2-0 (McGleish 80p, Johnson 90) W — Pos 11 — Att 4,618 — Opp pos 21 — Pts 64
Ref: G Hegley
U's: Brown S, Halford, White, Keith, Stockley, Brown W, Johnson, Izzet, Bowry, Williams* — sub Andrews
Opp: Turley, Roget, Edwards, Hunter!, Gray, Burgess, Bell", Hanlon, Kelly, Jack, Kitson, Dempster
Ernie Tippett's side hold their own until Barry Hunter is red-carded on 71 minutes for a second booking. Ritchie Hanlon handles a Johnson free-kick and McGleish nets the breakthrough goal from the spot. In the dying minutes Andrews sets up Johnson to net with his 'wrong' foot.

46 A 8/5 — PLYMOUTH — 0-2 (0-1) (Friio 17, Norris 47) L — Pos 11 — Att 19,859 — Opp pos 1 — Pts 64
Ref: A Hall
U's: Brown S, Halford, White, Keith, Stockley, Brown W, Johnson^, Izzet, Bowry*, Andrews — subs Pinault/Williams
Opp: McCormick, Aljofree, Connolly, Capaldi^, Gilbert, Coughlan, Norris, Friio!, Evans", Keith^, Hodges, Lowndes/Adams/Wotton
A big crowd, celebrating Argyle's promotion, enjoys Frenchman David Friio's smart opening goal. David Norris adds a second from a Tony Capaldi cross. Friio handles to stop a U's goal and is sent off, but McGleish misses the resultant penalty. Nathan Lowndes hits the crossbar.

Average 3,536 — Home 3,536 — Away 7,243

NATIONWIDE DIVISION 2 (CUP-TIES)   Manager: Phil Parkinson   SEASON 2002-03

Carling Cup

No		Opponent	Date	Att	Pos		F-A	H-T	Scorers, Times, and Referees
1	H	PLYMOUTH	12/8	2,367		W	2-1	2-1	Fagan 22, Pinault 40 / Evans 24 — Ref: J Ross
2	A	ROTHERHAM	23/9	2,474	11 / 22	L	0-1	0-1	Sedgwick 22 — Ref: T Leake

1 — Plymouth: Birmingham loanee Fagan lofts the ball neatly over Roman Larrieu and heads it into the unguarded net for his first Colchester goal. Long-serving Micky Evans powers in a header to equalise, but Izzet squares to Pinault, whose crisp low drive arrows past Larrieu for the winner.

2 — Rotherham: Chris Sedgwick drills in a firm shot to give Ronnie Moore's struggling Millers the lead. Chilvers clips Martin Butler's heels as he attempts to score and is sent off. Hadland, signed from Darlington, makes his first U's appearance. It is now 19 years since the club reached round three.

FA Cup

No		Opponent	Date	Att	Pos		F-A	H-T	Scorers, Times, and Referees
1	H	OXFORD	8/11	3,672	3 / 3:3	W	3-1	1-0	McGleish 38 — Ref: T Parkes
2	H	ALDERSHOT	6/12	4,255	8 / NL	W	1-0	0-0	Vine 83 — Ref: G Hegley
3	A	ACCRINGTON STAN	3/1	4,368	9 / NL	D	0-0	0-0	— Ref: P Joslin
3R	H	ACCRINGTON STAN	13/1	5,611	10 / NL	W	2-1	1-0	Keith 11, 84; Mullin 89 — Ref: P Joslin
4	A	COVENTRY	24/1	15,341	11 / 1:14	D	1-1	1-1	Adebola 30 (og); Joachim 33 — Ref: M Clattenburg
4R	H	COVENTRY	3/2	5,530	14 / 1:15	W	3-1	2-1	Vine 12, 43, 57; Joachim 25 — Ref: T Leake
5	A	SHEFFIELD UTD	15/2	17,074	14 / 1:5	L	0-1	0-0	Peschisolido 61 — Ref: D Pugh

1 — Oxford: Bowry's interception is fed to Vine, who supplies Fagan. The striker's bending shot hits a post and rebounds for McGleish to tuck in. It proves a deserved winner. Stockley is man-of-the-match against his former club, rising to the occasion after criticism from Oxford boss Ian Atkins.

2 — Aldershot: United are well on top against Conference opposition but produce only wayward shooting. Brown has two saves all game, one of them on 80 minutes later Vine goes on a probing run before shooting past Nikki Bull to put the U's in round three.

3 — Accrington Stanley: Stanley, the last part-timers left in the FA Cup, dominate the second half and Brown makes a number of vital saves. Rory Prendergast's effort is cleared off the line and Lutel James hits the bar. The U's go closest when Duguid's effort strikes a post and McGleish's late header the bar.

3R — Accrington Stanley: The biggest home crowd of the season sees Keith stab in a Fagan cross. Near the end Keith smashes in a fierce angled drive. Paul Mullin's header sets up a tense finale. Amid the excitement, Stanley's boss John Coleman tangles with stewards and his assistant jostles with Parkinson.

4 — Coventry: U's make their fans proud, dominating for most of the tie. Dele Adebola puts through his own goal with a spectacular diving header. The Sky Blues hit back as Julian Joachim is played through by Andy Morrell and as McKinney dashes out, the ball rebounds into the net off the striker.

4R — Coventry: Vine shrugs off Richard Shaw and sweeps the ball past Gavin Ward. Bjarni Gudjonsson's pull-back is knocked home by Julian Joachim. Vine regains the lead with a fine shot from Duguid's cross. He completes a classy hat-trick with a cool finish after a Keith swerving shot is spilled.

5 — Sheffield Utd: United put up a spirited display against Neil Warnock's outfit. Vine lets their best opportunity get away when he bears down on goal but allows Robert Page to get back and block his progress. Paul Peschisolido breaks the deadlock, heading home Alan Wright's free-kick at the near post.

LDV Vans Trophy

No		Opponent	Date	Att	Pos		F-A	H-T	Scorers, Times, and Referees
1	H	CHELTENHAM	14/10	1,324	13 / 3:16	W	3-1	1-1	Keith 40, Vine 65, 88; Devaney 18 — Ref: S Tanner
2	A	YEOVIL	4/11	3,052	3 / 3:6	D	2-2 aet	1-1	Andrews 41, McGleish 77; Edwards 11, Gall 66 — Ref: R Olivier (U's win 4-2 on penalties)

1 — Cheltenham: Martin Devaney shoots home after the ball cannons off Fitzgerald, but Keith levels from a Fagan pass. Ben Cleverley sees an effort strike the woodwork. Vine intercepts a poor back-pass and rounds the keeper to score. Vine makes the game safe by heading home from a Pinault cross.

2 — Yeovil: Kevin Gall's cross is converted by Jake Edwards and Yeovil dominate the first half. Andrews darts in to bundle home an equaliser. Gall blasts in a long ball, but McGleish heads a second leveller. In the penalty shoot-out, Brown saves Yeovil's first kick and the fourth is also missed.

Squad numbers in use / subs used

(Colchester United listed first; opponents in *italics*. Subs used shown after the semicolon.)

Carling Cup 1 — Plymouth: Brown S, Stockley, Myers, White, Fitzgerald, Keith, Pinault, Izzet, Duguid, McGleish, Fagan.
Larrieu, Worrell, Gilbert*, Adams^, Coughlan, Aljofree*, Norris, Bent, Evans, Capaldi, Kieth; Stonebridge/Friio/Wotton

Carling Cup 2 — Rotherham: Brown S, Stockley, Baldwin*, White, Chilvers!, Keith^, Bowry", Izzet, Duguid, Fagan; Hadland/Coote/Pinault.
Pollitt, Barker, Minto, Robinson, Swailes, McIntosh, Sedgwick*, Talbot^, Butler, Byfield, Monkhouse"; Warne/Robins/Hurst

FA Cup 1 — Oxford: Brown S, Stockley, Myers, Duguid, White, Chilvers, Pinault, Bowry", McGleish, Fagan, Vine.
Woodman, Ashton, Waterman, Bound, McNiven, Crosby, Wanless^, Hunt", Whitehead, Alsop, Basham*; Louis/Rawle/Hackett

FA Cup 2 — Aldershot: Brown S, Stockley, Myers, Duguid, White, Chilvers, Pinault, Izzet, McGleish, Vine, Andrews.
Bull, Warburton*, Rees, Chewins, Charles, Sterling, Shields, Challinor, D'Sane, Miller; Sills, Taylor

FA Cup 3 — Accrington Stanley: Brown S, Stockley, Myers, Fitzgerald, Johnson, Pinault, Duguid, Izzet, Fagan, McGleish, Vine*; Keith.
Speare, Howard, Halford", Hollis, Proctor*, Williams, Gouck*, Mullin, Prendergast, Cook, James; Flitcroft/Calcutt/Armstrong

FA Cup 3R — Accrington Stanley: Brown S, Stockley, Myers, Fitzgerald, Keith, Halford", Pinault, Izzet, Fagan*, McGleish, Andrews^; Vine/White.
Kennedy, Howard, Halford", Flitcroft*, Proctor, Williams, Cavanagh, Mullin, Prendergast, Cook, James; Calcutt/Smith

FA Cup 4 — Coventry: McKinney, Stockley, Keith, White, Pinault, Halford", Izzet, Duguid, Fagan*, Bowry", Vine; Andrews, Vine.
Ward, Konjic, Whing, Gordon, Davenport, Adebola*, Doyle, Joachim, McSheffrey, Morrell"; Gudjonsson/Warnock

FA Cup 4R — Coventry: Brown S, Keith, White, Halford, Pinault, Izzet, Duguid, Fagan*, McGleish^, Vine"; Andrews/Bowry.
Ward, Staunton, Shaw, Davenport, Warnock*, Doyle, Joachim, Gudjonsson", Morrell'; Gordon/McSheffrey/Adebola

FA Cup 5 — Sheffield Utd: Brown S, Keith, Stockley, Duguid, Pinault, Izzet, Andrews, Vine, McGleish, Tierney*; McGleish.
Kenny, Page, Whitlow, Wright, Montgomery, Jagielka, McCall, Peschisolido, Allison, Ndlovu", Boussatta"; Rankine/Parkinson

LDV Vans Trophy 1 — Cheltenham: Brown S, Duguid, Chilvers, Myers^, Fitzgerald, Pinault, Halford", Keith, McGleish, Fagan, Vine; Vine/Stockley/Baldwin.
Higgs, Victory, Duff*, Fyfe, Bird", Finnigan, McCann, Cleverley, Yates, Taylor", Devaney; Odejayi/Dobson/Spencer

LDV Vans Trophy 2 — Yeovil: Brown S, Stockley, Keith, White, Halford*, Pinault, Izzet, Andrews, Fagan, Gall, Crittenden; McGleish/Johnson/Baldwin.
Weale, Lockwood, Johnson, Skiverton^, Miles", Way, Terry, Williams, Crittenden, Gall, Edwards*; Reed/Stansfield/Gosling

Cup results

#	Venue / Opponent	Date	Pos	Res	Agg	H/T	Scorers	Ref	Att
3	A WYCOMBE	9/12	8	W	3-2 aet	2-1	McGleish 8, 39, Brown J 120 — Thomson 22, Johnson 69	Ref: M Cowburn	1,873 (24)
SS F	A NORTHAMPTON	20/1	11	W	3-2 aet	0-1	McGleish 61, 86, 95 — Walker 14, 51	Ref: P Crossley	4,304 (3:14)
SF 1	H SOUTHEND	10/2	14	L	2-3	1-2	Pinault 7, Andrews 75 — Const'ine 17, Broughton 42, Bramble 68	Ref: P Taylor	5,401 (3:22)
SF 2	A SOUTHEND	17/12	14	D	1-1	1-1	Izzet 3 — Broughton 45	Ref: M Ryan	9,603 (3:20)

(U's lose 3-4 on aggregate)

Line-ups (as read)

Wycombe: Brown S, Williams, Stockley, Myers, Duguid, White, Chilvers, Johnson G^, Izzet, Andrews*, Keith / Bowry* / Brown J — Simpemba, McSporran, Halligan, Faulconbridge

Northampton: McKinney, Harper, Stockley, Keith, White, Halford*, Reid^, Pinault, Izzet, Fagan, Smith — Asamoah*, Walker

Southend (1): Brown S, Flahavan, Stuart, Cort, Warren, Hunt^, Chilvers, Duguid, Izzet, Pinault, Gower, Jupp — Tierney*, Broughton!, Bramble^, Constantine^, Pettefer / Clarke / Wilson

Southend (2): Brown S, Flahavan, Stuart, Cort, Warren, Hunt, Chilvers, Duguid, Izzet, Pinault, Gower, Jupp — Halford^, Broughton, Bramble, Constantine, Pettefer

Match notes

McGleish punishes an error with a slick finish but Andy Thomson levels from a corner. Unmarked McGleish knocks in a corner before Roger Johnson heads in a free-kick. Bowry exits in a neck brace and his replacement, debutant Jermaine Brown, slots in a dramatic last-gasp winner.

Loanee Richard Walker nets a near-post header and appears to clinch victory from a Paul Trollope cross. But Ian Sampson is sent off for his second yellow card and sub McGleish arrives to transform the game. He converts two Andrews crosses, then wins it with an extra-time header.

In the southern final first leg, Pinault rifles a shot home after a corner. Leon Constantine cracks an equaliser and Drewe Broughton heads the visitors ahead. Brown's fumble lets Tes Bramble's mis-hit shot in. Broughton exits for a second yellow card. Andrews heads the U's second.

The aggregate scores are brought level early on when Izzet toe-pokes McGleish's pass into the net. Leon Cort's flick-on is neatly finished by Drewe Broughton. It's a feisty derby with eight bookings. Steve Wignall's men repel the U's, who are playing their 15th cup tie of the season.

League table

	Team	P	Home W	D	L	F	A	Away W	D	L	F	A	Pts
1	Plymouth	46	17	5	1	52	13	9	7	7	33	28	90
2	QP Rangers	46	16	7	0	47	12	6	10	7	33	33	83
3	Bristol City	46	15	6	2	34	12	8	7	8	24	25	82
4	Brighton *	46	17	4	2	39	11	5	6	11	25	32	77
5	Swindon	46	12	7	4	41	23	6	5	8	35	35	73
6	Hartlepool	46	10	8	5	39	24	10	5	6	37	37	73
7	Port Vale	46	15	6	2	45	28	6	4	13	28	35	73
8	Tranmere	46	13	7	3	36	18	4	9	10	23	38	67
9	Bournemouth	46	11	8	4	35	25	6	7	10	21	26	66
10	Luton	46	14	6	3	44	27	3	9	11	25	39	66
11	COLCHESTER	46	11	8	4	33	23	6	5	12	19	33	64
12	Barnsley	46	7	12	4	25	19	8	5	10	29	39	62
13	Wrexham	46	9	6	8	27	21	8	3	12	23	39	60
14	Blackpool	46	9	5	9	31	28	7	6	10	27	37	59
15	Oldham	46	9	8	6	37	25	5	13	3	29	35	57
16	Sheffield Wed	46	7	9	7	37	26	6	5	12	23	38	57
17	Brentford	46	9	5	9	34	38	5	6	12	18	31	53
18	Peterborough	46	5	8	10	36	33	7	8	8	22	25	52
19	Stockport	46	6	8	9	31	36	5	11	7	31	34	52
20	Chesterfield	46	9	7	7	34	31	3	8	12	15	40	51
21	Grimsby	46	10	5	8	36	26	3	6	14	19	55	50
22	Rushden & D	46	9	5	9	37	34	4	4	15	23	40	48
23	Notts Co	46	6	9	8	32	27	4	3	16	18	51	42
24	Wycombe	46	5	7	11	31	39	1	12	10	19	36	37
		1104	251	166	135	861	599	135	166	251	599	861	1490

* promoted
after play-offs

Appearances and Goals

Player	Lge	Sub	LC	Sub	FAC	Sub	LDV	Sub	G Lge	G LC	G FAC	G LDV	Tot
Andrews, Wayne	32	9			4	1	1	3	12			2	14
Baldwin, Pat	1		1										
Bowry, Bobby	18	6	1		1		1	2	1				1
Brown, Jermaine		1										1	1
Brown, Simon	40		2		6		5						
Brown, Wayne	16		2				1						
Cade, Jamie	6	9											
Chilvers, Liam	29	3			7		5		1				1
Coote, Adrian				1									
Duguid, Karl	30		2		6		4		2				2
Fagan, Craig	30	7	2		5		4		9			1	10
Fitzgerald, Scott	22	1	1		2		2						
Gerken, Dean	1												
Hadland, Phil		1		1									
Halford, Greg	15	3			2		4		4				4
Izzet, Kem	43				7	1	6		3		1		4
Johnson, Gavin	14	4			1	2	1		1				1
Keith, Joe	16	12	2		4	1	5	1	2				5
McGleish, Scott	25	9	1		6		4	2	10		1	6	17
McKinney, Richard	5												
Myers, Andy	21		1		2		2						
Pinault, Thomas	31	9	1	1	7		5		2		1		2
Stockley, Sam	44		2		6		5						
Tierney, Paul	2												
Vine, Rowan	30	5	1		5	2	4	2	6		4	2	12
White, Alan	30	3	2		5	1	5						
Williams, Gareth	5	2					2		2				2
(own-goals)									1				1
27 players used	506	87	22	3	77	7	66	14	52	2	8	14	76

Odds & ends

Double wins: (4) Chesterfield, Sheffield Wed, Stockport, Wrexham.
Double losses: (3) Plymouth, Port Vale, Swindon.

Won from behind: (1) Stockport (H).
Lost from in front: (2) Port Vale (H & A).

High spots: Two long cup runs in one season – 15 ties played in all.
Rowan Vine's classy hat-trick to enable the giant-killing of Coventry
Substitute McGleish's dramatic late LDVT hat-trick at Northampton.
Effective use of the loan system (Fagan, Vine, Brown and Williams).
Rip-roaring FA Cup excitement under the floodlights versus Accrington.

Low spots: Beaten in the Southern LDVT final by local rivals Southend.
Karl Duguid's post-Christmas crisis: 2 red cards and a bad knee injury.
A dreadful night v Port Vale - the season's lowest gate and biggest loss.

Player of the Year: Alan White.

Ever-presents: (0).
Hat-tricks for: (3) Rowan Vine (v Coventry, H, FAC); Craig Fagan
(v Notts County, H); Scott McGleish (v Northampton, A, LDVT).
Hat-tricks against: (0).
Leading scorer: (17) Scott McGleish.

COCA-COLA LEAGUE 1

Manager: Phil Parkinson — SEASON 2004-05

SQUAD NUMBERS IN USE

---

1 A 7/8 SHEFFIELD WED — Att 24,138 — W 3-0 (H-T 0-0)
Scorers, Times and Referees: Fagan 85, Stockley 89, Keith J 90. Ref: P Taylor

Davison	Stockley	Halford	Brown W	Chilvers	Watson	Johnson*	Bowry	Andrews^	Fagan	Keith J
Lucas	Collins	Lee*	Bullen	Heckingbo'm	McGovern	Brunt	Marsden	McMahon^	MacLean	Proudlock*

Subs used: Cade/May · Branston/Peacock/Hamshaw

Adam Proudlock goes close in the very first minute, but United soon settle. They launch a late goal blitz to shock the Owls. Fagan slots home from three yards before Stockley makes it two with a long-range effort and then a spectacular free-kick from Keith seals a tremendous victory.

---

2 H 10/8 STOCKPORT — Att 3,346 — Pos 22 — W 3-2 (H-T 3-0)
Scorers, Times and Referees: Watson 19, Andrews 30, Fagan 41; Cartwright 66, Beckett 79. Ref: C Penton

Davison	Stockley	Halford	Brown W	Chilvers	Watson	Johnson*	Bowry	Andrews^	Fagan	Keith J
Cutler	Adams	Williams	Mair	Geary	Lambert^	Bridge-Wilk'n*/Robertson*	Beckett	Cartwright	Feeney	

Subs used: Cade/May · Welsh/Barlow/Goodwin

U's make it six goals in 47 minutes play with a great start. Watson steams in to net Halford's headed pass. Andrews shoots home at the second attempt. Fagan heads in Watson's cross. Sammy McIlroy's men make a fight of it through Lee Cartwright's drive and Luke Bennett's header.

---

3 H 14/8 PETERBOROUGH — Att 3,754 — Pos 13 — W 2-1 (H-T 0-1)
Scorers, Times and Referees: Andrews 58p, Ireland 64 (og); Farrell 10. Ref: P Danson

Davison	Stockley	Halford	Baldwin	Chilvers	Watson	Johnson	Cade*	Keith J*	Fagan	Andrews
Tyler	Burton^	Kennedy	Legg	Newton	Woodhouse	Ireland	Willock^	Farrell*	Platt	

Subs used: May · Real/Clarke/Semmer

David Farrell races forward to beat Halford and fire Posh ahead. Craig Ireland impedes Johnson only for Mark Tyler to save the Fagan penalty. Ireland concedes another spot-kick, Andrews converting this one. Ireland's misery is complete when he heads a long-throw into his own net.

---

4 A 21/8 CHESTERFIELD — Att 4,028 — Pos 8 — L 1-2 (H-T 1-1)
Scorers, Times and Referees: Johnson 44; N'Toya-Zoa 9, 55. Ref: A Hall

Davison	Stockley	Halford	Brown	Chilvers	Watson	Johnson*	Cade	Keith J^	Fagan	Andrews
Muggleton	O'Hare	Nicholson	Bailey	Evatt	Niven	N'Toya-Zoa	Camp-Ryce*/Innes	Allott	DeBolla^	

Subs used: May/Hunt! · Smith/Folan

Senegalese Tcham N'Toya-Zoa nets a superb shot but Johnson hits back on the stroke of half-time. N'Toya-Zoa sweeps in his second before being badly fouled by U's sub Hunt, just seconds after he comes on. This leads to a brawl and Hunt's comeback game ends with a dismissal.

---

5 H 28/8 DONCASTER — Att 3,803 — Pos 19 — W 4-1 (H-T 3-1)
Scorers, Times and Referees: Fagan 16, Johnson 22, Halford 27, [Keith J 70]; Doolan 45. Ref: G Hegley

Davison	Stockley	Halford	Brown	Chilvers*	Watson^	Johnson	Cade*	Keith J*	Fagan	Andrews^
Warrington	Marples	Ryan	Foster	Fenton	McIndoe	Green	Doolan^	Coppinger*	Fort'ne-West/Blundell*	

Subs used: Baldwin/Andrews/Bowditch · Ipoua/Ravenhill/Mulligan

Fagan swoops to score after an error by Steve Foster, then Johnson rattles home the U's second. Stunned Rovers are hit again as Halford starts and completes a move for the third goal in 11 minutes. John Doolan robs Brown to blast home. Keith steps up to score direct from a free-kick.

---

6 A 30/8 HARTLEPOOL — Att 4,371 — Pos 8 — L 1-2 (H-T 0-1)
Scorers, Times and Referees: Keith J 90; Williams 38, Boyd 70. Ref: M Pike

Davison	Stockley	Halford	Brown	Chilvers^	Cade	Johnson	White"	Keith J	Fagan	Andrews^
Konstant'los/Nelson	Westwood	Strachan	Robson	Ross	Sweeney	Humphreys	Williams	Betsy	Boyd	

Subs used: Bowditch/Baldwin · Boyd

In a drab first half, Adam Boyd flicks on a long ball and Eifion Williams beats Brown and goes on to slot home. May's 30-yarder goes close. Gavin Strachan sends over a free-kick and Boyd loops a header past Davison. Keith scores a late consolation with another free-kick 'special'.

---

7 H 4/9 SWINDON — Att 3,868 — Pos 12 — L 0-1 (H-T 0-1)
Scorers, Times and Referees: Parkin 7. Ref: K Wright

Davison	Stockley	Halford	Brown	Chilvers^	Cade	Johnson	White"	Keith J	Fagan	Garcia*
Evans	Ifil	Mitchell	O'Hanlon	Igoe	Hewlett	Duke	Miglioranzi*/Howard	Henderson	Parkin	

Subs used: Hunt/Williams/Cade · May*/Nicholas

Sam Parkin stoops to head an early goal from David Duke's left-wing cross. With pacy Andrews sold to Palace in midweek, U's parade new Aussie signing Garcia, celebrating his 23rd birthday, and he goes close to a leveller. Andy King's men hold on in the face of United pressure.

---

8 A 11/9 BOURNEMOUTH — Att 5,944 — Pos 19 — W 3-1 (H-T 2-0)
Scorers, Times and Referees: Fagan 10, Williams 24, May 79; Stockley 74 (og). Ref: J Ross

Davison	Stockley	Halford	Brown	Chilvers^	Watson	Johnson	Danns*	Garcia*	Fagan	Williams
Moss	Howe	Broadhurst	Cummings	Maher	O'Connor	Spicer	Stock	Rodrigues^	Hayter	Holmes*

Subs used: May/Baldwin/Bowditch · Browning/Connell

Fagan goes close with a lob from the halfway line, and minutes later lofts the ball over Neil Moss from the edge of the area. Fagan delivers a pinpoint cross for Williams to net a powerful header. Debutant John Spicer hits the crossbar before Stockley slides the ball past his own keeper.

---

9 H 18/9 MK DONS — Att 3,460 — Pos 21 — L 0-1 (H-T 0-1)
Scorers, Times and Referees: McLeod 45. Ref: E Evans

Davison	Hunt*	Halford	Brown	Chilvers	Watson	Keith J	Danns*	Garcia	Fagan	Williams
Bevan	Lewington	Charley	Edds	Small*	Williams	Kamara*	Herve	N'imba-Zeh/McLeod	Cummins	Smart

Subs used: May/Bowditch · Puncheon/Oyedele

Allan Smart balloons a shot wide when presented with a great chance. Ben Chorley nods on a cross and unmarked Izale McLeod crashes the ball home from close range. Scott Bevan has an excellent match to keep the U's at bay. Stuart Murdoch's strugglers hang on for a shock win.

---

10 A 25/9 OLDHAM — Att 5,166 — Pos 18 — D 1-1 (H-T 0-1)
Scorers, Times and Referees: Halford 56; Eyres 22. Ref: P Armstrong

Davison	Hunt	Halford	Brown^	Baldwin	Watson	Keith J	Danns*	Garcia	Fagan	Williams*
Mawson	Arber	Holden	Haining	Boshell	Griffin	Johnson	Eyre^	Killen*	Eyres	Betsy

Subs used: Williams/Bowry · Appleby/Jack

Veteran David Eyres, now past 40, smashes a drive past Davison as the Latics pile on first-half pressure. Brian Talbot's team seems to have recovered from their midweek 0-6 mauling by Tottenham. But after the interval Halford climbs to flick home a header from a Watson corner.

---

11 H 2/10 PORT VALE — Att 3,230 — Pos 17 — W 2-1 (H-T 2-0)
Scorers, Times and Referees: Danns 10, 19; Matthews 83. Ref: M Atkinson

Davison	Hunt	Halford	Brown	Baldwin	Watson	Keith J	Danns^	Garcia^	Fagan	Williams*
Brain	O'Connor*	James	Collins	Pilkington	Reid	Birchall	Smith J	Matthews	Paynter	McMahon

Subs used: May/Bowry · May/Paynter

Danns, on loan from Blackburn, bundles home a cross from Halford, the ball going in off his face. Soon after, Danns wins a tackle and surges forward to crack a superb goal past Jonny Brain. With Davison struggling with an injury, Vale pull one back via Lee Matthews' deflected shot.

Match Log (Games 12–23)

Results Summary

No	Venue	Opponent	Date	Pos	Res	Opp Pos	Pts	Att	Score	HT	U's Scorers	Opp Scorers	Referee
12	A	WALSALL	9/10	5	L	18	19	5,203	1-2	0-0	Garcia 71	Bennett 73, Emblen 84	R Beeby
13	A	BLACKPOOL	16/10	6	D	22	20	6,464	1-1	0-1	Watson 80	Murphy 10	A Penn
14	H	WREXHAM	19/10	7	L	12	20	2,866	1-2	0-0	Danns 49	Roberts 59, Llewellyn 90	K Stroud
15	H	TRANMERE	23/10	11	L	6	20	3,420	1-2	0-1	Halford 83	Dagnall 29, Zola 81	K Hill
16	A	BRISTOL CITY	30/10	13	D	12	21	11,678	0-0	0-0			P Walton
17	A	BRADFORD C	6/11	15	D	5	22	7,851	2-2	2-1	Johnson 8, 39	Windass 23, 81	C Oliver
18	H	HUDDERSFIELD	20/11	14	D	11	23	3,972	0-0	0-0			M Russell
19	A	TORQUAY	27/11	13	W	20	26	2,984	3-1	0-0	Fagan 67, 72, Garcia 78	Gritton 74p	M Warren
20	H	BARNSLEY	7/12	14	L	18	26	2,927	0-2	0-1		Kay 34, 54	C Penton
21	H	HULL	11/12	17	L	2	26	4,046	1-2	0-1	Williams 73	France 11, Elliott 50	S Tanner
22	A	BRENTFORD	18/12	18	L	5	26	5,634	0-1	0-1		Salako 45	P Robinson
23	A	LUTON	28/12	18	D	1	27	8,806	2-2	1-1	Garcia 34, Halford 62	Vine 37, 48	A Kaye

Line-ups (U's / *opponents in italic*)

12 WALSALL — Gerken, Hunt, Johnson", Brown, Baldwin, Watson, Keith J, Halford*, Danns^, Garcia, Williams. Subs: Stockley, Bowry, May.
Murphy, Aranalde, Bennett, Osborn, Emblen, Wright, Kinsella, Wrack, Fryatt, Leitao, Merson. Sub: Paston.*

13 BLACKPOOL — Gerken, Stockley, Chilvers, Brown, Baldwin, Watson, Keith J, Bowry*, Danns, Izzet, May^. Subs: Fagan, Williams.
Jones, Grayson, Richardson, Coid, McGregor, Clarke, Edwards P, Evans, Wellens, Murphy, Taylor. Sub: Parker.*

14 WREXHAM — Gerken, Stockley*, Chilvers, Brown, Baldwin, Watson, Keith J, Izzet, Danns, Fagan, Garcia^. Subs: May, Johnson.
Baker, Smith, Roberts, Holt, Lawrence, Pejic, Bennett, Ferguson, Williams, Sam", Llewellyn. Subs: Crowell, Shaw.*

15 TRANMERE — Gerken, Hunt, Chilvers, Brown, Baldwin, Watson, Keith J, Izzet, Danns, Williams*, Garcia". Subs: Halford, Stockley, Cade.
Achterberg, Sharps, Roberts, Taylor, Jackson^, Goodison, Rankine, McAteer, Whitmore, Dagnall^, Hume". Subs: Harrison, Zola, Hall.*

16 BRISTOL CITY — Gerken, Stockley, Chilvers, Brown, Baldwin, Johnson, Keith J, Halford, Watson, Danns, Fagan.
Phillips, Bell", Hill, Butler, Smith, Dinning, Murray", Orr, Wilkshire, Lita, Brooker. Subs: Fortune, Gillespie, Catterill.*

17 BRADFORD C — Gerken, Stockley, Chilvers, Brown, Baldwin, Johnson, Keith J, Halford, Watson, Danns, Fagan.
Henderson, Wetherall, Swift, Bower, Holloway^, Emanuel, Kearney, Crooks, Windass, Muirhead, Adebola. Sub: Gavin.

18 HUDDERSFIELD — Gerken, Stockley, White, Brown, Baldwin, Johnson*, Keith J, Halford, Watson, Garcia, Fagan. Sub: Bowry.
Rachubka, Mirfin, Lloyd, Clarke, Holdsworth, Schofield, Brandon, Yates, Worthington, Carss, Abbott. Sub: Edwards.*

19 TORQUAY — Davison, Stockley, White, Brown, Baldwin, Johnson*, Keith J, Halford, Watson, Garcia, Fagan. Sub: Keith.
Dearden, Taylor, Villis, Canoville, Hockley^, Russell, Hill, McGlinchey, Kuffour, Bedeau, Gritton. Subs: Akinfenwa, Boardley.*

20 BARNSLEY — Davison, Stockley, Chilvers, Brown, Baldwin, Keith J, Bowry^, Halford, Watson, Garcia, Fagan!. Subs: Cade, Williams.
Turnbull, Reid, Hassell, Williams, Vaughan, Burns, Kay, Shuker, McPhail, Chopra, Boulding^. Subs: Carbon, Conlon.*

21 HULL — Davison, Stockley, Chilvers, Brown, Baldwin, Keith J, Bowry", Halford, Danns, Garcia, Fagan. Sub: Cade^.
Myhill, Dawson, Cort, Joseph, Delaney, France, Keane, Barmby", Hargreaves, Claridge*, Elliott. Subs: Lewis, Allsopp, Wilbraham.*

22 BRENTFORD — Davison, Stockley, Chilvers, Baldwin, Brown, Johnson, Bowry*, Halford, Danns, Garcia, Fagan. Sub: Cade*.
Nelson, Turner, Sodje, Talbot, Frampton, Hargreaves, Claridge, O'Connor, Rhodes, Burton, Salako. Subs: Williams, Bowditch.*

23 LUTON — Davison, Stockley, Chilvers, Baldwin, Brown, Johnson, Bowry", Halford, Danns, Garcia, Watson. Sub: Fagan.
Beresford, Foley, Davis, Coyne^, Davies, Robinson, Brkovic, Nicholls, Holmes^, Vine, Howard. Subs: Perrett, Showunmi.

Match Reports

12 WALSALL: Player-manager Paul Merson nets Merson's cross, but Garcia is on target as he steers home Hunt's cross. Young keeper Gerken makes some good saves, but the crisis-hit Saddlers level when Julian Bennett nets Merson's cross. Then Neil Emblen heads a winner from Merson's free-kick.

13 BLACKPOOL: Leam Richardson's cross is headed in by John Murphy. Gerken is in great form to keep the score down. The U's work hard and level near the end, Watson drilling home with the home side screaming for an alleged foul earlier in the move. Tempers flare and there is a last-minute brawl.

14 WREXHAM: Brown's shot from a Keith corner is blocked but the loose ball is netted by Danns. A Darren Ferguson free-kick is only half-cleared and Steve Roberts rockets the ball home to level. In injury time Chris Llewellyn gets clean through twice, missing the first chance but netting the second.

15 TRANMERE: The slide down the table continues, United falling behind when Gareth Roberts' corner is flicked on and youngster Chris Dagnall pokes home. Sub Calvin Zola makes it two, heading in Jason McAteer's flag-kick. John Achterberg flaps at a Watson free-kick and Halford pulls one back.

16 BRISTOL CITY: A mid-table battle ends deadlocked with few moments to thrill the crowd. The U's look stronger in the first half and Gerken is kept on his toes. He saves one effort from on-loan Tony Dinning with his knees. The U's look stronger later on and Brown has a free-kick well saved by Phillips.

17 BRADFORD C: Veteran Johnson heads the U's in front from Keith's corner. Fagan hits the post before Dean Windass slips the ball home from a tight angle. Johnson lashes home from the edge of the area after a cut-back from Fagan. Lee Crooks' pass finds Windass, who expertly drills an equaliser.

18 HUDDERSFIELD: Johnson goes close with a volley when Keith's corner reaches him and later he shoots a Halford pass over the bar. The returning Davison has very little to do in goal, but manager Peter Jackson's five-man defence is kept busy. The U's run of games without a win is stretched to nine.

19 TORQUAY: After a scrappy hour's play, four goals arrive in 11 minutes. Fagan's volley is deflected past Kevin Dearden and he swoops again after the ball hits the Gulls' bar. Martin Gritton scores from the spot after a Davison foul. Garcia nets a far-post header after Baldwin flicks on a corner-kick.

20 BARNSLEY: Antony Kay back-heads a corner from Jacob Burns into the net and doubles the lead by nipping ahead of Garcia to head Stephen McPhail's free-kick past Davison. The U's create very little. Fagan, cautioned for a late tackle on Chris Shuker, fouls Burns in injury time and is sent off.

21 HULL: Peter Taylor's men go ahead when Ryan France finds himself in acres of space in a breakaway raid. Stuart Elliott's shot bobbles out of the reach of Davison for his 16th goal of the season. The U's look toothless without banned Fagan but sub Williams converts a cross from Halford.

22 BRENTFORD: After a quiet first half, Stuart Talbot's corner is cleared to the feet of John Salako, who rifles home his fifth goal of the season. Veteran Steve Claridge, 38, debuts for Martin Allen's side, but is given a rest for the last half-hour. Both keepers are kept busy in a more eventful second half.

23 LUTON: Long range shots by Chris Coyne and Sol Davis go close before Garcia forces in a Fagan cross. Kevin Nicholls' cross ends up with ex-U's man Rowan Vine who levels. Vine cracks a second after Davison blocks Nicholls' shot. Halford levels when a big punt forward causes panic.

COCA-COLA LEAGUE 1 — Manager: Phil Parkinson — SEASON 2004-05

Column key: No | Date | Att | Pos | Pt | F-A | H-T | SQUAD NUMBERS IN USE | subs used | Scorers, Times, and Referees

---

24 — A SWINDON — 1/1
Att 6,468 · Pos 17 · Pt 30 · W · F-A 3-0 · H-T 2-0

- **U's:** Gerken, Stockley, Chilvers, Baldwin, Brown, Johnson^, Danns, Halford, Watson, Garcia*, Fagan
- **Swindon:** Evans, Ifil, Heywood, Gerrard, Robinson*, Igoe, Hewlett, Duke, Holmes, Howard, Parkin
- **Subs used:** White/Hunt — Slabber/Nicholas
- **Scorers:** Johnson 31, Danns 38, Garcia 47 · **Ref:** I Williamson

Gavin Johnson nets a bullet header from Watson's corner and the U's take control. Danns buries a shot from ten yards after Halford's cross is not cleared. Danns beats four men before teeing up Garcia, who side-foots past Rhys Evans. The win eases fears of a looming relegation scrap.

---

25 — H OLDHAM — 3/1
Att 3,873 · Pos 18 · Pt 31 · D · F-A 0-0 · H-T 0-0

- **U's:** Gerken, Stockley, Chilvers, Baldwin, Brown, Johnson, Danns, Halford, Watson, Garcia*
- **Oldham:** Pogliacomi, Holden*, Bruce, Appleby, Haining, Hall, Griffin, Hughes^, Vernon, Kilkenny", Betsy
- **Subs used:** Williams — Croft/Bonner/Eyre
- **Ref:** P Danson

The U's poor home form continues as they fail to break down the Latics. Danns goes on a long run but slices wide. Baldwin nearly grabs his first ever goal, but shoots wide. Halford goes close three times after the break. Only two home points have been won from the last 18 available.

---

26 — A MK DONS — 15/1
Att 3,833 · Pos 18 · Pt 31 · L · F-A 0-2 · H-T 0-2

- **U's:** Gerken, Stockley, Chilvers, Baldwin, Brown, Johnson, Danns, Halford, Watson, Williams^, Fagan
- **MK Dons:** Martin, Edds, Small^, Oyedele, Lewington, Chorley, Mitchell, Smith, Harding^, Rizzo^, Platt
- **Subs used:** Keith J/Garcia — McLeod/Palmer/Puncheon
- **Scorers:** Harding 2, Small 18 · **Ref:** R Booth

When Wade Small gets clear and lobs Gerken, Stockley tries to head clear but the ball falls to Ben Harding who converts. Dons debutant Clive Platt flicks a header to Small who finishes clinically. Williams misses a sitter for the U's and Gary Smith rattles the crossbar for the home side.

---

27 — H LUTON — 22/1
Att 4,309 · Pos 17 · Pt 32 · D · F-A 0-0 · H-T 0-0

- **U's:** Davison, Stockley, Keith J*, Baldwin, Brown, Hunt, Danns, Halford, Watson, Garcia*
- **Luton:** Beresford, Foley, Davis, Coyne, Davies, Keane, Underwood*/Robinson, Nichols, Vine, Howard
- **Subs used:** N'Dumbu-Nsungu — Holmes/Showunmi
- **Ref:** M Dean

Nearly four months without a home win, but the U's push Mike Newell's league leaders all the way. Danns, Watson and Keith all have shots well saved by Marlon Beresford. Steve Howard blasts a good chance over. African-born N'Dumbu-Nsungu, signed from Sheffield W, debuts.

---

28 — H WALSALL — 25/1
Att 2,616 · Pos 16 · Pt 35 · W · F-A 5-0 · H-T 4-0

- **U's:** Gerken, Stockley, Hunt, Baldwin, Brown, Johnson*, Danns, Halford, Watson*, Fagan, Keith J*
- **Walsall:** Murphy, Aranalde, Bennett, Osborn, Emblen, Wright, Kinsella, Wrack, Williams^, Leitao^, Merson
- **Subs used:** Chilvers/N'Dumbu-N'gu/Keith — Robinson/Braad
- **Scorers:** Fagan 18p, 22, Johnson 34, Williams 44, [Hunt 90] · **Ref:** M Thorpe

Neil Emblen pushes Danns and Fagan nets from the spot. Fagan converts a cross and Johnson volleys in a corner. Williams tucks in Halford's cross for the fourth. It's an unhappy return to Layer Road for Mark Kinsella. Saddlers' player-manager Paul Merson offers to quit afterwards.

---

29 — H BLACKPOOL — 5/2
Att 3,526 · Pos 17 · Pt 35 · L · F-A 0-1 · H-T 0-0

- **U's:** Davison, Stockley^, Chilvers, Baldwin, Brown, Johnson, Danns, Halford, Watson, Keith J*, Williams
- **Blackpool:** Jones, Edwards R, Grayson, Clare, Clarke, Southern, Edwards P, Evans, Wellens, Parker^, Lynch
- **Subs used:** N'Dumbu-Nsungu/Guy — Warhurst
- **Scorers:** Grayson 75 · **Ref:** B Curson

Brad Jones keeps the U's at bay, saving good goalbound efforts from Williams and Halford. Fagan's booking means another suspension looms. Steve McMahon's men break the deadlock in a rare raid, Keigan Parker's cross being forced past the scrambling Davison by Simon Grayson.

---

30 — A TRANMERE — 12/2
Att 8,098 · Pos 17 · Pt 36 · D · F-A 1-1 · H-T 0-1

- **U's:** Gerken, Hunt, Chilvers, Baldwin, Brown, Johnson, Danns, Halford, Keith J, Watson*, Williams*
- **Tranmere:** Achterberg, Sharp, Roberts, Jackson, Goodison, Harrison, McAteer, Beresford*, Hall^, Dagnall, Dadi
- **Subs used:** N'Dumbu-N*/Williams — Whitmore/Jennings/Jones
- **Scorers:** Keith J 65 — Dadi 8 · **Ref:** S Mathieson

Partly due to injuries, Parkinson shuffles his pack, but is hit by an early blow as Eugene Dadi pounces on a loose ball and goes round Gerken. Keith rattles the bar just before the interval and later Halford does likewise. Halford's effort is headed in by Keith for a deserved equaliser.

---

31 — H BOURNEMOUTH — 15/2
Att 2,820 · Pos 15 · Pt 39 · W · F-A 3-1 · H-T 0-0

- **U's:** Gerken, Hunt, Chilvers, Baldwin, Brown, Johnson, Danns, Halford, Keith J, Watson, Williams*
- **Bournemouth:** Moss, Howe, Cummings, Maher, Purches", O'Connor, Spicer, Elliott, Stock^, Hayter^, Fletcher
- **Subs used:** N'Dumbu-Nsungu — Connell/Browning/Rodrigues
- **Scorers:** Johnson 54, N'Dumbu Nsungu 82, [Danns 83] — Cummings 47 · **Ref:** K Friend

Warren Cummings tries his luck from distance and the ball loops in off Baldwin's shoulder. Keith's corner is headed home by Johnson. Sub N'Dumbu-Nsungu slots in after Neil Moss fails to hold a Halford free-kick. Danns makes the points safe by crashing home a fine third goal.

---

32 — H BRISTOL CITY — 19/2
Att 3,412 · Pos 16 · Pt 39 · L · F-A 0-2 · H-T 0-0

- **U's:** Gerken, Hunt*, Chilvers, Baldwin, Brown, Johnson, Danns, Halford, Keith J*, Watson, Williams
- **Bristol City:** Phillips, Bell, Carey, Ireland, Coles, Wilkshire^, Doherty, Brown, Lita", Brooker, Cotterill^
- **Subs used:** N'Dumbu-Nsungu/Williams — Galbourne/Skuse/Anyinsah
- **Scorers:** Brooker 51, Lita 71 · **Ref:** P Taylor

City skipper Stephen Brooker hits the U's bar in the first half and Brian Tinnion's side look the more dangerous throughout. The pressure tells and United are flattened by slick finishes by Brooker and Leroy Lita. Luke Wilkshire misses an open goal and City could have scored a hatful.

---

33 — A WREXHAM — 22/2
Att 2,391 · Pos 16 · Pt 40 · D · F-A 2-2 · H-T 0-0

- **U's:** Gerken, Hunt, Chilvers, Baldwin, Brown, Johnson, Danns, Halford, White, Watson, Williams^
- **Wrexham:** Foster, Holt, Pejic, Smith*, Lawrence, Ferguson, Edwards, Crowell, Jones, Armstrong, Llewellyn^
- **Subs used:** Fagan — Morgan/Sam
- **Scorers:** Danns 60, Brown 71 — Jones 50, Sam 80 · **Ref:** G Salisbury

Mark Jones' rather tame shot somehow eludes Gerken and hits the net. Halford's effort from a corner is blocked on the line but Danns heads in the loose ball. A carbon-copy incident then sees Brown knock in another rebound. A double substitution pays off as Hector Sam heads home.

---

34 — A HULL — 26/2
Att 16,484 · Pos 17 · Pt 40 · L · F-A 0-2 · H-T 0-2

- **U's:** Davison, Keith J, Chilvers, Baldwin, Brown, Johnson, Danns, Halford, White, Watson, Williams^
- **Hull:** Myhill, Dawson, Stockdale, Cort, Delaney, France, Ashbee, Green^, Barmby, Elliott, Ellison^
- **Subs used:** N'Dumbu-N*/Stockley/Guy — Lewis/Price
- **Scorers:** Cort 16, Barmby 33 · **Ref:** N Miller

Promotion-chasing Hull sign United's Fagan the day before this game, but he doesn't take part. Carl Cort gives them the lead, firmly heading in a corner. With Davison out of goal, Kevin Ellison hits the bar, but Nicky Barmby coolly slots the rebound home for the crucial second goal.

Matches 35–46

No	V	Date	Opponent	Att	Pos	—	Res	Score	Pts
35	H	5/3	BRENTFORD	3,066	18	5	L	0-1	40
36	A	8/3	PORT VALE	3,496	18	17	D	0-0	41
37	A	12/3	STOCKPORT	4,004	16	24	W	2-1	44
38	H	19/3	SHEFFIELD WED	4,169	17	4	D	1-1	45
39	A	25/3	PETERBOROUGH	4,084	16	23	W	3-0	48
40	H	28/3	CHESTERFIELD	3,471	14	13	W	1-0	51
41	A	1/4	DONCASTER	6,774	14	8	D	1-1	52
42	H	9/4	HARTLEPOOL	3,148	14	5	D	1-1	53
43	A	16/4	HUDDERSFIELD	10,831	14	9	D	2-2	54
44	H	23/4	BRADFORD C	3,351	15	12	D	0-0	55
45	A	30/4	BARNSLEY	8,162	16	13	D	1-1	56
46	H	7/5	TORQUAY	4,834	15	21	W	2-1	59

Home Average 3,534 — Away 7,256

---

35 — BRENTFORD (H) 5/3 — L 0-1

U's: Davison, Hunt, Chilvers, Baldwin^, Brown, Johnson, White", Halford, Watson, Williams, Keith M*; subs Keith J/Stockley/N'Dumbu-Ns
Brentford: Nelson, Pratley, Turner, Sadje, Talbot, Frampton, Tabb^, Hunt, Hutchinson, O'Connor, Burton*; subs Fitzgerald/Dobson

Tabb 58. Ref: P Prosser

Williams grazes the bar in the first half. The U's fall behind when Baldwin's back-pass is intercepted by sub Scott Fitzgerald, whose shot is parried by Davison to Jay Tabb, who makes no mistake. Keeper Davison ventures upfield for a late corner and has a header cleared off the line.

36 — PORT VALE (A) 8/3 — D 0-0

U's: Davison, Hunt, Chilvers, Baldwin, Brown, Johnson, White, Halford, Watson, Williams, Keith M*; subs Williams
Port Vale: Goodlad, Pilkington, James", Collins, Walsh, Cummins, Abbey, Smith", Sonner, Paynter, Matthews*; subs Birchall/Reid/Rowland

Ref: P Robinson

Two bookable offences in four minutes sees Chilvers sent off just before half-time. Michael Cummins suffers a similar fate soon after and then sub Levi Reid gets a straight red for a tackle on White. There is little else to keep the crowd interested, both sides guilty of wayward shooting.

37 — STOCKPORT (A) 12/3 — W 2-1

U's: Davison, Hunt, Keith J, Baldwin, Brown, Johnson, White*, Halford, Watson, Danns, Keith M; subs Williams
Stockport: Spencer, Goodwin, Raynes, Horwood, Briggs, Williams, Dolan, Jackman*, Hurst, Le Fondre, Feeney^; subs Allen/Armstrong

Danns 30p, 90 / Feeney 4. Ref: A Hall

Warren Feeney taps home his 12th of the season from a cut-back from the bye-line. Jim Goodwin impedes Johnson and Danns tucks away the penalty. M Keith hits the woodwork before Danns nets a late winner from Baldwin's flick-on. 'We got out of jail,' says a relieved Parkinson.

38 — SHEFFIELD WED (H) 19/3 — D 1-1

U's: Davison, Chilvers, Stockley, Baldwin, Brown, Johnson, Danns*, Halford, Watson, Goodfell'w^, Keith M; subs Williams/White
Sheffield Wed: Adamson, Wood, Bullen, Bruce", Heckingbot'm, Racastle*, McGovern, Brunt, Whelan, Peacock, Quinn^; subs Adams/Talbot/Collins

Heckingbottom 48 (og) / McGovern 63. Ref: R Beeby

Paul Heckingbottom attempts to clear a Williams cross but can only divert the ball into his own net. John-Paul McGovern sets off on a solo run and shoots low past Davison to equalise. Debutant Goodfellow, borrowed from Bristol City, gets clear of the defence but hooks his shot wide.

39 — PETERBOROUGH (A) 25/3 — W 3-0

U's: Davison, Chilvers, Stockley, Baldwin, Brown, Johnson*, Danns", Halford, Watson, Goodfellow^, Keith M; subs White/Hunt/Williams
Peterborough: Tyler, Legg, Arber, Ireland^, St Ledger, Plummer, Semple*, Woodhouse, Thomson, Willock", Clarke; subs Purser/Coulson/Onijube

Goodfellow 45, Danns 70, Keith M 83p. Ref: U Rennie

Goodfellow seizes on to a half-cleared corner and rams a low shot through a crowd into the net. Danns converts a Stockley cross before M Keith completes a comfortable win from the penalty spot. Barry Fry's men lack confidence in attack and now look certainties for relegation.

40 — CHESTERFIELD (H) 28/3 — W 1-0

U's: Davison, Chilvers, Stockley, Baldwin*, Brown, White^, Danns, Halford, Watson, Goodfellow^, Keith M; subs Garcia/Williams
Chesterfield: Muggleton, Bailey, Nicholson, Blatherwick, Evatt, Niven, Davies", McMaster*, Logan, Allott, Folan^; subs Allison/N'Toya-Zoa/O'Hare

Keith M 76. Ref: C Penton

Ian Evatt slices a good chance straight to Davison and Carlos Logan is off target with another. M Keith scores his second goal since joining on loan from Plymouth, sweeping home from close-range following Watson's corner-kick. The win means lingering relegation fears are banished.

41 — DONCASTER (A) 1/4 — D 1-1

U's: Davison, Chilvers, Hunt, Baldwin, Brown, White^, Danns, Halford, Watson, Goodfellow^, Keith M; subs Garcia/Williams
Doncaster: Turner, Priet", Mulligan, Fenton, McIndoe, Ravenhill^, Doolan, Coppinger*, Blundell, Roberts; subs Guy/Green/Fortune-West

Keith M 14 / Guy 76. Ref: T Leake

M Keith's shot is deflected and hits the net with Iain Turner wrong-footed. United defend the lead well, but are finally beaten when Gregg Blundell's cross enables Lewis Guy to slot his first goal for Dave Penney's men. Danns misses the U's best chance, but a draw is a fair result.

42 — HARTLEPOOL (H) 9/4 — D 1-1

U's: Davison, Chilvers, Hunt, Brown, Johnson, White, Danns, Halford, Watson, Jarvis", Keith M; subs Garcia
Hartlepool: Konstant'os, Nelson*, Clark, Westwood, Strachan, Butler^, Robertson, Sweeney, Humphreys, Daly", Boyd; subs Howey/Istead/Appleby

Johnson 39 / Sweeney 54. Ref: M Warren

Hugh Robertson crashes in a free-kick which hits both bar and post before going back into play. Jarvis, on loan from Norwich, drags an effort wide with only the keeper to beat. Johnson nets after a long-throw reaches him. Thomas Butler's cross eludes everyone and ends up in the net.

43 — HUDDERSFIELD (A) 16/4 — D 2-2

U's: Davison, Chilvers, Hunt, Baldwin, Johnson, White*, Danns, Halford, Watson, Garcia*, Keith M; subs Garcia/Jarvis/Williams
Huddersfield: Rachubka, Adams, Mirfin, Clarke T*, Clarke N", Fowler^, Schofield, Brandon, Ahmed, Booth, Abbott; subs Holdsworth/Collins/Mendes

Danns 19, Chilvers 90 / Abbott 20, Schofield 62. Ref: K Woolmer

Paul Rachubka palms Garcia's cross straight to Danns who makes no mistake. Pawel Abbott nets a free-kick with the U's wall complaining in vain they hadn't been ready. Danny Schofield blasts home a fine drive, but Rachubka fails to gather a corner and Chilvers pounces to equalise.

44 — BRADFORD C (H) 23/4 — D 0-0

U's: Davison, Chilvers, Hunt, Baldwin, Johnson, White, Danns, Halford, Watson, Jarvis", Keith M; subs Brown/White/Williams
Bradford C: Ricketts, Wetherall, Bower, Holloway, Bridge-Wilk'n, Schumacher, Butler^, Windass, Morrison^, Muirhead, Cooke*; subs Forrest/Emanuel

Ref: T Parkes

Keeper Donovan Ricketts is man-of-the-match as the U's fail to score but maintain their unbeaten run. Colin Todd's side are lucky to be level at the break but improve afterwards and Davison gets far more to do. Dean Windass and Lewis Emanuel both miss clear-cut chances to win it.

45 — BARNSLEY (A) 30/4 — D 1-1

U's: Davison, Chilvers, Hunt, Baldwin, Brown*, Johnson, Danns", Halford, Watson, Garcia*, Keith M; subs Williams/Jarvis
Barnsley: Flinders, Williams, Austin, Kay, Burns*, Tonge, Wroe, McPhail, Chopra, Nardiello^, Johnson; subs Shuker/Jarman

Johnson 88 / Nardiello 41. Ref: P Walton

Daniel Nardiello heads in at the far post after good work by Nicky Wroe. United improve after the interval and Johnson equalises from 25 yards after a short free-kick manoeuvre. Tykes' caretaker-manager Andy Ritchie is furious as he felt the free-kick should not have been given.

46 — TORQUAY (H) 7/5 — W 2-1

U's: Davison, Chilvers, Hunt, Baldwin, Johnson, Brown*, Danns", Halford, Watson, Garcia", Keith M; subs Jarvis/Brown/Izzet
Torquay: Marriott, Taylor, Hockley, Woodman, Garner^, Russell, Phillips, Hill, Woods, Aklulewa, Constantine*; subs Beuleu/Abbey

Danns 42, Keith M 89 / Woodman 90. Ref: K Friend

The Gulls need a point to avoid relegation but Danns pounces to score after Keith's effort is blocked. In the last minute Keith nets Watson's through ball. In the dying seconds Craig Woodman pulls one back from a free-kick, but MK Dons' win elsewhere ensures Torquay are down.

COCA-COLA LEAGUE 1 (CUP-TIES) Manager: Phil Parkinson SEASON 2004-05

Carling Cup

1 H CHELTENHAM 24/8 — Pos 3 W F-A 2:1 H-T 1-0 — Att 2,144 2:17

Scorers, Times: Fagan 12, Johnson 61 / Devaney 70. Ref: P Crossley

- Colchester: Davison, Stockley, Halford*, Brown, Chilvers, Watson, Johnson^, Cade", Keith J, Fagan, Andrews — subs used: White/May/Bowditch
- Cheltenham: *Higgs, Taylor, Wilson, Gill, Victory, Duff, Melligan, Bird*, McCann, Guinan^, Devaney"* — subs used: *Odejayi/Spencer/Vincent*

Fagan gives the visiting defence the slip and rifles in from a tight angle. Sub Bowditch sets up Johnson to drive home the second goal. Martin Devaney makes the most of poor marking to pull one back. Davison has to make several good saves and Damian Spencer hits a United post.

2 H WEST BROM 21/9 — Pos 6 W F-A 2:1 aet H-T 1-0 — Att 4,591 P:19

Scorers, Times: Fagan 29, May 117 / Horsfield 50. Ref: A Kaye

- Colchester: Davison, Hunt, Baldwin, Brown, Chilvers*, Watson, Danns, Keith J, Garcia, Williams", Fagan^ — subs used: Halford/May/Bowry
- West Brom: *Kuszczak, Gaardsoe, Moore, Albrechtson, Scimeca, Dyer, Contra^, Gera*, Koumas, Horsfield, Dobie"* — subs used: *Greening/O'Connor/Hulse*

Williams dummies over the ball and Fagan turns on the edge of the box to crack home a beauty. Geoff Horsfield burst through to beat Davison and bring Gary Megson's men level. In extra-time Lloyd Dyer blocks Garcia's effort on the goalline but May lunges in to force the winner in.

3 A SOUTHAMPTON 27/10 — Pos 11 L F-A 2:3 H-T 1-0 — Att 20,588 P:18

Scorers, Times: Danns 7, Halford 64 / Blackstock 50, 54, 80. Ref: M Jones

- Colchester: Gerken, Hunt, Johnson*, Brown, Baldwin, Stockley, Keith J, Watson, Halford, Danns — subs used: Garcia
- Southampton: *Niemi, Kenton, Lundekvam, Jakobsson, Van Damme, Svensson*, Prutton, McCann^, Nilsson, Ormerod, Best** — subs used: *Blackstock/Telfer/Fernandes*

Keith's corner is not cleared and Danns swoops to score. Dexter Blackstock comes off the bench at half-time and converts Paul Telfer's cross and then nets when Gerken spills Anders Svensson's shot. Fagan sets up Halford to fire the U's level before Blackstock nets a far-post header.

FA Cup

1 A MANSFIELD 13/11 — Pos 15 D F-A 1:1 H-T 1-1 — Att 3,202 2:12

Scorers, Times: Halford 25 / John-Baptiste 28. Ref: P Prosser

- Colchester: Gerken, Stockley, Chilvers, White*, Baldwin, Johnson, Keith J, Halford, Watson, Garcia, Fagan — subs used: Cade
- Mansfield: *Pilkington, Buxton, Dimach, J'n-Baptiste, Artell, Corden*, MacKenzie, Curtis, McLachlan, Asamoah !, Larkin^* — subs used: *Murray/Day*

The Stags recently suspended manager Keith Curle and are under the temporary command of Carlton Palmer. Halford heads home against the run of play, but skipper Alex John-Baptiste levels with a stunning 30-yard volley. Derek Asamoah is sent off for a two-footed lunge at White.

1R H MANSFIELD 23/11 — Pos 14 W F-A 4:1 H-T 2-0 — Att 2,492 2:12

Scorers, Times: Garcia 10, Curtis 14 (og), Fagan 67p, [Williams 90p] / Neil 86. Ref: K Hill

- Colchester: Davison, Stockley, Chilvers, White, Baldwin, Johnson", Keith J*, Halford, Watson, Garcia, Fagan^ — subs used: Bowry/Hunt/Williams
- Mansfield: *Pilkington, Dimach, J'n-Baptiste / Artell, MacKenzie, Curtis", Lloyd*, Murray', Larkin, Neil, Burton* — subs used: *Herron/Wood/McIntosh*

Garcia heads in a White cross and then Tom Curtis diverts Stockley's cross into his own net. Alex Neil pulls a goal back but another push, on Fagan, gives the U's a penalty. On Garcia, gives Williams a late penalty chance.

2 A RUSHDEN & D 4/12 — Pos 13 W F-A 5:2 H-T 3-0 — Att 3,077 2:21

Scorers, Times: Halford 4, 47, 90, Fagan 25, 35 / Broughton 82, Gray 86. Ref: T Kettle

- Colchester: Davison, Stockley, Chilvers, White^, Baldwin, Johnson, Bowry*, Keith J, Watson, Garcia", Halford — subs used: Bowditch/Brown/Cade
- Rushden & D: *Turley, Connelly, Gray, Allen^, Hawkins, Gulliver, Dove", Burgess, Broughton, Robinson, Hay** — subs used: *Bell/Gier/Kelly*

Halford heads the first and Fagan converts two Stockley passes. Garcia sets up Halford for the fourth goal. Ernie Tippett's side are outclassed, but pull two goals back as Drewe Broughton and Stuart Gray convert David Bell crosses.

3 A HULL 8/1 — Pos 18 W F-A 2:0 H-T 2-0 — Att 14,027 1

Scorers, Times: Williams 27, Fagan 29. Ref: P Joslin

- Colchester: Gerken, Stockley, Chilvers, Baldwin, Brown, Johnson, Watson, Keith J, Halford, Williams*, Fagan — subs used: Cade
- Hull: *Myhill, Dawson, Angus", Cort, Delaney, Price, Green, Wilbraham^, Facey, Keane*, Lewis* — subs used: *Allsopp/Wiseman/Fry*

With key men missing, Hull's long winning run is ended. Michael Keane's slip allows Halford to produce a fine pass for Williams to shoot under Boaz Myhill. Moments later Fagan pounces and pokes home a Watson corner. The U's look for more goals and go through comfortably.

4 A BLACKBURN 29/1 — Pos 16 L F-A 0:3 H-T 0-2 — Att 10,634 P:16

Scorers, Times: / Watson 21(og), Johnson 27, Matteo 51. Ref: H Webb

- Colchester: Davison, Stockley, Baldwin, Brown, Chilvers, Watson, Johnson*, Halford, Danns, Garcia, Fagan — subs used: Cade
- Blackburn: *Friedel, Neill, Todd, Matteo, Pedersen^, Thompson, Emerton", Tugay, Savage, Johnson, Gray* — subs used: *Nelsen/Stead/Reid*

Red faces all round as Davison completely misses Watson's bobbling back-pass and the ball trickles in. Jemal Johnson nets a cross by David Thompson and Mark Hughes' outfit take full control of the tie. Robbie Savage's free-kick is converted at the near post by Dominic Matteo.

LDV Vans Trophy

1 H SOUTHEND 29/9 — Pos 6 D F-A 1:1 aet H-T 0-1 — Att 3,469 2:11

Scorers, Times: Garcia 63 / Bramble 40. Ref: P Robinson (U's lose 3-5 on penalties)

- Colchester: Davison, Hunt, Baldwin, Brown, Bowry^, Watson, Keith J, Halford, Danns, Garcia, Williams* — subs used: Cade/Johnson
- Southend: *Flahavan, Wilson, Edwards, Barrett, Jupp*, Pettifer, Bentley !, Gower", Maher, Gray, Bramble* — subs used: *Hunt/Broughton/Corbett*

Tes Bramble nets a 20-yard volley but Garcia heads an equaliser. In extra-time Mark Bentley is sent off, but angrily claims his only offence was to leap clear of a fierce challenge. In the shoot-out, Brown's penalty goes wide and Jimmy Corbett wins it with his first touch of the game.

League table

	P			Home						Away				Pts
		W	D	L	F	A	W	D	L	F	A			
1 Luton	46	17	4	2	46	16	12	7	4	41	32			98
2 Hull	46	16	5	2	42	17	10	3	10	38	36			86
3 Tranmere	46	14	5	4	43	23	8	8	7	30	32			79
4 Brentford	46	15	4	4	34	22	5	11	7	23	38			75
5 Sheffield W *	46	10	6	7	34	28	9	9	5	43	31			72
6 Hartlepool	46	15	3	5	51	30	6	5	12	25	36			71
7 Bristol City	46	9	8	6	42	25	9	8	6	32	32			70
8 Bournemouth	46	9	7	7	40	30	11	3	9	37	34			70
9 Huddersfield	46	12	6	5	42	28	8	4	11	32	37			70
10 Doncaster	46	10	11	2	35	20	6	7	10	30	40			66
11 Bradford C	46	9	6	8	40	35	8	8	7	24	27			65
12 Swindon	46	12	5	6	40	30	5	7	11	26	38			63
13 Barnsley	46	7	11	5	38	31	7	8	8	31	33			61
14 Walsall	46	11	7	5	40	28	5	5	13	25	41			60
15 COLCHESTER	46	8	6	9	27	23	6	11	6	33	27			59
16 Blackpool	46	8	7	8	28	30	7	5	11	26	29			57
17 Chesterfield	46	9	8	6	32	28	5	7	11	23	34			57
18 Port Vale	46	13	2	8	33	23	4	3	16	16	36			56
19 Oldham	46	10	5	8	42	34	5	5	14	18	39			52
20 MK Dons	46	8	10	5	33	28	4	5	14	21	40			51
21 Torquay	46	8	5	10	27	36	4	10	9	28	43			51
22 Wrexham **	46	6	8	9	26	37	7	6	10	36	43			43
23 Peterborough	46	5	6	12	27	35	4	6	13	22	38			39
24 Stockport	46	3	4	16	26	46	3	4	16	23	52			26
	1104	244	149	159	868	683	159	149	244	683	868			1497

* promoted after play-offs
** Deducted 10 pts Administr.

Odds & ends

Double wins: (4) Bournemouth, Peterborough, Stockport, Torquay.

Double losses: (3) Brentford, Hull, MK Dons.

Won from behind: (3) Bournemouth (H), Peterborough (H), Stockport (A).

Lost from in front: (3) Walsall (A), Wrexham (H), Southampton (A, CC).

High spots: The eleven-match unbeaten run at the end of the season. The fine Greg Halford hat-trick in the emphatic cup win at Rushden. Beating West Brom in the Carling Cup.

Consistent defending (the 'meanest' in the division away from home).

Low spots: The mid-season slump (dropping from 4th to 18th).

Karl Duguid missing all season, and Kem Izzet most of it, due to injuries.

The freak own-goal that set Blackburn on their way in the FA Cup.

The relatively poor home form (9 losses, compared to only 6 away).

Player of the Year: Pat Baldwin.

Ever-presents: (0).

Hat-tricks for: (1) Greg Halford (v Rushden & D, A, FAC).

Hat-tricks against: (1) Dexter Blackstock (v Southampton, A, CC).

Leading scorer: (14) Craig Fagan.

Appearances and Goals

Player	Appearances								Goals					
	Lge	Sub	LC	Sub	FAC	Sub	LDV	Sub	Lge	Sub	LC	FAC	LDV	Tot
Andrews, Wayne	4	1	1						2					2
Baldwin, Pat	35	3	2		5		1							
Bowditch, Ben		5				1		1						
Bowry, Bobby	7	4	1	1	1		1							
Brown, Wayne	38	2	3	1	2	1	1		1					1
Cade, Jamie	4	5	1			3		1						
Chilvers, Liam	40	1	2		4	1		1	1					1
Danns, Neil	32	2	2	1	1		1		11			1		12
Davison, Aidan	33	2	2	1	3		1							
Fagan, Craig	25	1	3		5	1		1	8			2	4	14
Garcia, Richard	20	4	1	1	3	1	1		4			1	1	6
Gerken, Dean	13	1			2									
Goodfellow, Marc	4								1					1
Guy, Jamie		2												
Hunt, Stephen	16	4	2	1	1	1	1		1					1
Halford, Greg	43	1	2	1	5		1		4			1	4	9
Izzet, Kem	3	1												
Jarvis, Ryan	2	4												
Johnson, Gavin	36	1	2		4			1	9			1		10
Keith, Joe	27	4	3	1	4	1	1		4					4
Keith, Marino	12	4							4					4
May, Ben	5	9	2						1			1		2
N'Dumbu Nsungu, G	2	6				1			1					1
Stockley, Sam	33	4	2		5				1					1
Watson, Kevin	44	3	3		5		1		2					2
White, John	16	4	1		3									
Williams, Gareth	12	17	1		2	1	1	1	3		2			5
(own-goals)									2		1			3
27 players used	506	84	33	11	55	11	7	2	60	2	7	6	12	79

COCA-COLA LEAGUE 1

Manager: Phil Parkinson — SEASON 2005-06

No	Date		Opponent	Att	Pos	Pt	F-A	H-T	Scorers, Times, and Referees
1	6/8	A	GILLINGHAM	7,293		0	1-2	0-0	Danns 50 / Crofts 75, Byfield 89 / Ref: P Joslin
2	9/8	H	SWANSEA	2,950	23 *3*	0 L	1-2	0-1	Halford 67 / Forbes 35, Trundle 68 / Ref: J Singh
3	13/8	H	BARNSLEY	2,721	18 *15*	3 W	1-0	0-0	Iwelumo 48 / Ref: T Parkes
4	20/8	A	MK DONS	4,423	18 *22*	4 D	1-1	0-1	Chivers 79 / Wilbraham 23 / Ref: K Wright
5	27/8	H	OLDHAM	2,742	18 *3*	5 D	0-0	0-0	/ Ref: D Gallagher
6	29/8	A	SOUTHEND	7,344	22 *12*	5 L	1-3	1-2	Stockley 19 / Goater 3, 78, Cole 30 / Ref: R Styles
7	3/9	A	BRISTOL CITY	10,180	20 *18*	6 D	0-0	0-0	/ Ref: R Olivier
8	10/9	H	DONCASTER	2,721	15 *24*	9 W	3-2	3-1	Iwel'o 1, McDaid 23(og), Foster 27(og) / Forte 5, McIndoe 53p / Ref: P Taylor
9	17/9	A	PORT VALE	5,166	13 *8*	12 W	1-0	1-0	Iwelumo 34 / Ref: C Webster
10	24/9	H	HUDDERSFIELD	3,415	15 *3*	13 D	1-1	0-0	Elokobi 49 / Taylor-Fletcher 65 / Ref: M Russell
11	27/9	A	BRADFORD C	6,891	15 *6*	14 D	1-1	0-0	Halford 62 / Petta 84 / Ref: M Jones

Squad Numbers in Use, Subs Used, and Match Reports

1 — A GILLINGHAM
U's: Davison, Halford, Chivers, Baldwin^, Stockley, Brown, Watson, Duguid, Izzet, Danns, Iwelumo* — subs Williams/Yeates
Gillingham: Brown, Cox, Rose, Jackman, Hope, Hes'nthaler*, Pouton^, Flynn, Crofts, Spiller^, Byfield — subs Shields/Corneille/Jarvis
Duguid returns after 17 months injured. The Gills are caught napping as Danns nets from close in, sparking a spell of U's pressure in which Iwelumo and Halford miss sitters. Andrew Crofts dives to head in and near the end Darren Byfield nets a crisp shot on the turn to grab victory.

2 — H SWANSEA
U's: Davison, Halford, Chivers, Baldwin, Stockley, Brown, Watson*, Duguid*, Izzet, Danns, Iwelumo — subs Williams/Howell/Guy
Swansea: Gueret, Ricketts, Iriekpen, Tate, Austin, O'Leary, Martinez, Akinfenwa, Forbes, Trundle, Goodfellow* — sub McLeod
Adrian Forbes heads an Alan Tait cross in at the far post. A minute after Danns hits a post from 20 yards, Halford equalises after Willy Gueret parries a Williams shot. Within seconds Kenny Jackett's men regain the lead, Lee Trundle controlling a loose ball and staying cool to convert.

3 — H BARNSLEY
U's: Davison, Halford, Chivers, Baldwin, Stockley, Brown, Watson, Duguid, Izzet, Danns, Iwelumo — sub Williams
Barnsley: Colgan, Reid, Carbon, Williams*, Austin, Kay, Burns, McPhail, Tonge^, Hayes, Nardiello — subs Conlon/Shuker
New signing Iwelumo grabs his first goal for the club, netting a downward header from Duguid's excellent cross. Keeper Nick Colgan defies the U's attempts to grab a second, saving a Halford long-ranger, a Danns overhead kick and an Iwelumo effort that looked a goal all the way.

4 — A MK DONS
U's: Davison (sent off), Halford, Chivers, Baldwin, Stockley, Brown, Watson, Duguid, Izzet, Danns, Iwelumo — sub Gerken
MK Dons: Baker, Morgan, Lewington, Edds, Palmer, Small^, McClenahan*, Puncheon, McKoy", Wilbraham, McLeod — subs Oyedele/Kamara/Smith
Soon after Izale McLeod rattles the U's bar, a poor defensive header by Baldwin falls for Aaron Wilbraham, who scores. After 69 minutes, Davison lashes out at McLeod and is sent off. Ten-man U's rise to the challenge and Chivers powers home a header from a corner.

5 — H OLDHAM
U's: Gerken, Halford, Chivers, Baldwin, Stockley, Brown, Watson, Duguid, Izzet, Danns, Iwelumo^ — subs White/Williams/Howell
Oldham: Day, Tierney, Branston, Scott, Owen, Wellens^, Butcher, Warne*, Porter, Liddell — subs Edwards/Bonner
Ronnie Moore's side rarely threaten, but hold firm against home pressure. Latics hero Chris Day claws away an Iwelumo header and saves a low drive by Halford. Iwelumo shoots straight at Day from close range. The visitors are delighted to escape with a point after a real pounding.

6 — A SOUTHEND
U's: Gerken, Halford, Chivers, Baldwin*, Stockley, Brown, Watson, Duguid, Izzet, Danns, Iwelumo — subs White/Williams/Guy
Southend: Flahavan, Wilson, Hunt, Barrett, Edwards, Guttridge*, Cole*, Gower, Maher, Goater, Gray^ — subs Bentley/Lawson/Smith
A full-blooded Essex derby sees Shaun Goater thump home a pass from Luke Guttridge. From a throw-in, Stockley powers home a 25-yarder to level. Mitchell Cole lobs the ball over Stockley and blasts past Gerken. Williams hits the bar, but Goater goes clear to clinch a home victory.

7 — A BRISTOL CITY
U's: Davison, Halford, Baldwin^, White, Richards!, Brown!, Watson, Duguid, Izzet, Danns, Iwelumo — subs Howell/King
Bristol City: Phillips, Golbourne^, Keough, Carey, Heywood, Murray, Orr, Skuse, Brooker^, Brown!, Bridges — subs Gillespie/Smith G
Both teams are missing regulars for this clash live on Sky TV. Stockley is injured in the warm-up and Richards steps up for his debut. When Brown lashes out at Michael Bridges at a free-kick he is sent off and the U's are under more pressure. Izzet nearly nicks a win but hits the bar.

8 — H DONCASTER
U's: Davison, Halford, Baldwin, White*, Stockley, Brown, Watson, Williams, Izzet, Yeates^, Iwelumo^ — subs Stockley/Hunt/King
Doncaster: Warrington, Albrighton, McDaid, Mulligan*, Foster, McGuire, Ravenhill, McIndoe, Green^, Fort'ine-West, Forte — subs Predic/Roberts N
After just 44 seconds Iwelumo prods in a rebound after a long throw. Loanee Jonathan Forte shrugs off Baldwin to slide Rovers level. The ball flies in off Sean McDaid's head and then Steve Foster adds a second own-goal, diverting in Halford's cross. Michael McIndoe nets a penalty.

9 — A PORT VALE
U's: Davison, Halford, Baldwin, White, Stockley, Brown, Watson, Williams^, Izzet, Yeates*, Iwelumo — subs Baldwin/Hunt
Port Vale: Goodlad, Rowland*, Collins, Dinning, Pilkington, Birchall, Sonner, Cummins, Paynter, Lowndes — subs Bell/Cornes
Martin Foyle's side struggle to cope with Iwelumo, who misses an early chance badly, but compensates by bundling the ball home from close range after poor defending at a Watson corner. Vale look a little sharper after the break, but the U's hold on thanks to a solid defensive display.

10 — H HUDDERSFIELD
U's: Davison, Halford, Baldwin, Elokobi, Stockley, Brown, Richards, Williams^, Izzet, Yeates*, Iwelumo — subs Baldwin/Hunt
Huddersfield: Rachubka, Adams, Clarke T, Clarke N, Holdsworth, Schofield, Brandon, Worthington, Carss, Booth, Abbott* — sub Taylor-Fletcher
Peter Jackson's men are a stern test for the improving U's. Halford flicks on a corner and teenager Elokobi heads his first senior goal to reward home pressure. Sub Gary Taylor-Fletcher springs the offside trap and rounds Davison to equalise. Andy Booth and Williams both strike wood.

11 — A BRADFORD C
U's: Davison, Halford, Wetherall(?), Elokobi, White, Stockley, Muirhead^, Richards, Izzet, Yeates*, Iwelumo — subs Cooke/Emanuel/Cadamarteri
Bradford C: Howarth, Wetherall, Taylor, Edghill", Bower, Muirhead^, Crooks, Schumacher, Petta, Windass, Claridge* — subs Cooke/Emanuel/Cadamarteri
City fans barrack their own side during a dull game. United go ahead against the run of play when Halford curls home a 30-yard free-kick, with the keeper's positioning looking faulty. A late City corner is flicked on by Lee Crooks and the former Ipswich winger Bobby Petta heads home.

Matchday grid — matches 12–23

#	V	Date	Opponent	Att	Pos	Res	Pts	HT	FT	Scorers / (opp)	Referee
12	H	1/10	CHESTERFIELD	3,414	16 (6)	L	14	0-1	1-2	Iwelumo 90 / Larkin 25, Hall 49	Ref: R Beeby
13	A	9/10	BLACKPOOL	4,793	13 (9)	W	17	1-0	2-1	Halford 16, 90 / Wright 90	Ref: C Foy
14	H	15/10	BOURNEMOUTH	3,120	15 (9)	L	17	0-0	0-1	Keene 90	Ref: R Booth
15	A	22/10	TRANMERE	6,612	16 (21)	D	18	0-0	0-0	—	Ref: S Mathieson
16	H	29/10	YEOVIL	3,409	13 (12)	W	21	1-1	3-2	Iwelumo 43, 90, Cureton 68 / Bastianini 32, Harrold 51	Ref: M Messias
17	A	12/11	ROTHERHAM	3,715	11 (17)	W	24	0-1	2-1	Barker 55 (og), Iwelumo 85 / Burton 23p	Ref: G Salisbury
18	H	19/11	BLACKPOOL	3,031	8 (22)	W	27	2-0	3-2	Iwelumo 34, 54, Halford 81 / Murphy 67, Wright 90	Ref: G Hegley
19	H	26/11	GILLINGHAM	3,801	7 (21)	W	30	2-0	5-0	Halford 32, 52, Cureton 54, 66, Brown 70	Ref: J Singh
20	A	6/12	HARTLEPOOL	3,375	6 (15)	W	33	0-0	1-0	Cureton 60	Ref: M Dean
21	A	10/12	SWANSEA	13,320	6 (1)	D	34	1-1	1-1	Iwelumo 13 / Robinson 30	Ref: M Jones
22	H	17/12	MK DONS	3,400	4 (22)	W	37	1-0	2-0	Danns 13, Iwelumo 90p	Ref: P Melin
23	A	26/12	SWINDON	5,531	6 (24)	L	37	0-0	0-1	Fallon 90	Ref: K Friend

Line-ups (United / opponent, with substitutes):

12 Chesterfield — Davison, Halford, Chilvers, Elokobi, White*, Watson^, Richards, Williams*, Izzet, Yeates, Iwelumo; subs Danns/Garcia/Stockley. Chesterfield: Roche, Nicholson, Hazell, Blatherwick, Davies, Allott, Niven, Hurst*, Hall, Larkin, Allison; sub Clingan.

13 Blackpool — Davison, Halford, Chilvers, Brown*, White, Watson^, Richards, Danns*, Izzet, Yeates, Iwelumo; subs Richards/Garcia. Blackpool: Pogliacomi, Edwards*^, Butler, McGregor, Clarke, Grayson", Burns, Southern, Wiles, Wright, Vernon"; subs Morris/Doolan/Blinkhorn.

14 Bournemouth — Davison, Halford, Chilvers, Brown, White, Stockley, Watson, Danns, Izzet, Yeates*, Iwelumo; sub Williams. Bournemouth: Stewart, Hart, O'Connor, Gowling, Young, Fol'Shend'n'Stock, Cooper, Surman*, Browning, Hayter^; subs Cooke/Keene/Maher.

15 Tranmere — Davison, Halford, Chilvers, Brown, White, Stockley, Watson, Danns*, Izzet, Yeates*, Iwelumo; sub Cureton. Tranmere: Achterberg, Sharps, Goodison, Linwood, Roberts, Jackson, Rankine", Alston*, Facey, Greenacre^; subs Zola/Davies/O'Leary.

16 Yeovil — Davison, Halford, Chilvers, Brown, White*, Stockley*, Watson, Izzet^, Cureton, Yeates, Iwelumo; subs Garcia/Danns/Duguid. Yeovil: Weale, Jones, Miles*, Amankwaah Skiverton, Davies", Terry, Jevons, Johnson, Bastianini", Harrold; subs Guyett/Lockwood/Gall.

17 Rotherham — Davison, Halford, Chilvers, Brown, White*, Stockley, Watson, Izzet, Danns, Yeates^, Iwelumo; subs Duguid/Garcia. Rotherham: Cutler, Worrell, Barker, Hurst*, Gilchrist, Williamson, McLaren, Mullin, Monkhouse Burton", Butler; subs Hoskins/Newsham.

18 Blackpool — Davison, Halford, Chilvers, Brown, White, Stockley, Watson, Danns*, Cureton*, Yeates^, Iwelumo; subs Izzet/Duguid/Garcia. Blackpool: Pogliacomi, Warrender, Morris, Edwards, Armstrong* Clarke, Harkins^, Southern, Wiles", Murphy, Wright; subs Butler/Doolan/Prendergast.

19 Gillingham — Davison, Bullock, Chilvers, Brown, White, Stockley, Watson, Danns*, Cureton*, Yeates, Iwelumo; subs Izzet/Garcia. Gillingham: Clohessy, Cox, Williams, Johnson, Jarvis, Flynn, Crofts, Smith*, Spiller", Byfield; subs Garcia/Izzet/Duguid, Jackman/Harris.

20 Hartlepool — Davison, Halford, Chilvers, Brown, White, Stockley, Watson, Danns*, Cureton*, Yeates*, Iwelumo; subs Izzet/Duguid/Garcia. Hartlepool: Konstantop' Nelson, Warrender Morris, Armstrong* Clarke, Humphreys Butler*, Sweeney, Williams E McDonald, Trundle; subs Proctor/Clark/Daly.

21 Swansea — Davison, Gueret, Chilvers, Brown, White, Stockley, Watson, Danns, Cureton*, Yeates*, Iwelumo; subs Garcia/Duguid/Izzet. Swansea: Ricketts, Monk, Tate, Britton", Tudor-Jones Martinez, Akinfenwa* Trundle, Robinson"; subs Connor/Goodfellow/Forbes.

22 MK Dons — Davison, Halford, Chilvers, Brown, White, Stockley, Watson, Danns*, Cureton*, Yeates*, Iwelumo; subs Duguid/Garcia. MK Dons: Baker, Mills, McClenahan Morgan, Lewington Chorley !, Quinn^, Small, Mitchell, Smith*, Wiltraham; subs Edds/Rizzo.

23 Swindon — Davison, Evans, Chilvers, Brown, White, Stockley, Watson, Danns*, Garcia, Yeates, Iwelumo; sub Izzet. Swindon: Ifil, Smith, Nicholas, O'Hanlon, McDermott**Mifilinranni Brown, Holgate^, Shakes, Fallon; subs Pook/Bouazza.

Match reports

12 Davison drops a Paul Hall cross and although he blocks Colin Larkin's first effort, he is beaten as the ball runs loose. Elokobi hesitates fatally in another raid, and Hall swoops eagerly. The U's throw men forward but their only success is when Iwelumo fires a 20-yarder in off the bar.

13 Colin Hendry's men are jeered by home fans after Halford collects Izzet's neat chip and hits the first. The U's look sound at the back and it comes as a shock when Tommy Wright fires home on 92 minutes. But within seconds Halford nets a sweet drive from another through-ball.

14 The Cherries get a penalty when James Hayter goes down but the ref changes his mind after consultation. The U's have the majority of the play but cannot score. Iwelumo hits a post late on, then Stephen Cooke gets down the right to set up fellow sub James Keene to scramble a winner.

15 A hard-won point at Prenton Park with Watson and Brown typifying the U's spirit. Iwelumo goes close twice in the second half and Cureton, newly loaned from Swindon, makes an immediate impact. He brings one superb save from John Achterberg and fluffs another goal chance.

16 Argentine Pablo Bastianini heads Lee John's free-kick home. Yeates crosses for Iwelumo to head the equaliser. Matt Harrold slides Yeovil ahead but Cureton squeezes a shot in from an angle. Deep into injury time Yeates' low cross is missed by Cureton but Iwelumo swoops to net.

17 Stockley brings down Martin Butler and Deon Butler slots home the penalty for Mick Harford's struggling side. Shaun Barker tries to clear Watson's cross, but diverts the ball into his own net. Iwelumo bags another last-gasp winner, ramming home after Danns bursts down the left.

18 From a corner, Iwelumo volleys United ahead. Fouled by Peter Clarke, Iwelumo slots in another from the spot. John Murphy heads Simon Grayson's side back into it, but Halford buries a pass from sub Duguid. Tommy Wright nets a late consolation, but the U's remain in control.

19 Halford shoots the U's two up, his second a rocket from 25 yards. Loanee Cureton poaches two more in deadly fashion and Brown rams in the fifth. But for Tony Bullock's heroics it would have been worse for the managerless Gills. It's the U's first run of six straight wins in 17 years.

20 Dean McDonald hits a post and Davison saves well from Thomas Butler. Cureton taps the ball in after Dmitri Konstantopoulos knocks a cross by Yeates into the air. In heavy rain, the U's hold on to equal a club record eight straight wins. Home fans call for boss Martin Scott to be axed.

21 Iwelumo beats the offside-trap to beat Willy Gueret. Brown pushes Lee Trundle on the edge of the box and Andy Robinson curls in the free-kick. A golden chance to beat the league leaders and create a new club record vanishes when Danns' late penalty is superbly saved by Gueret.

22 Confident United start brightly and Danns fires the first past Matt Baker after a fine pass from Watson. Baker keeps the home side at bay with some fine saves. Ben Chorley is sent off for abusive language just after the hour. Baker pulls down Garcia and Iwelumo knocks in the penalty.

23 Teenager Ashan Holgate brings a fine save out of Davison and Rhys Evans does brilliantly to keep out a Yeates free-kick. The stalemate is finally ended in stoppage time when New Zealander Rory Fallon heads in Hameur Bouazza's cross to end United's 12-match unbeaten run.

COCA-COLA LEAGUE 1

Manager: Phil Parkinson

SEASON 2005-06

Column headings: No | Date | Att | Pos | Pt | F-A | H-T | Scorers, Times, and Referees | SQUAD NUMBERS IN USE (Colchester top row / opponents bottom row) | subs used

---

24 — A BRENTFORD — 31/12
Att 6,397 · Pos *5* 3 · Pt 40 · F-A 2-0 · H-T 1-0
Scorers: Yeates 30, 86 — **Ref:** P Walton

- Colchester: Davison, Halford, Chilvers, Brown, White, Elokobi, Watson, Danns*, Cureton^, Yeates^, Iwelumo
- Brentford: Nelson, Tillen, Turner, Sodje, Brooker*, Hutchinson, Tabb, Newman, O'Connor^, Owusu, Campbell
- subs used: Garcia/Izzet/Duguid | Peters^/Gayle/Lewis

A New Year's Eve lunch-time kick-off doesn't suit the off-colour Bees, and Yeates beats a defender before firing a shot in at Stuart Nelson's near post. Lloyd Owusu goes close, hitting a post, but Yeates wraps up the three points late on, after collecting a downfield punt from Davison.

---

25 — H NOTT'M FOREST — 2/1
Att 5,767 · Pos *9* 4 · Pt 43 · F-A 3-1 · H-T 0-0
Scorers: Danns 71, Yeates 90, Garcia 90; Tyson 90 — **Ref:** P Crossley

- Colchester: Davison, White, Chilvers, Brown, Duguid, Brown, Watson, Danns*, Garcia^, Yeates^, Iwelumo
- Nott'm Forest: Gerrard, Breckin, Thompson, Eaden, Morgan, Perch^, Southall, Commons^, Holt, Tyson^, Taylor^
- subs used: Izzet | Bopp/Lester/Gardner

Goal action comes late in the day, Danns cutting in and unleashing a fine shot. U's fans hearts sink when Nathan Tyson slides a through ball past Davison in the last minute, but there's more fun to come. Iwelumo's flick sets up Yeates, then Garcia hits a third with a great solo effort.

---

26 — A WALSALL — 14/1
Att 5,464 · Pos *16* 4 · Pt 46 · F-A 2-0 · H-T 0-0
Scorers: Danns 76, Iwelumo 88 — **Ref:** S Tanner

- Colchester: Davison, White, Chilvers, Brown, Duguid, Brown, Watson, Danns^, Garcia, Yeates, Iwelumo
- Walsall: Murphy, Gerrard, Fox, Roper, James, Pead, Wright, Smith, Leary, Timm^, Constable^
- subs used: Williams/Richards/Izzet | Atieno/Standing

Paul Merson's men are made to pay for missing many chances. The U's take control late on when Danns forces the ball in after Halford flicks on a Watson flag-kick. The victory is assured when Iwelumo replicates the first goal, heading home after Watson and Halford combine again.

---

27 — H BRISTOL CITY — 17/1
Att 4,022 · Pos *20* 2 · Pt 49 · F-A 3-2 · H-T 2-1
Scorers: Williams 27, Danns 45, 61; Murray 2, Stewart 90 — **Ref:** P Armstrong

- Colchester: Davison, White, Chilvers, Brown, Halford^, Baldwin, Watson, Danns*, Williams^, Yeates, Iwelumo
- Bristol City: Basso, Heywood, Carey, Woodman, Noble, Murray, Skuse", Orr, Savage^, Brooker, Cotterill
- subs used: Garcia/Izzet/Thorpe | Brown/Stewart/Russell

Scott Murray's deflected shot is cancelled out by Williams' 20-yarder. Danns, who has just become a father for the first time, fires a cracking goal before the break. He bundles in another before Marcus Stewart knocks in a consolation. The U's have now won 15 of their last 17 games.

---

28 — H PORT VALE — 21/1
Att 4,316 · Pos *14* 1 · Pt 52 · F-A 2-1 · H-T 0-0
Scorers: Garcia 74, 87; Husbands 79p — **Ref:** P Joslin

- Colchester: Davison*, White*, Chilvers, Brown, Halford, Baldwin, Watson, Danns, Williams^, Yeates, Iwelumo
- Port Vale: Goodlad, Tagwell, Fortune, James, Pilkington, Birchall^, Abbey, Husbands, Innes^, Cummins
- subs used: Garcia/Gerken/Thorpe | Constantine/Lowndes/Doherty

Keeper Davison limps off with a hamstring problem. A minute after coming on, sub Garcia scores from an Iwelumo flick. Brown's handball gives Michael Husbands his penalty chance. Garcia wins it from close range. A great day for Essex with the U's now top and Southend second.

---

29 — H BRADFORD C — 4/2
Att 4,503 · Pos *11* 2 · Pt 55 · F-A 3-1 · H-T 1-1
Scorers: Garcia 41, 53, Iwelumo 63; Windass 37 — **Ref:** M Russell

- Colchester: Davison, White, Chilvers, Brown, Halford, Baldwin, Watson, Danns*, Garcia*, Yeates, Iwelumo
- Bradford C: Ricketts, Stewart, Wetherall, Edghill*, Bower, Holloway, Penford, Bridge-Wilk'n, Sch'm'cher, Windass^, Cooke^
- subs used: Williams/King | Wright/Claridge/Cadamarteri

Mark Bower's cross is knocked home by veteran Dean Windass. Halford's clever cross is converted by in-form Aussie Garcia. Richards lofts a ball forward and Garcia heads over keeper Donovan Ricketts. Watson's corner is headed firmly home by Iwelumo to maintain the title chase.

---

30 — H SCUNTHORPE — 7/2
Att 4,416 · Pos *17* 1 · Pt 58 · F-A 1-0 · H-T 1-0
Scorers: Iwelumo 45 — **Ref:** K Wright

- Colchester: Davison, White, Chilvers, Brown, Halford, Baldwin, Watson, Danns, Garcia^, Yeates^, Iwelumo
- Scunthorpe: Evans, Byrne, Rose, Foster, Hinds, Goodwin, Taylor, Johnson^, Sparrow, Sharp, Keogh
- subs used: Williams/Stockley/MacKenzie | Keogh

Brian Laws' side pose more problems than expected and United are relieved when Iwelumo rises high to head home a Halford trade-mark long throw. Richard Hinds misses a great chance and Cleveland Taylor also goes close. Tom Evans blocks a Danns effort in the dying moments.

---

31 — A HUDDERSFIELD — 11/2
Att 13,515 · Pos *5* 2 · Pt 58 · F-A 0-2 · H-T 0-1
Scorers: Worthington 14, Graham 68 — **Ref:** G Salisbury

- Colchester: Davison, White*, Chilvers, Brown, Halford, Richards!, Watson, Danns, Garcia^, Yeates^, Iwelumo
- Huddersfield: Senior, Mirfin, Smith, McIntosh, Clarke N, Collins, Worthington, Booth, Brandon, Graham
- subs used: Baldwin/Williams/Elokobi | Tayl'r-Fletch

After Iwelumo hits the post early on, Gary Fletcher-Taylor's shot is diverted into the net of Jonathan Worthington to give Peter Jackson's men the lead. Richards is red-carded for impeding David Graham and the U's quickly fall two behind. Graham's clinical finish proves a killer blow.

---

32 — H WALSALL — 14/2
Att 3,810 · Pos *21* 2 · Pt 59 · F-A 0-0 · H-T 0-0
Scorers: — **Ref:** P Miller

- Colchester: Davison, Oakes*, Chilvers, Brown, Halford, Baldwin, Watson, Danns, Garcia^, Yeates, Iwelumo
- Walsall: Gerrard, Mills, Roper, Pead, Wright, James^, Smith, Keates, Barrowman^, Nicholls^
- subs used: Williams/Stockley | Demontagnac/Bradley

Maybe the upcoming Chelsea cup-tie has caused the U's to wobble. Failure to win means Southend stay top despite losing tonight to Brentford.

---

33 — A BARNSLEY — 25/2
Att 9,411 · Pos *5* 3 · Pt 59 · F-A 0-1 · H-T 0-0
Scorers: Howard 72 — **Ref:** B Curson

- Colchester: Davison, Elokobi^, Chilvers, Brown, Halford, Baldwin, Watson^, Danns, Garcia, Yeates, Iwelumo
- Barnsley: Colgan, Hassall, Austin, Heck'gbot'n, Kay, Shuker^, Devaney, Howard^, McPhail^, Hayes, Wright
- subs used: Stockley/Williams | Burns/McParland/Reid

United start brightly, but Andy Ritchie's side gradually come into the game. Davison saves well from Brian Howard, and Martin Devaney squanders a good chance. Devaney's cross finds Howard, who knocks the ball in at the second attempt. A late siege fails to yield an equaliser.

---

34 — H SOUTHEND — 4/3
Att 5,920 · Pos *1* 5 · Pt 59 · F-A 0-3 · H-T 0-3
Scorers: Eastwood 11, Maher 21, Wilson 32 — **Ref:** L Mason

- Colchester: Davison, Chilvers, Brown, Halford, Baldwin, Watson, Danns, Garcia, Gutteridge^, Yeates, Iwelumo
- Southend: Flahavan, Jupp, Wilson, Barrett, Sodje, Gower, Guttridge^, Maher, Goater*, Eastwood^, Bradbury
- subs used: Watson/Thorpe | Lawson/Moussa

Steve Tilson's men shock the U's with a heart-breaking three-goal first-half salvo. Luke Guttridge's cross is netted by Freddie Eastwood's firm header. Kevin Maher slots the second after good work by Eastwood. The contest is killed off when Che Wilson slides home from a tight angle.

No		Date		Res	Att	Pos	Pts
35	A	11/3	L	0-1	5,822	6 / 7	59

OLDHAM
Davison · Chilvers · Stockley · Brown · Halford · Duguid · Izzet! · Danns* · Watson · Yeates^ · Iwelumo · Elokobi/Thorpe
Grant · Branston · Swailes · Haining · Edwards · Hughes^ · Wellens · Butcher · Warne · Porter* · Taylor · Hall/Forbes
Butcher 90
Ref: D Drysdale
Izzet blasts an early chance over the bar and Danns hits the woodwork with a superb effort. Near the end Izzet is sent off after a bad tackle on Richie Wellens and moments later Richard Butcher cracks the winner with his left foot. It's now seven without a win for the goal-starved U's.

| 36 | H | 18/3 | L | 1-0 | 3,767 | 5 / 23 | 59 |

SWINDON — Iwelumo 15p
Davison · Chilvers · Baldwin · Brown · Halford · Duguid · Watson · Danns · Thorpe* · Yeates^ · Iwelumo · Izzet/White
Evans · Smith · Jenkins · Nicholas* · Gurney · O'Hanlon · Pook · Whalley* · Brown · Peacock* · Cureton · Benj'n/Comyn-Platt/Roberts
Ref: G Sutton
Thorpe gets his first full game in a bid to boost the attack, but a high number of chances go astray. Keeper Rhys Evans impedes Thorpe and Iwelumo fires in the penalty. Andy Nicholas hits a post and Jack Smith has a header well saved. Relief all round at the first win in nine games.

| 37 | A | 21/3 | D | 0-0 | 4,262 | 5 / 10 | 60 |

DONCASTER
Davison · Chilvers · Baldwin · Brown · Halford · Duguid · Watson · White · Thorpe^ · Yeates^ · Iwelumo* · Vernon/Izzet/Yeates
Blayney · Roberts S · McDaid · Lee · Mulligan · Thornton · Price · Horlock · Guy^ · Coppinger · Roberts N* · Armstrong/McCormack
Ref: M Pike
Rovers come out with all guns blazing and it needs resolute defending to keep them at bay. Busy Davison is the United hero with a remarkable series of fine saves. The U's best chance sees White fire inches wide after picking up a clearance from Jason Price. A point very well-earned.

| 38 | A | 25/3 | D | 0-0 | 4,608 | 4 / 11 | 61 |

SCUNTHORPE
Davison · Richards · Baldwin · Brown · Halford · Duguid · Watson · Danns^ · Thorpe* · Yeates · Iwelumo · Clarke/Izzet
Musselwhite Crosby · Rose · Foster · Stanton · Hinds · Taylor · Sparrow* · Barraclough Torpey · Keogh · Beagrie
Ref: P Taylor
Thorpe is lucky to escape a red card after an apparent head-butt. United battle hard and are denied a late winner by an assistant's flag. Irishman Clarke, on loan from Ipswich, nets on his debut in the 89th minute but the players celebrations cut short by the officials.

| 39 | H | 1/4 | D | 1-1 | 5,635 | 4 / 2 | 62 |

BRENTFORD — Iwelumo 31 / Tabb 6
Davison · Richards · Baldwin · Brown · Halford · Duguid · Watson · Danns · Thorpe* · Yeates · Iwelumo · Clarke
Nelson · Smith · Turner · Sodje · Frampton · Tabb* · Brooker · Newman · Owusu · Gayle" · Willock^ · Pratley/Rankin/Hutchinson
Ref: R Booth
A tense encounter opens with Jay Tabb netting for Martin Allen's men from a Paul Brooker corner. After missing several chances, Duguid crosses for Iwelumo to plant a header in the net. Yeates has a fine game and hits the bar, but the Bees somehow keep out a series of U's efforts.

| 40 | A | 8/4 | L | 0-1 | 22,680 | 4 / 8 | 62 |

NOTT'M FOREST — Perch 72
Davison · Richards" · Baldwin · Brown · Halford · Duguid · Watson · Danns · Vernon* · Yeates^ · Iwelumo · Clarke/Camp^-Ryce/Chilvers
Pederson · Breckin · Curtis · Morgan · Bennett · Perch · Clingan^ · Commons · Holt Ga · Holt Gr* · Tyson · Lester/Thompson
Ref: I Williamson
United field two new loanees, but a tight and evenly contested affair sees defences rule the day. The deadlock is broken luckily when Brown makes a fine tackle on Grant Holt, but sees his clearance cannon into the net off James Perch. Iwelumo volleys a late opportunity over the bar.

| 41 | H | 11/4 | W | 2-0 | 3,916 | 3 / 21 | 65 |

HARTLEPOOL — Danns 83, 90
Davison · Chilvers · Baldwin* · Brown · Halford · Duguid · Watson · Danns · Clarke · Yeates · Iwelumo" · Thorpe/Vernon
Konstantop'Nelson · Clark · Humphreys · Maidens · Bullock · Butler" · Williams D!/Turnbull · Boyd" · Barron/Williams E/Brown
Ref: T Kettle
Relegation-threatened Pool hit the woodwork three times, but struggle after Darren Williams is sent off on the hour mark for his second yellow card. There is great relief and joy for home fans as Danns bullets a header home and then fires into an empty net after a neat last-minute move.

| 42 | A | 15/4 | D | 2-2 | 3,649 | 3 / 15 | 66 |

CHESTERFIELD — Yeates 45, Iwelumo 73 / O'Hara 3, Hall 18p
Davison · Chilvers · Baldwin* · Brown · Halford · Duguid · Watson · Danns · Thorpe^ · Yeates · Iwelumo" · Camp^-Ryce/Clarke/Vernon
Roche · O'Hara · Downes · Picken · Bailey" · Kovacs · Allott · O'Hara · Niven · Hall^ · Larkin" · Allison/Smith/Davies
Ref: E Ilderton
A dreadful start as Jamie O'Hara fires a superb opener from 25 yards and then Paul Hall tucks in a penalty after a foul by Duguid. Parkinson changes his formation and Yeates beats three men to slide a goal back. Duguid finds space on the left and his cross is volleyed in by Iwelumo.

| 43 | H | 17/4 | W | 1-0 | 4,757 | 2 / 17 | 69 |

TRANMERE — Brown 63
Davison · Chilvers · White^ · Brown · Halford · Duguid · Watson · Danns^ · Clarke^ · Yeates · Iwelumo" · Camp^-Ryce/Thorpe/Vernon
Wilson · Sharps · Goodison · Tremarco^ · Roberts · Raven" · Jennings · Alston^ · O'Leary! · Facey · Greenacre · Harrison/McAteer/Davies
Ref: J Singh
A bad tackle on White by loanee Stephen O'Leary produces a red card. The ten men's resistance ends when Jason McAteer hauls down Yeates and Brown powers in the free-kick. With Blackpool netting a late equaliser at Brentford, United move into second as the excitement mounts.

| 44 | A | 22/4 | W | 2-1 | 6,231 | 2 / 16 | 72 |

BOURNEMOUTH — Chilvers 51, Vernon 51 / Cooke 8
Davison · Chilvers · White* · Brown · Halford · Duguid · Watson · Danns* · Vernon* · Yeates* · Iwelumo" · Thorpe/Izzet/Baldwin
Stewart · O'Connor · Broadhurst · Young · Purches" · Fol'Sher'n^ Cooke · Jennings · Browning" · Hayter · Fletcher · Pitman/Hart/Rix
Ref: D Gallagher
Brown's free-kick is headed in by Chilvers at the far post. The Cherries respond quickly, Stephen Cooke surging past Brown and slamming in a fierce shot. United exert plenty of pressure and are rewarded when Blackpool loanee Vernon blasts in his first U's goal from a Duguid cross.

| 45 | H | 29/4 | W | 2-0 | 5,741 | 2 / 20 | 75 |

ROTHERHAM — Barker 29 (og), Yeates 53
Davison · Chilvers · White · Brown · Halford · Duguid · Watson · Danns* · Vernon^ · Yeates* · Iwelumo" · Baldwin/Thorpe/Izzet
Cutler · Worrall · Barker · Hurst · Murdock · Robertson* · Williamson McLaren^ · Mullin · Shaw · Butler · Hoskins/Monkhouse
Ref: P Joslin
A must-win game and U's lay siege to the visiting goal. Danns' cross is headed towards his keeper by Shaun Barker but loops into the net. The crucial second comes when Yeates nets a cracking drive from 15 yards. Third-placed Brentford only draw, so promotion is there for the taking.

| 46 | A | 6/5 | D | 0-0 | 8,785 | 2 / 15 | 76 |

YEOVIL
Davison · Chilvers · White · Baldwin · Halford · Duguid · Watson · Danns* · Vernon^ · Camp^-Ryce*Iwelumo · Izzet/Thorpe
Collis · Cohen · Lockwood · Terry · Milos · Lindegaaul · Skiverton · Rocastle · Davies^ · Poole" · Jevons · Harrold/Williams
Ref: A Mariner
One point will be enough and a large following travels to Somerset. Davison and Brown are declared unfit, but the defence toils brilliantly in a scrappy, tense game. Both sides go close before the final whistle signals a huge party to mark the club's first promotion to the second flight.

Average 3,969
Home 3,969
Away 6,789

COCA-COLA LEAGUE 1 (CUP-TIES)

Manager: Phil Parkinson

SEASON 2005-06

Carling Cup

1 H CARDIFF — 24/8
- Att 1,904 C:21 | Pos 18 | **L 0-2** | H-T 0-2
- Scorers, Times: Purse 31p, Jerome 34. Ref: R Beeby
- U's: Gerken, Halford, Chilvers, Baldwin*, Stockley*, Brown, Danns, Watson^, Izzet, Yeates, Iwelumo
- Cardiff: Alexander, Loovens, Weston, Purse, Barker*, Cooper, Whitley, Koumas, Boland, Jerome^, Lee
- Subs used: Williams/Howell/Elokobi · Parry/Feretti
- Baldwin pushes Jeff Whitley in the back and Darren Purse sends Gerken the wrong way from the spot. Minutes later Alan Lee races clear and sets up Cameron Jerome to round Gerken and sweep into an empty net. A disappointing night for the U's, who fail to trouble Neil Alexander.

FA Cup

1 H LEAMINGTON — 5/12
- Att 3,513 NL | Pos 12 | **W 9-1** | H-T 2-0
- Scorers, Times: H'39, Br 44, Iw 48, Cur^ 60,70, Wat' 63, Davison [Yeates 67, Danns 89, 90] / Adams R 72. Ref: G Lewis
- U's: Davison, Halford, Chilvers, Brown, Duguid, Stockley*, Watson, Izzet, Cureton, Yeates, Iwelumo^
- Leamington: Morris, Tank, Rodman^, Adams R, Gregory, Adams J, Morgan, Blake, Thompson*, Parisi", Howell
- Subs used: Garcia/Danns/Williams · Eden/Kestall/Smith
- After 38 minutes of deadlock the floodgates open. Halford's fine free-kick is the first of nine U's goals in 51 minutes. When 0-7 down, the visitors get arguably the best of the day via Richard Adams' piledriver. Danns nets with the game's last kick to equal a 44-year-old club record.

2 A SHREWSBURY — 3/12
- Att 3,695 2:14 | Pos 7 | **W 2-1** | H-T 1-1
- Scorers, Times: Cureton 23, Iwelumo 50 / Edwards 45. Ref: S Tanner
- U's: Davison, Halford, Chilvers, Brown, Duguid, Stockley*, Watson, Izzet, Cureton*, Yeates*, Iwelumo
- Shrewsbury: Hart, Ashton, Hope, Whitehead, Herd, Smith^, Edwards, Sorel, Tolley, Stallard*, McMenamin
- Subs used: Garcia/Izzet/Duguid · McMenamin Langmead/Darby
- Cureton cracks in a loose ball from 15 yards. The home side's man-of-the-match Dave Edwards levels, sweeping in from close range. Iwelumo grabs a deserved winner, heading in Halford's pin-point cross. The managers Parkinson and Gary Peters clash and are sent from the touchline.

3 A SHEFFIELD UTD — 7/1
- Att 11,820 C:2 | Pos 4 | **W 2-1** | H-T 1-1
- Scorers, Times: Danns 33, Williams 72 / Kabba 5. Ref: A Leake
- U's: Davison, Halford, Baldwin, Brown, White, Duguid, Danns, Garcia*, Yeates, Izzet, Iwelumo
- Sheffield Utd: Barnes, Armstrong, Morgan, Kozluk, Ifill", Quinn*, Nalis, Jagielka, Tonge, Gillespie, Kabba^
- Subs used: Williams · Forte/Haidong/Montgomery
- Neil Warnock rests several regulars and the U's take advantage to outclass the Championship side. Steve Kabba steams in on a rebound to open the scoring early on. Danns lashes in an equaliser from close range, before sub Williams grabs a winner, glancing in a cross from Yeates.

4 H DERBY — 28/1
- Att 5,933 C:18 | Pos 1 | **W 3-1** | H-T 1-0
- Scorers, Times: Danns 44, 52, Garcia 59 / Smith 79. Ref: B Curson
- U's: Gerken, White, Baldwin, Richards, Halford, Duguid, Izzet, Danns, Garcia*, Yeates*, Iwelumo
- Derby: Camp, Hajto, Johnson, Nyatanga, Davies, Idiakez, Bisgaard, Thirlwell, Bolder^, Peschis'ido*, Smith
- Subs used: Stockley/Williams · Holdsworth/Holmes
- Iwelumo hooks on a long throw and Danns slides the ball home. The Rams are no match for in-form U's and Danns fires another after Garcia's effort is blocked. Garcia's downward header is parried by Lee Camp, but Garcia nets the rebound. Tommy Smith pulls one back from the spot.

5 A CHELSEA — 19/2
- Att 41,810 P:1 | Pos 2 | **L 1-3** | H-T 1-1
- Scorers, Times: Carvalho 28 (og) / Ferreira 37, Cole 79, 90. Ref: D Gallagher
- U's: Davison, White, Baldwin, Brown, Halford, Duguid, Danns, Watson, Garcia*, Yeates*, Iwelumo
- Chelsea: Cudicini, Johnson, Huth, Carvalho, Ferreira, Duff", Essien, Maniche^, Wr't-Phillips Diarra^, Drogba, Cole
- Subs used: Chilvers/Williams · Cole J/Lampard/Crespo
- An unforgettable day, made all the better when Garcia's cross is turned into his own net by Ricardo Carvalho. For nine glorious minutes the U's hold a deserved lead, before Ferreira touches in after Damien Duff's corner. Classy goals by Joe Cole bring the U's back down to earth.

Football League Trophy

2 H NORTHAMPTON — 23/12
- Att 1,719 2:5 | Pos 4 | **W 3-2 aet** | H-T 0-1
- Scorers, Times: Elokobi 57, Garcia 90, Danns 101 / Kirk 26, Bojic 67. Ref: C Penton
- U's: Gerken, Stockley, Elokobi^, Baldwin, Richards, Halford^, Izzet^, Danns, Williams, Garcia, Duguid
- Northampton: Poke, Bojic^, Low*, Taylor, Doig, Chambers, Rowson, Hunt', McGleish, Kirk, Mendes"
- Subs used: Iwelumo/Watson/Yeates · Crowe/Galbraith/Jess
- Andy Kirk nets an easy tap-in, but Elokobi levels, his shot squeezing under the body of teenage debutant Michael Poke. Pedj Bojic nets a low shot before Garcia secures a well-deserved victory by hammering home a powerful drive. In extra-time Danns secures a place in...

S QF — MK DONS (A) — 20/12
- Att 2,649 22 | Pos 4 | **W 2-1** | H-T 0-0
- Scorers, Times: Duguid 61, Danns 74 / Mills 56. Ref: K Hill
- U's: Gerken, Baldwin, Elokobi, Stockley, Richards, Williams^, Danns, King*, Duguid, Garcia, Guy^
- MK Dons: Martin, Crooks*, Morgan, Lewington, Mills, Edds, Small", McKoy^, Rizzo, McLeod, Wilbraham
- Subs used: Halford/Danns · Kamara/Quinn/Baldock
- Both teams are much-changed from the league meeting just a few days earlier. Pablo Mills gives the Dons the lead, powerfully heading in a corner. U's skipper Duguid levels minutes later with a fierce shot. Malvin Kamara's weak header falls perfectly for Danns to ram the winner.

S SF — CHELTENHAM (A) — 24/1
- Att 2,243 2:6 | Pos 1 | **W 1-0** | H-T 1-0
- Scorers, Times: Garcia 21. Ref: I Williamson
- U's: Gerken, Stockley, Elokobi, King*, Baldwin, Richards, Izzet, Williams, Garcia*, Duguid, Duguid
- Cheltenham: Higgs, Gill, Bell*, Bird, Caines, Townsend, Melligan^, Finnigan, Spencer, Gillespie, Wilson
- Subs used: White/Guy · Wylde/Armstrong/Odejayi
- A much-changed team tackles John Ward's side for a place in the Southern Final. Duguid's clever curling shot goes just wide. Halford goes close with a powerful run and shot. Garcia breaks the deadlock with a low, raking drive. Unmarked Garcia then misses an easy headed chance.

SF 1 — SWANSEA (A) — 7/3
- Att 7,285 4 | Pos 5 | **L 0-1** | H-T 0-1
- Scorers, Times: Akinfenwa 40. Ref: P Taylor
- U's: Gerken, Stockley, Elokobi, Chilvers, Danns, Williams", Garcia, Watson, Iwelumo, Duguid, Williams^
- Swansea: Gueret, Ricketts", Tate, Britton, Monk, Way, Forbes, McLeod", Watson, Robinson, Akinfenwa
- Subs used: Izzet/Guy/Baldwin · Knight/Martinez/McDonald
- Williams goes agonisingly close with a 25-yard free-kick effort. Iwelumo finds the net, but to United's dismay the goal is ruled out for offside. Ade Akinfenwa holds off challenges and strokes the only goal. Willy Gueret saves bravely when faced with Iwelumo bearing down on goal.

SF H SWANSEA

SF	H	SWANSEA	6	L	1:2	0-0	Danns 46
2	14/3						
	3,236	4					

Britton 52, Knight 56
Ref: P Crossley
(U's lose 1-3 on aggregate)

Line-ups

Baldwin	White*	Brown	Chivers	Watson
Ricketts	Tate	O'Leary^	Monk	Lowe

Gerken	Halford	Danns	Iwelumo	Yeates^	Duguid	Williams/Guy
Gueret	Britton	Tudor-Jones	Akintenwa		Robinson*	Martinez/Knight

Danns' shot is deflected past Willy Gueret, but Kenny Jackett's men level with a well-taken close-range effort by Leon Britton. The Swans clinch their place in the final at Cardiff – against Carlisle – when a right-wing cross causes defensive chaos and Leon Knight swoops to score.

League table

Pos	Team	P	W	D	L	F	A	W	D	L	F	A	Pts
1	Southend	46	13	6	4	37	16	10	7	6	35	27	82
2	COLCHESTER	46	15	4	4	39	21	7	9	7	19	19	79
3	Brentford	46	10	8	5	35	23	10	8	5	37	29	76
4	Huddersfield	46	13	6	4	40	25	6	10	7	32	34	73
5	Barnsley *	46	11	11	1	42	19	7	7	9	25	25	72
6	Swansea	46	11	9	3	42	23	7	8	8	36	32	71
7	Nott'm For	46	14	5	4	40	15	5	7	11	27	37	69
8	Doncaster	46	11	6	6	30	19	9	3	11	25	32	69
9	Bristol City	46	11	7	5	38	22	7	4	12	28	40	65
10	Oldham	46	12	4	7	32	24	6	7	10	26	36	65
11	Bradford C	46	8	9	6	28	25	6	10	7	23	24	61
12	Scunthorpe	46	8	8	7	36	33	7	7	9	32	40	60
13	Port Vale	46	10	5	8	30	26	6	7	10	19	28	60
14	Gillingham	46	13	4	6	31	21	3	8	12	19	43	60
15	Yeovil	46	8	8	7	27	24	7	3	13	27	38	56
16	Chesterfield	46	6	7	10	31	37	8	7	8	32	36	56
17	Bournemouth	46	8	6	9	25	20	7	4	12	24	33	55
18	Tranmere	46	8	5	10	32	20	7	4	12	18	22	54
19	Blackpool	46	8	7	8	33	27	6	4	13	23	37	53
20	Rotherham	46	8	6	9	31	26	5	7	11	21	36	52
21	Hartlepool	46	9	4	10	28	30	4	7	12	16	29	50
22	MK Dons	46	8	8	7	28	25	4	6	13	17	41	50
23	Swindon	46	9	5	9	31	31	2	10	11	15	34	48
24	Walsall	46	7	7	9	27	34	4	7	12	20	36	47
		1104	234	173	145	788	586	145	173	234	586	788	1483

* promoted after play-offs

Odds & ends

Double wins: (4) Blackpool, Hartlepool, Port Vale, Rotherham.
Double losses: (1) Southend.

Won from behind: (6) Bradford C (H), Bristol C (H), Northampton (H, LDV), Rotherham (A), Sheffield Utd (A, FAC), Yeovil (H).
Lost from in-front: (3) Chelsea (A, FAC), Gillingham (A), Swansea (H, LDV).

High spots: Promotion to English football's second tier for the first time.
The memorable display, including taking the lead, at mighty Chelsea.
The mid-season run of form: 20 wins in 22 games.
The thrilling finale in the January win over Nottingham Forest.
Creating a club record nine wins in a row – against Bradford City.
Equalling a 44-year club record with the 9-1 win over Leamington.
The FA Cup giant-killings of Derby and Sheffield United.

Low points: Neil Danns' late missed penalty at table-toppers Swansea.
Being 'doubled' by local rivals Southend – particularly the home beating.
The 'wobble' in February-March: 7 losses and a draw in 8 games.
Failing at the last hurdle to reach the LDV Vans Trophy final at Cardiff.

Player of the Year: Wayne Brown.
Ever-presents (not incl. FLT): (1) Chris Iwelumo.
Hat-tricks for: (0).
Hat-tricks against: (0).
Leading scorer: (19) Chris Iwelumo.

Appearances and Goals

Player	Lge	Sub	LC	Sub	FAC	Sub	FLT	Sub	Lge	LC	FAC	FLT	Tot
Baldwin, Pat	20	5			3		3	1					
Brown, Wayne	38		1		4		2		2		1		3
Campbell-Ryce, Jamal	1	3											
Clarke, Billy	2	4						1					
Chivers, Liam	33	1	1		2	1	2		2				2
Cureton, Jamie	7	1	1		2		4		4		1	2	7
Danns, Neil	38	3	1		4	1	3	1	8			7	15
Davison, Aidan	41		1		4		4						
Duguid, Karl	26	9	1		4	1	5		1				1
Elokobi, George	10	2					4		1			1	2
Garcia, Richard	9	13		1	3	2	4		5		1	2	8
Gerken, Dean	5	2			1		5						
Guy, Jamie		2					2						
Halford, Greg	45		1		5		3		7			1	8
Howell, Dean	1	3					3						
Hunt, Stephen		2					2						
Iwelumo, Chris	46		1		5		5		17			2	19
Izzet, Kemi	19	14	1		2	1	2	1					
King, Robbie		3					3						
Richards, Garry	12	3			1		4					1	1
Stockley, Sam	21	6	1		2	1	4						
Thorpe, Tony	5	9											
Vernon, Scott	4	3					1	1				1	1
Watson, Kevin	43		1		4		2	1					
White, John	32	3	1		4		4	1	1				1
Williams, Gareth	6	12	1		5		1	1	1		1		2
Yeates, Mark	42	2	1		5		4		5		1		6
(own-goals)									4		1		5
27 players used	506	106	11	3	55	11	55	12	58		6	17	81

COCA-COLA CHAMPIONSHIP

Manager: Geraint Williams — SEASON 2006-07

No	Date		Att	Pos	Pt		F-A	H-T	Scorers, Times, and Referees
1	A	BIRMINGHAM 5/8	24,238	21	0	L	1-2	0-1	Garcia 51 / Campbell 30, Bendtner 79 — Ref: K Stroud
2	H	PLYMOUTH 8/8	4,627	21	0	L	0-1	0-1	/ Summerfield 30 — Ref: R Booth
3	H	BARNSLEY 12/8	4,249	22	0	L	1-2	1-0	Halford 42 / Richards 57, Howard 78 — Ref: G Poll
4	A	WEST BROM 19/8	17,509	23	0	L	1-2	0-2	Guy 83 / Ellington 11p, Wallwork 41 — Ref: P Taylor
5	H	DERBY 26/8	4,574	22	3	W	4-3	2-1	Cureton 28, 30, 67, Iwelumo 49p / Lupoli 42, 80, Peschisolido 89 — Ref: P Walton
6	A	BURNLEY 9/9	10,039	20	6	W	2-1	1-0	Watson 26, Iwelumo 54p / Gray 88 — Ref: R Olivier
7	A	LUTON 12/9	7,609	20	7	D	1-1	1-1	Cureton 40 / Parkin 32 — Ref: K Friend
8	H	QP RANGERS 16/9	5,246	16	10	W	2-1	2-0	Iwelumo 9, Garcia 18 / Brown 76 (og) — Ref: A Wiley
9	A	LEICESTER 23/9	22,449	15	11	D	0-0	0-0	Ref: C Oliver
10	H	IPSWICH 29/9	6,065	13	14	W	1-0	1-0	Duguid 9 — Ref: L Probert
11	A	WOLVERHAMPTON 14/10	19,318	13	14	L	0-1	0-0	Bothroyd 51 — Ref: S Mathieson

Match reports

1. A baptism of fire in the Championship. DJ Campbell opens the scoring, but United rally after the break and deserve Garcia's leveller. Cameron Jerome is sent off for fouling Duguid, but Steve Bruce's men are hugely relieved as teenager Nicklas Bendtner rifles in Stephen Kelly's cross.

2. Garcia hits the woodwork with an early thunderbolt, then Duguid has a lob cleared off the line by Hasney Aljofree. Against the run of play debutant Luke Summerfield nets a fine half-volley. Cureton has a goalbound effort nodded off the line by Paul Wotton as the U's press in vain.

3. Graham Poll takes his first game since his much-publicised World Cup cards blunder. The Tykes conjure up a winner, Brian Howard powering home a 25-yard drive. Richardson heads an equaliser from Michael McIndoe's cross. Halford steams in to head Cureton's cross home. Marc

4. During a spell of early pressure Brown fouls John Hartson and Nathan Ellington nets the penalty. Ronnie Wallwork fires his first goal in 19 months and the U's are on the way to their fourth successive loss. Garcia and Richards go close before sub Guy's volley sets up a tense finale.

5. Cureton hits the bar with an overhead kick, but nets a volley from Duguid's throw and then heads in Watson's free-kick. Arturo Lupoli's sweet strike is followed by a foul on Garcia giving Iwelumo a penalty. A fine lob seals Cureton's hat-trick. The U's hang on as Derby pull two back.

6. Against the run of play, a swift counter-attack sees Watson convert a Cureton pass. Izzet is stretchered off, but the U's extend their lead when Iwelumo nets a penalty after Garcia is flattened by John McGreal. Intense Clarets pressure sees Andy Gray scramble a goal from close range.

7. Carlos Edwards' cross is headed in by Sam Parkin to give Mike Newell's men the lead. Cureton levels with a 20-yard drive. Richard Langley is fouled by Izzet, but his penalty hits the bar. For the second away game in four days, plucky United ride their luck and repel intense pressure.

8. Full of confidence, the U's take Rangers apart in the first half. Brown's effort from a corner is blocked but Iwelumo nets the rebound. Duguid heads on and Garcia volleys a smart goal. The U's miss many chances before Marc Nygaard's job beats Gerken and Brown can only help it in.

9. Brown clatters into Chris O'Grady but no penalty is given and United nearly capitalize at the other end when Patrick McCarthy's mistake lets in Cureton. Duguid misses a clear chance when set up by Cureton. Iain Hume gets clear on his own but Davison sprints out to clear the danger.

10. The first league derby between these sides in 49 years and Layer Road is a cauldron of noise. Duguid raises excitement to fever pitch, stabbing home after Cureton's cross is parried. Jon Macken bundles the ball home but the effort is ruled out. Loyal Duguid gives a real captain's display.

11. The curse of the Manager of the Month award strikes Williams with the first defeat in seven games. Jay Bothroyd nips in to steer home Rohan Ricketts' free-kick. Bothroyd later hits a post with his own 25-yard free-kick. United could have gained a draw but their strikers are out of luck.

Squad numbers in use / subs used

(U's line-up, with subs used, then opposition line-up in italics with subs)

1. Davison, Baldwin, Halford, Brown, Jackson, Watson, Duguid, Izzet^, Garcia^, Cureton" — subs: Iwelumo/White/Guy
Taylor, Tebily, N'Gotty, Kelly, Dunn, Clemence*, Danns, Johnson, Campbell*, Forssell" — Larsson/Bendtner/Jerome!

2. Davison, Baldwin^, Halford, Brown, Jackson, Watson, Duguid, Izzet*, Garcia, Cureton — subs: Iwelumo/Richards
McCormick, Doumbe, Aljofree, Connolly, Summerfield"d, Norris, Capaldi", Wotton, Hodges, Chadwick" — Ebanks-Blake/Sawyer/Djord'c

3. Davison, Richards, Halford, Brown, Jackson*, Watson, Duguid, Izzet, Garcia, Cureton^ — subs: Iwelumo/Guy
Colgan, Togwell", Reid, Hassell, Heck'gbor'm, Devaney, Kay, M'Indoe, Howard, Richards" — Wright/Wroe/Healy

4. Davison, Halford, Brown, Richards*, Izzet^, Watson, Duguid, Iwelumo, Garcia, Cureton — subs: Baldwin/Guy
Zuberbuhler, Robinson, Watson, Wallwork", Pdtry, Quashie, Greening, Ellington", Gera^, Hartson — Carter/Chaplow/Albrechtson

5. Davison, Baldwin, Halford, Brown, Iwelumo*, Watson, Duguid, Izzet, Garcia, Cureton" — subs: Guy/White
Camp, Leacock, Johnson M, Nyatanga, Idiakez*, Barnes, Bisgaard^, Howard, Lupoli, Smith R* — Smith T/Johnson S/Pesch'do

6. Davison, Halford, Brown, Barker, Watson, Duguid, Izzet*, Iwelumo, Garcia, Cureton^ — subs: White/McLeod
Jensen, Sinclair", Harley, McGreal, Thomas, Mahon, O'Connor, Hyde, Jones*, Gray, Lafferty — Noel-Williams/Elliott/Duff

7. Davison, Halford, Brown, Barker, Watson, Duguid, Izzet^, Iwelumo^, Garcia^, Cureton" — subs: McLeod/Guy
Beresford, Foley, Davis, Barnett, Heikkinen, Langley, Robinson, Edwards, Emanuel, Parkin, Vine — Vine

8. Gerken, Baldwin, Barker, Brown, Izzet, Watson, Duguid, Iwelumo, Garcia, Cureton" — subs: McLeod
Cole, Rehman, Stewart, Milanese, Rose, Ward, Baidoo, Birchan^, Jones*, Nygaard", Cureton — Czerkas/Donnelly

9. Davison, Baldwin, Barker*, Brown, Izzet, Watson, Duguid, Iwelumo, Garcia, Cureton — subs: Barker
Logan, Johansson, Kenton^, McCarthy, Wesolowski, Johnson, Hughes^, Porter, O'Grady*, Fryatt — Low/Stearman/Hume

10. Davison, Baldwin, Barker, Brown, Izzet, Watson, Duguid, Iwelumo, Garcia, Cureton — subs: Garcia
Price, Harding, DeVos, Naylor, Sito, Legwinski, Currie, Walton^, Noble, Macken*, Lee — Lee/Clarke/Bowditch

11. Davison, Halford, Brown, Barker, Izzet, Watson, Duguid, Iwelumo", Garcia, Cureton" — subs: McLeod/Guy/Jackson
Murray, Clapham, Breen, Craddock, Edwards, Olofinjana, Henry, Potter, Ricketts*, Johnson", Bothroyd^ — Clarke/Davies/Gobern

Match-by-match record (matches 12–23)

No	Venue	Opponent	Date	Col U pos	Result	Pts	Att	Opp pos	HT	FT	Referee
12	H	SHEFFIELD WED	18/10	10	W	17	5,097	21	1-0	4-0	R Beeby
13	A	COVENTRY	23/10	14	L	17	16,178	10	0-1	1-2	M Pike
14	H	SOUTHAMPTON	28/10	10	W	20	5,893	11	1-0	2-0	D Whitestone
15	A	NORWICH	31/10	10	D	21	25,065	16	0-0	1-1	D Gallagher
16	H	CARDIFF	2/11	9	W	24	5,393	1	0-0	3-1	J Moss
17	A	LEEDS	11/11	11	L	24	17,678	22	0-1	0-3	M Jones
18	A	SUNDERLAND	18/11	13	L	24	25,197	15	0-1	1-3	A Hall
19	H	SOUTHEND	25/11	11	W	27	5,954	24	0-0	3-0	S Bennett
20	H	HULL	28/11	7	W	30	5,373	23	1-1	5-1	P Miller
21	A	CARDIFF	2/12	10	D	31	13,512	3	0-0	0-0	M Pike
22	A	CRYSTAL PALACE	9/12	8	W	34	16,762	17	0-0	3-1	R Lewis
23	H	STOKE	16/12	6	W	37	5,345	7	2-0	3-0	K Wright

12 — H SHEFFIELD WED (18/10)
Scorers: Cureton 28, Halford 56, Iwelumo 61, [Duguid 83]

Colchester U: Davison, Halford", Barker, Brown, Baldwin, Izzet, Watson, Duguid, Iwelumo, Garcia*, Cureton^. Subs: McLeod/Guy/White.
Sheffield Wed: Jones, Hills, Boughera, Bullen*, Simek, Coughlan, Small, Folly, O'Brien, MacLean, Tudgay". Subs: Lunt/Burton/Talbot.

Cureton lobs the first goal after chasing a long pass. United dominate throughout apart from one bad miss by Steve MacLean. Halford nets a stunner from 30 yards. Iwelumo lashes in a through ball from the edge of the area. Duguid caps a tremendous night by cracking in a fine fourth.

13 — A COVENTRY (23/10)
Scorers: Guy 85. Coventry: John 45, Doyle 69

Colchester U: Davison, Halford, Barker, Brown, Baldwin, Izzet, Watson*, Duguid, Iwelumo", Garcia*, Cureton. Subs: Jackson/McLeod/Guy.
Coventry: Marshall, Ward, Duffy, Page, Clarke, Cameron", Hughes, Doyle, McKenzie", John*, Kyle. Subs: Tabb/Hutchison/Birchall.

Colin Cameron and Stern John combine well for the latter to stroke the ball past Davison. Michael Doyle snaps up his first goal in 18 months after John sets him up. Cureton goes close with a 25-yard drive before sub Guy pulls one back and the Sky Blues are left hanging on nervously.

14 — H SOUTHAMPTON (28/10)
Scorers: McLeod 3, Cureton 90

Colchester U: Davison, Halford, Barker, Brown, Baldwin, Izzet, Jackson, Duguid, Iwelumo, McLeod*, Cureton^. Subs: Jones.
Southampton: Davis, Bale, Lundekvam, Baird, Viafara*, Idiakez, Wright, Surman^, Dyer, Jones, Rasiak". Subs: Licka/Skacel/Wright Phillips.

Visiting manager George Burley receives plenty of stick on his return to Layer Road. McLeod ghosts in at the far post to net Cureton's early cross. Saints pressure comes to nothing and a loud penalty appeal is turned down. Late on, Cureton converts a long ball to settle the outcome.

15 — A NORWICH (31/10)
Scorers: Cureton 53. Norwich: Etuhu 72

Colchester U: Davison, Halford, Barker, Brown, Baldwin, Izzet, Jackson, Duguid, Iwelumo, Cureton^. Subs: Jones/Guy.
Norwich: Gallacher, Drury, Shackell, Doherty*, Colin, Robinson, Eagle^, Etuhu, Safri", Huckerby, Earnshaw. Subs: Fleming/Dublin/Hughes.

Iwelumo clatters into the keeper and is shown a yellow card. Jackson has a shot blocked but the ball finds ex-Canary Cureton who blasts it in. Darren Huckerby supplies Dickson Etuhu, who fires a 25-yard drive past Davison. Sub Dion Dublin goes close with a header just over the bar.

16 — H CARDIFF (2/11)
Scorers: McLeod 49, Guy 84, Cureton 90p. Cardiff: Chopra 66

Colchester U: Davison, Halford, Elokobi, Brown, Baldwin, Izzet, Jackson, Duguid, Iwelumo^, McLeod*, Cureton. Subs: Guy/Flood/Johnson/Kamara.
Cardiff: Alexander, Loovens^, McNaughton/Chambers, Purse, Parry", Scimeca, Ledley*, Chopra, Campbell. Subs: Flood/Johnson/Kamara.

Jackson slides a pass for McLeod who makes no mistake. Michael Chopra is on hand to sweep into an empty net for the leaders. Sub Guy shrugs off Darren Purse to net a low shot. In stoppage time Richie Jones is fouled by Stephen McPhail, who is sent off and the penalty netted.

17 — A LEEDS (11/11)
Leeds: Blake 36, 53, Cresswell 48

Colchester U: Davison, White*, Barker, Brown, Baldwin, Izzet, Jackson, Duguid, Iwelumo^, McLeod", Cureton^. Subs: Jones/Guy.
Leeds: Stack, Heath, Kilgallon, Foxe, Crainey, Lewis^, Derry, Blake, Douglas, Cresswell", Horsfield*. Subs: Moore/Westlake/Beckford.

The first ever league meeting with Leeds, and Dennis Wise's men go ahead when Robbie Blake shoots home Shaun Derry's pass. Richard Cresswell heads in Eddie Lewis' centre and Blake coolly chips in a penalty after White fouls Creswell. Cureton nets but the effort is ruled out.

18 — A SUNDERLAND (18/11)
Scorers: Iwelumo 79. Sunderland: Elliott 45, 53, Connolly 90

Colchester U: Davison, White^, Barker, Brown, Baldwin, Izzet, Jackson, Duguid, Iwelumo", Guy^, Cureton. Subs: Jones/Iwelumo.
Sunderland: Ward, Nyatanga, Varga, Leadbitter", Miller, Wallace^, Collins, Whitehead, Yorke, Elliott, Brown*. Subs: Connolly/Hysen/Kavanagh.

Sunderland are fast improving under Roy Keane and Stephen Elliott swivels to shoot them ahead. Elliott taps in the second after a well-worked move. Sub Iwelumo nets from close in from Halford's cross. Home nerves are settled as David Connolly converts Graham Kavanagh's pass.

19 — H SOUTHEND (25/11)
Scorers: Halford 68, Baldwin 74, Cureton 85

Colchester U: Davison, Halford, Barker!, Brown, Baldwin, Izzet*, Jackson, Duguid, Iwelumo*, McLeod, Cureton. Subs: Watson/Jones/Guy.
Southend: Flahavan, Francis, Prior, Sodje, Hammell, Camp", Bryce, McCormack^, Maher!, Gower!, Harrold*. Subs: Bradbury/Riera/Hooper.

An intense derby sees Kevin Maher red-carded for leaving Duguid on the floor. Mark Gower trips Duguid and departs too. Halford runs 50 yards before crashing in a fine goal. Baldwin scores after a rebound off the bar. Barker is sent off before Cureton sweeps in United's third goal.

20 — H HULL (28/11)
Scorers: Iwelumo 19, 54, 66, 79, Cureton 57. Hull: Forster 16

Colchester U: Davison, Halford, Barker, Brown, Baldwin, Izzet, Jackson, Duguid, Iwelumo^, McLeod*, Cureton. Subs: Watson/Ephraim/Guy.
Hull: Myhill, Ricketts, Turner, Coles, Delaney, Welsh", Livermore, Marney, Elliott, Forster, Fagan. Subs: Barmby/France.

Phil Parkinson endures a miserable return, despite Nicky Forster bundling Hull ahead. After this they are blown away, Iwelumo bagging four goals. He nets a header, a penalty and a shot on the turn. After his fourth he is subbed to a huge ovation. He also supplies Cureton for the other.

21 — A CARDIFF (2/12)

Colchester U: Gerken, Halford, Elokobi, Brown, Baldwin, Izzet, Jackson", Duguid, Iwelumo^, Watson*, Garcia^. Subs: Iwelumo/Cureton.
Cardiff: Alexander, McNaughton/Wright, Johnson, Purse, Parry, Scimeca, Ledley, Hughes, McAnuff, Watson*, Chopra. Subs: Thompson*/Campbell/Cooper.

Gerken superbly tips over a Ricardo Scimeca piledriver. The U's look dangerous on the break and Duguid goes close with a low drive. Watson clears a Roger Johnson header off the line. Cureton just fails to reach a cross by Guy. City are left hanging on for one point by the final whistle.

22 — A CRYSTAL PALACE (9/12)
Scorers: Duguid 63, Garcia 70, Iwelumo 90p. Palace: Morrison 87

Colchester U: Gerken, Halford, Barker, Brown, Baldwin, Izzet, Watson, Duguid, Iwelumo", Garcia*, Cureton. Subs: Soares/Morrison/Kuqi".
Crystal Palace: Turner*, Granville, Ward, Hudson, Lawrence, Hughes, McAnuff, Watson*, Kamara^, Chopra, Morrison. Subs: Flinders/Green/Scowcroft.

Palace look stronger early on, but lose keeper Iain Turner with a leg injury. Cureton's cross clips the bar and Duguid forces it home. Garcia makes it two with a cracking shot. Clinton Morrison nets a header but then Mark Hudson pulls down Garcia and Iwelumo converts the penalty.

23 — H STOKE (16/12)
Scorers: Cureton 2, 17, Garcia 63

Colchester U: Gerken, Halford, Barker, Brown, Baldwin, Izzet, Watson^, Duguid, Garcia^, Iwelumo, Cureton. Subs: Iwelumo/Ephraim/Jackson/Guy.
Stoke: Simonsen, Duberry, Higginbotham/Hoekstens, Hill, Brammer", Lawrence, Russell", Fuller, Sidibe", Hendrie, Fuller. Subs: Berger/Pericard/Eustace.

Stoke's long run of not conceding is ended after 75 seconds as Cureton's deflected shot loops in. Garcia helps Cureton add a second from eight yards. Ricardo Fuller twice misses badly before Garcia heads in Barker's cross for a killer third goal. Layer Road has become a real fortress.

COCA-COLA CHAMPIONSHIP   Manager: Geraint Williams   SEASON 2006-07

Column key: No · Date (venue/opponent) · Att · Pos · Pt · F-A · H-T · Scorers, Times, and Referees · SQUAD NUMBERS IN USE · subs used

---

24 — A PRESTON, 23/12
Att 14,225 · Pos 8 · Pt 37 · L · F-A 0-1 · H-T 0-1
Scorers, Times: Nugent 33. Ref: M Halsey

U's: Gerken, Halford, Barker, Brown, Baldwin, Izzet", Watson, Duguid*, Garcia, Iwelumo^, Cureton — subs used: Jackson/Guy/Ephraim
Preston (2): Nash, Pugh, Chilvers, St Ledger, Hill, Alexander, McKenna, Whaley, Sedgwick, Nugent*, Dichio^ — subs used: Miller/Neal/Wilson

Duguid collides with Carlo Nash and a post in the first minute and is taken off with an eye injury. Matt Hill's cross is headed down by Danny Dichio and David Nugent arrows a shot into the net. Nugent later performs a blatant dive and, having been booked, is lucky to stay on the field.

---

25 — H LUTON, 26/12
Att 5,427 · Pos 7 · Pt 40 · W · F-A 4-1 · H-T 2-0
Scorers, Times: Mcleod 23, Iwelumo 41, 65, Garcia 59, Vine 85p. Ref: P Crossley

U's: Gerken, Halford, Barker, Brown, Baldwin, Izzet, Watson, McLeod*, Garcia, Iwelumo^, Cureton^ — subs used: Jackson/Ephraim/Guy
Luton (19): Kiely, Heikkinen, Coyne, Barnett, Foley, Emanuel^, Morgan, Brkovic, Bell, Vine — subs used: Feeney/Davis

The U's give Luton a lesson in finishing in an otherwise even match. McLeod nods in an Izzet cross, before Iwelumo volleys a second. Garcia stretches to divert home a Watson free-kick and Iwelumo heads the fourth. Garcia pushes Chris Coyne and Rowan Vine fires in the penalty.

---

26 — H WOLVERHAMPTON, 30/12
Att 5,893 · Pos 6 · Pt 43 · W · F-A 2-1 · H-T 2-0
Scorers, Times: Cureton 4, Iwelumo 45, Collins 90. Ref: R Beeby

U's: Gerken, Halford, Barker, Brown, Baldwin, Izzet, Watson, McLeod*, Garcia, Iwelumo^, Cureton — subs used: Guy/Duguid
Wolverhampton (10): Murray, Breen, Collins, Little, McNamara^, McIndoe, Olofinjana*, Henry, Potter, Ricketts*, Clarke — subs used: Davies/Clapham/Edwards

Cureton is fouled by Neil Collins and cracks in the free-kick himself. Iwelumo takes Gerken's clearance and drives the ball past Matt Murray. The 11th home win in a row sends the U's into the new year at an all-time peak of sixth place. Collins nets a late consolation from close-range.

---

27 — A QP RANGERS, 1/1
Att 11,319 · Pos 6 · Pt 43 · L · F-A 0-1 · H-T 0-1
Scorers, Times: Jones 36. Ref: P Walton

U's: Gerken, Halford, Barker, Brown, Baldwin^, Izzet^, Watson, McLeod*, Garcia, Iwelumo, Cureton — subs used: Jackson/Ephraim/Guy
QP Rangers (20): Royce, Bignot, Kanyuka, Stewart, Mancienne, Lomas, Cook, Ward^, Blackstock, Jones*, Gallen — subs used: Baidoo/Furlong

A fine cross by danger-man Lee Cook finds Ray Jones, who loops a header into the far corner of the net. McLeod sends an inviting ball across the face of goal, but nobody is able to reach it. Gerken makes a spectacular save from Kevin Gallen. Jackson heads a good opportunity wide.

---

28 — H LEICESTER, 13/1
Att 5,915 · Pos 6 · Pt 44 · D · F-A 1-1 · H-T 0-1
Scorers, Times: Iwelumo 48p, Hume 19. Ref: D McDermid

U's: Gerken, Halford, Barker, Brown, Baldwin, Izzet, Watson, McLeod*, Garcia, Iwelumo, Cureton* — subs used: Ephraim
Leicester (18): Henderson, McCarthy, Kisnorbo, Maybury, McAuley, Williams, Hughes, Tiatto, Porter, Hume, Fryatt* — subs used: Cadamarteri

Matt Fryatt's pass sets up Iain Hume to beat Gerken. The referee, in his first Championship fixture, horrifies City by awarding a penalty for a push on Iwelumo by Patrick McCarthy, which is converted by Iwelumo.

---

29 — A IPSWICH, 20/1
Att 28,355 · Pos 8 · Pt 44 · L · F-A 2-3 · H-T 1-1
Scorers, Times: Duguid 15, Iwelumo 90p, Lee 31p, Legwinksi 56, Haynes 82. Ref: G Laws

U's: Gerken, Halford, Barker, Brown, Baldwin, Izzet^, Richards*, Ephraim^, Garcia, Iwelumo, Cureton* — subs used: Guy/Jackson/White
Ipswich (15): Price, Harding, Wright!, Bruce, Naylor, Peters, Williams, Roberts*, Legwinski, Clarke^, Lee* — subs used: Haynes/O'Callaghan/Richards

A huge crowd for a pulsating derby. Duguid nets from an Ephraim pass, but Richards' foul on Lee allows Town to level. Sylvain Legwinksi heads home and sub Danny Haynes' deft chip makes it three. David Wright is red-carded for the handball that gives the U's a late consolation.

---

30 — H PRESTON, 30/1
Att 5,085 · Pos 8 · Pt 47 · W · F-A 1-0 · H-T 0-0
Scorers, Times: Richards 67. Ref: C Foy

U's: Gerken, Halford, Barker, Brown, Baldwin, Izzet, Watson, Duguid, Garcia, Iwelumo, Cureton* — subs used: Richards/Guy
Preston (3): Lonergan, Pugh, Wilson, Chilvers, Hill^, Alexander, McKenna, Neal*, Sedgwick, Ricketts, Nugent — subs used: Whaley/Omerod

With Halford sold to Reading for a club record £2.5 million just before kick-off, Manchester City loanee Matthew Mills debuts for the U's. He is subbed by local product Richards and just moments later the latter scores his first senior goal, rising to head a winner from Watson's corner.

---

31 — H BIRMINGHAM, 3/2
Att 5,918 · Pos 9 · Pt 48 · D · F-A 1-1 · H-T 0-0
Scorers, Times: Izzet 55, Clemence 66. Ref: K Woolmer

U's: Gerken, White, Barker, Brown, Baldwin, Izzet*, Watson, Duguid, Jackson, Iwelumo, Cureton — subs used: Ephraim
Birmingham (4): Doyle, Taylor, N'Gotty, Jaidi, Sadler, Muamba^, Clemence, Johnson, Jerome", Vine" — subs used: McSheffrey/Bendtner/Larsson/Campbell

Steve Bruce's title challengers fall behind when Cureton's 20-yard drive beats Colin Doyle but rebounds off a post, Izzet reacting first to net the rebound. Gerken saves superbly from a Radhi Jaidi header, but from the resulting corner-kick Stephen Clemence heads home an equaliser.

---

32 — A BARNSLEY, 10/2
Att 11,192 · Pos 8 · Pt 51 · W · F-A 3-0 · H-T 2-0
Scorers, Times: Duguid 3, Cureton 10, Ephraim 83. Ref: C Webster

U's: Gerken, White, Barker, Brown, Baldwin, Izzet, Watson, Duguid, Jackson, Iwelumo^, Cureton* — subs used: Garcia/Ephraim
Barnsley (22): Colgan, Reid P, Eckersley, Hassell, Atkinson, McCann, Devaney, Mattis", Howard, Rajizi, Richards^ — subs used: Reid K/Ferenczi

Adam Eckersley fluffs an intended back-pass and Duguid nets an easy early goal. Watson cuts back a fine ball for Cureton to drive home the second. Jackson hits the bar twice, with a dipping shot and then a header, before sub Ephraim evades several tackles to drill in from 15 yards.

---

33 — H WEST BROM, 13/2
Att 5,611 · Pos 8 · Pt 51 · L · F-A 1-2 · H-T 0-0
Scorers, Times: Jackson 55, McShane 51, Kamara 52. Ref: M Atkinson

U's: Gerken, White*, Barker, Brown, Baldwin, Izzet*, Watson, Duguid, Jackson, Iwelumo, Cureton — subs used: Garcia/McLeod
West Brom (2): Kiely, Clement, Robinson, Davies, McShane, Chaplow, Koren, Carter, Kamara, Gera, Hartson* — subs used: MacDonald

Tony Mowbray's men go ahead as Paul McShane converts a near-post corner by Robert Koren. A minute later Diomansy Kamara surges past Mills and drives in a fine solo goal. Jackson pulls one back with a header, but Albion deserve to inflict the U's first home defeat in six months.

---

34 — A PLYMOUTH, 20/2
Att 12,895 · Pos 9 · Pt 51 · L · F-A 0-3 · H-T 0-1
Scorers, Times: Norris 12, Ebanks-Blake 59p, Gosling 67. Ref: R Olivier

U's: Gerken, White*, Barker, Brown, Baldwin, Izzet*, Watson, Duguid, Jackson, Garcia^, Iwelumo", Cureton — subs used: Ephraim/McLeod/Guy
Plymouth (11): McCormick, Timar, Sawyer, Connolly, Seip, Norris, Gosling^, Nalis, Ebanks-Blake*, Gallen", Sinclair — subs used: Fallon/Halmosi/Summerfield

Ian Holloway's FA Cup quarter-finalists strike first when David Norris surges forward to blast a fierce shot past Gerken. Brown hauls down Sylvan Ebanks-Blake, who gets up to convert the penalty. Teenager Dan Gosling puts the result beyond doubt with a cool piece of finishing.

35 — BURNLEY (H) 24/2
League: 10th (opp 16th) — Drawn — 52 pts · FT 0-0 (HT 0-0) · Att 4,934
Colchester: Gerken, Duguid, Brown, Barker, Mills, Watson, Izzet, McLeod*, Garcia, Iwelumo^, Cureton
Burnley: Coyne, McGreal, Caldwell, Thomas*, O'Connor, McCann", Gudjonsson, Elliott^, Akinbiyi, Gray, Lafferty
Subs: Ephraim/Guy · Duff/Branch/Harley
Ref: C Boyeson
United create more chances, but Steve Cotterill's side force Gerken into a number of saves. Without a win in 14 games, the Clarets go close when Ade Akinbiy's fierce drive is superbly saved. Garcia misses the best chance of all, heading over from close range from a Barker cross.

36 — DERBY (A) 2/3
League: 10th (opp 1st) — Lost — 52 pts · FT 1-5 (HT 0-3) · Att 26,704
Jackson 56 (How'd 62p, Barker 69 (og)) // Jones 2, Lupoli 20, Barnes 30
Colchester: Gerken, White", Brown, Barker, Mills, Watson^, Duguid, Jackson, Izzet, Garcia, Cureton*
Derby: Bywater, Moore, Johnson*, McFeely, Edworthy, Oakley", Teale, Jones, Barnes, Howard, Lupoli^
Subs: Iwelumo/Ephraim/Baldwin · Mears/Fagan/Macken
Ref: M Jones
Williams returns to his old club, but the U's are outgunned in front of live TV cameras. David Jones volleys in Steve Howard's cross and then Giles Barnes' pass is smashed in by Arturo Lupoli. Barnes drills a third before Jackson heads a consolation. Jones' shot ricochets in off Barker.

37 — COVENTRY (H) 10/3
League: 10th (opp 14th) — Drawn — 53 pts · FT 0-0 (HT 0-0) · Att 5,453
Colchester: Gerken, Duguid, Brown, Barker, Baldwin, Watson, Izzet, McLeod*, Garcia, Iwelumo, Cureton
Coventry: Marshall, Hall, Ward, Hawkins, Virgo, Osbourne, Tabb, Hughes, Doyle, Adebola, McKenzie*
Subs: Ephraim · Mifsud
Ref: K Stroud
Stephen Hughes produces the best effort of the game, forcing Gerken to make a fine save from his powerful shot. Iain Dowie's outfit claim a penalty when Duguid tangles with Jay Tabb, but Mr Stroud is not impressed. Frustrated United fail to give keeper Andy Marshall much to do.

38 — SHEFFIELD WED (A) 13/3
League: 10th (opp 12th) — Lost — 53 pts · FT 0-2 (HT 0-2) · Att 18,752
Simek 27, Mills 35 (og)
Colchester: Gerken, Duguid, Brown, Mills, Elokobi, Watson", Izzet, McLeod*, Garcia, Iwelumo, Cureton^
Sheffield Wed: Turner, Wood, Gilbert^, Bullen, Simek, Lunt, Brunt, Whelan", MacLean", Tudgay, Burton
Subs: Ephraim · Foly/Spurr/Lekej
Ref: D Gallagher
Williams tries a change of tactics, but a quiet game ends with defeat by two soft goals. American defender Frank Simek sees his pass ricochet off McLeod to set him up perfectly to drive past Gerken. The crucial second arrives as a Chris Brunt corner is headed into his own net by Mills.

39 — SOUTHAMPTON (A) 16/3
League: 10th (opp 8th) — Won — 56 pts · FT 2-1 (HT 2-1) · Att 18,736
Cureton 4, 27; Saganowksi 26
Colchester: Gerken, White*, Brown, Barker, Baldwin, Watson, Izzet, Jackson, Garcia, Iwelumo, Cureton*
Southampton: Bialkowski, Pele, Guthrie, Bale, Lundekvam, Baird", Wright, Surman, Dyer", Wr't-Phillips, Sagan'wksi^
Subs: Mills/Guy · Viafara/Rasiak/Best
Ref: T Kettle
United's bid for a play-off place gets back on track as Cureton swoops early to turn in an Iwelumo cross. Nathan Dyer and Andrew Surman combine to set up Marek Saganowski for the equaliser, but within a minute St Mary's is stunned as Cureton finds space to volley a fine goal.

40 — NORWICH (H) 31/3
League: 10th (opp 16th) — Won — 59 pts · FT 3-0 (HT 3-0) · Att 5,851
Cureton 52, Garcia 64, Iwelumo 73
Colchester: Gerken, White*, Brown, Barker, Baldwin, Watson, Izzet, Jackson, Garcia, Iwelumo*, Cureton*
Norwich: Warner, Shackell, Dohrty, Hunt, Croft", Safri, Lappin, Dublin, Huckerby, Martin, Chadwick
Subs: Guy/Ephraim
Ref: I Williamson
Iwelumo hits the bar as the U's take the game by the scruff of the neck. Cureton breaks the deadlock, turning in Iwelumo's nod-down from a Duguid cross. Jackson's cross reaches Garcia, who bags the second. Andrew Hughes' slip allows Iwelumo in to seal a great afternoon's work.

41 — SOUTHEND (A) 6/4
League: 9th (opp 23rd) — Won — 62 pts · FT 3-0 (HT 1-0) · Att 10,552
Cureton 1, 63, 79
Colchester: Gerken, White^, Brown, Barker, Baldwin, Watson, Izzet, Jackson*, Garcia", Iwelumo*, Cureton"
Southend: Flahavan, Hammell*, Clarke, Hunt, Sodje, McCormack, Foran", Gower, Maher, Bradbury, Eastwood
Subs: Guy/Ephraim/White · Campbell-Ryce/Harrold
Ref: K Friend
Good Friday lunchtime fun in the sun, covered live by Sky TV. Efe Sodje's slack header is neatly turned in by an alert Cureton in the opening seconds. Cureton's second is a 25-yarder into the corner. He completes a wonderful hat-trick, darting in to clip the ball past Daryl Flahavan.

42 — LEEDS (H) 9/4
League: 9th (opp 22nd) — Won — 65 pts · FT 2-1 (HT 0-0) · Att 5,916
Iwelumo 82, Cureton 90; Lewis 53
Colchester: Gerken, Duguid, Brown, Barker, Baldwin, Watson*, Izzet, McLeod*, Garcia^, Iwelumo, Cureton
Leeds: Ankergren, Michalik, Gray, Heath, Rui Marques, Lewis, Kishishev, Douglas !, Thompson, Healy*, Kandol, Blake
Subs: Ephraim/Guy
Ref: A Wiley
Eddie Lewis fires Dennis Wise's troubled side ahead and they look set to nick a win. A storming finish sees Iwelumo glance home Duguid's free-kick, and then in stoppage time Ephraim sends Cureton through to slot home a jubilant winner. Jonathon Douglas is red-carded for dissent.

43 — HULL (A) 14/4
League: 9th (opp 21st) — Drawn — 66 pts · FT 1-1 (HT 0-1) · Att 20,887
Cureton 63; Forster 25
Colchester: Gerken, Duguid, Brown, Barker, Baldwin, Ephraim*, Izzet, Jackson, Garcia, Iwelumo, Cureton*
Hull: Myhill, Ricketts, Dawson, Turner, Delaney, Livermore*, Parlour, Ashbee, Elliott^, Forster, Windass"
Subs: McLeod/Guy · Pelter/Parkin/McPhee
Ref: N Miller
A big crowd at the KC Stadium hopes to see Hull pull clear of the drop zone, but the U's are in determined mood. Ian Ashbee's cross falls for Nicky Forster, who diverts the ball in. Both sides go close, but Cureton gets a deserved equaliser, finishing well after combining with Iwelumo.

44 — SUNDERLAND (H) 21/4
League: 9th (opp 1st) — Won — 69 pts · FT 3-1 (HT 3-1) · Att 6,042
Brown 45, Garcia 82, Cureton 89p; Yorke 55
Colchester: Gerken, Duguid, Brown, Baldwin, Barker, Watson", Izzet, Jackson*, Garcia, Iwelumo^, Cureton"
Sunderland: Ward, Evans, Nosworthy, Collins, Leadbitter", Whitehead, Edwards, Connolly, Murphy^, Yorke, John*
Subs: Ephraim/Guy · Wallace/Stokes/Elliott
Ref: L Probert
Brown meets Watson's free-kick with a thunderous finish. Roy Keane's men bounce back as Dwight Yorke heads home Daryl Murphy's cross. With time running out, Garcia swivels and finishes clinically. Cureton tucks in a penalty to seal the first loss in 2007 for the champions-elect.

45 — STOKE (A) 28/4
League: 9th (opp 7th) — Lost — 69 pts · FT 1-3 (HT 1-0) · Att 20,108
Iwelumo 38p; Russell 53, Sidibe 57, Higginbotham 62
Colchester: Gerken, Duguid, Barker !, Brown, Baldwin, Watson, Izzet, Lawrence*, Garcia, Iwelumo^, Cureton^
Stoke: Simonsen, Hoefkens, Griffin, Fortune, Higginbotham, 'm Russell, Diao", Russell, Hendrie, Sidibe, Fuller^
Subs: Ephraim/Guy · Eustace/Pericard/Martin
Ref: G Salisbury
A play-off spot could be up for grabs if the U's can at least avoid defeat. Salif Diao's challenge produces a penalty and things look good. But Stoke storm back, Darel Russell netting a towering header, the first of three goals in nine minutes. Barker is off for tangling with Lee Hendrie.

46 — CRYSTAL PALACE (H) 6/5
League: 10th (opp 12th) — Lost — 69 pts · FT 0-2 (HT 0-2) · Att 5,857
Scowcroft 11, Watson 69
Colchester: Gerken, Duguid, Elokobi*, Brown, Baldwin", Watson, Izzet, Ephraim, Garcia, Iwelumo, Cureton
Crystal Palace: Speroni, Borrowdale, Hudson, Cort, Lawrence, McAnuff, Watson, Fletcher^, Kennedy, Scowcroft, Morrison"
Subs: White/McLeod · Soares/Ifill
Ref: R Beeby
United need a mathematical miracle to make the play-offs. Their chances get even slimmer when Jamie Scowcroft heads home Carl Fletcher's cross from a tight angle. Ben Watson's shot sneaks under Gerken. Chances are missed and a wonderful season ends with a disappointing result.

Average — Home 5,466 · Away 17,795

COCA-COLA CHAMPIONSHIP (CUP-TIES)

Manager: Geraint Williams

SEASON 2006-07

Carling Cup

			Att	F-A	H-T	Scorers, Times, and Referees	SQUAD	NUMBERS	IN	USE								subs used
1	A	MK DONS	23	0-1	0-0	McLeod 94	Gerken	Halford	Brown	White	Izzet	Watson	Duguid	Iwelumo	Garcia	Guy*	Cureton	
		22/8	2,747 2:4		aet	Ref: P Crossley	Bankole	Morgan	Edds	O'Hanlon	Harding*	Howe^	Mitchell	Tillen"	Taylor	Hastings	McGovern/Dyer/McLeod	

Martin Allen makes ten team changes for this competition, and the U's just four. The visitors look the more likely scorers, but Halford's free-kick whistles just over and Duguid misses with a late chip. In extra-time Izale McLeod's shot loops off Baldwin and into the net off the bar.

FA Cup

			Att	F-A	H-T	Scorers, Times, and Referees	SQUAD	NUMBERS	IN	USE								subs used
3	A	BARNET	6	1-2	1-0	Cureton 35	Gerken	Halford	Barker	Brown	Baldwin	Izzet^	Watson	McLeod"	Garcia	Iwelumo*	Cureton	Guy/Jackson/Duguid
		9/1	3,075 2:13		L	Yakubu 62, Puncheon 80	Harrison	Hendon	Yakubu	King	Bailey	Graham	Puncheon	Nicolau	Cogan*	Sinclair	Birchall	Hatch
						Ref: T Kettle												

Nicky Nicolau's slip allows Cureton to slam his 14th of the season. Barnet improve after the interval and defender Yakubu breaks through and sees his shot loop over Gerken. McLeod hits a post, but moments later Jason Puncheon strikes a sweet winner from the edge of the box.

	P	Home					Away					Pts
		W	D	L	F	A	W	D	L	F	A	
1 Sunderland	46	15	4	4	38	18	12	3	8	38	29	88
2 Birmingham	46	15	5	3	37	18	11	3	9	30	24	86
3 Derby *	46	13	6	4	33	19	12	3	8	29	27	84
4 West Brom	46	14	4	5	51	24	8	6	9	30	31	76
5 Wolves	46	12	5	6	33	28	10	5	8	26	28	76
6 Southampton	46	13	6	4	36	20	8	6	9	41	33	75
7 Preston	46	15	4	4	38	17	7	4	12	26	36	74
8 Stoke	46	12	8	3	35	16	7	8	8	27	25	73
9 Sheffield Wed	46	10	6	7	38	36	10	5	8	32	30	71
10 COLCHESTER	46	15	4	4	46	19	5	5	13	24	37	69
11 Plymouth	46	10	8	5	36	26	7	8	8	27	36	67
12 Crystal Pal	46	12	6	5	33	22	6	8	9	26	29	65
13 Cardiff	46	11	7	5	33	18	6	6	11	24	35	64
14 Ipswich	46	13	2	8	40	29	5	6	12	24	30	62
15 Burnley	46	10	6	7	35	23	5	6	12	17	26	57
16 Norwich	46	10	5	8	29	25	4	13	6	27	46	57
17 Coventry	46	10	5	8	30	25	5	4	14	17	37	56
18 QP Rangers	46	9	6	8	31	29	5	5	13	23	39	53
19 Leicester	46	6	8	9	26	31	7	6	10	23	33	53
20 Barnsley	46	9	4	10	27	29	6	1	16	26	56	50
21 Hull	46	8	3	12	33	32	5	7	11	18	35	49
22 Southend	46	6	6	11	29	38	4	6	13	18	42	42
23 Luton	46	7	5	11	33	40	3	5	15	20	41	40
24 Leeds **	46	10	4	9	27	30	3	3	17	19	42	36
	1104	266	123	163	827	612	163	123	266	612	827	1523

* promoted after play-offs
** Deducted 10 pts Administr.

Odds & ends

Double wins: (2) Southampton, Southend.
Double losses: (2) Plymouth, West Brom.

Won from behind: (2) Hull (H), Leeds (H).
Lost from in-front: (4) Barnet (A/FAC), Barnsley (H), Ipswich (A), Stoke (A).

High points: Finishing just six points short of the play-offs.
The potent goalscoring partnership developed by Cureton and Iwelumo
Geraint Williams becoming a contender for 'Manager of the Year'.
Beating local rivals Ipswich in front of a live TV audience.
The first league 'double' over Essex rivals Southend for 21 years.
Finishing as best-placed East Anglian club for the first time ever.
Attracting the highest average home attendances since 1970-71.
Becoming the only club to beat champions-elect Sunderland after Xmas.

Low points: Losing manager Parkinson to a Championship rival club.
Conceding three goals in nine minutes at Stoke, to end play-off hopes.
First-hurdle cup defeats to lower division clubs.

Player of the Year: Jamie Cureton.
Ever-presents: (1) Wayne Brown.
Hat-tricks for: (3) Jamie Cureton (v Derby, H & Southend, A),
Chris Iwelumo (v Hull, H).
Hat-tricks against: (0).
Leading scorer: (24) Jamie Cureton.

	Appearances						Goals		
	Lge	Sub	LC	Sub	FAC	Sub	Lge	LCFAC	Tot
Baldwin, Pat	35	3			1		1		1
Barker, Chris	38								
Brown, Wayne	46		1		1		1		1
Cureton, Jamie	44		1		1		23	1	24
Davison, Aidan	19			1					
Duguid, Karl	42	1				1	5		5
Elokobi, George	8	2							
Ephraim, Hogan	5	16					1		1
Garcia, Richard	33	3			1		7		7
Gerken, Dean	27		1		1				
Guy, Jamie	1	31				1	3		3
Halford, Greg	28		1		1		3		3
Iwelumo, Chris	41	5	1		1		18		18
Izzet, Kemi	45				1		1		1
Jackson, Johnnie	24	8				1	2		2
Jones, Richie		6							
McLeod, Kevin	13	11			1		3		3
Mills, Matthew	8	1							
Richards, Garry	3	2							
Watson, Kevin	38	2			1		1		1
White, John	8	8					1		1
(own-goals)									
21 players used	506	99	11	1	11	3	70	1	71

David Gregory holds off Torquay's Steve McCall during
the Third Division play-off final win at Wembley in 1998

Lomana Tresor Lua-Lua, perhaps
the most remarkable of all the
talent to come through the
Colchester youth system